BIRTH OF THE BATTLESHIP

Birth of the Battleship

British Capital Ship Design 1870-1881

JOHN BEELER

NAVAL INSTITUTE PRESS
Annapolis, Maryland

In Memoriam

H. W. 'Bert' Jones, 1936-1997

Frontispiece

HMS *Benbow*, 1885. (U.S. Naval Historical Center: NH61642)

First published in Great Britain by Chatham Publishing, 61 Frith Street, London W1V 5TA

Published and distributed in the United States of America and Canada by the Naval Institute Press, Beach Hall, 291 Wood Road, Annapolis, Maryland 21402-5034

Library of Congress Catalog Card No. 2001087069

ISBN 1-55750-213-7

Manufactured in Great Britain.

CONTENTS

Acknowledgements   7

Introduction   9

1. International Relations, Naval Rivals, Domestic Politics and Government Finance: The Context   13

2. Materials and Construction   30

3. Sails and Steam   47

4. Armament   65

5. Strategy, Economics, Politics and Design Policy   87

6. Design by Committee   108

7. The *Inflexible* and Mr Reed   122

8. From *Inflexible* to *Colossus*   138

9. The Coast Assault Paradigm Shaken: *Collingwood* and the 'Admiral' Class, 1879-81   157

10. The Cruiser Quandary   182

11. Conclusion   204

Bibliography   215

Index   221

ACKNOWLEDGEMENTS

THE SINGLE author's name on the title page of most history books belies the collaborative effort involved in their composition. This volume is certainly no exception, having benefited immeasurably from the wisdom, advice, assistance, and support of numerous individuals who graciously shared their expertise and time to make it a better piece of scholarship than it otherwise would have been.

First and foremost, I must express my gratitude to the staffs of the archives and libraries consulted in the course of research. Without their help and guidance, invariably rendered with both courtesy and efficiency, this study could scarcely have been started, much less completed. My heartfelt thanks, therefore, to the personnel of the Public Record Office (Kew), the British Library Main and Manuscripts Reading Rooms, the Ministry of Defence Library, the Bodleian Library of Oxford University, the Liverpool Record Office, the Northamptonshire Records Office, the Institute of Historical Research of the University of London, the University of Illinois Library (Urbana-Champaign), the Sterling, Beineke, and Mudd Libraries at Yale University, and the Law and Gorgas Libraries of the University of Alabama. Special thanks go to the archivists at the National Maritime Museum: Clive Powell, Alan Gidding, and the late David Topliss at Greenwich, and Meredith Wells, Imogene Gibbon, and Guy Robins at the Old Brass Foundry, Woolwich Arsenal.

The illustrative material, without which the text would be virtually incomprehensible, was supplied by the Naval Historical Center at the Washington Navy Yard and by the National Maritime Museum. Thanks to Edwin Finney at the former for having quickly and thoroughly trawled through the Center's immense holdings for the photographs herein, and to the Naval Historical Foundation for splendid reproductions of the originals. To Meredith Wells at the National Maritime Museum an additional thank-you for the invaluable assistance with the Ships' Plans.

I must also acknowledge the kindness of the Controller of Her Britannic Majesty's Stationery Office for permission to quote from Crown Copyright material, the Trustees of the National Maritime Museum for permission to quote from the papers of Sir Alexander Milne, Sir Geoffrey Phipps Hornby, and Sir William Houston Stewart, the National Trust for permission to quote from the Hughenden (Disraeli) papers, the Syndics of Cambridge University Library for permission to quote from the papers of Hugh C.E. Childers, and G.E. Ward Hunt for permission to quote from the papers of George Ward Hunt.

Numerous scholars and colleagues read and commented on part or all of the manuscript. Chapters 2 through 6 benefited from the careful scrutiny and constructive criticism of Professor John Lynn and Professor Emeritus John McKay, both of the University of Illinois, Professor Geoffrey Parker of Ohio State University, and Professor Sir Michael Howard. Professor Emeritus Robert Erwin Johnson of the University of Alabama graciously read and critiqued the entire text, as did Dr. Wade Dudley and Michael Kuric. All provided valuable advice and insights.

Three individuals deserve special thanks. Professor Andrew Lambert of King's College, University of London, has assisted my scholarship in more ways than can be counted, beginning with our first exchange of letters more than a dozen years ago. He has helped me comprehend the world-view of mid-Victorian administrators and naval officers, provided expert research recommendations, and, most recently, touted this manuscript to Chatham Publishing to mention but three prominent instances of his unfailing helpfulness. Professor Emeritus Walter Arnstein of the University of Illinois oversaw the composition of Chapters 2 through 6 in his capacity as my dissertation director. More fundamentally, he has influenced my understanding of history in general and Victorian Britain in particular in profound and myriad ways. My scholarly debt to him is incalculable. Last, but certainly not least, Robert Gardiner, publisher of Chatham Publishing, was not only willing to produce this book, but also graciously undertook the task of tracking down the Ships' Plans which enliven the text. It has been an unalloyed pleasure working with him.

Thanks are also due to Professor Emeritus Bryan Ranft of the University of London, Professor Geoffrey Till of the Royal Naval College, Professor Emeritus Donald Schurman of the Royal Military College of Canada, Professor Jon T. Sumida of the

University of Maryland, and Professor Nicholas A.M. Rodger of the University of Exeter, all of whom furnished valuable assistance at one or more stages of my research and writing. Dr. William Sutton has been, since our graduate student days, a tireless source of encouragement. Both Bill Nash and Paul Wirth furnished valuable creative assistance, and I am indebted to Scott Manring for many fruitful conversations on ramming tactics.

Numerous others have provided valuable help and advice. My mother, Anne Beeler, has been an unflagging source of support, both moral and financial, as have been my in-laws, Howard and Linda Crowson. Florrie, Ken, and Graham Jones and Sue and Emma Jordan have, over the years, become my second family and their house in Thetford, Norfolk my 'home away from home' while in England. My colleagues in the University of Alabama History Department have been paragons of collegiality and supportiveness. And no one could ask for greater encouragement and love than I have had from my wife, Amy. Both are reciprocated in full measure, along with sincere apologies for time spent apart while researching and writing.

All – family, friends, colleagues, scholars, archivists, and institutions – and many others too have had a hand in the creation of this book. Thanks to everyone, and to anyone whom I may have neglected to mention. I, of course, bear sole responsibility for any errors that remain.

John F. Beeler
Tuscaloosa, Alabama
19 November 2000

INTRODUCTION

Neanderthals of Naval Architecture? HMS *Inflexible*, an example of 'precocious hypertrophy' according to long-time *Jane's Fighting Ships* editor Oscar Parkes. (US Naval Historical Center: NH60025)

RELATIVELY LITTLE has been written about the ships of the mid-Victorian British Navy–Admiral Ballard's 'Black Battlefleet'–at least in comparison to the vessels of the Dreadnought era or even the preceding steam line-of-battle ships, whose period has attracted a recent flurry of scholarly attention.[1] Furthermore, almost without exception, the few works which have dealt with the warships of the 1860s, 1870s, and 1880s have shared two traits. First, their focus has been–often almost exclusively–technological aspects: design, armament, protection, hull dispositions, and the like.[2] Second, most take critical views of the ships, especially those of the 1870s and 1880s, the abilities of the men who designed them, the politicians who underfunded the Navy, even the British public which was, it is alleged, indifferent to the

1. See Andrew Lambert, *Battleships in Transition* (London, 1984) and *The Last Sailing Battlefleet: Maintaining Naval Mastery 1815-1850* (London, 1991); David K. Brown, *Before the Ironclad: Development of Ship Design, Propulsion, and Armament in the Royal Navy, 1815-1860* (London, 1990), Ann Giffard and Basil Greenhill, *Steam, Politics and Patronage: The Transformation of the Royal Navy, 1815-54* (London, 1994). The allusion to Ballard refers to his articles in *Mariner's Mirror* on the ships of the mid-Victorian Navy. Those relating to capital ships were later collected and printed in a single volume. See George Ballard, *The Black Battlefleet* (N. A. M. Rodger ed., Annapolis, 1980).

2. See James Phinney Baxter, *The Introduction of the Ironclad Warship* (Cambridge, Mass., 1933); Stanley Sandler, *The Emergence of the Modern Capital Ship* (Newark, Delaware, 1979); Oscar Parkes, *British Battleships, 1860-1950* (London, 1957); Robert Gardiner and Andrew Lambert (eds.), *Steam, Steel and Shellfire: The Steam Warship, 1815-1905* (London, 1992); David K. Brown, *Warrior to Dreadnought: Warship Development, 1860-1905* (London, 1997) and 'Wood, Sail, and Cannonballs to Steel, Steam, and Shells, 1815-1895', in J.R. Hill (ed.), *The Oxford Illustrated History of the Royal Navy* (Oxford, 1995). An exception is C.I. Hamilton's *Anglo-French Naval Rivalry, 1840-1870* (London, 1994), which nonetheless uses the comparative rates of technological change between the two forces as its point of departure.

service's glaring technological shortcomings and its weakness.[3] Modern authors have generally taken their cue from contemporaries such as Seymour Fortescue, who, in retrospect declared that 'the ignorance of the British public of everything regarding the navy' in the 1870s and 1880s 'can only be described as colossal'.[4]

These two interpretative tendencies go hand-in-hand, and are indeed closely connected. The fleets of the period 1860-90, Britain's included, were, in the words of a charitable authority, 'some of the strangest collections ever assembled, reflecting not only a rapid series of technical inventions but a state of anarchy in the ideas of naval architecture.'[5] As such, the tendency to focus on the ships' technological characteristics, reinforced by the peaceful service lives of most of them, is scarcely surprising. Moreover, the ships of the 1870s and 1880s stand in stark contrast to those of the 1890s, whose design had stabilised and whose numbers grew

rapidly, the consequence of greatly increased funding and a public increasingly stimulated by navalist propaganda. In other words, modern perceptions of the mid-Victorian British battlefleet are almost unavoidably coloured by comparison to that which followed in the 1890s. The ships have been criticised by subsequent standards, and, not surprisingly, they have been found wanting. At best they have been seen as curios, blending some characteristics of pre-Dreadnought capital ships with inexplicable hold-overs from earlier days – sails, most prominently. At worst they have been dismissed as bizarre evolutionary dead-ends: Neanderthals of naval architecture, doomed to extinction by the march of enlightened progress and modern technology.

Such a facile appraisal does justice neither to the men who designed and built the Black Battlefleet, nor, especially, to the complexity of the situation which confronted them. It ignores, for instance, the very real divide between the theoretical and practical limitations of technology as it developed during this transitional period. Likewise, by viewing technology narrowly, commentators have routinely neglected other, non-technological factors that influenced both design policy and the incorporation of technology itself. And, perhaps most perniciously, it implicitly – sometimes explicitly – portrays those responsible for warship design during

The basic layout of HMS *Dreadnought* (laid down 1870) – with a centreline turret at each end of the superstructure – foreshadowed the pre-Dreadnought battleships of the 1889-1904 era, leading many critics to charge that the failure to adhere to this design in the 1870s and 1880s is evidence of conservatism or incompetence at the Admiralty. (National Maritime Museum, London: 9311)

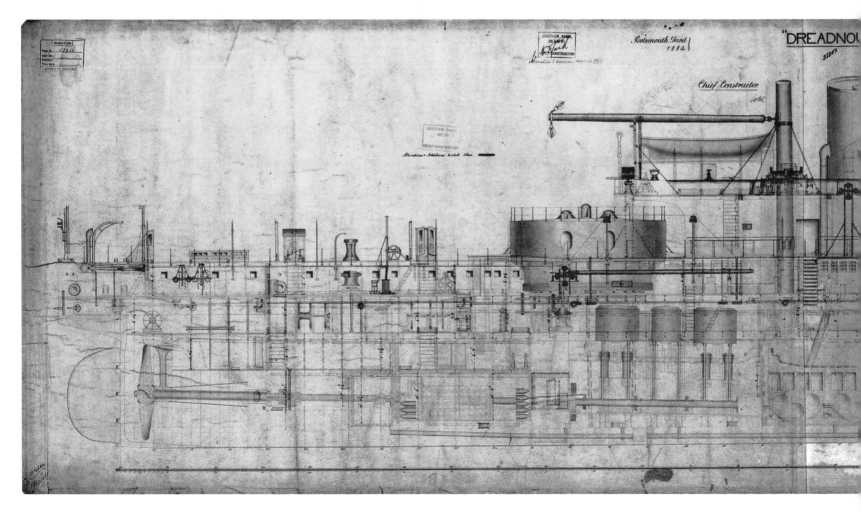

the period as blinkered, reactionary, incompetent, and even stupid. Consider, for instance, the case of Nathaniel Barnaby, Director of Naval Construction (D.N.C.) from 1875 to 1885, and, as such, the naval architect chiefly responsible for British warships for the fifteen years between 1870 and the latter date. One recent author flatly states that Barnaby was 'unsuited to his post', and was, more than any other contributor, responsible for 'the miscellaneous collection of bizarre and ill-assorted designs which composed the Navy's fleets and squadrons in the middle years of Queen Victoria's reign.'[6] The rest of the Board, however, was hardly absolved, for the 'chief fault' was not Barnaby's shortcomings, but rather 'organisational weakness of the Admiralty, and the personal failings of his superiors' which allowed Barnaby to exercise 'a dominant influence on questions he was incompetent to judge'. The whole administration thus stands condemned.

Yet there is no want of evidence in the Admiralty Papers in both the Public Record Office and the National Maritime Museum that Barnaby was not the Navy's chief designer – rather than its chief architect – by default. Indeed, he was not involved in the design of *Shannon, Temeraire, Ajax, Agamemnon, Colossus, Edinburgh, Conqueror,* and the 'Admiral' class at all. The designs of these vessels were merely drawn by Barnaby and his department, acting on very specific directions from the Board of Admiralty. Nor is Barnaby's competence and influence the only matter on which misapprehension exists. Recent scholarship has by and large failed to appreciate how Admiralty policy-makers wrestled with the ramifications of technological change in strategic, logistic, and operational spheres, nor, as a corollary, the degree to which they based design policy on strategic and logistic considerations.

The aim of this work is not to present a detailed technological or design history of the capital ships built by the British navy during this crucial period of transition. That has already been done.

3. See in particular N. A. M. Rodger, 'The Dark Ages of the Admiralty,' *Mariner's Mirror* 61/4 (1975), pp331-42; 62/1 (1976), pp33-46; 62/2 (1976), pp121-28, and 'British Belted Cruisers,' *Mariner's Mirror* 64/1 (1978), pp23-35; 'The Design of the *Inconstant*,' *Mariner's Mirror* 61/1 (1975), pp9-22;, 'The First Light Cruisers', *Mariner's Mirror* 65/3 (1979), pp209-30; Parkes, *British Battleships*, pp230-346; Sandler, *Emergence of the Modern Capital Ship*, pp248-9.

4. Seymour Fortescue, *Looking Back* (London, 1920), p149.

5. Theodore Ropp, *The Development of a Modern Navy: French Naval Policy, 1871-1901* (Steven Roberts ed., Annapolis, 1987), p27.

6. N.A.M. Rodger, 'The Dark Ages of the Admiralty, Pt. II: Change and Decay, 1874-80', *Mariner's Mirror* 62/1 (1976), p45.

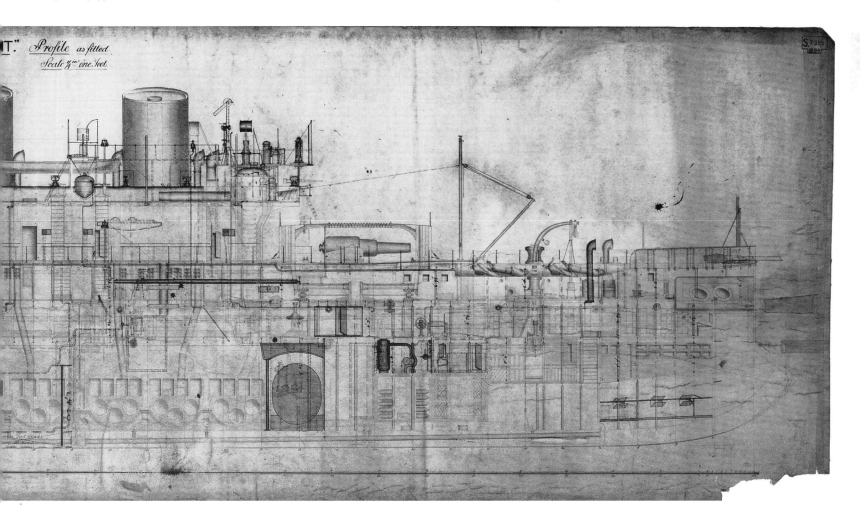

Rather, it is to delineate the general framework–political, economical, strategic, tactical, and technological–in which these designs evolved. Illuminating these parameters, it is hoped, will aid in comprehending why they turned out like they did. It can be thus read by itself, or in conjunction with other, more narrowly technological works. Moreover, it focuses on some aspects of the design process which are overlooked by other studies, in particular the administrative structure of the Admiralty and how it contributed to design policy, the intersection of strategic, logistical, and technological factors, and the design compromises which were the consequence of both these and other constraints. Finally, it seeks to present the products of the era on their own terms, rather than by comparison with later ships, much less in a technological/teleological framework, a 'Whig interpretation' of technological 'progress.' In so doing, it is hoped that the motives and actions of the men who designed these vessels, as well as the factors that circumscribed their options, will be better understood.

The historian's quest is to comprehend the past on its own terms, yet, typically, the past only 'speaks' to us when it appears to be of some utility in understanding present circumstances. Of what value, then, might a study of mid-Victorian British warship design policy be to non-specialists? Perhaps more than initially meets the eye. The conditions under which the Admiralty's administrators and technical staff laboured during the 1870s and early 1880s are in many respects strikingly similar to those confronting American policy makers and implementers in the post-Cold War era. Like Britain a century-and-a-quarter ago, the United States today faces no major challenges to its security. Also like Britain at that time, the U.S. is today the sole power with worldwide military commitments. America, indeed, currently undertakes a global policing role analogous to that played by Britain during the *Pax Britannica*. To make the argument in a more explicitly naval context, the U.S. Navy has inherited the Royal Navy's task of policing the seas and, more crucially, its deterrent function; today's carrier groups perform the 'forward presence' duties formerly carried out by Victorian Britain's overseas squadrons, the ballistic submarine force that of the British battlefleet.

Further similarities are evident on closer examination. Like post-Cold War U.S. armed forces, Victorian Britain's military services endured a process of 'downsizing' during the 1870s and early 1880s, partly as a consequence of diminished foreign threats, but at least as much as a result of politicians' desire to curry favour with a mass electorate through fiscal retrenchment. At the same time, however, rapid technological change tended, as it does today, to drive up the costs of weapons systems research and development. Moreover, given the imperatives of meeting global responsibilities and, more crucially, deterring would-be competitors from mounting challenges to naval hegemony, the Admiralty had to stay abreast of the march of technology. Such was the pace of techno-

logical change that a vessel which was state-of-the-art at the time of its design was usually obsolescent upon completion, sometimes by the time of its launch. Yesterday's battlefleet, policy-makers realised, made a poor deterrent. The Admiralty was thus forced to resolve the conflict between demands for economy emanating from their political overseers and countervailing pleas for efficiency from their service constituency. The U.S. Department of Defense faces precisely the same dilemma today, as anyone familiar with the divide between politicians' tax-cutting rhetoric and the Pentagon's 'doom and gloom' prognostications can attest. Indeed, the Admiralty's experience during the ironclad era furnishes the first historical example of defence policy formulation in an industrialised constitutional democracy during peacetime. As such, the manner in which the Board of Admiralty and its technical experts dealt with the financial, technological, strategic and tactical problems confronting them may furnish an instructive example for contemporary policy-makers.

This study is based principally on primary source research, rather than on earlier syntheses. Official publications consulted include *Hansard's Parliamentary Debates* and the *Parliamentary Papers*. Naval debates in Parliament were not restricted solely to matters of finance. The strength of the Navy, the designs of its ships, and their seaworthiness were often covered in minute detail. Likewise, the *Parliamentary Papers* are of value not only for the yearly Naval Estimates, but also for Reports of Committees, complete with minutes of evidence, on ships designs, on Admiralty administration, on dockyard management, and on a host of other subjects. Other official papers, consulted in the Public Record Office and the National Maritime Museum, include the Admiralty Papers. The most valuable of these collections are ADM1 (Secretary's In letters) at the Public Record Office, containing, among other things, interdepartmental correspondence and intelligence reports, and the 'Ship's Covers', at the National Maritime Museum, volumes containing the surviving papers relevant to the design of individual ships. Several collections of personal papers were also consulted, including those of the political figures Gladstone, Disraeli, Lord Halifax, Hugh Childers, Sir Stafford Northcote, Lord Carnarvon, Lord Cardwell, George Ward Hunt, and W.H. Smith. These have been supplemented by those of naval officers who served at the Admiralty during the 1870s, in particular Admiral Sir Alexander Milne, Admiral Sir Geoffrey Phipps Hornby, Admiral Sir William Houston Stewart, and Admiral Sir John Walter Tarleton. Of these collections the Gladstone, Disraeli, Milne, and Hornby papers are of especial value, all of them containing voluminous correspondence relating to expenditure, foreign threats, and all manner of naval matters. Research in published primary sources includes newspapers, pamphlets, memoirs, and journals, in particular the *Royal United Services Institution Journal* and the *Transactions of the Institute of Naval Architects*, along with works relating specifically to the Navy.

Chapter 1

INTERNATIONAL RELATIONS, NAVAL RIVALS, DOMESTIC POLITICS AND GOVERNMENT FINANCE: THE CONTEXT

Historical Assessments

FOR A CENTURY or more the suppositions that the pre-Naval Defence Act (1889) British battlefleet was both under strength and technologically antiquated were accepted without question. In *British Battleships, 1860-1950*, long regarded as authoritative, Oscar Parkes, for instance, states unequivocally that Britain, whose margin of national and imperial security had his-torically been measured by a battlefleet comparable to those of the second and third largest naval powers combined, could not, as of

The masts and sails carried by *Northampton* and similar 1870s-era ironclads are routinely put forward as evidence of the Royal Navy's conservatism. (U.S. Naval Historical Center: NH58049)

1880, boast even a 'one-power standard'.[1] 'To be sure, there was the British Navy,' writes A.P. Thornton in similar tones, '[b]ut in the 1870's [sic] its ships were sadly antiquated . . .'.[2] Another recent author remarks that the mid-Victorian period saw the fortunes of the navy 'at a low ebb'.

> It was small in size, by comparison either with its potential enemies or its potential duties. It was backward in technology and often reactionary in outlook. Its ideas of strategy were not so much misguided as non-existent.[3]

The origins of this interpretation date to the 1890s, when the writings of Alfred Thayer Mahan, Philip Howard Colomb, and other navalist-cum-publicists popularised the doctrine that not only Britain's national security but its great power status were dependent on the possession of a large fleet of capital ships, capable of beating back any challenges to its maritime supremacy through the strategy of the *guerre d'escadre*.[4] The ascendance of this doctrine coincided with–indeed was fuelled by–the height of European colonial competition in both Africa and Asia, and the emergence of Japan, the United States and, at the end of the decade, Germany, as naval powers to be regarded mistrustfully alongside traditional rivals France and Russia. In addition, the erosion of Britain's once-unrivalled economic and industrial dominance further encouraged the Social Darwinistic view that the nation and the navy should be prepared against all potential comers. The indictment also contained an explicitly political dimension. Admiral C.C.P. Fitzgerald wrote retrospectively;

> At about this time, there was a perfect craze for naval economy. It was not confined to the radical politicians. The Conservatives

were very nearly as bad. Both parties wanted votes and the only way to get popularity and votes was to reduce expenditure on the Army and Navy. As we were never going to have another war, it was obviously a waste of money to spend it on new ships of war.[5]

As long as such views predominated, the policies pursued by both Liberals and Conservatives in the years dominated by Benjamin Disraeli and William Gladstone regarding the Navy's numerical strength and its technical modernity were judged in a generally critical light. Politicians and civilian administrators, it has repeatedly been charged, neglected the necessity of maintaining an overwhelmingly strong naval force, ready on short notice, to overawe any would-be challengers. Again, subsequent commentators have echoed the charge. C.J. Bartlett, for instance, claims in the years after 1865 Disraeli and Gladstone 'actually entered into competition' in their embrace of Manchester Radical Richard Cobden's economical views on 'foreign policy, imperial defence, and governmental retrenchment', and Norman McCord neatly echoes Fitzgerald's earlier charges: '[i]n the mid-nineteenth century Britannia was determined to rule the waves, but not to pay the price of doing so efficiently. Both of the major political groups repeatedly tried to run the armed forces on a shoestring, rather than face the wrath of a tax-paying electorate.'[6]

In the past decade, however, several studies have disputed traditional assessments of Britain's naval position during the 1870s and 1880s.[7] The revised view is founded upon two principal premises. First, to comprehend the state of the Navy in the mid-Victorian era accurately it is necessary to seek answers from contemporary sources, rather than from those rendered *ipse post facto*. Post-Mahanian assessments of the size, strength and war-readiness of the pre-Mahanian fleet have been almost without exception

1. Parkes, *British Battleships, 1860-1950* (London, 1957), p232.

2. A.P. Thornton, *The Imperial Idea and its Enemies: A Study in British Power* (London, 1959), p29.

3. N.A.M. Rodger, 'The Dark Ages of the Admiralty, 1869-1885, Part I, Business Methods, 1868-74', *Mariner's Mirror* 62/1 (1975), p331. For similar assessments, see Richard Millman, *British Policy and the Coming of the Franco-Prussian War* (Oxford, 1965), p151; C. J. Bartlett, 'The Mid-Victorian Reappraisal of Naval Policy,' in Kenneth Bourne and D. C. Watts (eds.), *Studies in International History* (London, 1967), p207; and Jeffrey L. Lant, 'The Spithead Naval Review of 1887,' *Mariner's Mirror* 62/1 (1975), pp67-79, esp. p76.

4. See in particular Mahan's *The Influence of Sea Power Upon History, 1660-1783* (Boston, 1890) and *The Influence of Sea Power Upon the French Revolution and Empire, 1792-1812* (Boston, 1892), 2 vols. and Colomb's *Naval Warfare: Its Ruling Principles and Practice Historically Treated* (London, 1891). Other influential navalists of the period included professionals Lord Charles Beresford, Alexander Milne, Geoffrey Phipps Hornby and John Fisher, and journalists H.O. Arnold-Forster, W.T. Stead and James Thursfeld. The gathering strength of navalism during the 1890s was symbolised by the founding in 1894 of the Navy League. Phipps Hornby agreed to act as its first president. For historical treatment of navalism, see Arthur J. Marder, *The Anatomy of Sea Power: British Naval Policy in the Pre-Dreadnought Era, 1880-1905* (Hamden, CT, 1940), Jon T. Sumida's *In Defence of Naval Supremacy: Finance, Technology, and British Naval Policy, 1889-1914* (Boston, 1989), and W. Mark Hamilton's *The Nation and the Navy: Methods and Organization of British Navalist Propaganda, 1889-1914* (New York, 1986).

5. C.C.P. Fitzgerald, *From Sail to Steam* (London, 1916), p140.

6. Norman McCord, 'A Naval Scandal of 1871: The Loss of H.M.S. *Megaera*', *Mariner's Mirror* 57/2 (1972), pp131-2; Bartlett, 'The Mid-Victorian Reappraisal of Naval Policy', p189.

7. See John Beeler, 'A 'One-Power Standard?': Great Britain and the Balance of Naval Power, 1860-1885,' *Journal of Strategic Studies* 15/4 (1992), pp548-75, *British Naval Policy in the Gladstone-Disraeli Era, 1866-1880* (Stanford CA, 1997), and 'Steam, Strategy, and Schurman: Imperial Defence in the Post-Crimean Era, 1856-1905,' in Keith Neilson and Greg Kennedy (eds.), *Far-Flung Lines: Essays in Honour of Donald Schurman* (London, 1996); Andrew Lambert, 'The Shield of Empire, 1815-1895,' in J. R. Hill (ed.), *The Oxford Illustrated History of the Royal Navy* (Oxford, 1995), pp161-97, 'The Royal Navy 1856-1914: Deterrence and the Strategy of World Power,' unpublished paper, and 'Deterrence: The Critical Parameter of British Naval Power, 1850-1914,' unpublished paper; George Modelski and William Thompson, *Sea Power in Global Politics, 1494-1993* (Seattle, 1988).

8. Sydney Eardley-Wilmot, *An Admiral's Memories: Sixty-Five Years Afloat and Ashore* (London, 1927), p85.

9. See for instance Donald Schurman, *Imperial Defence, 1868-1887* (ed. John Beeler, London, 2000), p5.

10. B.R. Mitchell, *British Historical Statistics* (Cambridge, 1988), pp435, 536-7. The trade figures include imports, exports, and re-exports. The shipping figures are *net*, rather than gross, tonnage.

HMS *Rodney*, one of a class of six battleships laid down by Gladstone's government in the early 1880s as a response to the French Navy's modernisation. (U.S. Naval Historical Center: NH54832)

dismissive, but these assessments typically contrast the Navy of 1870 or 1880 with that of 1895 or 1900, rather than with the contemporary French, Russian, Italian, or American navies. Rear-Admiral Sir Sydney Eardley-Wilmot, for instance, derided the force assembled for the Jubilee Review of 1887 as a 'motley collection of ancient constructions', but he did so in the pages of his memoirs, published forty years after the Review took place.[8] It may appear obvious once pointed out, but it is important to bear in mind that in the event of war over the Eastern Crisis of 1878, the Royal Navy would have faced the existing Russian fleet – such as it was – rather than its own counterpart of twenty years later.

Secondly, and related to the first point, it has been stressed that the size of the mid-Victorian Navy failed to keep pace with the growth of the British empire, ocean-borne trade, and the merchant marine, all of which would require defending in the event of war.[9] The charge is indisputable; the size of the Navy in general and the battlefleet in particular remained static, perhaps shrank

slightly, between 1870 and 1885, during which time Britain purchased stock in the Suez Canal (1875), occupied Egypt (1882), saw its overseas trade swell from £547,100,000 per annum to £642,500,000, and its merchant tonnage increase from 5,691,000 to 7,430,000.[10]

But fixing the requisite level of British naval strength on the basis of its theoretical obligations in the event of a general European war – invariably, it might be added, on the presumption that Britain would fight without allies – is neither realistic in the realm of strategy nor, especially, in that of finance. Contemporary naval administrators, it is true, repeatedly rendered such assessments, as a perusal of the Admiralty Papers and other collections will quickly reveal, but their alarmist pronouncements were, it must be recalled, designed to extract increased funding from the government, and thus calculated to carry maximum impact or 'scare value'.[11] To others – as is equally true today – the fundamental factor was not the theoretical scope of the Navy's duties, but the existing foreign forces that could threaten the nation, empire, and sea lanes.[12] In short, the fitness and strength of the Navy is more accurately reckoned by comparing it to its contemporary rivals, and by calculating the demands which would be made of it by the same standard, rather than by nebulous theoretical calculations, much less retrospective indictments like Eardley-Wilmot's.

The British Battlefleet and the Guerre d'Escadre

Compared to contemporary foreign forces – both in terms of funding and *matériel* – it is clear that, so far from falling short of a 'one-power standard', the mid-Victorian navy consistently measured close to or above the two-power level laid down in 1817 as the basis for national security calculations.[13] Indeed, apart France, with the arguable exception of the United States during the American Civil War, there was no other naval rival worthy of the name during the mid-Victorian era. Britain invariably spent far more on its navy than did any would-be rivals with the sole exception of France. Between 1860 and 1890 German naval spending never reached a quarter of Britain's. Italy's barely broached 30 per cent, and then only during the last three years of the 1880s. Russia's, so far as is known, never reached 50 per cent. Austria-Hungary's remained consistently below 15 and typically less than 10 per cent, and the United States, whose naval expenditures ballooned to over twice Britain's in 1864-5, spent less than half from 1868 through 1875, and less than a third for the remaining years of the period.[14]

Unsurprisingly the mid-Victorian British battlefleet also dwarfed that of all rivals save France. The United States, it is true, had far and away the largest ironclad fleet during the mid-1860s, but that force consisted almost solely of small, shallow-draft monitors, ill-suited for anything beyond strictly coastal operations. Without a single sea-going, first-class ironclad, the United States Navy could pose a threat to neither the British Isles nor any part of the Empire except Canada. Moreover, even the monitors were in all respects inferior even to analogous British vessels, featuring laminated armour made up of 1in layers bolted together (rather than the solid plates found on British vessels), low-velocity smoothbore ordnance, and weak and unreliable steam machinery. Finally, following the Civil War virtually the entire Federal ironclad force was laid up. By 1874 the U.S. Navy had plummeted from its peak strength of forty-eight ironclads to twenty-eight; a year later it had dropped to sixteen.[15]

As early as January 1870 the Admiralty's Controller, Rear-Admiral Robert Spencer Robinson, reported to the Board that 'we may declare with tolerable certainty that as an aggressive Navy, capable of making serious attacks on . . . other powers, the Naval force of the United States is not very formidable.'[16] Two years later Royal Navy Captain E.A. Inglefield reported 'it is acknowledged by all American Naval authorities, that the present condition of their Navy is at a lamentably low ebb, and this opinion is supported by the reports of the Secretary of the Navy [in] 1870, 71, [and] 72 . . .'.[17] Inglefield, then in the midst of touring the United States added '[a]ll my observations during a visit to America of some months . . . tend in a great manner to confirm these views.' Later that year the British naval attaché, Captain Gore Jones, quoted United States' Admiral of the Navy, Civil War hero David Dixon Porter, who compared 'their navy in relation to European Navies as being like a man on foot armed with a pistol encountering a mounted man clad in armour and carrying a rifle.' Of the forty-eight monitors which made up the U.S. ironclad fleet, no less than thirty-six were 'laid up' – unable to go to sea – a further four were 'repairing,' two were 'in ordinary,' and four more were 'on the stocks' or otherwise unfinished.[18] In short, the effective ironclad fleet of the United States in 1873 was two ships, neither of them suited for service on the high seas.

Russia's ironclad navy was similar to that of the United States: in 1880 twenty-one of its twenty-eight armoured vessels were monitors, adequate enough for operations in the Gulf of Finland or along the Black Sea coast, but incapable of posing any threat to Britain outside the confines of those waters. Likewise, the limitations of Russia's industrial infrastructure meant that its warships were either purchased abroad or were markedly inferior to analo-

11. See, for instance, Memorandum to Cabinet on the State of the Navy (Copy), April, 1874, Memorandum on H.M. Fleet (Copy), Confidential, November 1875, Hughenden (Disraeli) Papers, Bodleian Library, Oxford University, B/XX/Hu/59; Carnarvon Papers, PRO: PRO30/30/6/ 115, fol 61; *Third Report and Final Report of the Royal Commissioners appointed to enquire into the Defence of British Possessions and Commerce Abroad*, Confidential, 25 May 1882, Carnarvon Papers, PRO: PRO30/6-52. See especially the *Digest of Evidence*.

12. *Hansard's Parliamentary Debates*, 3d ser., 210 (1872), col. 450. First Lord George J. Goschen succinctly remarked 'It cannot be said the we ought to have a certain absolute number of iron-clads, but that if our neighbours have much fewer, we also require much fewer. It is a question of proportion.'

13. Andrew Lambert, 'Preparing for the Long Peace: The Reconstruction of the Royal Navy 1815-1830,' *Mariner's Mirror* 82/1 (1996), p41.

14. Beeler, *British Naval Policy in the Gladstone-Disraeli Era*, pp192-3.

15. Ibid, pp199-201.

16. Spencer Robinson to Admiralty, 22 January 1870, PRO: ADM1/6177.

17. Inglefield to Admiralty, 20 April 1872, PRO: ADM1/6255.

18. Cited in Frederic Martin (ed.), *The Statesman's Yearbook* (London, 1874), pp575-6.

19. Beeler, *British Naval Policy in the Gladstone-Disraeli Era*, pp201-03.

20. Goodenough to Admiralty, 6 January 1871, PRO: ADM1/6198.

21. James W. King, *European Ships of War and Their Armament, Naval Administration, etc* (Washington, 1877), p167.

gous British types, and not infrequently both.[19] Finally, much of the Russian ironclad fleet dated to the early 1860s, yet was maintained on the Active List throughout the period, indeed into the early twentieth century. Thus, by 1880 the Russian fleet numbered only ten vessels of 1870 or more recent vintage. As early as 1871 the British naval attaché in Europe, Commodore James Goodenough, reported of the Russian battlefleet: '[t]here is now no turret vessel [which type accounted for seventeen of twenty-four Russian ironclads] fit to leave the Baltic, and the broadside vessels are inferior to the '*Warrior*' & '*Defence*,' the first broadside vessels built in England.'[20] Moreover, before the late 1880s only

one Russian vessel–the *Peter the Great*–measured up to the first-class seagoing ironclads of the British battlefleet. In the words of informed contemporary observer James W. King, Chief Engineer of the United States Navy, '[e]xcept for coast defence, the Russian fleet is rather numerous than powerful. The *Peter the Great* and the *Minin* [an armoured cruiser] are the only two vessels on the list which approach the modern standard of fighting efficiency.'[21]

Italy's armoured force was inconsequential prior to 1880, and

The Italian battleship *Dandolo* underway in the canal at Taranto, 1894. Her layout was copied for HMS *Inflexible*. (U.S. Naval Historical Center: NH66131)

The *Italia*, the largest and most revolutionary capital ship design of the 1870s and 1880s. (U.S. Naval Historical Center: NH88743)

only of interest to the British thereafter due to the size, power, and speed of four battleships – the *Duilio*, *Dandolo*, *Lepanto*, and *Italia*. These vessels boasted the most innovative designs of the period 1870-90, prompting the British *Inflexible*, modelled on the *Duilio*, but provocative designs aside, four ships do not a fleet make, and the Italian navy posed no threat to the Mistress of the Seas. Of its thirteen completed armoured vessels in 1885, nine were obsolescent and no fewer than seven predated the debacle at Lissa (1866). All but the four most modern ships were, by British standards, small, poorly protected, and weakly armed.[22]

Before 1875 Germany's battlefleet was little more impressive than Italy's, consisting of three seagoing ironclads and two tiny second-class vessels, little larger than gunboats. Thereafter the German navy grew steadily, albeit modestly. By the late 1880s it numbered eleven sea-going armoured vessels, although two were thoroughly obsolete. In combination with the French battlefleet it could arguably have posed a challenge to British control of the sea – the only combination of two powers capable of so doing between 1860 and 1890 – but the likelihood of a Franco-German alliance was, after 1871, insignificant. Furthermore, German naval strategy was explicitly defensive: the navy functioned as an adjunct of the Army, its task the defence of the Baltic and North Sea coasts. From its inception to 1888 Army officers commanded the German navy.[23]

The Austro-Hungarian navy was weaker than either the Italian or the Russian battlefleets; as of 1880 only two of its five ironclads above 5000 tons had iron hulls, and the largest vessel in the fleet was 7600 tons, smaller than some second-class British armour-clads. Beyond these powers not another country in the world had pretensions to high-seas naval capability; the Ottoman Empire's seventeen ironclads were largely coast-defence vessels, the Scandinavian countries were likewise content with coastal vessels, Argentina, Peru, and Chile had an ironclad or two apiece, and Japan had only six armoured vessels by 1890, none of them larger than 3700 tons.[24] Hence, the bulk of the British battlefleet was maintained close to home – in the Channel and the Mediterranean – to counter the threat posed by the sole navy that mattered, that of France.

Britain versus France

The only substantive challenge to British naval supremacy between 1850 and 1890 occurred at the dawn of the ironclad era – the late 1850s and early 1860s – when Napoleon III undertook an ambitious ironclad building programme. Beginning with *Gloire* (1858) France had, by 1861, laid down sixteen ironclads. Yet the very nature of the French challenge revealed the difficulties faced by any would-be naval rival. Their designer, Dupuy de Lôme, had attempted to overcome the daunting British superiority in sailing ships-of-the-line through the introduction of the steam line-of-battle ship *Napoleon* in 1847, and tried again to level the playing field

22. Martin, *Statesman's Yearbook* (London, 1881), pp313-14.

23. Beeler, *British Naval Policy in the Gladstone-Disraeli Era*, pp196, 227-8.

24. Roger Chesneau and Eugene Kolesnik, *Conway's All the World's Fighting Ships, 1860-1905* (London, 1979), pp219-20, 360-1, 364-5, 369-70, 372-4, 388-91, 401, 405-06, 410-11, 418.

25. Walker to the Board of Admiralty, 22 June 1858, quoted in Andrew Lambert, *Warrior* (London, 1987), p15.

through technological innovation by initiating the ironclad era. Incapable of besting Britain in an out-and-out naval race, Dupuy de Lôme sought to gain a temporary advantage via technological superiority.

British response to the French challenge, however, was prompt and unequivocal. As influential Surveyor of the Navy Baldwin Wake Walker stated to the Board of Admiralty in June 1858 on receipt of French intentions;

I have frequently stated that it is not in the interest of Great Britain, possessing as she does so large a navy, to adopt any important change in the construction of ships of war which might have the effect of rendering necessary the introduction of a new class of very costly vessels unless such a course is forced upon her by the adoption by Foreign Powers of formidable ships of a novel character requiring similar ships to cope with them, yet then it becomes a matter not only of expediency but of absolute necessity.[25]

Marengo (1869). Typical of the first and second generation French ironclads, which had wooden hulls. (U.S. Naval Historical Center: NH64448)

The moment of absolute necessity had arrived. With its naval supremacy thus threatened, by the end of 1861 Britain had laid down ten ironclads and ordered the armouring of another nine wooden-hulled vessels under construction. Until 1863 this ironclad race appeared to be neck and neck, but by the following year Britain's industrial and shipbuilding superiority had clearly asserted itself, and, as the historian of the Victorian French navy remarks, the first arms race of the industrial era quickly ended with 'the complete victory of England'.[26] By 1870, Britain had completed forty ironclads, France thirty. By 1890, the British had laid down or purchased ninety-six ironclad vessels of all types, the

French seventy-eight, but no less than eleven of the latter were floating batteries of less than 1600 tons displacement.

The British lead was considerably wider than appears on superficial examination, owing to a couple of corollary points. First, prior to the *Redoutable*, laid down in 1873, only two French ironclad boasted iron hulls; not only the *Gloire*, but her two sisters, plus the *Magenta* and *Solferino*, and nine of the ten *Provence* class vessels had wooden hulls, onto which iron armour was bolted.[27] By contrast, twenty-nine of the British armourclads completed by that date had iron hulls, which permitted internal subdivision and watertight compartmentalisation. Wooden hulls, being less rigid, could not be so constructed, giving the British a combat advantage too obvious to require elaboration. Following the collapse of Napoleon III's building challenge, moreover, French construction fell off sharply, both in terms of new ships and the rate at which

Colbert (foreground) and *Redoutable* at Brest. Like most French ocean-going ironclads of the 1870s, they were masted. (U.S. Naval Historical Center: NH74956)

existing vessels were completed. Between 1858 and 1865 the French commenced nineteen first-class, eight second-class (station), and six coast-defence ironclads. Over the course of the next decade, however, the figures were six, five, and six, respectively, while during the same period Britain began ten first-class, nine second-class, and ten coast-defence armourclads, further increasing her numerical advantage (fifteen completed vessels to eleven as of 1865), and giving her close to a two-to-one advantage in the most modern vessels.

This advantage was of especial note in light of the rapid rate of obsolescence caused by improvements in ordnance, armour, and steam technology. Perhaps the most tangible indicator that the world's navies had entered a period of rapid change brought about by mechanisation was the 'see-saw' between the offensive power of the big naval gun and the defensive power of armour plate, which began in the early 1860s and continued for two decades. When HMS *Warrior* was completed in 1861 her 4½in-thick iron plates were impervious to any gun then manufactured. They were not to remain so for long, however. The following year armour 5in thick was pierced in gunnery experiments and in early 1863 Controller Robert Spencer Robinson (admittedly something of an alarmist), warned that every British ironclad 'could be penetrated by shells at 800 yards', which was taken by most officers to be about the extreme range at which future battles would be fought.[28] The Admiralty's response was predictable. Beginning in the early 1860s the swath of armour for new ships was increased to 5½in. The primacy of defence over offence was reasserted, albeit temporarily. In *Bellerophon* (launched 1865) the thickest armour was 6in; in *Hercules* (launched 1868), 9in; and in *Devastation* (launched 1871), 14in.[29] In each instance, however, gun founders quickly designed and constructed larger, more powerful ordnance, and the once-impervious swath of armour was impervious no longer.

In such circumstances, ships only a few years old, often in their first commission, were no longer 'state of the art', their armour no longer proof to the latest ordnance, and their guns no longer able to pierce the armour of new designs being constructed. By 1867 Admiralty Secretary Lord Henry Lennox termed the four earliest British ironclads 'not perfect specimens'.[30] First Lord Hugh Childers was more specific in 1869, noting that the first generation British armoured ships – not one of which at that moment was as much as a decade old – were 'very badly protected,' and by 1872

Childers' successor George J. Goschen informed Parliament of the need 'to replace, as we have begun to do, our older ironclads by other ships . . .'.[31]

The same was true of the French battlefleet, even more so in fact, since wooden hulls were subject to rot along with stress from simple wear and tear, lacking the durability of iron. Thus the fall-off of the French ironclad programme after 1865 paid double dividends across the Channel. Until the mid-1880s the French battlefleet consisted largely of first- and second-generation ironclads, with their wooden hulls and thin armour plating, whereas the British reaped the harvest of continuing to lay down new vessels through the late 1860s and into the following decade. The front line British battle force was, therefore, not only more numerous than that of its main (only?) rival; it was also newer, more heavily armed, and more heavily armoured. The growing disparity was not lost on domestic observers. By 1873, Goschen sounded an unmistakable note of confidence in his annual presentation of the Naval Estimates, informing Parliament that Britain possessed 'twelve ships which were so strong' they had no peers in rival navies.[32] There can be no disputing Goschen's boast. France had been in many respects the technological innovator during the initial building race, but between 1865 and 1879, its designs lagged considerably behind those of Britain in terms of protection and fighting power. As regarded sea-going (as opposed to coast-defence) ironclads, the French continued to design and construct little apart from full-rigged, modestly-protected vessels until the end of the 1870s, whereas the British, as early as 1869, were constructing mastless, heavily-armed and protected 'breastwork monitors', the precursors, in many respects, of pre-Dreadnought battleships. Even the second-class British ironclads of the *Audacious* and *Swiftsure* classes, with iron hulls and 8in armour belts, were markedly superior to the similar-sized first generation French ironclads of the first class, many of which continued to be so designated well into the 1880s. Most of the contemporary French second-class ironclads, by contrast, were half the displacement of their British counterparts, and wooden-hulled. *Audacious* and *Swiftsure* could, and did, take their place in the British line of battle whereas the six French *Almas* were solely 'station battleships', suitable for no greater task than showing the flag overseas.

As a further indication of confidence regarding their superiority, the British were quicker to strike obsolescent ships from the Active List than were the French. By 1885 only two first- or second-genera-

26. Theodore Ropp, *The Development of a Modern Navy: French Naval Policy 1871-1904* (ed. Stephen Roberts, Annapolis, 1987), p10. See also C.I. Hamilton, *Anglo-French Naval Rivalry, 1840-1870* (Oxford, 1993), p316. For a year-by-year breakdown of ships completed between 1863 and 1870, see Stanley Sandler, *The Emergence of the Modern Capital Ship* (Newark, DL., 1979), pp255-6.

27. The same was true of the five French coast-defence rams and eight small 'station' ironclads laid down during the 1860s. See *Conways 1860-1905*, pp298-9, 301-02.

28. Sandler, *Emergence of the Modern Capital Ship*, p101.

29. Parkes, *British Battleships*, pp102, 120, 195.

30. *Hansard*, 3d ser., 185 (1867), col. 1846.

31. Ibid., 3d ser., 194 (1869), col. 898; 3d ser., 210 (1872), col. 450. See also Sandler, *Emergence of the Modern Capital Ship*, pp101-03. Sandler notes that as early as 1863 the 4½in armour of the first British ironclads was no longer impervious to the latest ordnance.

32. *Hansard*, 3d ser., 215 (1873), cols. 44-45.

tion British ironclads remained on the list of battleships, whereas three times that number of first-generation French vessels were so listed. And despite the soundness of their iron hulls, *Warrior* and *Black Prince* were reclassified as armoured cruisers in 1881, owing to their thin armour. Had the British felt any alarm at French pretensions it would have been a simple enough matter to forestall such re-classification, knowing that much of the mid-1880s French battlefleet was inferior even to the very first British ironclads.

The *matériel* mismatch was equally evident in funding. During the 1860s French naval spending ranged from £6.4 to £8.8 million, between 60 and 80 per cent of the analogous British figure. But the humiliating defeat in 1870-1 necessitated a drastic re-prioritisation in French national security policy. The navy of Napoleon III had played an insignificant role in the conflict, passively blockading the north German coast while the army met its ignominious fate. For the subsequent decade, therefore, the bulk of French resources and energy were turned to military reform and renewal. The navy was allowed to languish, giving Britain an unlooked-for 'peace dividend'. In January 1872 Admiralty intelligence reported that the French Minster of Marine had issued a circular 'calling attention to the absolute necessity for rigid economy in the present state of financial difficulty.' The Admiralty itself added '[t]he diminution of ships and men forms only a portion of the saving to be effected in the Navy.'[33]

From 1871 through 1878 French naval spending never broached 60 per cent of the British level, dropping below 50 per cent in 1874 and 1875. This diminution also coincided with a period of rigid economy in British naval administration and is thus even more marked than first appears. The Minister of Marine drew up a new building programme in 1872, which was to be the construction standard for the next two decades, but that year's budget underfunded shipbuilding, allotting only 49 million of the 64 million francs earmarked for new construction.[34] The French assembly regarded the 1872 budget, in turn, as the norm for the subsequent five years. Only in 1879 did French spending again climb above 60 per cent of the British figure. As the Admiralty's Parliamentary Secretary, George John Shaw-Lefevre, noted in an 1880 Admiralty report, 'for three or four years succeeding the Franco German War, very little was done towards adding to the *matériel* of the French Fleet. It was described by the Minister of Marine in 1874 as perishing from want of means; and as the build-ing of ironclads was maintained in England during this period the superiority of the British fleet was assured.'[35]

When, in the early 1880s, the level of French naval funding finally rose significantly the service was confronted with the need to replace the ageing and thoroughly outmoded battlefleet of Napoleon III. The French Programme of 1879 called for a fleet strength of twenty-six battleships (including seven coast-defence battleships), ten station (cruising) battleships, and an additional twelve coast defence vessels, including four torpedo vessels.[36] Within two years, however, this program was whittled to twenty squadron battleships, eight station ironclads, and a dozen coast-defence battleships. Even so, implementation remained problematic. True, the naval budget climbed fairly dramatically, topping out at £8.8 million, or 82 per cent of the British figure, in 1883: a higher sum and percentage than was ever reached during the arms race of two decades earlier. Yet new construction barely kept pace with the phasing-out of the first generation French ironclads. Between 1876 and 1885 seven squadron battleships were completed and another seven launched, but by the latter date eleven of the first generation ironclads had been removed from the active list, and a further three followed suit by 1890.[37]

The British navy scare of 1884, fuelled by W.T. Stead's 'Truth About the Navy' articles in the *Pall Mall Gazette*, was a belated, hysterical, and largely unjustified response to the ambitious French replacement shipbuilding of the early 1880s.[38] By the time Stead published, the French naval budget, which had climbed rapidly between 1878 and 1883, was on the decline again. Discerning spectators were quite aware of not only French aims, but also the means used to finance them. As Admiralty Secretary George Otto Trevelyan informed the House of Commons in 1882; '[T]he whole of the extraordinary French Estimates for rebuilding their Fleet had hitherto been provided, not out of revenue, but as an increase to the National Debt.'[39] The practice of financing naval reconstruction through loans ceased after 1883, however, with dramatic consequences for the building program. During the first half of the decade France laid down four battleships, but no further such vessels were begun until 1889.[40]

The expansion of the French Navy in the early 1880s, along with many other capital improvements, was financed by loans. When these dried up, the navy was forced to take a major cut in its budget, which fell from 217.2 million francs (£8.8 million) in 1883 to

33. Goodenough to Admiralty, 3 January 1872, PRO: ADM1/6238.

34. Ropp, *Development of a Modern Navy*, pp33, 41.

35. Shaw-Lefevre to Admiralty, 1 August 1881, PRO: ADM1/6608.

36. Ropp, *Development of a Modern Navy*, p363.

37. *Conway's 1860-1905*, pp286-7.

38. Realised by astute contemporaries. See John Knox Laughton's anonymous article 'Past and Present State of the Navy,' *Edinburgh Review* (April 1885), pp492-513. 'The alarm has really sprung from ignorance and misrepresentation: ignorance of the facts of our navy as it has been, misrepresentation of the state of our navy as it is.'

39. *Hansard's.*, 3d ser., 268 (1882), col. 1063.

40. *Conway's 1860-1905*, pp303-04. *Dupuy de Lôme* was begun in 1888 and *Amiral Charner* in 1889.

41. Ropp, *Development of a Modern Navy*, p140.

42. *Conway's 1860-1905*, pp29-31, 64-6.

43. Beeler, *British Naval Policy in the Gladstone-Disraeli Era*, pp152-3, 161-2, 277.

Amiral Baudin, part of an ambitious French shipbuilding programme of the late 1870s and early 1880s, which was aimed not at challenging British naval superiority but at replacing the outmoded 1860s-era ironclads. (U.S. Naval Historical Center: NH66054)

171.6 million (£7.8 million) in 1885. As a result, the whole armoured shipbuilding program nearly ground to a halt.[41]

The Stead scare broke after France's naval situation had taken this unmistakable turn for the worse but nonetheless generated a crash construction programme. Between 1884 and 1888, during which time France began no battleships or armoured cruisers, the British began five of the former, seven of the latter, and one coast-defence ironclad, in addition to four battleships laid down in 1882.[42]

Empire, Sea Lanes, and the Guerre de Course

There was, of course, another dimension to command of the sea. Contemporary navalists were fond of pointing out the vastness of the British Empire, the length, extent, and exposure of the sea lanes connecting Empire to Home Islands, the unrivalled size of the British Merchant Marine, and the centrality of seaborne commerce to the survival of the Empire. The Navy, they routinely charged, lacked the necessary vessels to defend this commerce in time of war.[43] Indeed, the arrival of the steam age, in addition to complicating the task of blockading enemy fleets, seemed likewise to make the task of interdicting enemy commerce raiders far more difficult. The performance of Confederate cruisers, in particular CSS *Alabama*, which captured and destroyed upwards of seventy Union merchant vessels during its two-year career, pointed to the apparent menace such vessels posed. More alarming, *Alabama* was small (1050 tons), relatively poorly-armed, and dependent

The armoured cruiser HMS *Warspite* (launched 1884) was in part a response to the threat of commerce-raiders. (U.S. Naval Historical Center: NH52505)

largely on its sails rather than its engines. The scale of Britain's seaborne commerce, the fact that most of it was carried in sailing ships until well into the 1880s, and its vulnerability even to vessels as weak as the *Alabama* all seemed to lend weight to navalist apprehensions.

Yet again it is necessary to consider the issue from the practical standpoint as well as the theoretical. Certainly the task of protecting seaborne commerce grew both in terms of scope and complexity during the early steam era. Piecemeal enlargement of the empire during the pre-1880 period, if nothing else, added to the demands which would have been made on the service in wartime, as did the steady growth of Britain's Merchant Marine and overseas trade. Likewise, it cannot be doubted that the advent of steam did heighten the menace posed to merchant ships in general, and sailing vessels in particular. On the other hand, however, it is plain that the Admiralty did, beginning in the early 1870s, consider systematically the material and operational requirements necessary to meet the *guerre de course* threat. First Naval Lord Alexander Milne repeatedly produced memoranda pointing to the defenselessness of most British trade routes, urging the construction of a large cruiser force with which to interdict enemy raiders.[44] His proposals initially bore only modest fruit—a substantial unarmoured shipbuilding program was implemented in 1876-7—but

44. Milne, 'Paper Relative to Unarmoured Ships, and Proposal for an Establishment' (Copy), Confidential, December, 1874, NMM: MLN/144/3/1 'Position of Cruising Ships for Protection of Trade' (Copy), December 1874, ibid.; 'Unarmoured Ships' (Copy), Confidential, 11 November 1875, ibid., MLN/144/4/2; see also Bryan Ranft, 'The protection of British seaborne trade and the development of systematic planning for war, 1860-1906,' in Bryan Ranft(ed.), *Technical Change and British Naval Policy, 1860-1939* (London, 1977), p2.

45. See Beeler, 'Steam, Strategy, and Schurman', *passim*; Ranft, 'The protection of

British seaborne trade', pp1-10; Schurman, *Imperial Defence, 1868-1887, passim*; W.C.B. Tunstall, 'Imperial Defence, 1815-1870', in *Cambridge History of the British Empire* Vol 2 (Cambridge, 1940), pp807-41; and, 'Imperial Defence, 1870-1897', *Cambridge History of the British Empire* Vol 3, pp230-54.

46. Ranft, 'The protection of British seaborne trade', p2.

47. Ibid, p5.

48. Ibid, pp5-8.

the situation was not allowed to languish. Indeed, the question of defending a world-wide network of coaling stations – the logistical network which would give a steam-age navy the same strategic reach as its sail-powered predecessor – was turned over to the War Office in 1875, and, following the Russian 'war scare' of 1877-8, resulted in the creation of first a Colonial Office Defence Committee (chaired by Milne) and, in 1879, the appointment of Lord Carnarvon's Royal Commission on Colonial Defence (1879-82).[45] Implementation of the latter's proposals regarding coaling station defence was hesitant, owing to the political climate for much of the 1880s, but by the end of the decade the matter was receiving both political and fiscal attention.

Additionally, from the mid-1870s onward the Navy gave serious attention to its anti-commerce-raiding operational strategy. Again, Milne provided the impetus, maintaining that cruisers should be stationed at important strategic 'choke points', such as the mouth of the English Channel, where trade routes converged and the density of merchant shipping was greatest.[46] The enemy threat would be concentrated, he thought, in these areas. Subsequent Admiralty policy followed Milne's lead, most notably in the form of a Foreign Intelligence Committee paper of 1884, and another report the following year which advocated both this course and 'an all-out offensive against enemy ports, coaling stations, and cruisers

as soon as war started.'[47] These strategies have since come in for a great deal of criticism. The renunciation of the traditional and time-tested anti-commerce-raiding strategy of convoy in favour of 'offensive' methods has been roundly criticised, especially in the wake of the latter's disastrous failure to stem the German submarine campaigns of the First World War.[48] Yet it should not be overlooked that at the time that it evolved – the 1870s and 1880s – and even with regard to surface raiders in the early twentieth century, it was a viable strategy. Given the limitations of steam technology in the pre-steel era, coupled with the paucity of coaling stations available to enemy corsairs and the impossibility of coaling at sea, ships bent on commerce destruction would either be tied to their bases, owing to the frequent need to refuel, or else have to operate primarily under sail. In either event, the risk of interdiction by a British cruiser was markedly increased, and in the latter the likelihood of achieving severe depredations similarly reduced. For that matter, precisely the same strategy was used to hunt down German surface raiders during the opening months of the Great War and regardless of the space devoted to *Emden*'s exploits it must also be

The Russian proto-armoured cruiser *General Admiral* (1873). Ships such as this drew domestic British attention to the threat of the *guerre de course*. (U.S. Naval Historical Center: NH60734)

stressed that it worked: all of Germany's cruisers at sea in August 1914 had been chased down by December.

Furthermore, it is easy to exaggerate the real threat as it existed in the 1870s and early 1880s. To be sure, there was more of the empire and more overseas trade to be protected in the event of a war, but there was not a great deal from which it needed defending. So far from seizing on the opportunity to build fast steam-powered cruisers with which to menace British trade, most of the Empire's naval rivals contented themselves with building traditional, slow, unprotected sail/steam cruisers, suited more to the peacetime duties of maritime police forces than to the *guerre de course*. France, to cite the most prominent example, laid down only three cruisers capable of more than 15kts during the 1870s, and all were unprotected vessels, vulnerable even to light-calibre ordnance.[49] Only in 1882 did the French Navy begin work on its first fast protected cruiser.

Much historical attention has been dedicated to the Russian Navy, which began building proto-armoured cruisers in the early 1870s. These vessels were aimed explicitly at menacing British trade.[50] Yet even in this case the threat was more apparent than actual. The vessels in question – *General Admiral* and *Gerzog Edinburgski* – were too slow under steam for their designed task, owing to the deficiencies of their domestically-produced engines. Worse still, from the Russian standpoint, they would, owing to geographical constraints, had to have operated from Vladivostok, far from any heavily-travelled British trade routes. The danger posed by two such vessels operating far from the main arteries of the Empire was not one with which the Admiralty needed to be unduly concerned, and thus it comes as little surprise to find that most of the dire warnings emanating from navalists pointed to latent dangers, rather than existing ones. Additionally, no potential naval adversary possessed the comprehensive logistical network of coaling stations overseas that would be necessary to sustain a concerted *guerre de course*. Indeed, as Thomas Brassey remarked in 1889, 'we find the resources of our neighbours for the conduct of

naval operations in distant waters slender indeed in comparison with those which we command.'[51]

Hence, notwithstanding the *Jeune École*'s emergence in the mid-1880s, the *guerre de course* was not a threat that seriously endangered Britain until the advent of practical submarines armed with torpedoes in the early twentieth century. To be sure, throughout the 1870s and early 1880s the Navy lacked the requisite vessels to protect Britain's vast and far-flung commerce in the event of a large-scale naval conflict. But no other power possessed a fleet of commerce raiders capable of posing that large-scale threat. Britannia, in sum, ruled the waves by default, if by no other means.

The Domestic Context

Of course, numerous contemporary charges of inadequate funding can be found, despite the favourable foreign situation. These naturally emanated from the usual sources: hawkish politicians and disgruntled professionals whose unhappiness with peacetime defence spending may be taken for granted. Yet curiously, their perceptions continue to inform modern assessments of mid-Victorian naval policy. 'It is doubtful,' writes one recent authority, 'whether Britain was able at any other time to purchase security at so cheap a price', and there can be no question that the £10-12 million annually allotted the Navy was tiny by the standards of the 1910-14 era, when the service's yearly budget routinely nudged the £40 million mark.[52]

As is the case with after-the-fact indictments of the battlefleet's condition, it is important to keep in mind that contemporaries did not see matters from the perspective of hindsight. What they saw, instead, was a service whose cost grew rapidly and alarmingly as a consequence of technological change. During the 1830s naval spending had never risen above £6 million a year, and through the subsequent decade it never topped £7.5 million.[53] But, as the *Times* unhappily editorialised in March 1867, although '[t]here used . . . to be some notion of a respectable and judicious average of naval

---

49. *Conway's 1860-1905*, pp317-19.

50. N.A.M. Rodger, 'British Belted Cruisers', *Mariner's Mirror* 64/1 (1978), pp24-5.

51. Thomas Brassey, *Naval Annual* 3 (Portsmouth, 1889), p231.

52. C.J. Bartlett, 'The Mid-Victorian Reappraisal of Naval Policy', p189.

53. B.R. Mitchell and Phyllis Deane, *Abstract of British Historical Statistics* (Cambridge, 1962), p397.

54. *The Times*, 23 March 1867, p8.

55. Ibid. 2 March 1876, p9 and 21 April 1874, p 9. Actually, £10 million was never spent in any one year between 1866 and 1880, save in one extraordinary instance, on what the contemporary political world knew as the 'effective' portion of the Navy. Among the various heads printed in the Navy Estimates were Votes 16 and 15, the former of which covered the sums disbursed for Half Pay and Retired Pay for naval officers and the latter pensions of various kinds. These Votes covered what was sometimes termed the 'deadwood' in the Estimates. Half Pay was the naval officer's equivalent of the dole and Retired Pay his pension. These outlays, particularly in the case of Half and Retired Pay stipends,

was expenditure over which the Admiralty and the government could exert relatively little control. The sums applied to these heads were not trifling; Half Pay and Retired Pay cost the Navy almost £700,000 in 1867-78, and the figure had, by 1879-80, climbed to little short of £900,000, thanks primarily to the workings of a recently-introduced mandatory retirement scheme. Similarly, civil and military pensions accounted for the better part of three-quarters of a million pounds in 1867-8, and had topped £1.1 million twelve years later.

There was also another component of naval expenditure from which the service received no benefit whatsoever, namely, the cost of transporting soldiers overseas for the Army. As might be imagined, expenditure on of this service could vary widely from year to year, contingent on the amount of action which the Army saw and where it occurred. Hence, sums expended on Conveyance of Troops ranged from a low of below £200,000 a year for the four years from 1872-3 through 1875-6 – sinking to £141,425 in 1874-5 – to a high of almost £850,000 in 1878-9, the consequence of British intervention in the affairs of the East, most notably the dispatch of Indian troops to Malta. Not only did the Navy gain nothing from this duty and its attendant expense; wear and tear on troopships ultimately swelled the costs of shipbuilding and repair.

56. Ibid. 17 November 1876, p7.

expenditure . . . steam and iron have long since broken through that.'[54] The cost of building a machine-age navy destroyed the 'respectable and judicious average of naval expenditure' which had been maintained during the 1830s, 1840s, and for much of the 1850s. By the late 1860s it was widely maintained that if Britain did not possess its requisite level of naval strength it was certainly not 'for the want of paying for it'. The naval budget more than doubled between 1849 and 1861, from £6.2 to £12.5 million. The *Times* doubtless spoke for many of its readers when observing that while the Navy should not be allowed to waste away, neither did they 'want to spend more than 10 millions' on it, but with the exception of Gladstone's first administration (1868-74), when the Naval Estimates were kept to roughly that level, the country typically paid £11 million and upwards.[55] Hence, notwithstanding the carping of professionals, from the contemporary perspective the 'strength of the British Navy [was] unmatched, if vastness and costliness be taken as affording the practical measure of its power.'[56]

In sum, then, the relatively modest margin of numerical superiority over the French battlefleet between 1865 and 1890 should not obscure the fundamental realities on which British naval policy was founded during the mid-Victorian era. If it appears in retrospect that Britain was content with something nearer a one- rather than a two-power standard, it was due to the fact that there was not another naval power in the world apart from France capable of challenging, much less endangering, naval supremacy on the high seas. Moreover, behind the numbers were telling factors which reinforced Britain's hegemony: unrivalled shipbuilding facilities, both in the Royal Dockyards and the private sector, equally unrivalled financial resources to draw on in the event of an arms race, and, not least of all, the psychological advantage born

The launch of HMS *Colossus*, 1882. (U.S. Naval Historical Center: NH61371)

of the navy's tradition of victory, stretching back through Nelson, Howe, Hawke, Drake, and numerous other heroes.

This favourable assessment should not, however, imply that the Navy was lavished with funds for building the fleet on which national and imperial security depended. Like all peacetime defence establishments in constitutional mass democracies, it had to lobby strenuously for its funding, and was not capable of maintaining the level of naval strength desired by the professionals at the Admiralty. Moreover, there were a host of factors outside the Admiralty's control that influenced the speed and degree to which the Navy underwent its technological transformation. As a consequence, those responsible for designing and building the Navy's vessels were continually faced with difficult choices: about the types of ships best suited to performing the myriad tasks demanded of a world-wide force, about size and power of engines, about coal capacity, about weight of guns and thickness of armour *versus* displacement and cost, and about innumerable other quandaries, both great and small.

In addition, Admiralty policy-makers were forced to contend with public opinion, for the choices it made often aroused hostile comment in Parliament and the press. Every point on which differing opinions existed – and these were numerous indeed – had the potential to generate criticism and disagreement outside as well as inside Whitehall. As Walter Bagehot noted in the course of his celebrated explanation of the structure and functioning of the British constitution;

[t]here are two cries against the Admiralty which go on side by side: one says, 'We have not ships enough, no 'relief' ships, no

Openly imitative of a French ironclad design, *Collingwood* (launched 1882) is used by critics as more evidence of the Admiralty's reactionary mentality. (U.S. Naval Historical Center: NH75973)

navy, to tell the truth'; the other cry says, 'We have all the wrong ships, all the wrong guns, and nothing but the wrong; in their foolish constructive mania the Admiralty have been building when they ought to have been waiting; they have heaped a curious museum of exploded inventions, but they have given us nothing serviceable'.[57]

Most commonly, however, the Admiralty was regularly accused of lagging behind in matters of technology. The Navy, declaimed the *Times* in early December 1874, was 'always lagging' in the 'technological race'.[58] 'It was so with the introduction of steam power to the Navy, and with the application of armour plating to our ships. We followed, instead of leading, in these two important changes.' This charge was neither new nor unusual by 1874. Numerous organs of the press had during the latter 1860s engaged in an acrimonious campaign against the Admiralty with the aim of pressuring it to adopt the design theories of Captain Cowper Phipps Coles, one of the inventors of the turret system of mounting and protecting heavy ordnance.[59] And, in 1872, during one of the periodic domestic alarms regarding the state of the Navy's *matériel* the *Times* charged '[i]f during the last two years we had been building a different kind of Navy, it might never have been necessary to startle the public from their slumbers. But the time has come when silence would be treason.'[60] In sum, '[t]wo short years have sufficed to derange the whole fabric of our maritime ascendancy.'

Such contemporary charges of technological backwardness, of Admiralty foot-dragging, continue to inform modern assessments. Oscar Parkes coined the catch-phrase 'the Dark Ages of the Victorian Navy' to describe the decade between 1873 and 1883.[61] And even Stanley Sandler, ordinarily sympathetic to administrators, both civil and naval, facing technological dilemmas, attributes the Admiralty's failure after 1871 to follow the progressive recommendations of a Committee on Designs for Ships of War to the combined effects of 'conservative influence in the Admiralty and economy-minded political leaders at Westminster'. Furthermore, he regards the period from 1870 to 1885 as having been one of 'stagnation in British warship design'.[62]

On the most obvious level these charges contain a kernel of truth. As the *Times* pointed out, the British did lag behind in many technological innovations. France was the first country to embark on the construction of a sea-going ironclad and had been, for that matter, faster in converting its wooden sailing battlefleet to steam. Moreover, contemporaries, and more notably naval historians, focused on the retention of sails and muzzle-loading ordnance into the 1870s and even the 1880s, the Admiralty's apparent slowness in adopting the Whitehead – that is to say, the self-propelled – torpedo, and other instances of apparent reluctance to embrace new technology, to buttress the argument that the British Navy during the early ironclad era was beset with conservatism bordering on, if not plunging over the precipice into, reaction, foot-dragging, and sometimes downright ineptitude.[63]

It is crucial to bear in mind, however, that technology does not exist in a vacuum; it has consequences beyond the narrow realm of efficiency – not least among them cost – and, moreover, choices regarding design and technology are necessarily based at least in part on non-technological considerations. Contemporary critics did not always base their critiques on the same considerations which informed the decisions of naval policy-makers, and subsequent commentators have too often failed to take in the full scope of policy considerations before rendering judgement on the technological results of those policies. The following chapters will thus attempt to place design policy within the context of politics, economics, industrial and shipbuilding infrastructure, and naval strategy, the framework in which that policy evolved.

---

57. Walter Bagehot, *The English Constitution* (reprint ed., Ithaca, NY, 1963), p205.

58. *The Times*, 3 December 1874, p9.

59. Sandler, *Emergence of the Modern Capital Ship*, pp177-233. Sandler provides a comprehensive summary of the struggle between the Admiralty and Coles in his chapter 'Captain Coles and the Turret Warship.' See also his article ''In Deference to Public Opinion': the loss of H.M.S. *Captain*', *Mariner's Mirror* 59/1 (1973), pp57-68.

60. *The Times*, 21 October 1872, p 9.

61. Parkes, *British Battleships*, pp230.

62. Sandler, *Emergence of the Modern Capital Ship*, pp247-8.

63. Parkes, *British Battleships*, pp217, 230-1, 260-1; N.A.M. Rodger, 'Dark Ages of the Admiralty, Part II,' *Mariner's Mirror* 62/1 (1976), pp45-6; Sandler, *Emergence of the Modern Capital Ship*, pp248-9.

Chapter 2

MATERIALS AND CONSTRUCTION

'The Admiralty has not yet recognised the great truth that the wooden navies of the world have ceased to exist as effective instruments of war.'

The Times, 11 March 1868

'Engineers and shipbuilders are, I think, generally of opinion that steel must eventually displace iron in shipbuilding, both for hull and machinery. I do not fully understand why the rate of progress towards this desirable end is so slow.'

Nathaniel Barnaby to the Institution of Naval Architects, 1875

IN 1859 the Royal Navy gained a crucial technological advantage over the rest of the maritime world through the decision to construct HMS *Warrior*, the first British sea-going ironclad, wholly out of iron. It was an eloquent testimonial to the nation's industrial lead over its rivals, especially France, whose ironclad navy was largely extemporised by bolting armour plate on wooden hulls. No other country in the world could compete with British iron production or shipbuilding.[1] However, during the course of *Warrior*'s construction, and even well into the 1860s, the Navy continued to advance the construction of several wooden steam battleships laid down in the late 1850s in response to the perceived naval challenge mounted by Napoleon III. As the future D.N.C. Sir William White observed in the *Quarterly Review* several years later,

[t]he conduct of our naval affairs from 1858 to 1860 appears almost inexplicable; and the Admiralty Boards holding office during that period cannot be freed from censure for their sins both of omission and commission. They simply yielded to a *vis inertia* which carried them smoothly on in a well-worn track long after it should have been left; and instead of initiating a policy, or relying, as the French did, upon the skill of their naval architects, they waited for the pressure of public opinion before venturing on anything like extensive changes . . .[2]

White, however, was misinformed. The source of the inertia, as matters would have it, was not Whitehall, but rather Number 10 Downing Street, the foremost advocate of the policy being none other than Lord Palmerston.[3] It might be added that Palmerston's motives were not the products of hide-bound traditionalism, as alleged by subsequent critics. Indeed, they might be viewed more as a rational manifestation of caution imbued by years of experience or, more prosaically, a hedging of technological bets owing to the seriousness of the stakes. With Britain's naval supremacy in the balance, and with the superiority of sea-going ironclads still undemonstrated – despite the success of the armoured floating batteries used in the Crimea – Palmerston could not justify a wholesale switch to iron, despite enthusiastic endorsements of such a policy

by his subordinates Parliamentary Secretary to the Admiralty Lord Clarence Paget and Chancellor of the Exchequer William Ewart Gladstone.[4] The former based his advocacy on grounds of technological superiority, the latter on those of economy.[5]

Only in 1861, with irrefutable evidence of France's wholehearted commitment to ironclads, was Britain's policy of simultaneously augmenting the wooden battlefleet abandoned, although even at this late date the Admiralty still entertained doubts as to the ultimate success of *Warrior* and her sister-ship *Black Prince*. That year Surveyor Baldwin Wake Walker was ordered 'to report as to their fitness for use as transports or other duties should it be deemed advisable at any time to strip off their armour plates.'[6] It was by no means the last instance of caution on the part of government or Admiralty regarding the composition of the Navy.

As late as 1871 Controller of the Navy Captain Robert Hall envisioned a continuing role for the wooden battlefleet. In the event of a great clash at sea, he speculated, in which both ironclad fleets were severely mauled, 'the Power having a few wooden screw line of battle ships at command might, by manning them with the crews of the iron-clads under repair, seize great and possibly decisive advantages.'[7] Moreover, argued the Controller, since France had yet to scrap all of its remaining ships-of-the-line, 'I think we should have some also' and he urged that ten be kept in a state of readiness. Hall's opinion was certainly well behind the times by that point, even though there were still two wooden battleships putatively under construction.[8] Still, as late as 1867 First Lord of the Admiralty Henry Corry maintained in a Cabinet memorandum that unarmoured battleships were useful, and that six under construction or in ordinary should be 'brought forward' to replace those on active service in need of repair.[9] But as far as the actual building of wooden battleships was concerned, a vote in the House of Commons in April 1861 on Radical M.P. William Lindsay's motion 'calling for an end to the construction of wooden capital ships marked the end of the [wooden] steam battleship.'[10]

This triumph for the advocates of iron turned out to be incomplete, however, since the battlefleet was but one element of the British Navy. Through the remainder of the 1860s the more zealous of the economic Radicals and Free Trade Liberals, often along with the ardent navalists in Parliament, called for the complete abandonment of wooden shipbuilding in the Navy, regardless of the type, size, or intended use of the vessel. Shipbuilder and Liberal M.P. Joseph Samuda, for instance, objected in 1867 to the Admiralty's plans to build composite gunboats (wooden hulls over iron frames), to replace wooden vessels suffering from rot: '[h]e doubted whether a composite ship was longer lived than a wooden one . . . The restoration should have been in iron and not wooden ships.'[11] A year later Hugh Childers, speaking in opposition, chided First Lord Corry for want of zeal in the pursuit of economy, reminding him that the means by which the Government might economise on naval expenditure were 'by a reduction in the number of men, by a general watchful economy throughout the Estimates, and by ceasing to build wooden ships . . .'.[12]

In 1867 the *Times*, fulminating on the system of maintaining overseas squadrons, proclaimed that 'protection by wooden ships is no protection at all, except against enemies who will undertake to confine their operations to wood.'[13] The course to be adopted was clear, stated the 'leading journal': '[l]et them go, then, and let us waste no unavailing regrets over them.' The advice was not heeded. Through the 1870s, the rate of unarmoured shipbuilding, a substantial proportion of it consisting of wooden or composite vessels, trailed closely behind that of ironclad construction. Several cogent factors, however, contributed to continued wooden warship building, even when a stronger and more durable alternative was widely and cheaply obtainable. What seems upon superficial examination to have been hostility to change was, when appreciated in context, a pragmatic decision, dictated largely by logistic, geographic, and technological constraints.

That iron was a more durable material than wood for the construction of ships' hulls was, by the mid-1860s, no longer a matter of dispute.[14] In 1863, it is true, Lord Clarence Paget maintained in the House of Commons 'that the question of wood *versus* iron is one which may be argued any way', but he was speaking specifically of the ability to absorb the blows of heavy artillery.[15] Regardless of Paget's context, though, in the course of the same debate Radical M.P. William Lindsay, himself a ship owner, cited the testimony of eminent private-sector shipbuilders John Scott Russell and John Laird, as well as Navy Controller Spencer Robinson, all of whom held iron to be the superior shipbuilding material.[16] Moreover, Lindsay himself, speaking from personal knowledge,

1. Paul Kennedy, *The Rise and Fall of the Great Powers* (New York, 1987), p51; B.R. Mitchell, *European Historical Statistics* (2nd rev. ed., New York, 1980), pp412-13. In 1860 British pig iron production was 3,772,000 metric tons. Its closest European rival, France, produced 898,000 metric tons.

2. White quoted (approvingly) in Parkes, *British Battleships*, p14.

3. Philip Guedalla (ed.), *Gladstone and Palmerston*, (New York, 1928), p114. Palmerston wrote to Gladstone on 29 November 1859 'there are good opinions both ways as to Line of Battleships but I own I think the balance of argument strongly in Favour of having as many of them as needed to over match those which could be brought against us. I take it the Command of the Ocean will still be with the Power that can fit out the strongest Fleet of Line of Battle Ships.' See also Palmerston to the Duke of Somerset, 25 September 1859, quoted in Andrew Lambert, *Warrior*, p29.

4. Palmerston to Gladstone, 29 November 1859 printed in Guedalla, *Gladstone and Palmerston*, p114. 'Whether Iron plated ships will stand such shot as improved Science will bring to bear against them remains to be seen. . . .' His caution was seconded, it might be added, by no less an authority than the Surveyor of the Navy, Sir Baldwin Wake Walker, who, in a memorandum to the Board on 27 July 1858, stated that ironclads 'must be regarded as an addition to our force, as a balance to those of France, and not calculated to supersede any existing class of ship; indeed no prudent man would, at present, consider it safe to risk upon the performance of ships of this novel character, the Naval Supremacy of Great Britain.' Baldwin Walker quoted in Lambert, *Warrior*, p16.

5. Andrew Lambert, *Battleships in Transition* (London, 1984), p78. 'Gladstone . . . alone among the Cabinet [Paget was not of Cabinet rank] had a realistic conception of the needs of Britain's defence. He regarded the danger of invasion as altogether "visionary", yet he favoured a strong Navy and tried to ensure that the Navy Estimates were expended on the most useful vessels. Having decided that ironclads must be the ships of the future he consistently opposed spending money on wooden ships, calling for the transfer of moneys voted for timber to the construction of ironclads. In this he clashed with Palmerston, who considered it necessary to match the French in both types of battleship.' See also Parkes, *British Battleships*, p14; Guedalla, *Gladstone and Palmerston*, p114. Gladstone wrote to Palmerston on 19 February 1861: 'I am not opposed to applying a larger *share* of our Ship-building force and expenditure to iron-cased or shot-proof vessels.' In fact, he maintained to Palmerston that he had written to Somerset on this very matter, but 'that was with a view to the substitution of work on Shot-proof ships for a part of our vast expenditure on Wooden Line of Battle Ships, of which I doubted the utility.'

6. Quoted in Parkes, *British Battleships*, p30.

7. Remarks of Hall on the *Report of the Committee on Designs for Ships of War*, 26 July 1871, PRO: ADM1/6212.

8. Lambert, *Battleships in Transition*, p82. Work on them had been suspended for years, however.

9. Memorandum by Henry Corry for the Cabinet (Copy), Confidential, 2 December 1867, Milne Papers, NMM: MLN/143/3/10, p2.

10. Lambert, *Battleships in Transition*, p82.

11. *Hansard's Parliamentary Debates*, 3rd ser., 186 (1867), col. 347-48.

12. Ibid., 3d ser., 192 (1868), col. 70.

13. *The Times*, 8 April 1867, p8.

14. E. Pellew Halstead, 'Iron-cased Ships', *Journal of the Royal United Services Institution* 5 (1861), p126. In 1861 Halstead provided a lengthy list of iron's advantages: '1. Greater facility for procuring, selecting, and maintaining throughout the fabric, any requisite standard of strength in the material used; without any process of 'seasoning', and with a certainty unattainable with any wood. 2. Greater facility in producing any form, however finely modified. 3. Greater facility for combining a maximum of strength, with a minimum of material. 4. Complete adaptability to vessels of every size. 5. Greater facility of imparting 'strength of material' to every subordinate portion, and in every direction throughout the structure. 6. Greater lightness with equal strength. 7. Greater roominess in ships of equal external dimensions. 8. Shorter period for construction. 9. Less expense, tonnage for tonnage, in all large-sized ships. 10. Greater durability. 11. Less liability to repair, and far greater facility for it when required. 12. Superior security against the effects of leakage – however caused – and also against fire – by the greater facility of employing watertight bulk-heads, partial or complete, longitudinal or transverse, in any number, and for any purpose, considered requisite.' Against this impressive run-down Halstead could list only two drawbacks: compass deviation caused by the iron hull, a problem which had been largely solved by the time he presented his paper, and rapid fouling of the hull. Twenty-seven years prior to this Macgregor Laird, of the pioneering iron shipbuilding firm at Birkenhead, had given a similar list of advantages in testimony to a Select Committee on Steam Navigation to India, without mentioning any drawbacks. See Daniel Headrick, *The Tools of Empire: Technology and European Imperialism in the Nineteenth Century*, (New York, 1981), pp28-9.

15. *Hansard*, 3rd ser., 169 (1863), col. 1351.

16. Ibid, cols. 1334-45.

was forthright: 'in an iron ship the various parts were practically welded into one another, so that the whole structure became almost a solid body, and formed a vessel infinitely stronger and more durable for all purposes than a wooden ship.'[17] As a consequence, he continued, 'for the last ten years he had not built a wooden ship, having come to the conclusion that iron ships were . . . altogether a better investment than wooden ones.'

Furthermore, the escalation of size and weight of capital ships

The stem of HMS *Howe*, prior to launch in 1885. British shipyards, both public and private, could turn out battleships like *Howe* faster than foreign yards. (U.S. Naval Historical Center: NH75914)

and the introduction of steam worked to the disadvantage of wood, even prior to the ironclad era.

> [T]he use of steam machinery placed new demands on the fabric of the [wooden] ship, both by its weight and the vibration . . . While these problems were overcome it was at the cost of a marked increase in the amount of timber and iron worked into the later ships. This pushed up the weight of the ship and brought fresh demands for increased engine power.[18]

The concurrent escalation in the size and weight on naval ordnance only served to exacerbate the situation still further. 'Basically', writes Andrew Lambert, 'wood was [by 1850] no longer a suitable material for the construction of warships that had to carry a concentrated weight of engines and artillery.'[19]

But what applied to large warships was not true of small vessels of the so-called 'non-fighting navy' – sloops, corvettes, gunvessels, and gunboats – and the circumstances of their deployment made the continuance of wooden construction in many ways preferable to a wholesale switchover to iron. In their study of the role of the gunboat in British colonial and imperial policy during the second half of the nineteenth century, Anthony Preston and John Major maintain that the Navy should have made the shift to iron construction, and that it did not was a consequence of Admiralty penny-pinching. 'Iron construction would have been ideal', they remark in reference to gunboat construction during the mid-Victorian era, 'but in 1868 the Admiralty would never have sanctioned the construction of an unarmoured iron fighting ship.'[20] However, this verdict overlooks salient facts. By 1868 the large unarmoured frigate *Inconstant* was already well in hand and *Volage*, another frigate, was being laid down. Both had iron hulls.[21] Moreover, in 1864 the Navy laid down two iron-hulled armoured gunboats and by the middle of the 1870s wooden shipbuilding in the Royal Dockyards had ceased.[22] Of course, not all shipbuilding was carried out in the Dockyards, and although the last wholly wooden Royal Navy vessel was launched in 1874, when Thomas Brassey published his first *Naval Annual* in 1886 the service was still building composite ships.[23]

Moreover, notwithstanding its durability, iron had significant drawbacks for shipbuilding. First, it did not mix well with seawater. Iron, noted Paget during the course of the 1863 debates on shipbuilding, 'is adapted to very large constructions, it lasts longer, but it greatly interferes with speed and steerage, owing to the immediate deposit of grass and shells, necessitating continual docking and painting.'[24] 'Timber hulls', notes a more recent authority, 'would not foul as did iron hulls, which, if not scraped regularly, suffered from bottoms which resembled a "lawyer's wig"'.[25]

This problem was of course universal, regardless of where a ship served, although it was unquestionably more severe in tropical waters, where marine growth was most rapid. For merchant vessels operating on regular schedules, and with regular access to docking facilities, it was not an insurmountable obstacle to efficient sailing or steaming. Likewise, for British warships operating in European waters, within reasonable proximity of the Dockyards, regular cleaning and painting were feasible. But elsewhere on the world's oceans the situation was very different. The Navy lacked dry-dock facilities in the Pacific, for instance, until 1886, and the facility constructed at Esquimalt, Vancouver Island, could not be used without considerable inconvenience and loss of time by ships patrolling the South American coast.[26] Likewise, although there was a dock at Hong Kong capable of admitting second-class ironclads, so much difficulty attended its use that 'British Admirals preferred to avail themselves of the Japanese Navy's excellent facilities and dock their flagships at Nagasaki or Yokohama.'[27]

Because of its strength and structural rigidity, iron quickly became the material of choice for large ships in the British Navy, once iron armour had demonstrated its effectiveness. As Oscar Parkes suggests, however, there was a price attached to this conversion, that being that iron ships intended for duty on distant stations often had their hulls sheathed with a layer of wood, followed by a skin of copper sheeting. Copper was the one material which did significantly retard the growth of marine life on a ship's hull, but one could not simply copper an iron hull. In contact with each other and seawater the two metals generated electricity, turning the hull into a battery. The charge produced by this 'galvanic action' negated the virtues of copper as a deterrent to fouling and, equally serious, rapidly corroded the iron. Even in wooden-hulled ironclads a current was created if armour plates and copper came in contact with each other, as was demonstrated by a report on the French ironclad *Gloire* in the early 1860s. When the vessel 'was docked a few months since . . . the copper was as much covered with barnacles and weeds, as if the hull had been of iron . . . the armour-plating was greatly affected by oxide, and showed holes five or six millimetres (nearly a quarter on an inch) deep in many

places.'[28] Thus a shield of wood was needed between the two metals.

Sheathing iron hulls first with wood then copper was both heavy and expensive, but short of embarking on a large-scale dry-dock construction programme around the world, it was the only practical policy. Sending ships on distant stations home periodically for cleaning was pointless; by the time a ship returned to its station the hull would be thoroughly foul again. To have rotated ships in commission more frequently would have required a larger number of vessels for reliefs and, as it was, in the 1870s the Admiralty had recurring problems finding ships to spare for this purpose in the first place. Coppering iron hulls in this manner was expensive, but it was undeniably cheaper than the logical alternatives, and for the economy-minded politicians and naval administrators of the 1860s, 1870s, and early 1880s, this was reason enough.

If a hull was wood, however, rather than iron, the need for an additional layer of wood to act as a shield vanished, and the copper sheeting could be fastened to the ship itself. And if the vessel was small rather than large, and did not carry heavy engines and ordnance, then iron's superior strength and rigidity became largely irrelevant, and the problem of fouling was not so obviously offset by other virtues. Hence, any pressing reason to convert to iron vanished. That wood lacked iron's durability was undeniable, but this one advantage was insufficient to tip the scales when constructing small ships. For capital ships the need to strengthen and enlarge the hull in order to carry the increased burdens of steam machinery and heavy ordnance 'helped to make the iron-hulled ship cheaper to build as well as cheaper to maintain', but again what applied to large vessels was not equally applicable to their smaller counterparts.[29] The latter did not require the same extent of strengthening or enlarging, and the relative lack of strain on the hull meant that the incidence of maintenance was lessened as well. Of course, the fact that the hull itself could be coppered reduced the expense of one element of maintenance considerably.

17. Ibid, col. 1334.

18. Lambert, *Battleships in Transition*, p117.

19. Ibid. Both the British and the French did, of course, build several wooden-hulled ironclads, but in the case of the former the motives were entirely expediency and economy – the conversion of wooden hulls to ironclads was cheaper and probably quicker than building iron-hulled vessels from scratch – and in the case of the latter the constraints on iron shipbuilding from an inadequate ferrous metals industry. On the British timber-hulled ironclads, see Sandler, *The Emergence of the Modern Capital Ship* , pp43-6.

20. Anthony Preston and John Major, *Send a Gunboat!* (London, 1967), p93.

21. George Ballard, 'British Corvettes of 1875: The *Inconstant and Raleigh*', *Mariner's Mirror* 22/1 (1936), pp43-53 and 'British Corvettes of 1875: The *Volage, Active, and Rover*', *Mariner's Mirror* 23/1 (1937), pp53-67; Fred Mitchell and Conrad Dixon, *Ships of the Victorian Navy* (reprint ed., Southampton, 1987), pp65, 103.

22. *Conway's 1860-1905*, p111; Mitchell and Dixon, *Ships of the Victorian Navy*, pp40, 48.

23. Thomas Brassey, *Naval Annual* 1, (Portsmouth, 1886), pp188-94.

24. *Hansard*, 3rd ser., 169 (1863), col. 1348.

25. Sandler, *Emergence of the Modern Capital Ship*, p43. See also Halstead, 'Iron-cased Ships,' p126. Halstead was equally graphic. The two objections to iron hulls were, he stated, compass deviation and 'the great an rapid fouling of the ship's bottom, due to the facility for adhesion, offered to every marine substance, by the surface of every material yet applied for the protection of the bottom from corrosion; and this objection – costing its annual tens of thousands among all concerned, remains to the present day. . . .' Various remedies were proposed and tried by the Admiralty during the 1860s and 1870s, but none proved efficacious. As Parkes observes, zinc and a patent formula known as 'Muntz metal' after its inventor were both tried to reduce fouling, 'but were inferior in this respect to copper'; Parkes, *British Battleships*, p157.

26. Parkes, *British Battleships*, p157.

27. N.A.M. Rodger, 'British Belted Cruisers', *Mariner's Mirror* 64/1 (1978), p28. The most serious drawbacks of the Hope dock at Hong Kong were that the route to the dock was beset with strong cross-currents, and the entrance was so shallow that ironclads had to remove virtually every moveable item – coal, guns, water, ammunition, plus the upper masts – and even then could only enter at the highest of spring tides.

28. Quoted by John Laird in *Hansard*, 3rd ser., 173 (1864), col. 1149.

29. Lambert, *Battleships in Transition*, p66.

Another point which told in favour of building small vessels of wood, rather than iron, was, ironically enough, that wood was in many respects the superior material for absorbing solid shot, if not necessarily explosive shells. Experiments conducted at Woolwich in 1845 by firing solid shot at iron plating of various thicknesses revealed that plates struck at high velocity shattered, producing numerous dangerous splinters.[30] Moreover, when plates as thick as five-eighths of an inch or more were struck, 'the shot were [*sic*] shivered to fragments from the force of impact'; and on one occasion during the firing, 'a sentry on his post was struck by a splinter at a distance of from 200 to 300 yards from the target, and obliquely in front of it, the piece taken out of his leg being a fragment of shot.' As a consequence the Admiralty concluded that 'ships of iron' are condemned as unfit for the 'purposes of war'. Several large iron frigates being built for the Navy at that time were converted into transports; the 'trials at Woolwich had indicated that the thin shell plating [used for iron hulls] was no substitute for a wooden hull when it came to protection.'[31] Indeed, as Andrew Lambert suggests, the wooden warship persisted—in all navies—after merchant ships of iron were becoming common,

> because the hull of a wooden battleship was far better protection than the thin plating of an iron ship. The disastrous experience of the 1845 iron frigates [those which were converted to transports] convinced many that iron would never be used, and until the idea of fitting armour plates onto an iron hull with a substantial wooden backing [to absorb the force of impact] was adopted, wooden-hulled ironclads proved far stronger than those built entirely of iron.[32]

Of course, shot penetrating wooden hulls also produced splinters, but the resilience of wood actually offered greater resistance to shot and, when penetrated, did not tend to shatter completely, much less cause disintegration of the shot. Moreover, the effects of explosive shell, supposedly the death-knell of the wooden warship, have been considerably overrated by most naval historians.

> It must be emphasised that for all the startling results of shell practice the effects of shell-fire in combat were unimpressive. At Sinope [1853], six Russian sail of the line, three of them 120-gun ships, took several hours to destroy a similar number of frigates and corvettes at close range: with tolerable gunnery equal results would have been expected from solid shot practice.[33]

Therefore, 'the shell guns of the 1840s and 1850s did not revolutionise naval warfare.'

Multiple factors, in sum, militated against the use of iron in smaller, unarmoured ships of war, even beyond the 1870s. Wooden ships may not, by that point, have been cheaper to build —no contemporary seems to have made a close comparison of cost—but they seem unquestionably to have been cheaper and more practical to maintain, especially on distant stations where repair facilities were minimal at best. And although most of the ships of the 'non-fighting navy' ran little risk from large-calibre modern ordnance over the course of their careers, in the event they did become embroiled in a fracas, their wooden hulls were actually a boon rather than a detriment. Contemporaries, moreover, recognised the advantages of wooden hulls in this type of vessel. The repeated onslaughts on this aspect of Admiralty shipbuilding policy which had so characterised the naval debates of the early 1860s dwindled as the decade progressed, and following Childers' strictures in 1868 they virtually disappeared from Parliamentary discourse. George Ward Hunt, in enumerating the vessels building in the dockyards in 1875, listed, along with eight ironclads and eight iron-hulled corvettes, 'six composite corvettes, nine composite sloops, [and] five composite gunboats . . .'.[34] Not one voice was raised in objection to this policy in the debate which followed.

Charges that the Navy was 'behindhand' in embracing iron construction were largely spurious in specific reference to ironclads. From the start the Admiralty's preference was iron. Although in 1858 the Controller, Sir Baldwin Walker, had initially proposed building a wooden-hulled vessel, by early 1859 the ability of an iron hull to resist heavy ordnance when a layer of wood was interposed between hull and armour plates had been demonstrated, and Walker switched to advocating iron hulls.[35] His recommendation was followed by Sir John Pakington's Board when ordering *Warrior*.[36] Iron, moreover, remained the material of choice for British capital ship construction until it began to be supplanted by steel in the late 1870s.

During the course of the 1860s, though, the Navy did build a number of wooden-hulled ironclads. Of forty-one armoured vessels constructed or purchased during the decade fourteen had wooden hulls, but of them five were small experimental vessels and another seven started out as wooden battleships and were converted in the course of construction. Only two were designed from the start as wooden-hulled ironclads intended for general service with the fleet, and even in these two instances an eye to economy entered the Admiralty's calculations. Their construction was put forward as a way to utilise a vast surplus of timber accumulated between 1859 and 1861, before it was too rotten to be of any value.[37] Moreover, all of these ships, as Stanley Sandler points out, were authorised primarily from motives of economy. 'Here was an inexpensive method of keeping Britain's lead in armoured ships.'[38] Lord Clarence Paget further maintained that the Admiralty had been forced to adopt this course by outside pressure:

> [W]e were positively driven by the House of Commons, and, I will admit, by public opinion, not to confine ourselves to iron

34

armoured ships, but to convert what wooden ships we had in the dockyards into armour-plated vessels, in order to, as it was said, to put ourselves in a proper state of defence.[39]

Iron hulls were therefore the rule rather than the exception for British ironclads during the 1860s and 1870s, and during the first decade of the ironclad era they gave the Navy a substantial technological edge over the closest and most serious maritime rival, France. Virtually all French ironclads constructed prior to 1872 had wooden hulls, and these ships suffered from substantial weaknesses in terms of both strength and fighting efficiency.[40] Although Controller Spencer Robinson and First Sea Lord Sir Sydney Dacres could, in the midst of a self-induced panic triggered by the outbreak of the Franco-German War in 1870, claim that Britain's ironclad force was inferior to that of France–at least in terms of sheer numbers–with the cessation of hostilities, not to mention Spencer Robinson's departure from the Admiralty, calmer and more balanced heads prevailed, and more rational assessments of the technological disparity between the two battle-fleets were soon forthcoming.[41] Little more than a year later Admiralty clerk Augustus Spalding compiled a report on the

French fleet in which he 'specially observed in comparing the French and English Ironclads that nearly all the French ships are *wooden* hulls plated with iron, in most cases not above 5 inches in thickness, and they are consequently almost of obsolete type when considered in connection with our ships such as "*Hercules*", "*Monarch*", "*Agincourt*", "*Glatton*", "*Devastation*" &c both as regards construction and powers of defence'.[42]

In fact, stated Spalding, the French armoured ships were no better than the wooden-hulled British ironclads and if, as was reported in the French press, they were beginning to suffer from problems of rot, '[t]he superiority of all the English Ironclads with iron hulls over the French ships is proved to be greater than ever.'[43] To this litany Dacres, who had sounded such an alarmist note a year previously, meekly added '[t]his is a very comprehensive and good report.'

Iron hulls conferred advantages beyond simple durability. An 1877 intelligence report on the French battlefleet by naval attaché Captain Nicholson listed the drawbacks to large ships accruing from wooden construction. It, he said, 'increases the danger from fire . . . prevents their being built with double bottoms, and renders impossible that rigidity of structure without which, after a

30. Halstead, 'Iron-cased Ships,' pp130; Lambert, *Warrior*, pp10-11.

31. Lambert, *Battleships in Transition*, p19.

32. Ibid, p117; Parkes, *British Battleships*, p12. Parkes notes that the efficacy of wooden backing for armour plate was demonstrated by tests conducted by the Admiralty in 1858: 'the *Meteor* with the 20-in. of wood putting up a far better resistance than the iron-hulled *Erebus*, in which the frames were displaced by concussion.'

33. Lambert. *Battleships in Transition*, p92. The further example of the wooden Austrian battleship *Kaiser* at the Battle of Lissa in 1866 is cited. That vessel was in the thick of the action, suffered repeated hits from Italian shells, had by far the largest casualties in the Austrian fleet, and yet was capable of fighting the following day. Lambert attributes the misconception of the effect of shells on wooden ships to J.P. Baxter's, *The Introduction of the Ironclad Warship* (Cambridge, Mass, 1933).

34. *Hansard*, 3d ser., 222 (1875), col. 1653.

35. Lambert, *Warrior*, pp13, 18.

36. Parkes, *British Battleships*, pp12.

37. Ibid, pp49-58, 68-77, 84-101, 108-14, 146-9. One of the two ships, *Lord Clyde*, suffered from premature decay as a consequence of the materials used, and had a very short service career, even by wooden ship standards.

38. Sandler, *Emergence of the Modern Capital Ship*, p44.

39. *Hansard*, 3d ser., 177 (1865), col. 1411. See also Sandler, *Emergence of the Modern Capital Ship*, p44.

40. Spalding to Admiralty, 25 September 1871, PRO: ADM1/6214,. Frederic Martin (ed.), *The Statesman's Yearbook* (London, 1871), pp69-71. According to the intelligence report by Admiralty clerk Augustus Spalding, of the entire French ironclad fleet, then numbering some sixty-two vessels, counting floating batteries and some small armoured gunboats, only two seagoing ironclads and seven floating batteries had iron hulls.

41. Spencer Robinson and Dacres to Childers (Copy), 6 August 1870 PRO: ADM1/6159. Throughout the 1860s, Spencer Robinson consistently rated the British ironclad fleet inferior to its cross-Channel rival, in order to lend weight to his campaigns for enlarged and accelerated shipbuilding programmes. In late 1867, for instance, he wrote that a 'comparison was made between the armoured ships of England and those of France; it was pointed out [in the autumn of 1866] that, on the whole we were manifestly inferior in the number of our ironclads to that Power, taking into account those that were build-

ing . . . The inferiority in the number of ironclad ships which existed in 1866 still exists in 1867.' Spencer Robinson counted thirty-nine English ironclads to forty-six French. (Remarks of Spencer Robinson in Report on the State of the Steam-Ships of the Royal Navy, 12 December 1867, Milne Papers, NMM: MLN/143/4/1)

He was not alone. In November 1867 First Sea Lord Admiral Sir Alexander Milne prepared a memorandum in which he claimed that France outnumbered England in ironclads by fifty-seven to '37 or 39' (Milne Memorandum 'Naval Preparations; Our present state,' 7 November 1867, MLN/143/3/8). The following month Henry Corry drafted a memorandum for the Cabinet which put the ratio at fifty-two to forty-one in favour of France (Memorandum by Corry for the Cabinet [Copy], Confidential, 2 December 1867 MLN/143/3/10). At no time after 1865 was Britain's lead in completed ironclads endangered. Spencer Robinson, Milne and Corry thus serves as a wonderful examples of what defence analyst Edward Luttvak has termed 'amoral navalism'; professionals agitating for the enlargement of the force at their disposal without any regard for either the constraints imposed by politics and foreign policy (or any other factors, for that matter), or the actual menace posed by rival forces.

In 1870 Spencer Robinson counted the British ironclad force at thirty-nine ships, and that of France at forty-one, claimed further that France had the superiority of numbers in heavy guns, and concluded that '[a]t this moment an alliance between France and so small a naval power as Holland would turn most seriously the Naval preponderance against England . . .'. With all of this Dacres cordially concurred, pointing out especially that '[t]here is no doubt that we are outnumbered by some ten vessels of the special service class [ie coast and harbour defence vessels] of French ships.'

42. Spalding to Admiralty, 25 September 1871, PRO: ADM1/6214.

43. Spalding's report alluded to one French ship in particular, *Normandie*, which 'has been ordered to be broken up as her hull was seriously affected with rot.' It might be added, though, that reports of the impending demise of other wooden French ironclads were apparently exaggerated. Another intelligence report, this one by naval attaché Captain Nicholson in 1877, stated that there was little, if any, evidence to suggest a large-scale rot problem in the early French ironclads: 'I believe that they are still good strong vessels'(Nicholson to Admiralty, 15 November 1877, PRO: ADM1/6425). This assessment received the concurrence of Controller Houston Stewart. By this point, however, they were clearly obsolete. The 1880 *Statesman's Yearbook* noted bluntly that other then eight recent ironclads, most of the French battlefleet was 'of antiquated construction. . . .'(74). The French realised this themselves, and as noted, much of the impetus for the increased level of French shipbuilding in the late 1870s and early 1880s came from the realisation that the ships built during the Second Empire were in dire need of replacement.

The French *Redoutable*, launched in 1876, was the first armoured warship to use a significant amount of steel in her hull construction. (U.S. Naval Historical Center: NH74912)

heavy shock (from ram or torpedo) watertight compartments are hardly to be depended upon.'[44]

The French decision to build ironclads with wooden hulls offered eloquent testimony to the superior development of the British industrial infrastructure during the 1850s and 1860s, for it was born of necessity rather than choice. The historian of the late nineteenth century French Navy, Theodore Ropp, minces no words: 'the French decided to build nearly all their ironclads with wood hulls because of the backward condition of the French iron industries.'[45] Moreover, Britain's advantage extended to the dockyards as well, where she enjoyed 'a distinct qualitative superiority over the French, not the least of which was the ability of British yards, in spite of the novelty of the work, to complete ironclads with more rapidity than could the French yards.'[46] Such considerations doubtless led Lord Henry Lennox, Secretary to the Admiralty 1866-8, to assert confidently to his friend Disraeli that if

44. Nicholson to Admiralty, 15 November 1877, PRO: ADM1/6424. Nicholson understated the matter of watertight compartments. The lack of rigidity in large wooden-hulled vessels made watertight compartments impossible, with or without an additional 'heavy shock'. The action of the sea alone was ample to open joints and seams.

45. Theodore Ropp, *The Development of a Modern Navy* (Stephen Roberts ed., Annapolis, 1987), p10.

46. Sandler, *Emergence of the Modern Capital Ship*, p62. See also Parkes, *British Battleships*, p108. Parkes notes by the mid-1860s it was so clear that 'the French battleship programme was badly in arrears' that the British could afford to slacken their own pace of construction.

47. Lennox to Disraeli, Very Confidential, 12 January 1867, Hughenden (Disraeli) Papers, British Library of Economic and Political Science (microfilm copy), B/XX/Lx/256.

48. Ropp, *Development of a Modern Navy*, p36.

49. Ibid, pp36-7. See also Brassey, *Naval Annual*, 1 (1886), pp224-31. According to Brassey all of the French battleships launched during the 1870s, *Redoutable* included, had hulls of a combination of iron and steel, rather than being entirely steel, as Ropp states. Brassey describes the arrangement in *Requin*, a French battleship launched in 1885: 'the outer plating is iron, the rest of the hull is built of steel'(p230). This accords with Barnaby's observation, quoted below, that he was prepared to go one better than the French and construct the entire hull of steel. This quibble does not alter the fact that the French embarked on large-scale utilisation of steel well before the British did.

50. David Landes, *The Unbound Prometheus: Technological Change and Industrial Development in Western Europe from 1750 to the Present* (Cambridge, 1969), p251.

51. Parkes, *British Battleships*, p291. Specifically, the stem and stern posts.

52. Admiralty to Portsmouth Dockyard, 13 March 1879, PRO: ADM12/ 1045/91.1.

the United States could, following the outbreak of the Civil War,

with but a few dockyards, and almost no establishment . . . build and convert a sufficient number of Monitors to spread a network of these defences along their Coasts and Rivers, surely England with her vast resources & exorbitant Establishments could do more, and in less time should such a contingency arise.[47]

For Lennox there was no mistaking the advantages which followed from Britain's industrial superiority.

Ironically, however, by the mid-1870s the British advantage in construction materials had eroded. The crucial development in this respect was the French decision in 1872 to undertake naval reconstruction, following the Franco-German debacle, using steel rather than iron for its armoured ships. The French shipbuilding programme of 1872, 'definitely ended the construction of battleships with wooden hulls . . . Although the program specified iron, the designer of the *Redoutable* proposed the immediate introduction of steel.'[48] The advice was followed. 'The *Redoutable* and the first two coast defence ships of the [1872] programme . . . marked the definite change from iron to steel in French naval shipbuilding policy.'[49]

Steel offered substantial advantages in terms of construction, chiefly, as David Landes notes, by combining the virtues of pig and wrought iron: 'it is hard, elastic, and plastic.' Furthermore;

[i]ts strength in proportion to weight and volume makes possible lighter, smaller, and yet more precise and rigid–hence faster–machines and engines. And the same combination of compactness and strength makes steel an excellent construction material, especially in shipbuilding, where the weight of the vessel and space left for cargo are of primary importance.[50]

But only with the construction of *Colossus* and *Edinburgh*, both laid down in 1879–seven years after *Redoutable* was begun and over a year after her completion–were any British capital ships to utilise steel extensively in their construction, and even in these instances some of the heavier hull pieces were still made of iron.[51] Britain clearly lagged behind France in switching to the new shipbuilding material. As late as March 1879 Portsmouth Dockyard requested a scheme of prices for steel from the Admiralty so as to avoid being overcharged by suppliers. The Admiralty had to respond that such a list would be sent out when it had been drawn up.[52]

The failure to effect a rapid switch to steel shipbuilding was, however, largely the result of shortcomings in the British ferrous metals industry, rather than of excessive caution, conservatism, or some more malevolent influence in the counsels of the Admiralty.

HMS *Edinburgh* and her sister-ship *Colossus* were the first British capital ships to have predominantly steel hulls. (U.S. Naval Historical Center: NH88837)

As early as 1875, the D.N.C., Nathaniel Barnaby, speaking to the Institute of Naval Architects, admitted that a visit to French dockyards the previous fall confirmed that 'there was an extended use of steel, which argued greater confidence in the material than we have ourselves.'[53] Barnaby himself maintained that matters should not continue in this path: 'I am ready for my part,' he declared, 'to go further than the French architects have gone, and build the entire vessel, bottom plates and all, of steel, but,' he added, 'I know that at present the undertaking will involve an immense amount of anxiety and care.' Anxiety and care or not, though, the D.N.C. was not prepared to leave matters unchanged: '[w]e ought not be behind any other country in this matter, and it shall not be my fault if we are.'[54]

Two factors slowed the transition to steel construction in the British Navy: cost and quality. Not surprisingly, the two were related. The high-quality steel necessary for maritime applications was markedly more expensive than iron. In 1875 Barnaby acknowledged that as far as the Admiralty were concerned, steel of sufficient quality was still too costly:

It must not be supposed that the question of cost does not press hardly upon constructors of ships . . . so it happens that we do not feel at liberty to build of the best possible material when that material is very costly. We use the material which, all things considered, including price, is, in our judgement, the best for the purpose.[55]

As of 1867 steel was over two-and-a-half times more costly than iron.[56] But during the next decade the gap rapidly narrowed. By 1870 the differential had dropped to about one-and-a-half times, and when Barnaby made his observations steel was roughly 20 per cent more expensive. In 1878 another lecturer at the Institute of Naval Architects proclaimed that steel's cost, 'having regard to the reduced weight required – will warrant the shipowner, from a commercial point of view, in adopting the lighter and stronger material.'[57] This pronouncement garnered the hearty approval of M.P. Joseph Samuda, himself a shipbuilder. 'I concur entirely in that which . . . [the lecture] intends to advocate, namely, a substitution, almost a universal substitution of steel for iron in shipbuilding . . .'[58]

Yet the late 1870s did not witness a wholesale transformation of the British shipbuilding industry – least of all the Royal Dockyards – to steel construction.[59] As of 1880 some 38,000 tons of merchant shipping built of steel 'were added to the register of the United Kingdom', but this figure was dwarfed by the 487,000 tons of iron shipping completed that year. Five years later the ratio was still about three to two in favour of iron, although by 1890 it had been completely and dramatically reversed to almost twenty to one in favour of steel.[60] The primary factor for this slow transformation, despite the essential equality of iron and steel prices by 1875, was structural problems involved in the use of steel in shipbuilding. The quality of steel produced in Britain, at least before 1880, was not uniformly suitable for the purpose.

Despite the fact 'that no country had a greater stake in the old way of doing things', Britain was nonetheless the world's largest steel producer during the 1850-90 period.[61] In 1875 British steel production amounted to 719,000 metric tons: over 150,000 tons more than France's and Germany's combined output, and very

53. Nathaniel Barnaby, 'On Iron and Steel for Shipbuilding' *Transactions of the Institute of Naval Architects* 16 (1875), p131.

54. Stanley Sandler takes a rather dim view of Barnaby's progressivism, observing that 'he must be held responsible for a personal conservatism that could write favourably of wood as a warship building material in the twentieth century' (Sandler, *Emergence of the Modern Capital Ship*, pp248-9). Barnaby's words as an active naval designer in 1875 seem to this writer a more reliable indicator of his views than his reminiscences (in *Naval Development in the Century*[London, 1902]), written over fifteen years after his retirement, and when he was well over seventy years old.

55. Barnaby, 'Iron and Steel for Shipbuilding', p133.

56. Landes, *Unbound Prometheus*, p260. The citations of cost are based on French prices, according to Landes, 'but the trend was substantially parallel in the other producing countries' (p260n). Indeed, from the difficulties encountered by the British steel industry in producing steel of uniform quality, the gap between the costs of the two metals may have been greater than in France.

57. B. Martell, 'On Steel for Shipbuilding', *Transactions of the Institute of Naval Architects* 19 (1878), p1.

58. Ibid, p23.

59. Sidney Pollard and Paul Robertson, *The British Shipbuilding Industry, 1870-1914* (Cambridge, Mass., 1979), pp6-7. Pollard and Robertson go so far as to claim that British caution and slowness to change was 'one of the greatest strengths of the industry and contributed to Britain's continued dominance 1914 by reducing overhead charges and allowing the British to produce vessels as a lower cost than was possible in many of the

highly capitalised yards in other countries.'

60. Landes, *Unbound Prometheus*, p260.

61. Ibid.

62. Mitchell, *European Historical Statistics*, pp420, 424. The output for all of Europe, including Russia, was 732,000 metric tons. The figures for France and Austria are incomplete as they only include Bessemer steel (p424). French production was 239,000 tons, German, 318,000 tons (p420).

63. J.H. Clapham, *An Economic History of Modern Britain, Vol. 2: Free Trade and Steel, 1850-1886* (Cambridge, 1932), pp56, 62.

64. Landes, *Unbound Prometheus*, pp259-60. Landes, it should be noted, does attribute some of the British reluctance to shift to steel in general, and the Admiralty's in particular, to human, rather than technological factors. 'Nor should one underestimate the strength of inertia and conservatism in these matters – the scepticism of the British Admiralty, the reluctance of French railway men, that steel rails could outlast iron by a factor of six to one.' Given Barnaby's pronouncements in 1875, however, the charge against the Admiralty seems unsubstantiated. Penny-pinching, in all probability, was a more significant factor.

65. Barnaby, *Naval Development in the Century*, pp50-1.

66. Martell, 'On Steel for Shipbuilding', pp1-2.

67. Landes, *Unbound Prometheus*, p263.

68. Tom Kemp, *Industrialisation in Nineteenth Century Europe* (2nd rev. ed., London, 1985), p179.

HMS *Iris* (launched 1877) was the first steel-hulled British warship. (U.S. Naval Historical Center: NH65958)

nearly as much as that of all of continental Europe.[62] But quantity was not reflective of quality. The great economic historian J.H. Clapham maintained that Henry Bessemer 'spent his strength against the iron-bound obstinacy of the War Office and the Admiralty', but also admitted that if steel 'was to be adopted it must be proved markedly superior' because of its higher cost. 'Proof was not forthcoming, and for the next ten years [1864-74] steel shipbuilding was almost unheard of.'[63] Landes observes that 'the homogeneity of early Bessemer steel left something to be desired, and even the open hearth variety, costlier to begin with, was not good enough for more exacting uses–large rolled plates, for example.'[64] These, of course, were precisely the sorts of plates used for building ships' hulls. Barnaby confirmed the charge in his memoirs.

[He] saw every plate and angle bar which gave trouble at the [dock]yards, and he is satisfied that, apart from questions of treatment, steel was frequently supplied from all the best English works of a quality decidedly inferior to that which was making, at the same time, at the Terre-Noire and the Creusot works in France by another process; viz. the Siemens.[65]

And a lecturer at the Institute of Naval Architects in 1878, while extolling the virtues of steel for shipbuilding, implicitly acknowledged that there had been problems with the metal to that date:

The time has now come when it is said by many others besides the manufacturers, that steel can be used with as much confidence as

iron . . . Experience has now abundantly proved that mild [low carbon] steel can be manufactured by either the Bessemer or Siemens process, possessing qualities of ductility in connection with tensile strength and general uniformity, which renders it much superior to the iron in ordinary use, and fully meriting the high praise which has been claimed for it by the manufacturers.[66]

As for why British steel producers lagged behind the best firms in France in terms of the quality of their product, Landes suggests that an unscientific approach was largely the culprit:

Stimulated by necessity, the continental steelmasters worked at the basic process with a scientific will: they achieved and maintained a proper mix and produced a metal of good, uniform quality. The British tinkered and improvised, and the irregularity of their product merely confirmed the doubts of consumers, which in turn discouraged experiment and investment. The whole situation was self-reinforcing.[67]

A similar charge is levelled by Tom Kemp: 'the steelmakers surely displayed more than an excusable degree of complacency of the sort which had its origins in the period of Britain's undisputed industrial pre-eminence.'[68]

Whatever its origins, the uneven quality of British steel had a substantial impact on Admiralty shipbuilding policy during the latter

HMS *Mercury* (launched 1878) was identical to her sister-ship *Iris* apart from a straight rather than a clipper bow. (U.S. Naval Historical Center: NH88880)

half of the 1870s. Contemporary observations have been echoed by those of subsequent historians. David K. Brown notes that:

> the lead in steel manufacture had been taken by the French Creusot works. English steel was usually made by the Bessemer process and gave an unpredictable and often brittle material. Steel was used in the interior of British ships, but was too unreliable for use in the vital outer bottom or its framing.[69]

Likewise, although he attributes some of the British slowness to adopt steel to the 'timidity of the Admiralty' – an allegation difficult to sustain in light of Barnaby's pronouncements – Theodore

Ropp also cites the 'decidedly inferior quality of English steel' as another factor.[70] Elsewhere he notes:

> Throughout the 1870s and early 1880s the English steel-makers lagged behind the French. Heavy investments in ironworks made the English slow to change to steel, and a good supply of ore suitable for the Bessemer process made them reluctant to adopt the open hearth process.[71]

Moreover, the sluggishness with which the British Navy turned to steel for hull construction affected other elements of naval *matériel* as well; guns and projectiles – both of which were to be made of iron well after the French and Krupp had shifted to steel – and, especially, armour.[72]

The Navy's designers were also beset with other problems which

69. David K. Brown, *A Century of Naval Construction* (London, 1983), p48.

70. Ropp, *Development of a Modern Navy*, p37; Clapham, *Economic History of Modern Britain*, Vol 2, p62. Clapham also makes much of the Admiralty's conservatism, but allows that '[t]he reluctance of shipbuilders to experiment much with steel plates before the mid 'seventies is easily understood. Iron had not been generally adopted for steamers before the decade 1855-65; only for some of the best sailing ships during the decade 1860-70. Quick change to yet another more expensive, more experimental, material was hardly to be expected in so ancient a craft, in view of the policy and rulings of Lloyd's and the Admiralty.'

71. Ropp, *Development of a Modern Navy*, p64.

72. Ibid, p66. The French had been conducting tests with steel shells since the early 1870s. Regular production of cast steel shell by the French firm Terre-Noire began in 1877, and by 1884 a steel shell fired at a 16in-thick English armour plate, 'supposedly capable of resisting the French 13.4 inch gun . . . went completely through it and was picked up

unbroken 150 yards beyond.' In contrast, states Ropp, 'the English had not even begun experimenting with steel projectiles in 1884.' Ropp may be wrong about the date at which the French started to experiment with steel projectiles. A report by D.N.O. Sir Astley Cooper Key states the French to have been using steel shot (presumably solid) as early as 1867 (Cooper Key to Admiralty, 13 June 1867, PRO: ADM1/6012). See also Pollard and Robertson, *The British Shipbuilding Industry*, p14. They claim that private British shipbuilders were equally slow to switch to steel, and they date its introduction to 'the late 70s'.

73. Philip H. Colomb, *Memoir of the Right Honble Sir Astley Cooper Key, G.C.B., D.C.L., F.R.S., etc* (London, 1898), p325.

74. *The Times*, 18 December 1871, p9.

75. *Engineer*, 24 April 1874, p275. By the spring of 1875 the *Times* itself was reporting extensively on tests of the new gun. See the *Times* (London), 4 May 1875, p5; 2 June 1875, p7; 28 July 1875, p5; 18 July 1876, p4; 26 July 1876, p5; 27 July 1876, p7; 7 August 1876, p4; 11 August 1876, p11; 18 September 1876, p9.

complicated their task, paramount among which was the armour-armament see-saw which raged from the 1860s onward. Every time the Admiralty essayed to build a ship impervious to the state-of-the-art ordnance of the moment, it served up a challenge to Woolwich and private industry to develop a larger and more powerful gun. As Philip Colomb remarked in his biography of Sir Astley Cooper Key, '[a]s soon as the gun-producer had demolished the last armour-plate he washed his hands of matters until another plate beat him, and then the armour-producer in his turn stood aside.'[73] When Woolwich began testing a 12in, 35-ton gun in 1871, the *Times* briefly reviewed ordnance developments of the previous dozen years:

Our first ironclad, the *Warrior*, carried the old 68 pdr., with which, in fact, at 200 yards distance she could have made no impression on a ship armoured like herself. But soon afterwards the *Bellerophon* was armed with 12-ton, or 250 pdr., the *Hercules* received guns of 18 tons weight, throwing 400-pd. shot; and the *Monarch* had her 600-pdrs.[74]

All of these advances, the newspaper's editors apparently believed,

paled in comparison to the new piece of ordnance then being tried: 'the biggest gun ever manufactured in England', whose production they deemed one of the 'remarkable events' of 1871. And, exercising their predictive skills, they added that it was probable that no larger gun would ever be made.

Their predictive skills, as matters turned out, were woefully deficient. By April 1874 the journal *Engineer* reported;

[O]nly two years ago the sobriquet of 'Woolwich infant' was playfully applied to a gun which had just been constructed at the Royal Arsenal at Woolwich, of the then unprecedented size of 35 tons. Recent events have, however, proved that the name was by no means ill-chosen, for a decision has been arrived at which will necessitate our viewing this gun actually in the light of a mere baby, as series of monstrous successors having been designed which will put its nose out of joint altogether.[75]

HMS *Benbow*'s massive 16.25in guns were indicative of the desire to deliver a single, overpowering knock-out blow with gunfire. (U.S. Naval Historical Center: NH61641)

41

Foremost among these was a new piece of ordnance which would, 'it is expected, be of a weight slightly over or slightly under 81 tons'.[76] What this meant in more intelligible terms was a gun firing a 16.25in diameter shell weighing 1700lbs, which moved the *Engineer* to reflect on the dizzying pace of escalation in ordnance size:

When we consider that it was positively stated when the 7 in[ch] [7-ton] gun was produced that we had attained the highest point we should ever reach in weight of metal, it seems almost incredible that in less than a decade we should be in possession of artillery twelve times as heavy.

Nor, as far as contemporaries could see, was the 81-ton gun the limit. By late 1876 the Navy requested that the Ordnance Department to work up 'designs of Guns for requirements of the Navy Heavier than the 80 [*sic*] Ton Gun.'[77] Specifically, the Admiralty wanted to ascertain 'the external dimensions & weight of a gun that would penetrate 36" of iron at 1,000 yards . . .'.[78] The 81-ton gun had been designed to pierce 20in of armour at that range.[79] The War Office's reply to the Admiralty has not survived, but the dimensions of such a gun would have created insurmountable difficulties for designers saddled with substantial constraints as to the size and displacement of the ships they could build. As it happened, the 81-ton gun was to be the largest muzzle-loader employed by the Navy, and it was furthermore to be mounted in *Inflexible* alone.[80] But even so, this piece of ordnance was capable of penetrating the thickest armour – at least under testing-ground conditions – carried by every British ironclad save the one in which it was mounted, reinforcing, in turn, a dilemma for naval architects which was to muddy the waters of design for the whole of the 1870s.

Throughout the 1860s it had been possible for designers to offset the increasing size and power of naval ordnance by providing for greater thicknesses of armour from one ship to the next. The cost to this tactic was, of course, increased displacement. It would not have been a critical problem had there been no limitations on size and displacement, but was a real difficulty given the Admiralty's general preference for ships of moderate dimensions. The *Warrior*, launched in 1860, carried 950 tons of armour and another 350 tons of teak backing on a displacement of 9210 tons.

Hercules (1868), by way of comparison, carried 1322 tons of protection on a displacement of only 8680 tons. This trend continued for the remainder of the decade. *Monarch*'s 1364 tons of armour (1868) accounted for 16.5 per cent of her total displacement, as opposed to *Hercules*' 15.3 per cent, while *Devastation* (1871), although about 1000 tons larger than *Monarch*, carried no less than 2540 tons of armour, or over 27 per cent of her total displacement. But although *Devastation* was, at the time of her design, 'impervious to any gun afloat except the largest at close quarters', subsequent escalation in the power of ordnance rendered the 1ft-thick belt of armour she carried inadequate by the time she was commissioned.[81]

By 1871 the dilemma was too obvious to be ignored. The Report of an Admiralty Committee on Designs stated that before the rapid increase in gun size;

the question of how to unite in one ship the power of sailing, steaming, and carrying both heavy guns and armour, although difficult, did not appear to be insoluble, and was met with remarkable ability, and a very large measure of success by the Constructive department of the Navy.[82]

The continued growth of the power and weight of ordnance, however, rendered the continuation of this balancing act impossible and this was a crucial consideration in the Committee's recommendation to abandon sails in first-class ironclads. Moreover, noting that by that point armour manufacturers were capable of rolling plates up to 24in thick, the Committee unhesitatingly stated that 'we see no reason to doubt that it is within the resources of science . . .' to build guns capable of penetrating these plates. But, the Report continued, 'it is certain that no first-class sea-going ship of war of manageable size can be made to carry *complete* protection of anything like 24 inches in thickness . . .'.

One alternative to complete armour protection, and that which was advocated by the Committee on Designs, was reduction in the scope of coverage, concurrent with the increase in thickness. This practice, in fact, predated the Committee's report. The so-called 'belt and battery' or 'box-battery' ships designed by Edward J. Reed in the 1860s carried an armoured belt at the waterline for the whole length of the ship, but of the upper works only the central battery, in which a ship like *Hercules*' heavy ordnance was

76. *Engineer*, 24 April 1874, p275.

77. War Office to Admiralty, 15 January 1877, PRO: ADM12/985/59.4a.

78. Admiralty to War Office, 16 November 1876, PRO: ADM12/ 985/59.4a.

79. Director of Naval Ordnance to Controller's Department, 31 March 1875, NMM: PRO138/19, fol. 211; Ian Hogg and John Batchelor, *Naval Gun* (Poole, 1978), pp88-9. The 81-ton gun actually pierced 23ins of iron during its trials.

80. A decade later the battleships *Benbow*, *Victoria*, and *Sans Pareil* were to be provided with 16.25in, 110-ton breech-loading guns. See Parkes, *British Battleships*, pp320-1, 330-4.

81. Parkes, *British Battleships*, pp16, 198, 199.

82. *Report of the Committee on Designs for Ships of War*, 26 July 1871, PRO: ADM1/6212.

83. Ibid.

84. Reed charged that this was true of *Inflexible* anyway.

85. Nathaniel Barnaby, 'On some Recent Designs for Ships of War for the British Navy, Armoured and Unarmoured,' *Transactions of the Institute of Naval Architects* 15 (1874), p9.

86. Ibid, p17. In the discussion which followed Barnaby's paper, one of the members of the Committee on Designs, Dr. Joseph Woolley, disagreed with the D.N.C.'s prediction.

Like all British ironclads from *Inflexible* onwards, the 'Admiral' class battleship *Anson*'s armour was restricted to the ship's central portion and an armoured deck. (U.S. Naval Historical Center: NH75958)

mounted, was protected. Another possible solution, as will be seen when considering *Inflexible*'s design, was to secure 'the requisite reserve of buoyancy by other means than armour plating'. Were this aim accomplished, the Committee observed, 'the area of armour might be diminished, and its thickness increased in a corresponding degree.'[83] 'The ship would then comprise a strongly plated central citadel, surrounded and supported by an unarmoured raft constructed on a cellular system [*ie* with extensive watertight compartmentalisation]. . .'

But there were limits to the applicability, not to say the practicality, of this design tactic. The thicker the armour, of course, the smaller the coverage which could be afforded on a given displacement, and eventually the armoured portion of the ship would no longer be sufficiently buoyant to offset flooding in the unarmoured ends.[84] This limitation was recognised by Reed's successor as Chief Constructor, Nathaniel Barnaby, who boldly stated to the

Institute of Naval Architects in 1874 that '[m]y belief is, that in the *Inflexible* we have reached the extreme limit in thickness of armour for sea-going ships.'[85] Although Barnaby's prediction was not universally accepted by his contemporaries, he turned out to have been correct: *Inflexible* was to carry thicker armour than any ship subsequently built for the Royal Navy.[86]

An alternative, or at least a complement, to reduced armour coverage was championed by Barnaby himself: the substitution of horizontal for vertical armour. By replacing side armour with an armoured deck, the crew and guns would be deprived of protection but, on the other hand, the vital machinery, as well as a ship's buoyancy and stability, would be protected. Moreover, since designers did not have to take the danger of plunging fire into account–the short ranges at which contemporary ordnance was used ensured a near-horizontal trajectory–the armoured deck need not have been anywhere near as thick as side plates which would be exposed to direct, rather than glancing, blows. By the early 1870s Barnaby was incorporating this novel feature in his designs, the armoured cruiser *Shannon* (laid down 1873) being the first ship so constructed. In his description of the vessel Barnaby

HMS *Inflexible* had thicker armour than any other contemporary British or foreign ironclad. (U.S. Naval Historical Center: NH65955)

stressed that although 'the [side] armour has been omitted from the bow of the ship . . .', its replacement by a 3in-thick armoured deck 5ft below the waterline made the bow 'for a length of 60 feet quite impregnable to shot.'[87]

This novelty did not gain immediate acceptance. The armoured deck was initially received with 'suspicion and distrust' in naval circles, but over time it 'was to be accepted as a normal and adequate method of safeguarding the waterline in lieu of, or as an adjunct to, [side] armour', and as such Oscar Parkes considers it to have been 'Barnaby's chief contribution to naval architecture'.[88] Reflecting in 1878 on the advisability of conducting stability exper-

iments on *Inflexible* – following the recommendations of a Committee appointed to consider that question – Barnaby noted that Italy was building two large ironclads completely devoid of a waterline armour belt, and thought that '[i]t may be that the experiments would justify the complete abandonment of side armour in *first class ships* . . .'.[89] But the Admiralty was not prepared to go to such extremes. Side armour continued to be a feature of British ironclad designs, and, for most of the 1870s, it continued to consist of wrought-iron plates.

Wrought iron, although lacking the hardness of cast iron, was the better of the two for armour plate. Its malleability rendered it capable of absorbing the force of a shot, whereas cast iron shattered when struck, as did steel, for that matter. Though the last material was harder than either type of iron, it was incapable of

87. Barnaby to Stewart, 24 March 1873, NMM: ADM138/43, fol. 12.

88. Parkes, *British Battleships*, p236.

89. Barnaby to Stewart, [1878], NMM: ADM138/49.

90. *The Times*, 19 December 1877, p6.

91. *The Times*, 20 December 1877, p7.

92. Parkes, *British Battleships*, p396.

93. As late as January 1879 the use of compound armour on *Ajax* and *Agamemnon* had not been settled, the Dockyards being informed, when they requested details on the armour scheme, 'that it cannot be given because the nature of the turret armour is not fully determined' ('*Ajax* and *Agamemnon*, major alterations affecting the rate of construction,' 20 January 1879, NMM: ADM138/60).

94. Foreign Office to Admiralty, 28 June 1880, PRO: ADM12/1059/52.5.

withstanding the blows delivered from heavy artillery in trials conducted in the 1860s at Woolwich and Shoeburyness, the Army's artillery testing range. Even as late as 1877, the *Times*, reporting on armour-plate trials, noted that 'the conclusion to be drawn . . . is that further experiments will have to be made before a perfect substitute for iron is produced'.[90] None of the steel plates tested were 'enabled to survive the ordeal, their complete disintegration being effected at the third shot.' The editors remained optimistic that steel armour would eventually supplant iron, but for the time being 'the great difficulty' was 'how to keep the new armour from cracking and falling off under fire'.

Well before 1877, however, experiments were being conducted on compound armour – a face of steel over wrought iron. In theory the hardness of steel would be combined with the resilience of wrought iron, thus resulting in a superior armour plate. As early as 1867 tests with compound plates had confirmed their greater powers of resistance, but when struck hard the welds joining the two materials often broke and the plates separated. By late 1877, however, the *Times* reported significant advances in the technique of manufacturing compound armour by pouring molten steel on

HMS *Ajax* and her sister-ship *Agamemnon* incorporated compound armour on their turrets. (U.S. Naval Historical Center: NH64225)

red-hot iron plate. 'The face of the iron plate became partly fused by the overlying liquid steel, and a complete union, or weld, was thus effected between the metals.' 'The two plates,' it added, 'are inseparably joined together, and the bond was actually stronger than the iron plate.' The initial results from testing this new armour plate impelled the *Times* to proclaim that '[i]ron armour, in fact, has had its day; the utmost protection has been derived from it which it is capable of rendering; and it is to steel, if to anything, that we must look for an effective shield against heavy ordnance.'[91]

The Admiralty quickly availed itself of the new development. After brief initial hesitation, the Board decided to use compound armour on *Inflexible* (launched 1876). The advantage gained was significant: 12ins of compound armour equalled the protection afforded by 15ins of wrought iron, which meant a considerable savings in weight when the switch was made.[92] Thus, not only *Inflexible*, but *Ajax* and *Agamemnon*, also under construction in 1877, were furnished with compound armour turrets.[93] The subsequent two ironclads – *Colossus* and *Edinburgh* – had wholly compound protection. Moreover, the British Navy kept abreast of naval rivals in incorporating compound armour. The Board was informed in June 1880 that the French had adopted steel-faced armour 'for all Ironclads now building'.[94] By 1884, however,

France had made the shift to completely steel armour, while the British clung to compound plates until the *Royal Sovereign* class, authorised in 1889. Subsequent improvements in armour were to emanate from the United States and especially, Germany, until by the late 1890s the British, and everyone else, were using Krupp patent armour, a nickel-steel alloy.[95]

As if the armour/ordnance see-saw (and its ancillary quandaries as to how and where ships were to be armoured), was not enough to befuddled naval designers, to further perplex the issue by the early 1870s there was a counter-argument that advocated the complete abandonment of armour. The logic of the argument was that insufficient armour was worse than no armour at all, owing to the danger of flying fragments once penetrated. Since it was obviously impossible to make armour plate which could not be pierced sooner or later, it might as well be abandoned. The weight thus saved could then be more fruitfully employed by increasing the size and number of the guns, as well as securing greater speed, and these alterations would, it was thought, largely offset the lack of protection.

This anti-armour view was not advocated solely by radicals. Indeed, it was enunciated in the Report of the Committee on Designs, the members recording their belief that the time when 'the gun will assert a final and definitive superiority' over armour was fast approaching.[96] Given the prospect, the Committee wondered whether 'when these probabilities become accomplished facts, ship armour will retain any value, or whether it ought not rather to be abandoned as a mere costly encumbrance.' Ultimately, they favoured retaining armour:

> Even assuming that absolute impenetrability to shot proves to be unattainable, it is still our opinion that the time has not come to throw off armour altogether, but that it is necessary that the first ranks of our ships of war should continue to carry armour of as great resisting power as possible.[97]

Several authorities, some of them very distinguished, came to the opposite conclusion. No less a figure than Sir William Armstrong maintained that armour should be reduced, even abandoned. In 1874 Dr. Joseph Woolley, one of the Committee members, told the Institute of Naval Architects that he foresaw the abandonment of protection.[98] His opinion was shared by former First Lord Sir John Pakington, whose Board had ushered in the ironclad era in 1859: 'I cannot help thinking we do see ahead of us the day when this struggle between different classes of armour ships will be abandoned.'[99] Pakington also revealed a conviction curious in one who had been in large part responsible for *Warrior*, but which also serves admirably to demonstrate just how confusing the armour *versus* ordnance question was by 1874. 'For sea-going purposes (and, of course, I allude only to sea-going purposes) we shall revert to the wooden ships, so far as the external ship is concerned.' By 1876 the *Times* had added its voice to the fray, remarking that '[i]t appears clear, even to a landsman, that a continuous addition to the thickness of the armour in the present type of ship means either a continual reduction of offensive power, or a very large increase in size.'[100] This being the case, the newspaper's editors wondered;

> whether armour should be abandoned, or whether another type of ship should be adopted. Once relieved of the dead weight of very heavy armour, the gain in flotation [buoyancy] would enable a comparatively small vessel to mount a very heavy armament and attain a very high speed.

The Admiralty never took the advice proffered by Armstrong, Woolley, Pakington, and others, but the existence of the anti-armour discourse helped further to cloud already very murky waters. The *Times* provided a succinct assessment of the dilemma facing the Board a few months after it had itself doubted the wisdom of retaining armour. 'It is naturally, at the present time,' it was stated, 'a matter of great anxiety to professional constructors to have to decide on any form of ironclad construction; and it is, perhaps, a still greater anxiety to the Government, not only to have to make up its mind what sort of ironclads to build, but to have to decide whether or not to build ironclads at all.'[101] For that matter, having decided whether or not to build ironclads, the Admiralty was still faced with numerous other dilemmas, among them the size and power of steam engines and guns, the amount of space to be given to coal, and whether to retain sails, to mention only a few of the most obvious. All of these questions, and others as well, hinged in part on the state of technology, but all were also tied inseparably to economic and strategic considerations.

---

95. Parkes, *British Battleships*, p396. The ratio of resistance power was: 5¾in Krupp = 7½in Harvey (another nickel-steel alloy, developed by American Augustus Harvey in 1891) = 12in compound = 15in wrought iron.

96. *Report of the Committee on Designs for Ships of War*, 26 July 1871, PRO: ADM1/6212.

97. Ibid. The rationale was that '[a]fter making every allowance for the disadvantages that attend the use of an enormous dead weight of very costly armour, which after all is not absolutely impenetrable to certain special guns, we cannot lose sight of the indisputable fact that in an action between an armour-clad and an unarmoured ship (assuming they carry guns of equal power) the former has, and must have, an immense advantage in being able to penetrate the sides of her adversary at a distance which

she herself is impenetrable; and, further, in being able to use with effect those most destructive projectiles "common shells", which would fall harmless from her own armoured sides.'

98. Remarks of Joseph Woolley on Barnaby, 'On Some Recent Designs for Ships of War for the British Navy, Armoured and Unarmoured', *Transactions of the Institute of Naval Architects* 15 (1874), p17.

99. Remarks of Sir John Pakington, p18, ibid.

100. *The Times*, 25 February 1876, p4.

101. *The Times*, 8 September 1876, p3.

Chapter 3

SAILS AND STEAM

'We have had steam and sail fighting a battle in our ships for thirty years. It is a battle which steam has been constantly winning, and sails constantly losing.'

Philip H. Colomb, 'Steam-Power *versus*
Sail-Power for Men-of-War,'
Journal of the Royal United Services Institution (1878)

'My opinion has always been that sail power in certain descriptions of war vessels is indispensable.'

Admiral Henry Boys, 1883

THE MOST visible and symbolically charged issue surrounding technological change during the 1870s and early 1880s was whether to retain or abandon masts and sails – in the entire Navy generally but in particular on ironclad ships.[1] The controversy was launched in 1869 by First Lord Hugh Childers' Board's decision to build the 'mastless' breastwork monitor HMS *Devastation*, a first-class, seagoing ironclad. Hitherto only coast-defence armoured ships relied solely upon steam for motive power. But, as Edward J. Reed was to argue in successfully advocating his design for *Devastation*, 'no practicable spread of canvas can give these ships as much security on a lee-shore as their double screws [propellers] and quadruple engines provide, and because the adoption of even a small amount of sail power would render it necessary to double the crew, to build deckhouses for their accommodation, and to embarrass and compromise the fire of the guns, and the essential qualities of the ship as a monitor'.[2] Reed's views won over Childers and the Board, although there were to be repeated objections in Parliament when the First Lord unveiled plans to build the novel vessel and over the four years of her construction and trials.[3] George Bentinck M.P., for instance, steadfastly and frequently maintained that no ship was fit for seagoing duties unless it carried a full spread of canvas, and he was by no means alone.[4]

Professional opinion on the subject of sails was divided, but throughout the 1870s a large majority favoured retaining a moderate spread of sails in seagoing ironclads. Admiral Sir Sydney Dacres (1805-84), Second Sea Lord on the Conservative Board of 1866-8 and First Sea Lord on the Board which approved *Devastation*, was '[p]robably the only Service officer holding high office who advocated the complete abolition of masts and sails [on ironclads] in the 1860s. . .'.[5] During his two stints at the Admiralty Dacres 'persistently urged the monitor design for British ironclads'.[6] None of his colleagues or successors at Whitehall for the next decade went so far. Robert Spencer Robinson, generally portrayed as the epitome of the progressive professional, 'did not advocate' at any point, 'the total abolition of sails for ironclads', and denounced the idea of so doing: 'I do not hesitate to condemn these recommendations as fatal to our maritime greatness.'[7]

---

1. This, of course, was as much a professional as an administrative and design question, which generated a heated controversy among officers which stretched over many years. For a sample of pro-sail arguments, see J.H. Selwyn's 'On the True Economies of England's Naval Power', *Journal of the Royal United Services Institution* 15 (1871), pp157-75, and Gerard Noel's 'On Masting Ships of War, and the Necessity of Still Employing Sail-power in Ocean-going Ships of War', *Journal of the Royal United Services Institution* 27 (1883), pp543-75. Anti-sail views were aired by Philip H. Colomb in 'Great Britain's Maritime Power, how Best Developed as Regards Fighting Ships and etc', *Journal of the Royal United Services Institution* 22 (1878), pp1-55, and especially 'Steam-power *versus* Sail-power for Men-of-War,' *Journal of the Royal United Services Institution* 22 (1878), pp530-55, and C.C.P. Fitzgerald in 'Mastless Ships of War', *Journal of the Royal United Services Institution* 31 (1887), pp115-33. To get some idea of the range of opinion on the subject in among naval officers, see Thomas Brassey, *The British Navy: Its Strengths, Resources, and Administration* (London, 1882), vol 3, pp36-44.

2. Reed to Admiralty (Copy), 5 February 1869, PRO: ADM1/6138. Reed was later to contradict this argument, as is noted below.

3. *Hansard's Parliamentary Debates*, 3d ser., 195 (1869), cols. 99-128. When the proposal to build the first two seagoing breastwork monitors was laid before the House of Commons there was a lengthy debate (2 April 1869), in which Henry Corry moved the reduction of the Dockyards Vote by the amount to be spent on them. He argued, among other things, 'that it was unsafe to send a ship to sea without masts and sails as a ship which was to make long

voyages'(col. 113). Corry's motion was defeated by 122 votes to 46 after a substantial debate.

Of course, in the wake of the *Captain* disaster the question of the *Devastation* type's safety was reopened. There was another debate on the design in 1871 (*Hansard*, 3d ser., 208 [1871)] cols. 1147-75). Then, in 1873, when *Devastation* was about to begin her trials, the subject came up again. George Goschen defended the design at length during his speech on the Navy Estimates that year (*Hansard*, 3d ser., 215 [1873] cols. 48-53), but this attempt to forestall criticism failed. There were debates in both the Lords (*Hansard*, 3d ser., 215 [1873] cols. 332-343) and Commons (*Hansard*, 3d ser., 215 [1873], cols. 567-90) over the propriety – to say nothing of the safety – of sending her to sea.

4. Ibid, 3d ser., 215 (1873), col. 579. Typical of Bentinck's comments was that from the 1873 debate over *Devastation*: 'he condemned all those of our ironclads which could not be handled under canvas.'

5. Sandler, *Emergence of the Modern Capital Ship*, p84. Sandler undoubtedly means for ironclads alone. No Navy officer is known to have advocated the total abandonment of sails in the 1860s. See also Brassey, *The British Navy* Vol 3, p39. Brassey quotes Dacres thusly: 'No turret ship ought to have a mast. Ironclad ships cannot sail.' The date of this pronouncement is not recorded.

6. Sandler, *Emergence of the Modern Capital Ship*, p84.

7. Ibid; Spencer Robinson Minute on the *Report of the Committee on Design for Ships of War*, 25 November 1871, PRO: ADM1/6221.

HMS *Shannon* dressed overall at the 1887 Spithead Naval Review. The argument that masts and sails were necessary to maintain the courage and resourcefulness of British seamen has been overstated. (U.S. Naval Historical Center: NH54848)

Among subsequent Naval Lords during the next decade, not one unambiguously urged the abolition of masts and sails. Dacres' successor as First Sea Lord, Admiral Sir Alexander Milne (1872-6), argued in 1874 for the need to have a strong Channel Squadron made up of ships 'of the same character [*ie* of similar design], so as to manoeuvre together, and to act under canvas.'[8] Milne's colleague, Third Sea Lord Rear-Admiral Lord Gilford (later Earl of Clanwilliam), simultaneously advanced a version of the argument popular among advocates of sail, namely that masts and canvas

were necessities for building the strength, character, and every virtuous quality of British seamen, and for training officers. An over-reliance on steam, Gilford asserted, 'induces carelessness on the part of those who would act differently if they were trimming or working the sails and ropes of a vessel not under steam . . . This constant steaming and useless expenditure of coal produces ignorance in the rising young officers of all ranks.'[9]

In the correspondence surrounding the design of the second-class ironclad HMS *Shannon* in 1873, the Controller, William Houston Stewart, the Director of Naval Ordnance (D.N.O.), Captain Sir Arthur Hood, Second Sea Lord John Walter Tarleton, Junior Sea Lord Frederick Beauchamp Seymour, First Lord George J. Goschen, and Milne took the necessity for sails for granted. Hood went so far as to recommend a modification in the planned rig, for he argued the plan proposed by the Constructor would require the large topgallant sail be furled in a brisk breeze, leaving *Shannon* 'spreading a very small area of canvas, as compared to a vessel having the usual ship rig; a point of considerable importance where long passages under sail have to be made.'[10]

Given *Shannon*'s intended role as an ironclad for service abroad, the unanimity of opinion was scarcely surprising. But this consensus extended as well to HMS *Temeraire*'s design, which, although originally conceived as a second-class ironclad for service on distant stations, emerged, after protracted debates, as a much larger ship, suited for and ultimately employed in service in European waters. *Temeraire* was given a brig (two-masted) rig, largely, it appears, on the recommendation of Admiral Geoffrey Phipps Hornby, who had reported to the Admiralty 'what is wanted for heavy ships which are not at all adapted to sail is a rig which will combine a large power of setting sail when the wind is favourable with a great facility for stripping masts when wind is foul or when going into action.'[11]

The Board's advocacy of sails continued into the latter years of the decade. As late as 1878 First Naval Lord Admiral George Wellesley and Arthur Hood, then Second Sea Lord, argued for equipping HMS *Neptune*, one of the 'Russian war-scare' purchases, with a full rig, although Controller William Houston Stewart warned that 'the sailing qualities of the *Neptune*... will prove to be *nil* and that the spars and sails should be reduced'.[12]

Outside the Admiralty confusion in naval circles on the question of sails was equally evident. Edward Reed continued to espouse reliance on sails for seagoing ironclads, even after the mastless *Devastation* had proved a success. In 1875 he wrote in *Naval Science* 'an object of the greatest importance in a National Navy is to make

the officers and men expert seamen, and as this object is better attained the longer the time spent under sail alone, the comparative length of voyages performed by ironclads is not itself a disadvantage, but the contrary.'[13] Indeed, Reed publicly maintained that, contrary to appearances, 'it was always our intention to furnish the *Devastation* and other similar ships with the means of setting a purely supplemental, but nevertheless considerable, spread of canvas, after having secured for their fighting and steaming qualities the first ruling consideration, and we see no sufficient reason for not even now giving these ships a single square sail, a certain number of fore-and-aft sails, for use in the event of both engines or both screws failing.'[14] His recommendation was not followed, and his successor, Nathaniel Barnaby, was far less wedded to the traditional form of power, stating in 1871 that sails should be restricted to second-class ironclads for service on distant stations and maintaining that sail power on a 'very powerful ship' was 'practically unattainable'.[15]

Among the earliest naval officers to call for the complete abandonment of sails was, not surprisingly, John Fisher, who as a commander in 1871, stated categorically that '[m]asts and sails should be done away with. The room and weight they now represent should be taken by coal.'[16] Four years later Captain Philip Howard Colomb lent weight to Fisher's argument with a study calculating the weight taken up by masts, sails, and their accoutrements on board ships on the China Station, as well as figuring the amount of resistance caused by masts and rigging when steaming into the wind. He concluded that the sailing apparatus wasted more coal than it saved. '[T]he weight of masts, sails, and rigging, equal to 520 tons had led to the consumption of 1,031 tons of coal, while the coal saved by the use of sails had been but 453 tons.'[17]

Colomb's and Fisher's view attracted numerous detractors, however.[18] Gerard Noel, in a paper delivered to the Royal United Services Institution in 1883, the avowed purpose of which was to try to 'win back some of the wavering to a sounder faith in sail power . . .', stated that '[m]asting, in addition to its value in other

8. Remarks of Milne in Memorandum on the State of the Fleet, Confidential, 18 April 1874, Hughenden (Disraeli) Papers, British Library of Economic and Political Science (microfilm copy), B/XX/Hu/59.

9. Remarks of Gilford, 18 April 1874, ibid.

10. Minutes by Stewart, 24 March 1873; Hood, 26 March 1873; Milne, 2 April 1873; Tarleton, n.d., and Seymour, n.d.; and Goschen, 7 April 1873 on the design for HMS *Shannon*, NMM: ADM138/43, S.2970, fols. 13, 18, 19, 20, 21.

11. Proposals for Masting and Rigging *Temeraire*, 5 August 1875, NMM: ADM138/19, no fol.

12. Precis of Correspondence relating to the Rig of '*Neptune*,' entries of 22 March 1878 and 24 May 1878, NMM: ADM138/47, no fol.

13. [Edward J. Reed], *Naval Science* 4 (1875), p261.

14. [Edward J. Reed], 'On Future Maritime Propulsion', *Naval Science* 2 (1873), p309n.

15. *Report of the Committee on Designs for Ships of War*, 26 July 1871, PRO: ADM1/6212.

16. Fisher quoted in Brassey, *The British Navy*, Vol 3, p41.

17. Colomb cited in ibid, p42. Colomb's research and conclusions were presented in the paper 'Steam-power *versus* Sail-power for Men-of-War,' delivered to the Royal United Services Institution in 1878. See *Journal of the Royal United Services Institution* 22 (1878), pp530-55.

18. Parkes, *British Battleships*, p278; Sandler, *Emergence of the Modern Capital Ship*, p78. Sandler offers a similar synopsis.

Alexandra's reduced sail plan. The ship was re-rigged in 1889-91 and she was also re-boilered. (National Maritime Museum, London: 47036)

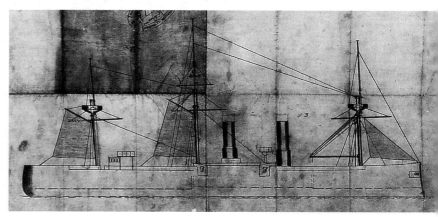

respects, is the best means of keeping the men in healthy employment of mind and body, and all the qualities conducive to good discipline.'[19] Similar arguments were advanced by, among others, Richard Vesey Hamilton, Beauchamp Seymour, and Henry Boys, all of whom served at the Admiralty during the 1870s.[20] Vesey Hamilton, furthermore, reminisced that once '[h]e had the misfortune to be driven on shore, and to have to throw out all of his

The twin propeller shafts, standard on first-class ironclads from *Devastation* onwards, can clearly be seen in this photograph of *Howe*'s stern at Pembroke prior to her launch. (U.S. Naval Historical Center: NH75913)

coals, what, then, could he have done without sails?'[21] While a disabled steamship might suffer a similar fate, with the adoption, from *Devastation* onwards, of twin propellers driven by separate engines, a ship's being rendered helpless by mechanical breakdown was improbable.

Yet proponents of sail were remarkably persistent. A scathing 1887 attack on the more than vestigial continued presence of masts and canvas by Charles Cooper Penrose Fitzgerald suggests that the issue was still very much alive even at that late date. 'Our Admirals,' he charged, 'have always so highly commended and attached so much value to the smart shifting of topsails . . . that we seem to have lost sight of the fact that it has nothing to do with the fighting efficiency of a ship of the present day.'[22] By this date, however, the Admiralty itself had long since abandoned the practice of fitting sails to new ironclad designs. The last first-class armoured vessel to carry canvas was HMS *Inflexible*, laid down in 1874. The last ever armoured ship to be provided with a wind-trap was *Imperiuse*, a cruiser designed for service on distant stations, laid down in 1881. The four 'Russian war-scare' purchases of 1878 did, it is true, all carry sails, but all had also been designed for other navies. In point of fact, the Admiralty was in advance of the opinions of many Navy officers in this regard.

But such progressivism did not spare the Navy's administration from charges of conservatism. The Report of the Committee on Designs for Ships of War provided a reasoned and seemingly convincing reinforcement of the arguments used by Reed against sails for *Devastation*. The Committee, composed of distinguished naval officers and men of science did, it is true, harbor a minority which held that 'it will always be necessary that this country should possess very powerful iron-clad ships, with a sufficient amount of sail power to enable them to economise coal in proceeding to distant stations.' But the majority, 'with much hesitation and reluctance . . . arrived at a contrary opinion.'[23] 'We all view with regret', they continued;

> what presents itself to the minds of most of us as the inevitable failure of the attempt to unite in one ship a very high degree of offensive and defensive power with real efficiency under sail; and we should unanimously hail as a most valuable acquisition, and as a triumph of Naval Architecture, a vessel in which these apparently irreconcilable elements should be combined. But at present we find ourselves compelled to regard the attainment of this very desirable object as an insoluble problem.

Barnaby supported this verdict in his comments on the Report, as did then Commander-in-Chief of the Mediterranean Squadron, Admiral Sir Hastings Yelverton, who in October 1871 informed the Admiralty '[t]he combination of Ironclad efficiency with that amount of sailing power which necessitates large Masts and Yards is a dream from which, I trust, we have all awoke. Either our

HMS *Imperieuse* (launched 1883), the last British ironclad with sailing rig. (U.S. Naval Historical Center: NH60121)

Ironclads must be exclusively steamers for war purposes alone, or failures. The attempt to unite the two powers in an armoured ship is out of the question.'[24]

Yet in the face of this body of professional and scientific opinion the Admiralty pursued a contrary course. In 1872, following the publication of the Committee on Designs Report, First Lord George J. Goschen blandly informed the House of Commons of his Board's intention to build further masted ironclads. 'I am bound to say', he stated, 'that we do not concur in that part of the Report of the Committee which refers to . . . seagoing ships of the first class.'[25] Here, it would seem, is confirmation of the charges of conservatism made by both contemporaries and recent writers.[26] But the subject is not as straightforward as first appears, and it is worth taking a look at the considerations which propelled the Board to adopt its policy in defiance of such weighty authority.

The sail issue was not simply one of technology: it must be seen as part of a larger question, which involved geographic and strategic factors as well. The Committee Report advocating abandoning sails also contained a crucial context for this recommendation:

19. Gerard Noel, 'On Masting Ships of War, and the Necessity of Still Employing Sail-power in Ocean-going Ships of War', *Journal of the Royal United Services Institution* 27 (1883), pp543, 555.

20. Hamilton quoted in Brassey, *British Navy*, Vol 3, p44; Seymour quoted in discussion on Noel's paper, ibid, p575; Boys quoted in comments on C.C.P. Fitzgerald, 'Mastless Ships of War', *Journal of the Royal United Services Institution* 31 (1887), p129.

21. Hamilton quoted in Brassey, *British Navy*, Vol 3, p44.

22. Fitzgerald, 'On Mastless Ships of War', p117; Thomas Brassey, *Naval Annual* 1 (Portsmouth, 1886), p72. Brassey stated in 1886 '[s]hips capable of cruising under sail will always be required in the Navy, both for the training of seamen, and for a certain portion of the duties which the Navy will be required to undertake in war. For ocean cruising, and when operating at a distance from a reliable source of coal, an ample spread of canvas is essential.'

23. *Report of the Committee on Designs for Ships of War*, 26 July 1871, PRO: ADM1/6212. The

Report was also printed in the *Parliamentary Papers*, 1872, Vol. 14, ppi-xlix, 1-363. The members of the Committee were: Lord Dufferin and Clandeboye (Chairman), Sir William Thomson, Admiral George Elliot, Rear-Admiral A.P. Ryder, Rear-Admiral Geoffrey Hornby, Rear-Admiral William Houston Stewart, Reverend Dr. Joseph Woolley, Professor Arthur Rankine, William Froude, Captain Arthur Hood, Captain James Goodenough, George W. Rendel, Peter Denny, G.P. Bidder, T. Lloyd, and Lieutenant-Colonel Pasley (Secretary).

24. Yelverton to Admiralty, 5 October 1871, PRO: ADM1/6187, N. 402.

25. *Hansard*, 3d ser., 210 (1872), col. 452.

26. Sandler, *Emergence of the Modern Capital Ship*, p88. 'Until approximately 1868 the Admiralty had some reason for resisting any call for a mastless, seagoing ironclad. . . . After the loss of H.M.S. *Captain*, the success of the *Devastation*, and the introduction of compound engines and twin screws [*ie* 1873-4], justification for such a conservative policy became almost impossible.'

we believe that our transmarine possessions, and other important interests in distant parts of the world, will be more efficiently protected by the establishment, where requisite, of centres of naval power, from which ships of the 'Devastation' class may operate, than by relying upon cruising ships . . . of limited fighting power . . . .[27]

In other words, the Committee envisioned a world-wide chain of naval bases capable of supporting a purely steam navy.

Much of the raw material for such a logistical network certainly existed by the mid-Victorian period. Aside from the famous outposts of British imperial power at which forces might be stationed – the Cape, Gibraltar, Bombay, Hong Kong and others – there were a number of key strategic points already utilised as bases by the various overseas squadrons. In the Mediterranean were, in addition to Gibraltar, Malta and, after 1878, Cyprus. On the routes to India, apart from the Cape, there were Aden, Mauritius, and Trincomalee. In the Far East were Singapore, Australia, and New Zealand. In the New World there were, on the Atlantic coast, Halifax, Bermuda, and the West Indian Islands. In the Pacific there was Esquimalt (Vancouver), and British ships were allowed by the Chilean government to use Valparaiso. Realising the Committee's recommendation would seem to have been a fairly simple task.

However, it was not simple at all. Most importantly, it also involved considerable expense. First, employing distant stations as naval bases for steamships meant establishing coal depots at each, all requiring continual replenishment from Britain or, more precisely, from South Wales, whence came the 'smokeless' coal preferred for purposes of steam navigation. The frugal governments of the 1860s, 1870s, and 1880s were ill-inclined to sanction the cost, especially in light of the existing balance of naval power. Reed's *Naval Science* stated unequivocally that '[i]t requires but a small acquaintance with the course of our political administration to see clearly that such a scheme as that of the Committee is one which could not, or at least would not, be adopted in this country.'[28] Nor, for that matter, was the government immediately prepared to bear the expense of fortifying these naval bases, as per the recommendation of the Carnarvon Commission on Colonial Defence a decade later.[29]

But the issue was not solely, nor even largely, one of national security *versus* governmental parsimony. The state of steam technology in the 1870s also exerted a very real influence on what types of ships the Admiralty chose to build, and where they could be deployed. The mastless *Devastation* had bunkerage for 1800 tons of coal, which with her simple (that is to say single-expansion) steam engines was good for about 9200 miles at 5kts, 4700 miles at 10kts, and 2700 miles at her full speed of 12.5kts.[30] This operational radius was more than adequate for service in European waters and, to be sure, it was in this theatre that Reed envisioned the ship would operate. '[T]his design', he wrote to Hugh Childers in February 1869, 'has been prepared to fulfil, on the smallest dimensions compatible with very large coal supply, the conditions of a modern man-of-war, adopted in all respects for Channel and Mediterranean purposes.'[31] True, Childers, Goschen, and

27. *Report of the Committee on Designs for Ships of War*, 26 July 1871, PRO: ADM1/6212.

28. [Anonymous], 'The Report of the Committee on Admiralty Designs,' *Naval Science* 1 (1872), p167. Reed included a disclaimer denying authorship of this article, but it is nonetheless a faithful representation of both his and Spencer Robinson's views.

29. *Royal Commission appointed to make enquiry into the condition and sufficiency of the means of the Naval and Military Forces provided for the Defence of the most important sea-ports within our Colonial Possessions and Dependencies* (generally known as the Carnarvon Commission), Confidential, Carnarvon Papers, PRO: PRO30/6/13. The Commission was appointed in 1879, issued its First Report in 1881, and its Second and Third Reports the following year. In the first of these it recommended, among other things, that colonial ports 'should entirely rely on their defence on military works and fortifications', that special consideration be given to fortifying coaling stations 'as the efficiency of Her Majesty's fleet to keep the sea depends on the security of the coaling stations' that many more coaling stations should be established, and that the fleet should be greatly enlarged, especially as regards cruisers for hunting down commerce raiders.

30. Parkes, *British Battleships*, p195.

31. Reed to Admiralty (Copy), 5 February 1869, PRO: ADM1/6138.

32. Andrew Lambert, *Battleships in Transition* (London, 1984), pp18-19; Daniel Headrick, *The Tools of Empire: Technological Change and European Imperialism in the Nineteenth Century*, (New York, 1981), p36. Headrick dismisses these drawbacks as the spurious arguments of a reactionary Admiralty establishment dead-set against technological change (pp36-7). In fact, the argument that the iron gunboats designed and built for the East India Company in the 1840s were kept secret so as to avoid a summary veto from the Admiralty lacks persuasiveness. First of all, Headrick never explains *how* the Admiralty could have forced the East India Company to cease and desist. Secondly, he acknowledges that the Admiralty was aware of the ships' existence, and musters no evidence to indicate that the Board made any attempt to interfere with their construction (p36). Thirdly, the charge that the Admiralty was immovably opposed to steam technology and iron ships is indefensible. There were legitimate, in fact grave, objections to the employment of paddle wheels on ships which might face the destructive effects of heavy artillery, and these extended to the use of iron in ship construction as well. The ½ to ⅝in plate used for hulls was proof against small arms, or the antiquated artillery that gunboats like the *Nemesis* faced in China, but the power of large naval ordnance simply shattered thin iron plate, far more completely and dangerously, in fact, than it did the heavy wooden planking of large warships. Moreover, as K.T. Rowland points out, the screw propeller, the alternative to paddle wheels, which obviated the major objections to steam power in fighting ships, was quickly adopted by the Admiralty (K.T. Rowland, *Steam at Sea: A History of Steam Navigation*, [Newton Abbot, 1970], pp95-103). Within three years of the device's patent in 1836, the Admiralty had built a screw frigate.

Moreover, the inefficiency of early steam engines, although acknowledged by Headrick, is not given adequate weight. It was one thing for a steamship company, operating on a regular schedule, carrying passengers, and in all probability, enjoying the income from a mail contract, to make the shift to steam. It was expensive, true, but there were no logistical difficulties to refuelling, and the enhanced profits would, hopefully, offset the higher cost. The Navy, however, did not operate under the same circumstances. Lacking both regular timetables and assured supplies of coal wherever the service might take them and, most crucially, hobbled by the grave inefficiency of early steam engines, warships had to continue to rely on the wind.

A more plausible explanation for the East India Company's secretiveness might by the desire to conceal its interventionist activities in Burma and China from Parliamentary critics, most notably the anti-colonial Radicals.

33. The damp and heat produced by boilers and engines also contributed to rapid rotting.

34. Lambert, *Battleships in Transition*, pp34-5.

The compound engines of HMS *Northampton* (launched 1876) marked a great increase in efficiency and economy under steam, but not enough to permit the abandonment of sails. (U.S. Naval Historical Center: NH58650)

subsequent naval administrators also maintained *Devastation* could, if need arose, serve on the far side of the Atlantic. But while its coal supply was adequate to make the round trip at low speed without refuelling, even short-term operations in American waters would have required a stockpile of coal near the scene. *Devastation* could not operate outside European waters unless serious logistical hurdles–foremost among them the availability of coal, dry docking, and repair facilities–were first overcome.

The adoption of the compound engine from the early 1870s onward did significantly increase economy of coal consumption. *Devastation*'s range was 4700 miles at 10kts; *Dreadnought* (launched 1875), some 2000 tons larger and carrying no more coal that her half-sister, had a range of 5700 miles at the same speed, thanks to more efficient engines. Yet *Dreadnought* was little more suited for service on the Pacific Station, in the Far East, or in the Indian Ocean than was *Devastation*. Furthermore, the maintenance problems involved with steam machinery in the early ironclad era, especially in regard to boiler upkeep, made the employment of purely

steam vessels on distant stations problematic even had ample coal been available.

By the late 1860s the steam engine had been employed for maritime applications for over half a century, but for the whole of the period serious shortcomings in the state of steam technology gravely restricted the circumstances under which it could be practically utilised.[32] Even after the screw propeller provided an alternative to paddle wheels, which were objectionable in warships on numerous counts, the British battlefleet did not undergo a wholesale transformation from sail to steam. The Navy ordered its first steam-powered ships-of-the-line in 1848, only after the French had first made the decision to build such vessels. On the purely technological level, the steam engines of the day were still extremely inefficient and the weight of engines, boilers, water, and coal wrought havoc on wooden hulls.[33] The engines themselves typically operated on pressures of no more than '10-15lb. per square inch (psi), figures that remained standard throughout the 1850s for large naval engines'.[34] At such low pressure coal consumption was prodigious for the relatively small horsepower produced. In 1858, while Junior Naval Lord, Milne calculated the average horsepower of the steam battlefleet at 650 per vessel. The thirty-five steam battleships, forty-seven frigates, sixty-five sloops and sixty gun vessels

Like most British ironclads of this period, *Collingwood* was fitted with locomotive or 'Scotch' boilers. (U.S. Naval Historical Center: NH61370)

stationed in home waters consumed between them, according to Milne, 6940 tons of coal daily. In making contingency plans for war, he presumed coal consumption to be 'reduced to the mere expenditure of 2 days steaming for each ship in a week', yet added 'I have great doubts in my own mind how far it will be practicable to keep the ships supplied, with any certainty, to enable them to act as steam vessels when none stow more than from 5 to 9 days Coal.'[35] Not surprisingly, sails remained the primary motive power for the Navy's warships, especially large vessels, through the end of the wooden warship era. Nor did the situation alter during the early ironclad era.

The advent of the compound engine in the 1860s did lead to significant gains in economy. The ability to exploit more fully the steam's expansive power was the key to the compound engine's superior efficiency. Its basic premise was explained to the Royal United Services Institute by the civil engineer G.B. Rennie in 1875: 'in contradistinction to the ordinary or simple engine, [it] has two or even more cylinders for using the same steam, that is, after the steam has done its duty in one cylinder, it is discharged into another, and in some cases into another, until the maximum effect is obtained out of the steam by its expansion.'[36] 'This,' notes modern authority K.T. Rowland, 'was one of the really important advances in marine engineering . . . due to the tremendous amount of fuel, amounting to between 30 and 40 per cent, which could be saved when compared to a single-expansion engine of the same power.'[37] The compound engine, therefore, offered the enticing combination of increased efficiency and reduced operating cost, at least in theory. Practical engines of the type appeared in 1853, when engineer John Elder took out a patent for his design, the first to be installed in a seagoing ship. By the early 1860s merchant shipping firms, especially those engaged in transoceanic hauling, were beginning to employ compound engines in significant numbers.

The crucial factor in the equation was not the engine itself, however, but a boiler capable of withstanding high-enough pressures to generate the steam needed for the compound engine to work efficiently and economically. 'Compound engines required double the pressure sufficient for the simple type' in order to operate efficiently, 'and the frequent failure of the early installations in the Navy and Merchant Service through insufficient *steam power* delayed their general acceptance for a long time.'[38] Early marine boilers were rectangular (hence the name box-boilers), and their design and structure rendered them incapable of withstanding pressures greatly in excess of 30 psi. Nathaniel Barnaby explained that internal stresses in the box-boiler,

> were principally resisted by numerous straight iron stay rods [but] [a]s the demand arose for higher steam pressures the unsuitability of this form had to be recognised. It was not possible to increase the number of stay rods without making the inside of the boiler inaccessible and without seriously increasing the weight.[39]

In 1862, therefore, concurrent with the growing use of the compound engine by private ship owners, the cylindrical, or 'Scotch' boiler was introduced in maritime applications. Its superiority to the box-boiler was unmistakable. 'From about 1870 onwards,' writes Rowland, 'the 'Scotch' boiler became the most popular in the British merchant marine; its sturdy construction and reliability made it suitable for pressures of 60 psi and above.'[40] The Chief Engineer Surveyor to Lloyd's Shipping Register observed to the Institute of Naval Architects in 1878,

> [d]uring the last few years several important improvements have been made in the detail of marine engines and boilers by which the wear and tear has been lessened and the durability increased. The pressures meanwhile have been slowly but steadily advancing from 60 lbs. to 75 lbs., now a common pressure, and in a few instances 90 lbs. has been reached. These gradual increases have also, I am assured by those engaged in working the steamers, been attended by a marked economy.[41]

Within a few years of the cylindrical boiler's introductions into merchant service the Royal Navy was experimenting with it. In the late 1860s the Admiralty fitted both rectangular and cylindrical boilers in two classes of small warships—the *Amethyst* and *Thetis* class corvettes—and 'the success of the latter in service led to their adoption in the *Dreadnought* and *Alexandra*'.[42]

The progress of technology should not, however, hide the operational problems encountered in the switch to cylindrical boilers or, for that matter, compound engines. The Institute of Naval Architects was informed of the former's drawbacks in 1876:

> [t]he anxiety attending upon the construction and the working of the marine boiler is much greater now than formerly; its first cost is largely increased, the expense of repair is much more, and the duration of its life is much less. . . .[43]

---

35. Draft of Milne's response to 'Three Questions put by the Queen to the Members of the Board of Admty Early 1858,' Milne Papers, National Maritime Museum, MLN/142/2 [1]. Milne also worked up a table on coal requirements, for both vessels at home and abroad.

Abstract C.

Average Quantity of Coal required,

At Home

No Ships &c	No	Average Horse Power	The Total Horse Power	Coals required
Ships Line	35	650	22.750	
Frigates	47	450	21.150	
Sloops	65	300	19.500	
G Vessels	60	100	6000	
[total]			69.400=	6940 Tons per day
Steaming 2 days in a week				13,800
at that rate in the Month				55.520
In three Months				166.560
One Years Store				666.240= £666.240 at 20s./per ton

Note. The Expenditure of Coal per day in Steam vessels is about ⅒th of the horse power.

Abroad

No Ships &c	No	Average Horse Power	The Total Horse Power	Coals required
Ships Line	30	650	19.500	
Frigates	70	450	31.500	
Sloops	95	300	28.500	
G Vessels	18	100	1.800	
[total]			81.300=	8130 Tons per day
Steaming 2 days in a week=				16.260
at that rate in the Month				75.040
In three Months				225.120
One Years Store				900.480=£2.200.000 at 45s/per ton

36. G. B. Rennie, 'On the Comparative Merit of Simple and Compound Engines', *Journal of the Royal United Services Institution* 16 (1875), p200.

37. Rowland, *Steam at Sea*, pp119-20. 'There were also other advantages arising from the increased regularity of the turning movement which yielded a higher propeller efficiency and decreased the stresses and strains developed in the engine frame, shafting, and bearings.'

Curiously enough, Edward J. Reed was an implacable foe of compound engines for warships, at least during the early and mid-1870s. See [Edward J. Reed], 'The Machinery of Ships of War,' *Naval Science* 1 (1872), pp323-4. 'As an engine peculiarly adopted for high-pressure steam, we regard the general introduction of the compound engine into the merchant and mail services, and in special service ships attached to the Navy, as being only a question of time; but that any advantage would be gained by its exclusive adoption for out ships of war, as strongly recommended by the Committee on Designs, appears to us very doubtful. Beyond the single fact of its proved economy in the consumption of fuel it has nothing to recommend it for modern ships of war, and we think our readers will allow that there is a fair prospect of equally good results in this respect being obtained with simple engines, at what has now become the ordinary working pressure. The inter-dependence of the cylinders of the compound engine renders it extremely liable to total disablement in an action, and the dissimilarity of the spare gear, owing to the difference in dimensions of the cylinders, slide-valves, &c, together with the comparatively unmanageable size of some of the principal parts, presents serious obstacles to rapid repair.'

38. Parkes, *British Battleships*, p210.

39. Nathaniel Barnaby, *Naval Development in the Century* (London, 1902), p124.

40. Rowland, *Steam at Sea*, pp135-6.

41. W. Parkes, 'On the Use of Steel for Marine Boilers, and Some Recent Improvements in Their Construction', *Transactions of the Institute of Naval Architects* 19 (1878), p172.

42. Parkes, *British Battleships*, p210.

43. J. Fortesque Flannery, 'On Water Tube Boilers', *Transactions of the Institute of Naval Architects* 17 (1876), p259.

Moreover, 'the feeling in favour of still higher steam pressure is checked chiefly by the difficulty of designing a boiler which will sustain it safely and efficiently.' 'The great drawback' to increasing steam pressure, J. Milton stated in 1877, 'is the want of a boiler strong enough and at the same time quite safe.' The problem remained unsolved through the latter 1870s: 'up to the present time,' Milton continued,

> the ordinary cylindrical boiler is . . . the only one which can be said to be reliable. But with this boiler we have now reached the maximum strength. The shell plates of some of these boilers now at work are 1¼ inch; in thickness greater than this it is, at least with our present appliances, almost impossible to properly close the joints.[44]

Problems with the construction and the maximum pressures tolerated by cylindrical boilers were exacerbated for many years by additional factors involving operation and maintenance. Before the late 1860s the Navy's ships generally employed sails far more often than engines. Under these circumstances boiler deterioration was fairly gradual. Once steam became the sole, or even the primary source of power, the rate of deterioration accelerated dramatically and the need for frequent repair and replacement escalated to become, in the judgement of contemporaries, distressingly common. Moreover, the widespread adoption of the surface condenser, in which exhaust steam from the pistons was condensed, then piped back into the boiler, plus distilling apparatus for desalinating feed water, thus enabling marine engines after 1855 to operate on fresh water rather than salt water, made the situation still worse.[45] These two innovations, it was anticipated, would increase the service life of machinery and, especially, boilers.

Polyphemus at speed. Like many other Royal Navy vessels of the 1870s and 1880s, her original boilers were very short-lived. (U.S. Naval Historical Center: NH65885)

Hopes were quickly disappointed, however: 'the surface condenser with the use of fresh instead of salt water was responsible for the growing incidence of boiler defects which began to cause concern to both the Admiralty and the Merchant Marine during the 1870s.'[46] By 1865 it was apparent in the latter service that 'the use of "fresh" water, which was continuously circulated through the system, was having the opposite effect to that which had been anticipated . . . the insides of boilers were now subject to corrosive attack from the recirculated water which became . . . "excessively foul".'[47] A.E. Seaton, author of a contemporary text on marine engineering, described the problem:

> boilers, especially those in H. M. Navy, showed signs of premature decay, such as was not customary with those receiving water from a jet condenser. It was found to be due to the highly corrosive power of redistilled water on the bare surface of the iron, and to the impossibility of keeping a protective scale on the surface when such water was used.[48]

Navy boilers were particularly vulnerable because they were not in constant use, and intermittent use – alternately filling, then emptying boilers – was more damaging than continual employment.

As early as the mid-1860s it was suggested that adding lime and soda would neutralise boiler water. This expedient helped somewhat, but 'the problem remained acute for many years'.[49] In 1873 First Lord Goschen noted three small warships needed new boilers after only four years, and that those of a fourth had to be replaced after seven years. 'They found,' he told the House of Commons, 'that boilers employed in the Navy did not last so long as they did in former days.'[50] Moreover, Goschen 'was sorry to say [that] it would be necessary to deal with the boilers of six of our ironclads.' The following year Goschen's successor, George Ward Hunt, appointed an Admiralty Committee to look into the matter.[51] The Committee, in turn, was to sit for the duration of Hunt's tenure at the Admiralty, studying the problem without reaching any defini-

tive conclusions. In 1878 former (and future) Secretary to the Admiralty George John Shaw-Lefevre commented pointedly upon its apparent inactivity.

> It was most unsatisfactory that Committee had been four years in existence and had not yet completed its work. . . . The evidence before the Committee showed that boilers in the Navy did not last more than five or six years; and it was clear, therefore, that nearly a whole set of boilers for the Navy had been worn out while the Committee was making its investigations.[52]

Only in 1880 was the final Report issued. It recommended placing 'sacrificial anodes' in boilers. These 'protect[ed] steel and other metals from electrochemical corrosion. The anodes gradually corrode away in preference to the steelwork [or iron] and [were] periodically replaced.'[53]

But even in top condition cylindrical boilers could not generate sufficient pressure to render the Navy's engines efficient and economical enough to permit the complete abandonment of sails on all vessels:

> 'Scotch' boilers were fitted in a number of naval vessels during the nineteenth century, but as the demand for higher performance increased, it was obvious to naval engineers that the fire-tube boiler was not suitable for the more exacting conditions of naval service.[54]

The ultimate solution to the problem was the development and adoption of a practical and safe water tube boiler, in which the fire circulated between and around small-diameter tubes carrying the water, rather than being channelled through flues in the boiler. By the end of the century pressures of 300 psi were being generated in such boilers. The type also offered a number of additional advantages. With the reduction of tube diameter, the need for thickness to contain the pressure was correspondingly reduced; a cylinder 1ft in diameter needed be only $\frac{5}{16}$in thick to withstand

150 psi. But while water tube boilers had, by 1876, been in industrial use for some time, problems plagued attempts to employ them at sea. Inadequate water circulation in the tubes made them prone to rapid overheating and explosion. Moreover, noted Fortesque Flannery in 1875,

> the metal exposed to the direct action of the fire is at the same time subjected to the tensile strain of internal pressure . . . any flaws will be stretched out, the flame will penetrate them, and promote their increase to the bursting point.[55]

The water tube boiler was not a practical alternative to the cylindrical type in the British or any other navy prior to the late 1880s, for that hurdle could only be surmounted by the switch from iron to steel. '[I]t is evident. . . ,' writes Rowland, that those

> who were responsible for the early development of the water-tube boiler were hampered by having to use iron as the material of construction: corrosion of boiler tubes was often rapid and with disastrous results. Another source of trouble was the accumulation of scale in the tubes . . . this restricted circulation and sometimes caused local overheating and tube failure.[56]

Uniform, high-quality steel was a prerequisite for the marine water tube boiler. As Milton put it in 1877, '[a]ll the latest inventions for generating high-pressure steam, in the shape of water-tube or sectional boilers have failed when set to work at ocean steaming'.[57] Without water-tube boilers, compound engines–to say nothing of triple- and quadruple-expansion units–could not be utilised with maximum efficiency.

The chief hurdle to adopting compound engines was the greater number of moving parts, which increased maintenance and the risk of breakdown. Engine wear-and-tear, moreover, was more rapid in ships of war than in merchant vessels, owing to the Admiralty's insistence that all machinery be below the waterline to reduce the risk of being struck by gunfire. This dictate necessitated

44. J. Milton, 'Strength of Boilers', *Transactions of the Institute of Naval Architects* 18 (1877), p318. See also Flannery, 'On Water Tube Boilers', p260. The latter placed the limit of thickness at 1⅜in, noting that a boiler of 12ft diameter would require a shell 1½ft thick to withstand 120 psi.

45. Rowland, *Steam at Sea*, p106. The surface condenser was first patented in the 1830s, but had been largely ignored by both naval and merchant interests for many years owing to problems of clogging. After 1855 improvements in the design, plus the switch from tallow to other forms of engine lubrication, eliminated the problems which had been encountered earlier.

46. Ibid, p136.

47. Ibid, p106.

48. A. E. Seaton, *A Manual of Marine Engineering: Comprising the Designing, Construction, and Working of Marine Machinery* (London, 1907), pp228-9. Seaton adds that there were further problems caused by chemical elements in suspension in the water becoming sediment and accelerating the corrosion.

49. Rowland, *Steam at Sea*, p106.

50. *Hansard*, 3d Ser., 215 (1873), col. 61.

51. Ibid, 3d ser., 218 (1874), col. 854.

52. Ibid, 3d ser., 238 (1878), col. 1429. See also Rowland, *Steam at Sea*, p136. The Committee did issue a preliminary report in 1878.

53. Rowland, *Steam at Sea*, pp106, 136. See also the 'Final Report of the Committee appointed by the Admiralty to inquire into the causes of the deterioration of Boilers, &c, and to propose measure which would tend to increase their durability; with Appendices containing results of Experiments,' *Parl. Papers* 1880, Vol. 13, p417.

54. Rowland, *Steam at Sea*, p136.

55. Flannery, 'On Water Tube Boilers', pp261-2.

56. Rowland, *Steam at Sea*, pp137.

57. Milton, 'Strength of Boilers', p318. See also Parkes, *British Battleships*, p392, for a synopsis of the adoption of the water tube boilers.

near-total abandonment of the vertical cylinder arrangement which minimised friction in cylinders and which was thus standard in merchantmen. Instead, the Navy's engines, save those in ships of very deep draught, had horizontally or diagonally situated cylinders, which in turn caused greater friction and wear, especially in the former. This drawback did not, however, dull Admiralty interest in the compound engine.

> The rapid diminution of overseas coal stocks in the numerous coaling stations throughout the world had long been a source of concern, particularly as most of the coal had to be transported in colliers from Britain. Consequently any improvement in thermal efficiency, however marginal, was worth investigating.[58]

By 1860, the same time the engine type was beginning to come into widespread use in the merchant service, the Admiralty began conducting experiments with it, fitting one vessel in a class of three with compound engines and the other two with the standard single-expansion variety, to carry out comparative trials. Despite the high incidence of maintenance problems, the greater efficiency of the compound engine was clearly demonstrated. 'The Admiralty,' however, 'remained to be convinced of the overall superiority of the compound engine because of the mechanical defects which were present in most of the early versions.'[59]

Early experience did not deter further experiments, though. Compound engines were installed in another five small vessels in the late 1860s, and their performance again demonstrated the savings advantage of the type in coal consumption. Moreover, in 1863 the Admiralty, again for experimental purposes, decided to equip a small ironclad, HMS *Pallas*, with the new engines. Again, maintenance was a problem: a report of their performance in 1868 observed '[t]hey are of course more complex than single cylinder engines, & they perhaps have been more often defective than Engines of simpler construction have been in performing the same amount of work.'[60] But again also, gains in economy and efficiency were demonstrable. The engines had 'been fairly successful' in 'obtaining a high rate of economy of fuel'. By 1871 the compound engine's superior economy was unmistakable, maintenance problems notwithstanding. The Committee on Designs of Ships of War displayed no ambivalence: 'its use has recently become very general in the Mercantile Marine, and the weight of evidence in favour of the large economy of fuel thereby gained is, to our minds, overwhelming and conclusive.' The Committee therefore recommended

> that the use of compound engines may be generally adopted in ships of war hereafter to be constructed, and applied, whenever it can be done with due regard to economy and to the convenience of the Service, to those already built.[61]

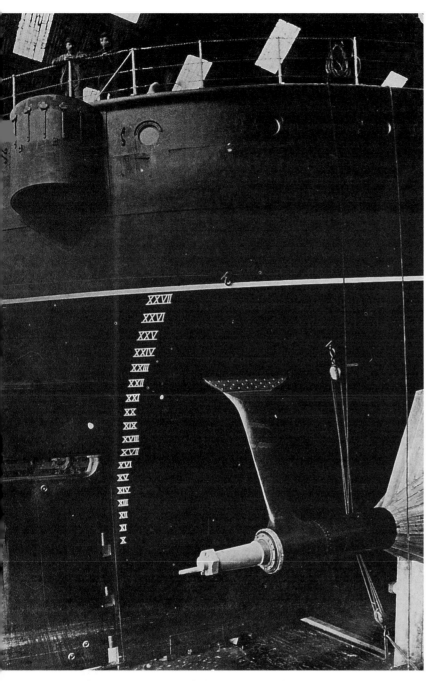

One of *Howe*'s propeller shafts, driven by vertical compound engines generating 11,500 ihp. (U.S. Naval Historical Center: NH75915)

58. Rowland, *Steam at Sea*, p121.

59. Ibid., pp121-2.

60. Thomas Lloyd to Controller, 12 November 1868, PRO: ADM1/6082.

61. *Report of the Committee on Designs for Ships of War*, 26 July 1871, PRO: ADM1/6212.

62. Ibid.

63. Richard Sennett, 'On Compound Engines', *Transactions of the Institute of Naval Architects* 16 (1875), p91.

64. James W. King, *European Ships of War and Their Armament, Naval Administration, etc.* (Washington, 1877), p192.

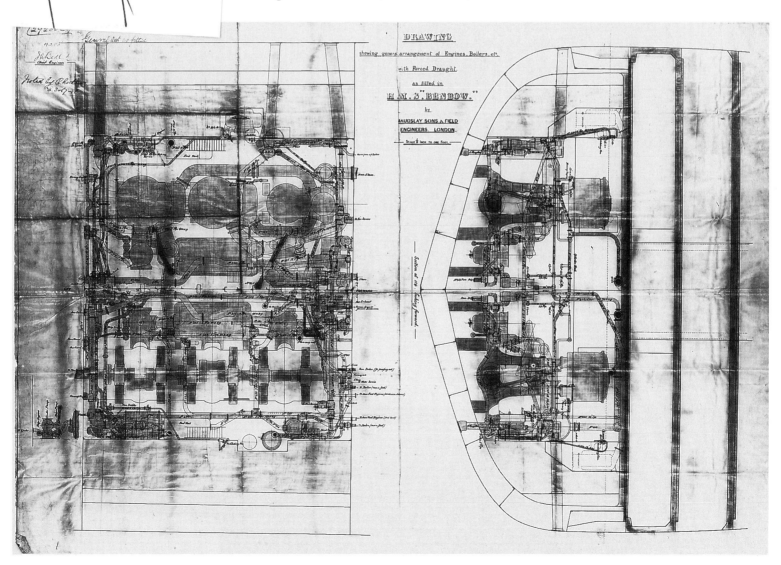

...lon sails on first-class iron-
...eeded at the Admiralty.
...gines the Committee was
...e Navy was in the midst of
... engines, and Nathaniel
...ee report observed '[t]he
...s already made or making
...h the Committee as to their
... engineer Richard Sennett
...cts that 'we seldom hear of
...pound engines.'[63] Two years
...mes W. King published a
...rld in which he noted that
...ed and ordered to be con-
...moured ships of large size,'
...ships, and '[a]ll of these ves-
...ats and one sloop, have been
...nd system.'[64]

...technological conservatism,

the Admiralty was not, as the contemporary phrase had it, badly 'behindhand' in its response to developments in maritime steam technology during the late 1860s and 1870s. The British Navy and the merchant marine adopted the surface condenser and the cylindrical boiler contemporaneously, and the slight lag on the part of the Navy in making a large-scale shift to compound engines was probably, as Rowland notes, due to the large number of mechanical problems in the early models installed in Her Majesty's ships. This performance illuminates the Admiralty's approach to novel technology: new machinery was adopted when it had been demonstrated by experience in the merchant service, in foreign navies, and often through the Navy's own experiments, to be both useful and reliable.

Overhead (left) and cross-sectional (right) plans of *Benbow*'s engines. The former shows, at top, the small-diameter high-pressure cylinder and two larger low-pressure cylinders of the ship's compound machinery, while the latter reveals the twin-shaft arrangement and watertight bulkhead between the two engine-rooms, as well as the vertical cylinders. (National Maritime Museum, London: 8382)

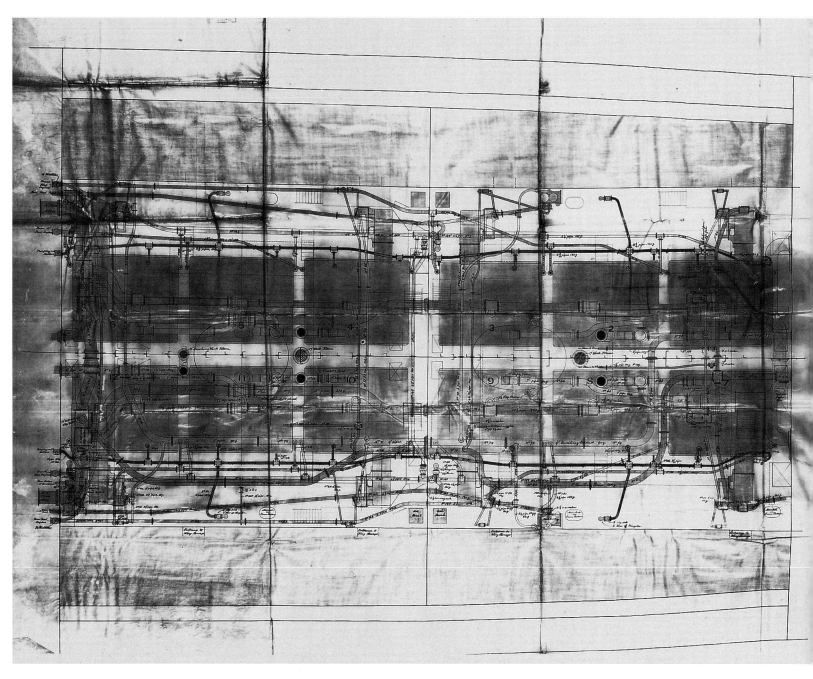

Modern commentators have almost without exception assumed that by 1870 the technological means existed to build a wholly steam-powered navy capable of operating world-wide.[65] This judgement is erroneous. Only after the tandem developments of high-pressure boilers and triple-expansion engines, neither of which made their appearance in Navy vessels prior to the early 1880s, and the gradual extension of the chain of defended coaling stations around the world was it practical to abandon sails on more than the fleet in European waters.[66] Although behind the times in advocating the retention of sails in 1883, Gerard Noel nonetheless touched on a salient fact when critiquing arguments against canvas. He pointed out that Philip Colomb had in 1878 presupposed the existence of 'no less than 75 coaling stations, 25 of which are not in our possession, and most of the remaining 50 are not fortified or protected in any way. When these important positions are all under our flag, and all rendered practically secure from capture or destruction we may reasonably trust our ships abroad without sail power'.[67]

Moreover, modern writers have generally failed to appreciate that the greater efficiency of compound engines was often more theoretical than real. Geoffrey Phipps Hornby testified in 1887 to the Hartington Commission, 'I drew out a list in 1874, just before I left the Channel Squadron, in which it appeared that of the 27 or 28 ironclads which we had, there were only five that would have been fit for war for over two years, the boilers were all so defective'.[68] In 1876, while in command of the

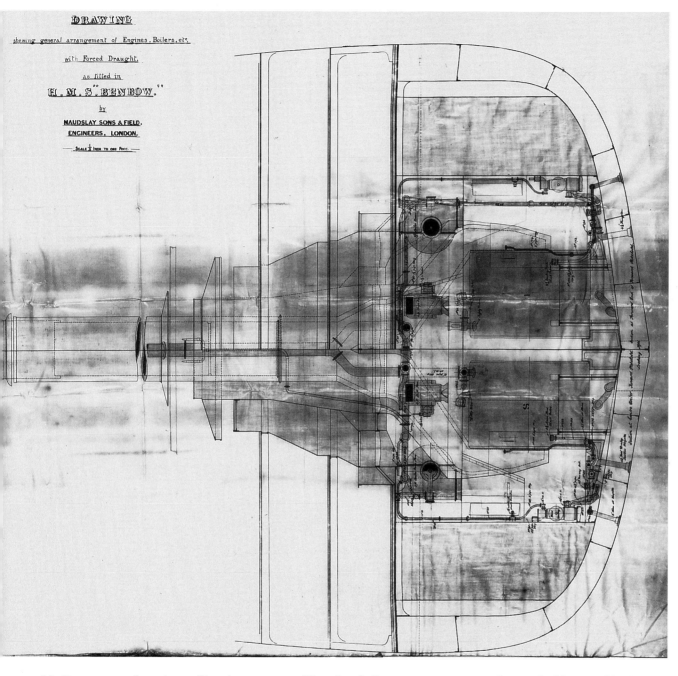

DRAWING

shewing general arrangement of Engines, Boilers, etc.

with Forced Draught.

as fitted in

H. M. S. "BENBOW."

by

MAUDSLAY SONS & FIELD,

ENGINEERS, LONDON.

— Scale ¼ Inch to one Foot. —

Overhead (left) and cross-sectional (right) plans of *Benbow*'s boilers. (National Maritime Museum, London: 8380)

Mediterranean Squadron, Hornby wrote to First Lord George Ward Hunt;

I should have been much surprised if the *Hercules*' boilers had proved fit for further service; but in my opinion, the country is stronger when such ships are shipping new boilers [*ie* when having them replaced] than when they are at sea 'making believe,' but really delaying effective ships. No one looks at the real cost of bad boilers. The *Monarch* . . . has burnt since leaving Malta 331 tons [of coal], while this ship has burnt 160; and, I believe, this

---

65. See, for instance, Sandler, *Emergence of the Modern Capital Ship*, pp86-7; Parkes, *British Battleships*, p221; N.A.M. Rodger, 'British Belted Cruisers,' *Mariner's Mirror* 64/1 (1978), pp29-30.

66. Parkes, *British Battleships*, pp330, 393. Triple expansion engines, operating on steam pressure of 135 psi., were first installed in ironclads in *Victoria* and *Sans Pareil*, both laid down in April 1885. The boilers of the early and mid-1870s typically operated at 60-70 psi., assuming they were in good repair, which was often not the case. By 1880 boiler pressures were up to around 90 psi., but only with adoption of the water tube boiler – first

used in battleships in the latter half of the 1890s – were pressures in excess of 200 psi. reached.

67. Noel, 'On Masting Ships of War', p550.

68. *Report of the Royal Commission appointed to make Enquiry into the Civil and Professional Administration of the Naval and Military Departments and the Relationship of those Departments to each other and to the Treasury* (generally known as the Hartington Commission), Strictly Confidential, PRO: HO73/35/3, p106.

Representative of early 1870s overseas designs, *General Admiral* and other foreign masted ironclads prompted the Admiralty to continue designing similar vessels. (U.S. Naval Historical Center: NH72161)

fairly represents the difference between steam at 60 lb. to [*sic*] steam at 16 lb.[69]

Those who accept the Committee on Designs Report at face value are quick to conclude that subsequent naval administrators

69. Mary Augusta Egerton, *Admiral of the Fleet Sir Geoffrey Phipps Hornby, G.C.B. A Biography* (Edinburgh, 1896), pp205-06.

70. Sandler, *Emergence of the Modern Capital Ship*, pp87, 88, 247.

71. [Edward J. Reed], *Naval Science* 1 (1872), p165; Parkes, *British Battleships*, pp204-5. Parkes cites Reed as commending the Admiralty for having 'most wisely' rejected the recommendation of the Committee.

72. Sandler, *Emergence of the Modern Capital Ship*, p78.

73. Parkes, *British Battleships*, pp115-16, 154-55. The most noteworthy of these expedients was the notorious 'lifting screw': a propeller which could be disconnected from the engine and hoisted up above the waterline in a contrivance not unlike that of a modern elevator shaft. Another – this one attended by fewer design and logistical headaches – was 'feathering' the screw; the nautical equivalent to putting a straight-drive car in neutral. The screw was disconnected from the engine shaft and allowed to rotate freely while a ship was under canvas, thus offering less resistance than a connected propeller. Unfortunately for naval architects, not to mention seamen and officers, 'feathering' produced only a marginal improvement in a vessel's performance under sail. With the adoption of twin screws in most ironclads from about 1870 on, the lifting screw, always a nuisance to operate, became completely impractical.

74. *Hansard*, 3d ser., 210 (1872), cols. 452-53.

75. Ibid., 3d ser., 215 (1873), col. 53. See also Sandler, *Emergence of the Modern Capital Ship*,

pp165-6. Sandler implicitly contradicts his own argument by admitting that the recommendations of the Committee on Designs for imperial defence 'proved far too radical and expensive to be implemented, particularly at a time when colonial relations with the mother country were unsettled. . . . Admirals Ryder and Elliot [Committee members who issued a dissenting Report] pointed out just how expensive it would have been for the Admiralty to have carried out the majority recommendation that mastless turret ships should operate from global "centres of naval power". In the whole of the Pacific, east of 180° longitude, no such centre existed south of Vancouver Island. In the western Atlantic there was nothing of value south of Trinidad except the Falkland Islands. In the Mediterranean, Malta was the only centre. Gibraltar was considered an extremity, while in the east no centre of naval power existed north of Shanghai. In Africa the ports were too widely spaced. Although the dissenting report agreed on the need for coaling ports, repair bases and docking facilities appeared out of the question at a time of peace, when it was difficult enough to obtain funds for a powerful ironclad fleet even for European waters. In fact the committee's majority recommendations found favour in almost no public quarter.'

76. [Edward J. Reed], *Naval Science* 1 (1872), p165.

77. Brassey, *Naval Annual* 1 (1886), p229. According to Brassey the French battleship *Marceau*, launched in 1884, was 'rigged with three lower masts with light top masts, but will carry fore and aft canvas only'.

78. King, *European Ships of War*, p143.

and designers were behaving retrogressively by failing to heed its recommendations.[70] In point of fact, however, the strategic, economic, and technological circumstances of the 1870s and early 1880s would have rendered the wholesale abandonment of sails for the ironclad fleet–to say nothing of the unarmoured 'peacetime' navy–not merely impractical, but foolish. Reed's *Naval Science* bluntly observed '[o]n the question of ocean-cruising ironclads the conclusions of the majority of the Committee were so manifestly unsound that it is surprising they could ever have been entertained.'[71] Stanley Sandler is certainly correct that 'Board policy . . . of combining steam and sail [was] a process that generally resulted in the perpetuation of the worst features of both systems of propulsion.'[72] Masts and sails not only increased wind resistance when steaming, but their weight and the space devoted to their spare hamper also reduced coal bunkerage. Likewise, the very form of a steamer's hull, plus the drag induced by the screw, had deleterious effects on a vessel's efficiency under sail and generally even worse ones on its handiness. None of the various expedients tried by naval designers to overcome the latter problems were of more than marginal utility.[73] But the conditions of the time made it impossible to abandon sails completely, no matter how unsatisfactory were the results of masting ironclads. As Goschen stated to the House of Commons, by way of justifying his Board's decision not to heed the Committee on Designs' recommendation,

> [i]t is a matter of great anxiety to differ from the Committee; but they have proceeded, as they frankly admit, on the rule of not looking at the existing Fleets of foreign countries, but at the future requirements of naval warfare . . . .We, on our own part have looked at the matter as a practical one, and we have asked what would be our position in the event of war, not in the remote future, but with the Navies of other countries such as we are now familiar with . . . .[74]

'[T]here are,' he continued,

> a large number of first-class ironclad cruisers belonging to other countries which can cruise under sail, and we should be in a dangerous position in regard to our distant possessions in the event of hostilities if we were not able to match these ships, which would be able to elude vessels carrying a limited quantity of coal.

A year later he added it 'was not a scientific question; it became rather a matter of common sense.'[75] This pronouncement drew approval from Reed's *Naval Science*: 'the Admiralty in the Estimates for the present year [1872-3] have gone in direct opposition . . .' to the Committee's advice, 'and, in point of fact, they [the Committee] stand almost entirely alone and without support.'[76]

Nor was British design policy regarding sails more conservative than that of France, which continued to design and construct first-

Notwithstanding her steel hull, *Redoutable* was typical of French ironclads of the 1870s in having masts and yards. (U.S. Naval Historical Center: NH74887)

class ironclads with masts and sails even longer than did its cross-Channel rival.[77] Indeed, King noted in 1877 that the French ironclad fleet contained 'no representatives of the mastless seagoing type to match the English *Dreadnought, Devastation, Thunderer,* and *Inflexible* [which was later given masts] . . . or analogous vessels of other nations . . . all [French] seagoing ships are rigged.'[78] The

Italians, it is true, abandoned sails on new ironclads in the early 1870s, but their navy was designed and built to operate exclusively in the narrow confines of the Mediterranean.[79]

In sum, the Admiralty's decision to continue to build sailing ironclads was not, for the greatest part, a manifestation of conservatism or foot-dragging, much less incompetence, although there were a few specific instances in which the continued provision for sails toppled over the brink separating common sense from silliness.[80] That the Navy did not undergo a complete transformation to reliance solely on steam for motive power was not, as some have implied, the result of a failure to utilise the most up-to-date refinements of steam engines and their ancillary devices. Nor, as modern critics of the Admiralty of the 1870s have alleged, was the failure to transform the Navy from sail to steam during that decade a consequence of conservatism, obstinacy, or incompetence at Whitehall. The tendency has been to note the development and acceptance of the compound engine in merchant applications and, simultaneously, the Navy's continued adherence to masts and sails, and to conclude either that it was slow to adopt the new technology, or backwards in retaining the old, or a combination of the two, for that matter. It was neither; the assumption that the compound engine obviated the need for sails in all applications is not borne out by a close examination of contemporary sources. An all-steam navy was only attainable in the steel age.

Simply because sails and steam did not mix well, and because the compound engine had become practical—at least on a theoretical level—by 1870, it does not follow, as Sandler argues, that 'the Board of Admiralty could . . . hardly plead technological hindrances to the abolition of masts and sails.'[81] Such a conclusion can be maintained by viewing only technological factors, and then only by viewing them in a purely theoretical context. The retention of sails was the consequence of simple pragmatism, of a realistic appraisal of the circumstances under which the Navy had to operate during the 1870s. The issue of sails, in short, was largely a red herring: superficially an indicator of want of progressivism in naval administration and design policy, but on closer examination a manifestation of a thorough appreciation of the limitations imposed by financial, geographic, strategic, and technological factors. While there were certainly cogent arguments against the continuation of the practice, there were, for at least a decade after the Committee on Designs sat, more telling ones in its favour, at least for certain types of vessels. Ironclads intended for service beyond European waters, plus of course the so-called 'non-fighting' navy needed a supplement to their engines when employed on distant stations.

---

79. The Italians laid down only four ironclads during the 1870s. None had masts and sails. On Italian designs, see Theodore Ropp, *The Development of A Modern Navy* (Stephen Roberts ed., Annapolis, 1987), pp80-6; Brassey, *Naval Annual*, 1 (1886), pp246-7, 250; *Conway's 1860-1905*, pp340-1.

80. There was really only one such case: the decision to mast *Inflexible*. For particulars, see Chapter 7.

81. Sandler, *Emergence of the Modern Capital Ship*, p87.

One clear instance where masts and sails were of no value. *Inflexible's* 18,000 sq ft of sail could barely have moved her 11,000-ton bulk. (U.S. Naval Historical Center: NH65879)

Chapter 4

ARMAMENT

'We do not by any means wish to dictate, but we think a mixed committee of naval and military men might, at a trifling expense, collect valuable evidence as to the expediency, the possibility and the cost of introducing heavy breech-loaders for cupolas [turrets] and other confined positions. If heavy breech-loaders are desirable, and the Russians can make them, surely we can supply ourselves.'

The Times, 16 January 1871

NAVAL ARMAMENT during the mid- and late-Victorian era fell into three categories; underwater weapons— mines and various forms of torpedoes, guns—the traditional armament of the Navy's ships since the dawn of the modern era—and the ram bow, championed by many naval officers and commentators during the latter years of the nineteenth century. The first two remain potent weapons to the present day. The third has long since vanished, although more than a few contemporaries thought it the most potent of the three. The ram formed an integral part of a ship's hull, however, and will thus be considered in the context of design rather than as a weapon.

Underwater weapons

In the 1860s and 1870s the term 'torpedo' applied to any sort of submerged or floating explosive device. Hence, what today are called mines were but one form of torpedo to the mid-Victorians, and the torpedo of the present day—the locomotive or 'fish' torpedo—was but one of several co-existing devices. Among the more noteworthy in the British Navy's arsenal were the spar torpedo, the outrigger or Harvey torpedo, as well as the locomotive or Whitehead variety. The first of these, as implied by the name, was simply an explosive charge mounted at the end of a long pole. It was supposedly detonated on contact with an enemy ship, having been conveyed there by a courageous or suicidal crew in a small, speedy launch. The Harvey torpedo was trailed from a line astern or, by employing a boom, alongside or ahead of a ship. The Whitehead, of course, was used in the fashion familiar to readers of naval literature today: launched from one ship and travelling under its own power underwater to strike (it was hoped) an enemy vessel.

All were in their infancy in the late 1860s and the efficacy of every type was still very much open to debate. The mine's performance in both the Crimean and the American Civil Wars had produced few demonstrable results, the most famous being the destruction of the USS *Tecumseh* at Mobile Bay in 1864. The spar torpedo could claim one notable success, William Cushing's audacious attack on the Confederate ironclad *Albemarle*, also in 1864.

The Harvey and Whitehead torpedoes both dated, as far as market availability was concerned, to the latter half of the 1860s. As of 1870, therefore, it was clear neither to Britain nor to any other naval power that the latter weapon would eventually prove to be the most potent and practical type, although within a decade it was evident that spar and Harvey torpedoes were as great, if not greater, menaces to the attacker as to the intended victim. Indeed, the spar torpedo was never to enjoy widespread popularity or employment in the Royal Navy, partly because of the obvious danger to the user, and partly because by the early 1870s the Whitehead torpedo appeared to be appropriate for any situation in which the spar torpedo might be used.

The Harvey torpedo, developed in 1867, was extensively tried by the War Office Committee on Floating Obstructions in 1868, but the Admiralty initially displayed little interest in the weapon, informing its inventor, Commander Frederick Harvey, R.N. that 'altho' he has shewn much ingenuity in the construction there are many difficulties in its application on actual service & my Lords are not disposed to incur expense in further experiments with it'.[1] Harvey 'expresse[d] surprise at their Lordships' decision', and requested a copy of the Report which advised against further experiments.[2] It was not forthcoming. Yet the Admiralty eventually adopted the weapon for employment in the fleet. On 2 September 1870 Harvey was informed that 'My Lords consider it desirable that his Torpedo should be adopted for the Naval Service & he is to make any claim he thinks he is entitled to.'[3]

The Harvey torpedo was almost exclusively a defensive weapon.[4] It may, theoretically, have been possible to manoeuvre a ship close enough to an intended victim to strike the latter with a torpedo

---

1. War Office to Admiralty, 19 March 1868, 17 April 1868; Director of Naval Ordnance to Admiralty, 3 July 1868; Admiralty to Harvey, 7 November 1868, PRO: ADM12/814/59.8.

2. Harvey to Admiralty, 25 November 1868, PRO: ADM12/814/59.8.

3. Admiralty to Harvey, 2 September 1870, PRO: ADM12/852/59.8.

4. An 1871 article by Commander W. Dawson, R.N., entitled 'Offensive Torpedo Warfare', *Journal of the Royal United Services Institution* 15 (1871), pp86-111, contains a nice 'artist's conception' of an attack with the Harvey torpedo. See plate between pp104-05.

trailing from a boom, but at that range most officers would have used the weapon of preference – the ram – rather than the torpedo. Yet as a deterrent to ramming, the Harvey and even the spar torpedo were thought to have virtues. As Philip Colomb suggested in 1865, 'would not the knowledge that every ship in an indented line had a torpedo extended from her bows, which required only a gentle *rub* to call it into action, be a wholesome disturber of the nerves of any adventurous ram-captain who might be disposed to try the new weapon?'[5] The Harvey's vogue was brief, however. With the incorporation of launching tubes for the Whitehead into British warship designs from the early 1870s onward, it was quickly apparent that the locomotive torpedo could be used to counter ramming attacks. By late 1878, when then Captain Harvey forwarded a list of design improvements for his weapon to the Admiralty, he was thanked and informed that there was 'no inten-

tion of increasing the stock of his torpedoes now in hand'.[6] Two years later Naval Ordnance Store depots were instructed to return all remaining Harvey torpedoes to Woolwich.[7]

The Whitehead was originally the invention of an Austrian, Johann Luppis, and was powered by a motor which ran on compressed air, but the refinements which made it a viable, if not wholly practical (or effective) weapon, were the contributions of an expatriate Englishman living in Fiume, one Robert Whitehead.[8] Most famous of his improvements was the depth-regulating device, the so-called 'Whitehead secret'. Luppis had been at work on the device since 1860. He joined forces with Whitehead in 1864, and three years later the essential elements of the design were in place. By 1868 the pair had managed to sell the weapon to the Austrian government, and were looking for buyers overseas, among them the Royal Navy. In late August of that year the Commander-in-Chief of the Mediterranean Squadron, Vice-Admiral Lord Clarence Paget reported that 'Mr. Whitehead is desirous of submitting his invention to H.M. Gov[ernmen]t'.[9]

The evolution of British Whitehead torpedoes, built under licence. (U.S. Naval Historical Center: NH84470)

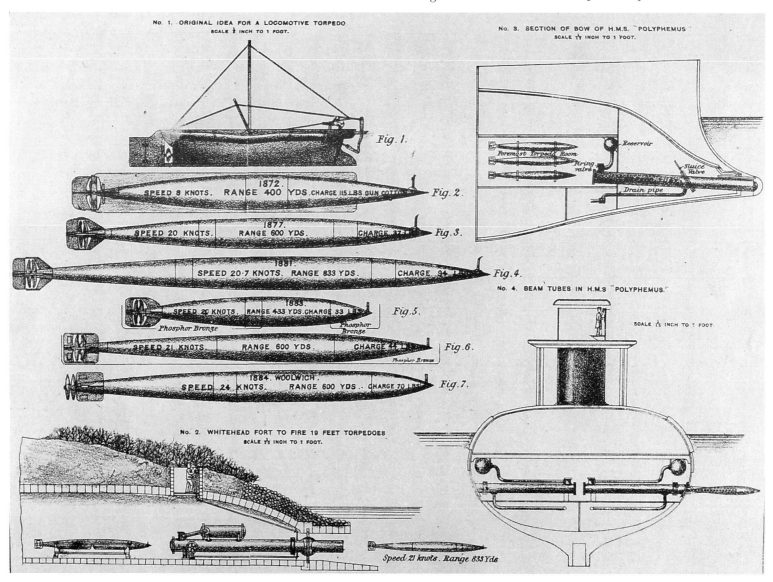

The Admiralty quickly expressed interest. The D.N.O., Rear-Admiral Sir Astley Cooper Key, saw no objection to testing it 'when Mr. Whitehead makes his proposition'.[10] But when the subject was brought to the attention of Chancellor of the Exchequer George Ward Hunt the response was not encouraging. Henry Corry reported to Disraeli on 16 November that the Navy had asked Ward Hunt 'whether he would authorise a trial of the torpedo, and whether, if the results were altogether satisfactory, he would authorise a grant of public money in payment for the secret.' Ward Hunt would have none of it. He was 'not prepared to assent to the proposition of the Admiralty as regards the invention.' Corry then appealed to Disraeli, claiming that the Chancellor would have come to a different conclusion had he known of the weapon's potential.[11] Furthermore, Corry warned the Prime Minister that Whitehead was then 'in Paris negotiating the sale of his secret to the French Government–to the exclusion of other nations'. Consequently, the First Lord added,

I cannot undertake the responsibility of refusing to make even a trial of the invention, and if it were not for the Elections I should have brought the matter before a Cabinet. As that is impossible at present [the Cabinet being dispersed to the constituencies], and as time presses . . . I think it my duty to refer the question to you . . . .

Disraeli, ordinarily hostile to 'bloated' armaments expenditures, in this instance agreed with Corry. 'This appears to me to be a matter of grave importance,' he wrote to Ward Hunt, '& I agree with the F[irst] L[ord] of the Adm[iralt]y, that our decision involves a very grave responsibility.'[12] Therefore, '[m]y impression is that the

experiment should be tried . . .', although he added that 'the present moment w[oul]d be inconvenient.' He was right on the last point. The Conservatives were out of office within a month of Disraeli's letter to Ward Hunt, and the Whitehead question was lost in the shuffle which accompanied the change of ministries.

It was to be more than a year before the Admiralty again took up the question of purchasing the 'Whitehead secret'. This delay, however, had nothing to do with 'naval obscurantism, but rather . . . the reluctance of other departments to co-operate'.[13] The lack of haste was doubtless partly attributable to the fact that France had not purchased the weapon after all.[14] In August 1869 the Foreign Office did issue a circular to diplomatic officials through Europe instructing them to gather 'secret information' regarding other Powers' 'Experiments with Torpedoes', and it is apparent that Liberal First Lord Hugh Childers' Board was interested in the weapon.[15] In July 1869 the new D.N.O., Captain Sir Arthur Hood, sent naval observers to Fiume to witness trials of the torpedo. Their report was favourable and further extensive tests were conducted in England during the fall of 1870. In November Hood reported 'the satisfactory result of trials' with the device, and his opinion that 'the torpedo can be improved upon'. Accordingly, he recommended that 'the secret of the Invention should be purchased'.[16] Hood's judgement was seconded by the Committee overseeing the trials, which stated unequivocally '[a]ny nation failing to provide itself with submarine locomotive torpedoes would be neglecting a source of great power both for offence and defence'.[17] The Treasury was informed in mid-November 'probably the torpedo will be purchased', although haggling over the price delayed completion of the transaction until mid-1871.[18]

5. Philip Colomb, 'Modern Naval Tactics', *Journal of the Royal United Services Institution* 9 (1865), p23.

6. Admiralty to Harvey, 20 December 1878, PRO: ADM12/1021/5.1.

7. Admiralty to Naval Ordnance Store Depots, 17 July 1880, PRO: ADM12/1060/59.8.

8. Alan Cowpe provides a comprehensive account of the early history of the Whitehead torpedo in the Royal Navy: 'The Royal Navy and the Whitehead Torpedo,' in Bryan Ranft (ed.), *Technical Change and British Naval Policy, 1860-1939* (London, 1977), pp23-36.

9. Paget to Admiralty, 25 August 1868, PRO: ADM12/814/59.8.

10. Ibid; Cowpe, 'The Royal Navy and the Whitehead Torpedo', p23. Cowpe notes Cooper Key's 'open-mindedness' on this issue, a point worth stressing since, in most cases, he was rather less receptive to technological change.

11. Corry to Disraeli, 16 November [1868], Wadenhoe (Hunt) Papers Northamptonshire R.O., Northampton, WH285. 'It is to be regretted [Corry wrote to the Prime Minister] that he was not in London, as I think if he had seen the papers, and heard what Admiral Key and General Lefroy–representing the Gunnery departments of the Admiralty and War Office–have to say on the subject, he would have come to a different conclusion.'

12. Disraeli to Hunt, 16 November 1868, Wadenhoe (Hunt) Papers Northamptonshire R.O., Northampton, WH286.

13. Cowpe, 'The Royal Navy and the Whitehead Torpedo', p23.

14. Robinson to Admiralty, 1 December 1870, PRO: ADM12/852/59.8.

15. Foreign Office to Admiralty, 17 August 1869, PRO: ADM12/832/59.8. The Foreign Office's directive netted reports from Italy, Russia, Sweden, Belgium, Greece, France, and the United States (ADM12/832/59.8, [1869], *passim*).

16. Hood to Admiralty, 3 November 1870, PRO: ADM12/852/59.8. The experiments had been conducted by a special Committee on Whitehead's Torpedoes, whose report was printed in October 1870 (Controller's Department to Admiralty, 27 October 1870, PRO: ADM12/846/5.1a).

17. *Report of the Committee on Whitehead Torpedoes*, 28 October 1870, quoted in Cowpe, 'The Royal Navy and the Whitehead Torpedo', pp23-4.

18. Controller's Department to Admiralty, 1 December 1871, PRO: ADM12/852/59.8. Luppis and Whitehead initially demanded £20,000, for which sum 'the secret & the right to use their invention will be imparted to H.M. Govt.'. D.N.O. Arthur Hood recommended that the Admiralty counter with an offer of £15,000, but Controller Spencer Robinson thought 'it would be better to pay the sum of £20,000 & take every means to secure the invention exclusively for England and Austria . . .'. The First Sea Lord, Admiral Sir Sydney Dacres, concurred with Hood: 'he [Dacres] does not recommend the divided right of Austria and England to use this apparatus as suggested.' The upshot of this departmental wrangle was that 'Messrs. Luppis & Whitehead informed that important departmental arrangements have to be made regarding torpedoes, after which a reply [to their demand] will be sent.'
When the Admiralty's offer was finally made, in February 1871, it was for £15,000, the Board claiming that £20,000 'is excessive . . .' (Admiralty to Luppis and Whitehead, 15 February 1871, PRO: ADM12/874/59.8). The inventors countered with a demand for £18,000 in early March, but in June Luppis and Whitehead accepted the offer of £15,000 (Luppis and Whitehead to Admiralty, 7 March 1871, 6 April 1871, PRO: ADM12/ 874/ 59.8; Luppis and Whitehead to Admiralty, n.d., PRO: ADM12/874/59.8; Agreement of the British Government with Messrs. Luppis and Whitehead, 11 June 1871, PRO: ADM-116/146). By December 1871 arrangements were being made in the following year's Navy Estimates to cover the cost of supplying Whitehead and Harvey torpedoes to the fleet (Controller's Department to Admiralty, 6 December 1871, PRO: ADM12/874/59.8).

This photograph of *Imperieuse* shows the deployment of her anti-torpedo nets on the starboard bow. (U.S. Naval Historical Center: NH65954)

Certainly the Admiralty displayed no reluctance to try and adopt the new weapon. Even Cooper Key, not the most progressive of naval administrators, favoured it. Indeed, Britain was the first country apart from Austria to purchase the 'Whitehead Secret', and this in turn prompted other European powers to follow suit rapidly.[19] Corry's Board was interested in the weapon from the time it was first brought to their attention. The ensuing lag of two and a half years before the invention was finally purchased was attributable to a variety of factors: the fortunes of politics, trials of the weapon, and bargaining with its inventors. The most time-consuming of these – testing the torpedo – so far from being a manifestation of conservatism, was another instance of the Admiralty's cautious yet open-minded approach to technological novelties, an approach which resisted plunging headlong into uncharted technical waters, but which also minimised the risk of being left behind by bolder rivals. Furthermore, in 1873 a separate school

for torpedo instruction, HMS *Vernon*, was established at Portsmouth, and that year the Admiralty approved Commander John A. Fisher's 'Short Practical Course of Torpedo Instruction', which was to 'be carried out in the *Vernon* under the supervision' of its author. The course lasted a month, and was 'compulsory in the case of Gunnery Lieutenants & Sub Lieut[enant]s & Voluntary in case of Gunners, Gunnery Instructors, & Seaman Gunners'.[20] Enlisted personnel who passed the course were to be ' "rated Trained Torpedo Men", with an extra 1d. a day in pay'. True, a similar school had been established in France four years earlier and a special Torpedo Corps of the United States Navy was also created in 1869,[21] but by 1868 the Admiralty had appointed a Torpedo Instructor to the Navy's Gunnery Training Ships, HMS *Cambridge* and *Excellent*, and in March of that year the War Office was 'informed that Torpedo classes have been established on b[oar]d . . .' the two ships.[22]

Debates about whether the British Navy was quick or slow on the uptake with regard to the Whitehead torpedo take on a slightly ludicrous aspect when the effectiveness of early models is considered. Although the torpedo ultimately proved the most formidable of underwater weapons, in its original incarnation it was formidable in theory alone.[23] Henry Corry claimed in 1868: 'the professed performance of the torpedo is so marvelous that one could hardly believe it', although a larger factor in his eagerness to try the weapon was probably 'the *fact* of the Austrian Government having paid Mr. Whitehead £20,000 for his secret, after a series of experiments conducted by scientific officers at Fiume'.[24] Its 115lb explosive charge could, no doubt, cause grave damage to the hull of any ship it struck. The problem was getting it there. Whitehead's torpedo, as originally marketed, had a range of only 400yds, and a top speed of 8kts.[25] Any vessel venturing close enough to its intended target to launch such a short-range weapon faced grave danger from gunfire. Moreover, assuming the boilers were in reasonably good condition, every seagoing British ironclad of the 1860s and 1870s was capable of more than 8kts under steam. A successful attack might have been launched at night against an anchored ship with a careless lookout, or at an already disabled vessel, but under any other circumstances it is difficult to envision a torpedo attack with the early models of the Whitehead. It was 'fairly good up to 200 yards (with a speed of 9 knots at that distance), and though this was remarkable enough, [it] was far from being an actual instrument of warfare.'[26]

In addition to speed and range deficiencies, early Whitehead torpedoes laboured under other disabilities. The depth-regulating apparatus garnered the praise of contemporaries, but they were less enthusiastic about the steering gear. In 1870 the Admiralty received a report regarding 'the constant deviation to the left of Whitehead's torpedoes'.[27] In 1882 Thomas Brassey observed '[i]t has occurred that a torpedo, launched for practice from an English ship of war, turned around and ran back to the ship.'[28] The event was not unique. Brassey added 'it is not feasible to launch a fish [Whitehead] torpedo right ahead with any success, even when at moderate speed; for, as might have been expected, it

commenced to diverge immediately upon entering the water, and pursued a most erratic course across the bows of its own ship.'[29]

These teething problems were gradually overcome. By the mid-1880s Woolwich Arsenal, which manufactured the weapons under license, had developed models with speeds of 24kts and ranges up to 600yds, but only during the Russo-Japanese War, more than thirty-five years after the weapon's appearance, did it achieve unequivocal success in action.[30] Hood was right when he surmised in 1870 that the Whitehead 'can be improved upon' but there was a great deal of improvement to be done before it was to be a practical engine of war. In 1872 civil engineer Robert Mallet, F.R.S., noted that none of the underwater weapons 'can as yet be said to have arrived at the stage of assured practical success'.[31] Regarding the Whitehead specifically, Mallet added

> even though the self-propelling torpedo be constructed on a large and expensive scale . . . so as to ensure as straight and unswerving a course in the initial direction as possible, still the chances of striking the hull of a distant ship are very small.

Rather than conservatism, the British and other navies which purchased the 'Whitehead secret' during the early years of its existence displayed considerable foresight and perseverance.

Guns

Naval ordnance provided another set of difficult choices for administrators, both civilian and professional. For more than three centuries before 1850 the primary naval gun had been a smoothbore muzzle-loader. The type had, of course, been refined or modified over time, perhaps most notably by the introduction of the 'carronade', a large-calibre short-barrelled gun, in the late eighteenth century, but the essentials of the design were unchanged.[32] This general stasis ended in the middle of the nine-

19. Theodore Ropp, *The Development of a Modern Navy* (Stephen Roberts ed., Annapolis, 1987), p112.

20. Admiralty to Commanders-in-Chief of Devonport and Portsmouth Dockyards, 15 January 1873, PRO: ADM12/920/59.8.

21. Foreign Office to Admiralty, 12 January 1869, 14 August 1869, PRO: ADM12/832/59.8.

22. Admiralty to War Office, 5 March, 1868 PRO: ADM12/814/59.8. The War Office had proposed that the two Services 'undertake joint Torpedo Instruction' with the costs to be split between them. The Admiralty replied that since the Navy's own course had already been implemented, 'My Lords have no occasion to avail themselves of the Royal Engineers at Chatham, the Gunnery ships having the requisite means of instruction.' The War Office was informed, however, that 'Their Lordships will . . . be glad to send an Instructor occasionally to Chatham to learn the improvements which may take place . . . ,' and lest it appear that the Admiralty's policy was all take and no give, it generously added that 'My Lords would be also glad to know in what way Chatham Yard can be made available for assisting the R[oya]l Eng[inee]rs in giving Torpedo Instruction.'

23. Cowpe, 'The Royal Navy and the Whitehead Torpedo', p25. Cowpe stresses this point. Noting the high praise it garnered from trials, he points out that it 'was still a prim-

itive weapon with a range of only 200 yards and a speed of 9 knots, while its value was in any event dependent on its rather limited chances of hitting its target. Again, therefore, its powers were, if anything, overestimated.'

24. Corry to Disraeli, 16 November [1868], Wadenhoe (Hunt) Papers, Northamptonshire R.O., Northampton, WH285.

25. E.P. Gallway, 'The Use of Torpedoes in War', *Journal of the Royal United Services Institution* 29 (1885), plate between pp472-3.

26. Ropp, *Development of a Modern Navy*, p113.

27. Captain Arthur to Admiralty, 19 December 1870, PRO: ADM12/846/5.1a.

28. Thomas Brassey, *The British Navy; Its Strengths, Resources, and Administration* Vol 2 (London, 1882), p149n.

29. Ibid, Vol 3, p466.

30. Gallway, 'The Use of Torpedoes in War', plate between pp472-3.

31. Robert Mallet, 'Subaqueous Torpedoes', *Naval Science* 1 (1872), p271.

32. Ian Hogg and John Batchelor, *Naval Gun* (Poole, 1978), pp17-24.

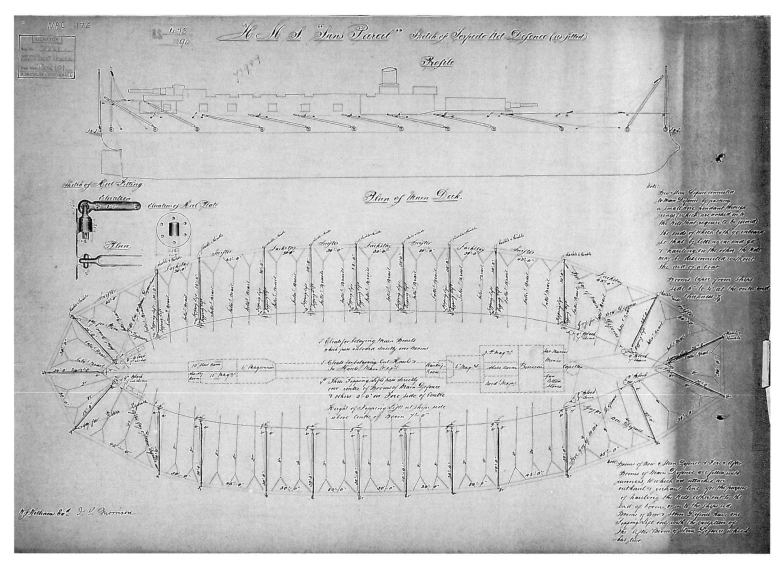

Plan of *Sans Pareil*'s anti-torpedo net defence. The same type of protection was used on most British ironclads and battleships from *Inflexible* onwards. (National Maritime Museum, London: E2282)

teenth century, owing principally to three factors: the incorporation of shell-firing guns in warships, the introduction of rifled naval ordnance, and the development and gradual improvement of breech-loading guns.[33]

The naval shell gun was pioneered by France in the late 1830s, and adopted soon thereafter by other navies. It has long been argued that this development sounded the death-knell of the wooden warship, so vulnerable to fire, but Andrew Lambert has recently suggested that the effect of shells has been much exaggerated. 'It must be emphasised that for all the startling results of shell *practice* the effects of shell-fire in combat were unimpressive . . . A combination of inaccurate artillery and poor fuses' ensured that shell guns never duplicated their performance on the testing ground, nor lived up to the expectations of their inventor, Joseph Paixhans.[34]

Of greater immediate significance to the British Navy was the

33. Ibid, p29; Lambert, *Battleships in Transition*, p92.

34. Lambert, *Battleships in Transition*, p92.

35. The former reason is usually cited, but Lambert points out that the smaller Armstrong breechloaders, especially the 20pdr, were used for many years without complaint. Only the larger calibres suffered from the problem. The cause, Lambert argues, was that metallurgy was not sufficiently advanced in 1860 to produce a strong enough breech piece for the bigger guns. See also Philip H. Colomb, *Memoir of the Right Honble Sir Astley Cooper Key, G.C.B., D.C.L., F.R.S., etc* (London, 1898), pp330-1.

36. Hogg and Batchelor, *Naval Gun*, p68.

37. Colomb, *Cooper Key*, p36. It might be noted that although the large Armstrong breech-loader was abandoned by the Navy, his method of constructing gun barrels, which involved shrinking successive layers of wrought iron coils around an inner steel tube became the standard process for manufacturing British naval ordnance.

38. Hogg and Batchelor, *Naval Gun*, pp69-70; Oscar Parkes, *British Battleships*, pp36-7; Stanley Sandler, *The Emergence of the Modern Capital Ship* (Newark, Delaware, 1979), pp92-3.

39. Parkes, *British Battleships*, p37; Sandler, *Emergence of the Modern Capital Ship*, pp92-3.

1860 decision to employ the breech-loading gun design of Sir William Armstrong. The advantages offered by Armstrong's gun were numerous: it was lighter than previous naval ordnance, its rifled bore greatly increased accuracy, and the breech-loading design itself facilitated loading. Consequently, the 7in Armstrong gun, throwing a 110lb shell, was adopted as the principal heavy gun in the British fleet. But this decision was quickly regretted. First, the breech-closing apparatus, consisting of a large screw, was subject to jamming, and even to being blown out of the gun upon firing. The latter phenomenon, which occurred with enough frequency to cause the weapons to be dubbed 'them two-muzzled guns' in the service, was the consequence either of incomplete or improper closure of the breech – which lacked an effective locking device – or of structural weakness of the breech piece.[35] Second, and related to structural weakness, the 110pdr could not deliver a hard enough blow to pierce even 4½in of wrought iron armour.[36] Indeed, the old 68pdr smoothbore throwing solid shot was a better armour-piercing weapon. In 1864, therefore, the Navy reverted to muzzle-loading guns, for the moment a 100pdr smoothbore of 9.5in calibre, weighing 6½ tons, known as the 'Somerset gun' after the then First Lord of the Admiralty.

The 'Somerset gun' was but a temporary expedient. The same year the Captain of the Gunnery Ship *Excellent*, Astley Cooper Key, reported that an experimental 7in rifled muzzle-loader was 'more than equal to naval requirements'. After further trials the gun, weighing 7 tons, was adopted as the heavy armour-piercing, or rather armour-battering, naval gun.[37] The weapon was not without its drawbacks. The method of rifling, which imparted spin to the projectile for increased accuracy, consisted of projecting studs at the base of the shell, which engaged grooves in the interior of the barrel.[38]

The studs tended to sheer [off] . . . the increasing spiral [of the rifling] led to gun damage and sometimes jamming of the shot; there was 'wobbling and hammering in the bore', and 'puffing' during the flight, which indicated that a projectile was misbehaving.[39]

Representative of British ordnance of the late 1860s and early 1870, this 12in, 25-ton muzzle-loading rifle was mounted aboard the ram *Hotspur*. (U.S. Naval Historical Center: NH71213)

In short, according to Oscar Parkes, the decision to abandon breech-loaders left the Navy saddled 'with a faulty system of artillery which was to endure through the next fifteen years'.

There can be little doubt that the 'Woolwich system' of rifling was imperfect. In 1868 an Ordnance Select Committee of the House of Commons pressed for the reintroduction of breech-loaders, claiming among other things that they were easier to load, quicker-firing, and allowed for greater protection of the gun crew. The Committee, minus one dissentient was of the 'opinion that a system of breech loading for heavy guns is most desirable', and it urged 'a re-consideration of the question whether the construction of the heavier natures of guns is to continue to be exclusively on a muzzle loading principle'. On the recommendation of the D.N.O. Cooper Key, the Board of Admiralty deigned not to follow the Select Committee's advice.[40]

The Navy's decision suggests conservatism or outright obstructionism, not to mention penny-pinching, since Cooper Key based one of his objections to breech-loaders on the cost of re-arming the fleet. Certainly the D.N.O. was a man of innate caution, yet factors beyond conservatism were involved.[41] First, the Ordnance Select Committee admitted that the advantages of breech-loading were 'abstract,' and it could 'not disguise the serious expense which must be incurred before any conclusion can be come to as to the actual adoption of any system of breech loading'. Second, Cooper Key did not dispute the 'firm advantages' obtained through 'the power of loading at the breech', but two questions accompanied his admission:

Is any one of the known systems of breech loading as applied to heavy guns so efficient as to be worthy of adoption, [and] [h]as any proved itself sufficiently satisfactory to authorise the experiments that would be necessary to ascertain its merits with guns of 10 [inch] calibre and upwards?

By 1870 both Prussia and France employed breech-loading systems for large ordnance, the former having made the switch in 1859, the latter a year later, at the time Britain made the abortive transition to Armstrong breech-loaders. Cooper Key's questions were nonetheless valid for both of the methods of breech closure – the 'interrupted screw' of the French system and the wedge apparatus in the Krupp ordnance used by Prussia – had obvious shortcomings.[42] Although both systems were less prone to spectacular breech failure in the manner of the Armstrong gun, neither boasted a perfect seal at the breech, and gas leaks were endemic to each. The Krupp system of closure was so imperfect, in fact, that in 1873 naval attaché Admiral A.P. Ryder reported:

There is a great escape of gas, so that it is necessary to have a leather guard on the trigger line to protect the man's hand . . . The Gun Captain's clothes have been known to catch fire – and they sometimes wear 'pinafores' to protect themselves.[43]

The interrupted screw design for breech closure, seen here on *Rodney*'s 13.5in guns, had been adopted by France in 1860, but only in the early 1880s by Great Britain. (U.S. Naval Historical Center: NH55603)

Rather unnecessarily Ryder added 'I imagine no great accuracy of fire can be expected under the circumstances'.

A greater drawback, in terms of efficiency, was the loss of muzzle velocity consequent upon the leakage of propelling gases, and so pronounced was this problem in rival ordnance systems that as of 1870 English heavy guns boasted substantially higher muzzle velocities. In 1867 Cooper Key compared a 9in British gun with a 9.5in French piece. The British weapon was, he maintained, the more powerful despite its smaller bore. 'The initial velocity of the [French] steel shot of 317 lb. is 1,102 ft. [per second] that of the English 9-in shot of 250 lbs. being 1,370. The range of the French gun with 4° elevation is 1,712 yards that of [the] English gun at 3° elevation being 1,848 yards.'[44] According to him, the British muzzle-loading rifle was superior in other respects as well. Despite the necessity of ramming powder and shell the entire length of the barrel, he claimed the British gun was quicker to load and fire. 'In rapidity of fire the Muzzle Loading gun has the advantage. The various manoeuvres involved in opening and closing the breech delays the operation of loading even when all is in good order.' Captain Arthur Hood of HMS *Excellent* seconded Cooper Key's opinion: 'taking into consideration the weight of the breech plug, and the various movements required in loading, I feel satisfied that a more rapid fire can be delivered and sustained with our 12 ton Gun than with the French 14 ton Gun.'[45] Neither officer offered statistical evidence to back up his claim nor did Cooper Key go beyond the vague generality that 'very good results' had been 'obtained from our own Muzzle Loading guns up to 12 tons weight—both as regards rapidity of fire and perfect safety.'[46] Regarding muzzle velocity, however, there was no dispute, and since this was the most important criterion when employing heavy guns against ironclads, Cooper Key confidently asserted

[t]he superiority rests in a marked degree with the English Gun, and I have no hesitation in offering an opinion that our mode of construction is more certain—of greater strength and more durable than that of the French—while the muzzle loading system is from its simplicity and freedom from risk of damage also superior to the French system of breech loading.[47]

The situation was much the same when comparing British guns and Krupp's breech-loading heavy ordnance during the late 1860s. Aside from the problem of gas leakage so vividly described by Ryder, the German method of securing the breech—a wedge screwed in to hold the breech plug in place—substantially slowed the rate of fire. In 1867 Hood reported that although '[t]he breech closing arrangement of this gun is in my opinion decidedly more secure and safe than that adopted by the French . . . the mode of opening and closing the breech is more complicated and requires considerably more time.'[48] Hood added

We were informed that this [Krupp] Gun could be fired at the

rate of one round in 2½ minutes—I have seen five rounds fired at a target from our 12 Ton Gun in the *Bellerophon* (the ship rolling from 3 to 5 degrees, and good practice [accuracy] made) in 1 minute 36 seconds.

As of the late 1860s, therefore, British muzzle-loading rifled ordnance was in important respects superior to rival systems. It is possible, of course, that Cooper Key, Hood and Ryder were prejudiced in favour of their own guns, but it was more common for naval officers to denigrate their own *matériel* and exaggerate the qualities of rival ships and weapons. In addition, Theodore Ropp, acknowledges that early French breechloaders were 'imperfect,' and Parkes admits that in 1868 'the wisdom of the Admiralty in preferring to retain the muzzle-loaders was justified, at any rate for the next few years'.[49]

However, Parkes is also correct in suggesting that the British muzzle-loaders' superiority was ephemeral. In 1872 a French Army officer, Captain de Bange, invented what contemporaries termed a 'plastic gas check' manufactured of malleable metal, which secured a complete seal at the breech, being forced into the space between gun barrel and breech plug by the gas pressure in the bore when the gun was fired.[50] After testing, it was officially adopted by the French in 1873. From this point on the gap between the power of British and foreign ordnance steadily narrowed. As late as 1876 Admiralty tables of muzzle velocities showed that the British 12.5in, 38-ton gun still had the advantage over the corresponding French piece. But the Krupp 12in gun had a higher muzzle velocity than the slightly larger British gun.[51] By 1877 at the

40. Director of Naval Ordnance to Admiralty, 15 September 1868, PRO: ADM1/6083. Other virtues of breechloaders listed by the Committee were the ability to build longer guns without 'practical inconvenience', less likelihood of damaging the gun through jamming or other mishaps, savings of labour, easier aiming, and easier inspection of the bore for signs of wear.

41. Colomb, *Cooper Key*, pp350-1.

42. The 'interrupted screw', which was eventually to be adopted by the British, was described by Cooper Key in an 1867 report: 'The breech plug is centred in the rear—it has a worm of 13 threads on its surface—three equal & equidistant portions of which are removed—each portion equal to ⅙ of the whole circumference. The corresponding portions of the female screw inside the breech are also removed—so that the plug can be pushed in—and by ⅙ of a turn it is screwed up' (Cooper Key to Admiralty, 13 June 1867, PRO: ADM1/6012).

43. Ryder to Admiralty, 9 May 1873, PRO: ADM1/6286.

44. Cooper Key to Admiralty, 13 June 1867, PRO: ADM1/6012. Elsewhere in his report Cooper Key noted that 'our 8-in Gun of nine tons is almost equal in penetrating power to the French 9.45-in Gun of 14 tons—and our 7-in Gun of 6 ½ tons superior in penetrating power to the French 7.6-in Gun of 8 tons weight.' His opinions were seconded by Captain Arthur Hood of *Excellent*, who wrote in the same report that 'our 12 ton gun is proved to possess considerably superior power to the Fr[ench] 14 ton Gun as an Armour penetrating Gun, it is two tons lighter and considered to be equally durable, it is also free from . . . the possibility of being disabled in action, owing to the derangement or damage of some part of the breech loading arrangements . . .'. Further confirmation of the superior velocity of English ordnance was provided the following year in a report by naval attaché Captain Hore: 'The [French] gun in question (of 27 centimetres [calibre])

though weighing 21.7 tons is very inferior in power and range to our 18 ton gun' (Hore to Admiralty, 4 March 1868, PRO: ADM1/6072).

45. Cooper Key further argued that 'when the action of the breech is impeded by deposit, by darkness—or by any of the delays inherent in a complicated mechanised operation this delay must become more serious—and with high elevation the difficulty will be much increased.' This argument was largely spurious, however. Cooper Key overlooked, ignored, or suppressed the fact that all the circumstances he enumerated would result in 'delays' and 'much increased difficulty' in the case of British ordnance as well. Deposits in the bore would hinder loading just as much, if not more, for a muzzle-loader, and darkness would also delay loading one, regardless of its mechanical simplicity. Furthermore, at high elevations, loading a large muzzle-loader was not merely a matter of 'much increased difficulty', it was one of outright impossibility. The gun barrel would have to be depressed before it could be loaded, and then raised back to firing elevation, an operation which, regardless of its difficulty, substantially impeded the rate of fire.

46. Cooper Key to Admiralty, 15 September 1868, PRO: ADM1/6083.

47. Cooper Key to Admiralty, 13 June 1867, PRO: ADM1/6012.

48. Ibid.

49. Ropp, *Development of a Modern Navy*, p14; Parkes, *British Battleships*, p187. Parkes, as noted earlier, stated that the muzzle-loading system was 'faulty', a somewhat contradictory view to that quoted above.

50. Hogg and Batchelor, *Naval Gun*, pp74-5.

51. Table shewing the Power of Heavy Guns with Service and Experimental Charges, 1876, PRO: ADM1/6382. The muzzle velocity given for the British gun was 1451ft/sec, that of the French gun 1371ft/sec, and the Krupp gun 1461ft/sec.

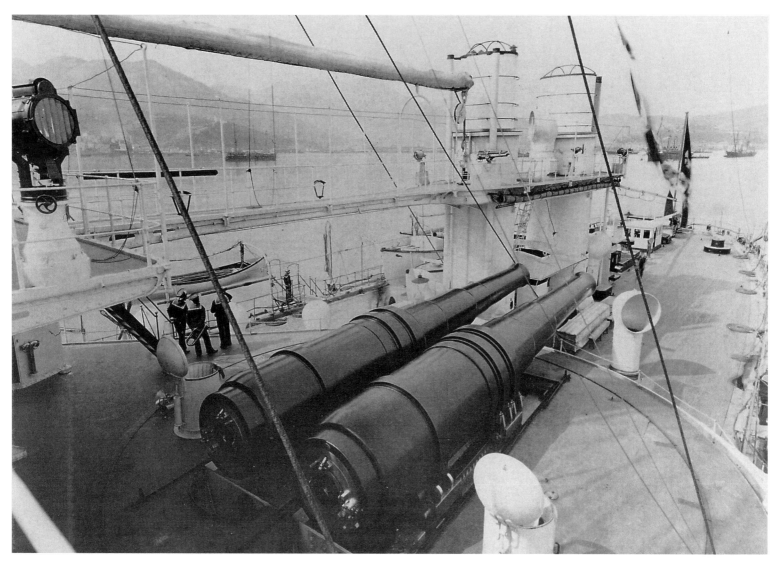

The 17in breech-loading rifled guns of the Italian ironclad *Lepanto* (launched 1883) show the improvements introduced in foreign ordnance while the British Admiralty was still agonising over the switch from muzzle-loaders. (U.S. Naval Historical Center: NH88704)

latest, British guns were inferior to those in use in France and Germany.[52]

This worsening situation did not escape public scrutiny. On 5 April 1875 Captain Philip Nolan, R.N. rose in the House of Commons to 'call attention to the present exceptional position of the country as regarded the manufacture of muzzle-loading ordnance', and 'said, in his opinion they [the British] had displayed extraordinary courage, or rather hardihood, in defying the general opinion' on the Continent.[53] He added that at a recent meeting of the Institute of Civil Engineers, 'all the speakers expressed a decided preference for the breech-loading principle, and the President stated further that Sir Joseph Whitworth and Sir William Armstrong', two prominent armaments manufacturers, 'were both in favour of it'.[54] At root, charged Nolan, the resistance to breech-

loaders was the product of a reactionary mentality. Referring to the problems encountered with the early Armstrong guns, he cited a United States Navy report which concluded that the British had abandoned breech-loading because it had 'been found to fail' and then, said Nolan, there 'arose a prejudiced belief that as we had failed in a solution of the problem, the problem must be necessarily incapable of solution'.[55] But, he maintained, 'it was a mere question of time as to when we were to take up breech-loading, and therefore in adhering to our present system we were only postponing the evil day'.[56]

Defence of muzzle-loading fell to Lord Eustace Cecil and Gathorne Hardy, the Assistant Secretary and the Secretary for War, respectively. The former reviewed the conclusions of the various committees which over the previous fifteen years had been appointed to study the question, stressing a report issued in 1871 comparing the two systems of loading. This committee, concluded Cecil, 'stated that the muzzle-loading gun was superior in range and accuracy, in point of simplicity, facility of repair, easy working, rapidity of fire, and original cost'.[57] All the same, admitted the

Assistant Secretary for War, Nolan 'had made some very strong observations', and he cited a foreign report on the subject which stated that 'the immediate future was for breech-loading . . .'.[58] Still, Cecil maintained that it was 'perfectly certain that they should not adopt a gun loading by the breech, unless they could find one that was superior to all known guns that were loaded by the muzzle'. Such a weapon, he argued, was yet to be found, for he expressed hopes of 'converting' Nolan 'to the opinion that the time for action in this matter had not yet arrived'.[59] Likewise, Gathorne Hardy 'declined to follow the hon. and gallant Gentleman [Nolan] to his conclusions'.[60] He did assure the House, however, that the government was 'determined to keep their eyes wide open and not to shrink from any expenditure that might be incurred when they were certain of being on the right track'.[61] There the matter rested in the House of Commons.

Three and a half weeks later the ordnance question was aired in the House of Lords, when former First Lord of the Admiralty the Duke of Somerset reviewed the arguments for and against the Service ordnance and breech-loaders before 'predict[ing] that breech-loaders would become essential to the Navy' and recommending 'that we ought to try them without delay'.[62] In the ensuing debate even Army Commander-in-Chief the Duke of Cambridge, whose conservatism was a byword in military and political circles, observed,

> when we find that Continental nations are adhering to the breech-loading guns, after having made a fair trial of them in the field [during the Franco-German War], we must feel that to a certain extent we have retrograded in going back to muzzle-loaders.[63]

Yet the Duke advocated 'proceed[ing] with the greatest possible caution', there being no reason 'why we should rush headlong to the adoption of the breech-loading guns'.[64] The government spokesman, the Duke of Richmond, was quick to assure peers that the Secretary for War, whose responsibilities included overseeing ordnance design and manufacture, was 'by no means wedded to any one system over another, and that whatever system may be shown to be the most perfect, he holds that should be adopted by this country'.[65] Similar assurances were forthcoming from another Ministry spokesman, the Earl of Malmesbury, who urged the Lords not to 'suppose that the Government regard the matter as settled'.[66] The Times wanted more than assurances, however, and in commenting on the Lords' debate, noted that neither Malmesbury nor Richmond had stated categorically 'that Mr. Hardy would himself initiate experiments.'[67] 'Unless this be done,' the paper continued, 'and done systematically, we shall find ourselves in a year's time no nearer advanced towards a better system of construction'. 'If breech-loaders are sufficiently advanced for all Europe to be armed with them,' it concluded, 'they must be sufficiently advanced to be subjected to experiment.'

The Times was well advised to question the Government's pronouncements and assurances on the matter, for the question of ordnance was not resurrected in Parliament for another three years, and then only briefly. In 1878 Viscount Bury assured the Duke of Somerset that Ordnance authorities were testing new designs of both weapons and armour.[68] Still, as the paper noted that year, in Britain 'the simpler ruling system [ie muzzle-loading] still has the preference'.[69] Only in 1879, and then as a consequence of the bursting of one of the heavy guns on board HMS Thunderer, a tragedy which killed or injured forty-five officers and men, was the question of ordnance fully reopened. The explosion resulted from accidentally double-loading the gun, but public attention was soon focused on the British system of ordnance, if for no other reason than, as the Times observed, 'it could not by any possibility have happened if the gun had been a breech-loader'.[70] By 17 March Lord Elphinstone, claiming that the Admiralty 'have no prejudice in favour of muzzle-loading',

52. Sandler, *Emergence of the Modern Capital Ship*, p110. Sandler notes, '[b]y clinging to the muzzle-loader long after it had been discarded on the Continent [not entirely; the Italian Navy continued to use muzzleloaders into the late 1870s], the Royal Navy probably slipped behind other European naval powers in naval ordnance by the 1870s. Captain Key's arguments against the breech-loader in the 1860s could hardly be expected to hold true a decade later.'

The lack of precision as to exactly when the British guns were superseded in point of power is inescapable. Conflicting figures for muzzle velocity were printed owing to the size of the powder charge and the weight and type of shell, so that there are doubts as to minor details. There can be no such doubts about the overall picture, however.

53. *Hansard's Parliamentary Debates*, 3d ser., 223 (1875), col. 304. Prior to this there were calls periodically to investigate the ordnance situation. As early as 1871, for instance, the *Times* was advocating a committee to 'collect valuable evidence as to the expediency, the possibility, and the cost of introducing heavy breech-loaders' (The *Times*, 16 January 1871, p4).

54. *Hansard*, 3d ser., 223 (1875), col. 309.

55. Ibid., col. 309.

56. Ibid., col. 311.

57. Ibid., col. 313.

58. Ibid., col. 314.

59. Ibid., col. 315.

60. Ibid., col. 318.

61. Ibid., col. 319.

62. Ibid., col. 1868.

63. Ibid., col. 1874.

64. Ibid., col. 1873.

65. Ibid., col. 1875.

66. Ibid., col. 1871.

67. *The Times*, 1 May 1875, p11.

68. *Hansard*, 3d ser., 239 (1878), col. 1273.

69. *The Times*, 18 May 1878, p12.

70. *The Times*, 31 March 1879, p9.

informed the House of Lords that an Ordnance Committee would take up the subject.[71] It was high time, as far as the *Times* was concerned. On 4 April a leading article declared that '[t]his important decision has not been taken a moment too soon', for 'it must be evident even to the most indifferent of observers that there is something very wrong in our present system of naval armament'.[72]

By the late 1870s there was a further reason for making the switch to breech-loaders. The latter half of the decade witnessed several developments in the chemistry and manufacture of gunpowder. The propelling agent used for British ordnance was a variety of 'black powder' more explosive than the formulae used in most foreign weapons. In 1867 Spencer Robinson noted that the French used 'a less explosive gunpowder' which was one of the reasons they were able to use breech-loaders safely even prior to de

Bange's invention of the gas check.[73] British gunpowder burnt almost instantaneously upon ignition, producing a very powerful explosion, which in large part accounted for the higher muzzle velocities of the country's ordnance. But this explosive powder subjected ordnance to severe stress, and British muzzle-loaders were constructed with massively reinforced breeches to contain the force of the detonation. Even this precaution was not entirely sufficient, however. British gunpowder was practical in small-calibre guns, but in larger pieces 'the sudden propulsive force generated by the explosion was [by the late 1870s] proving too much for the guns and shells'.[74]

Faced with this problem, chemists and manufacturers at home and abroad (foreign guns were confronted with the same problem, albeit on a lesser scale), turned to creating less explosive forms of propellant. First, during the late 1860s, the powder was formed into larger chunks to slow the rate of ignition, 'pebble powder' as it was called. By the late 1870s 'prismatic powder', a superior alternative to black powder, had been developed by

This sketch of *Inflexible*'s gun mountings clearly suggests the cramped conditions inside the turrets and also shows the layout of the hydraulic loading machinery outside them. (National Maritime Museum, London: 7771)

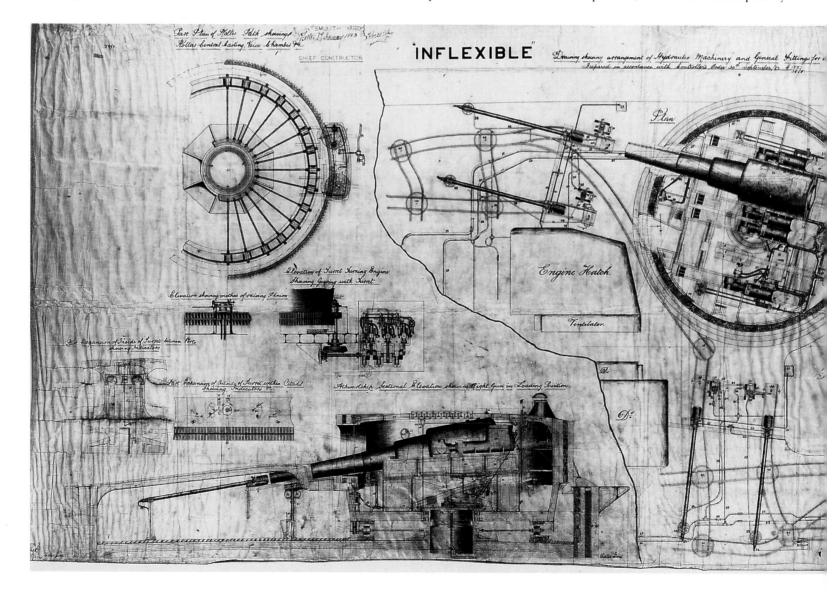

United States ordnance expert Arthur Rodman. Prismatic powder was chemically similar to black powder, but instead of being manufactured in separate grains, was pressed into hexagonal blocks. When ignited, this very dense powder burnt from the surface inward, first generating relatively low pressure, then, as flame split the prisms and penetrated further into the powder, the rate of ignition accelerated and with it pressure in the gun barrel. This breakthrough exacerbated existing problems with British ordnance, however. When prismatic powder was used in the short, stubby British muzzle-loaders, although the stress on the gun was much reduced, 'it meant that by the time the shell left the muzzle quite a large proportion of the powder was still unburned . . . [a]nd, of course, unburned powder was contributing nothing to the shell's velocity.'[75] It also meant that power and velocity could be increased, not by enlarging the bore or powder charge, but simply (and more safely) by lengthening the barrel, to take advantage of the greater expansive power of the new propellant.

But lengthening the barrels of British muzzle-loading ordnance

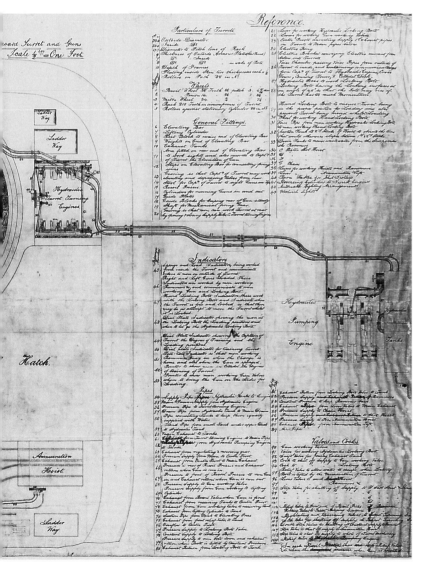

was anything but a simple matter. The escalation of the size of heavy naval ordnance from 1865 to 1875 from 12 to 25 tons, then from 25 to 35 to 38 tons, and finally to 81 tons – had already created formidable difficulties in loading. Common shells for the 81-ton guns on *Inflexible* weighed 1700lbs, the powder charge for each round another 450lbs. Even the much smaller 35-ton gun used a combination of shell and powder weighing 810lbs.[76] The difficulty of manually transporting such heavy burdens to the mouth of the gun, then ramming them the entire length of the barrel, forced the Navy in 1875 to adopt hydraulic loading machinery, another invention springing from the fertile mind of Sir William Armstrong.[77] Ironically, the retention of an obsolescent form of technology virtually necessitated the rapid incorporation of a new and largely untested machine.

Moreover, the size of the 38- and 81-ton guns had forced the designers of the ships in which they were mounted to improvise a system whereby the guns were loaded from *outside* their turrets.[78] The loading gear was concealed beneath an armoured *glacis* which was outside the turret, somewhat below the level of the guns. To load the turret was rotated around to face the *glacis*, and the guns were then depressed to line up with the hydraulic rammer. This time-consuming process contributed largely to the notoriously slow rate of fire of Britain's largest muzzle-loading guns. In 1867 Arthur Hood could extol the rapidity of fire of the 12-ton gun, but at the bombardment of Alexandria in 1882 *Inflexible*'s four 81-ton guns were fired a total of 208 times in the course of the ten-and-a-half hour engagement, an average of one round per gun every

71. *Hansard*, 3d ser., 244 (1879), col. 1016.

72. *The Times*, 4 April 1879, p9.

73. Robinson to Admiralty, 13 June 1867, PRO: ADM1/6012.

74. Hogg and Batchelor, *Naval Gun*, p76.

75. Ibid, pp76-7. The 'prisms' were also bored through, which enhanced the pattern of ignition.

76. Brassey, *British Navy*, Vol 2, pp104-05. Another problem posed by the huge increase in the size and weight of naval ordnance was the need to develop gun carriages capable of withstanding both the weight of the gun and the stress of firing. The old wooden carriages of the smoothbore era were as antiquated as the ships in which they were mounted with the coming of the ironclad era. Sandler includes a very comprehensive account of the development of modern naval gun carriages in his *Emergence of the Modern Capital Ship*, pp105-10.

77. Parkes, *British Battleships*, p198. Parkes notes only that 'the hydraulic system was introduced' in the *Thunderer* '[s]oon after her completion'. In fact, the gear was incorporated considerably earlier, while the ship was under construction. A note in the *Times* in August 1875 details trials of the machinery being installed in the ship (*The Times*, 4 August 1875, p4). The Ship's Cover for *Devastation* and *Thunderer* (NMM: ADM138/23) contains a 'Precis of a report relating to the trials of the Gun Machinery & hand loading gear of H.M. Ship *Thunderer* with remarks from Their Lordships and Officials'. Contained therein is an entry noting a report on the trials of the machinery by Captain Thomas Brandreth of HMS *Excellent* dated 18 August 1875. Also, on 11 October 1875 Houston Stewart 'congratulated their Lordships [for] having so readily adopted & tested a plan which enables them to work the largest guns than can be produced.'

78. See Parkes, *British Battleships*, pp198, 255.

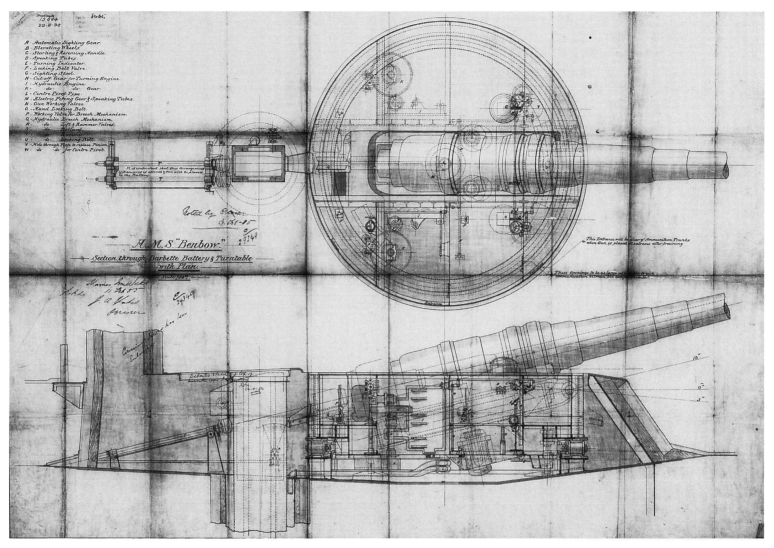

Like *Inflexible*'s muzzle-loaders, the breechloaders of the 'Admiral' class also had to be trained and elevated to align with fixed loading machinery. This is one of *Benbow*'s 16.25in guns.
(National Maritime Museum, London: 8435)

eleven minutes.[79] Immense difficulties would have followed an attempt to lengthen British muzzle-loading ordnance to exploit the capabilities of the new form of powder. Nor was lengthening the sole difficulty to be faced. The practice of 'chambering' guns militated still further against the feasibility of retaining muzzle-loading guns. '[I]t was . . . discovered that a greater amount of large-grained powder could be burned without increase in the maximum pressure if the charge were 'air-spaced' – that is, by making the powder chamber larger than the actual charge.'[80]

Yet the Navy retained its muzzle-loading ordnance through the later 1870s and well into the 1880s, although after 1872 it steadily lost ground to competing systems.[81] By the final years of the decade well-informed observers clearly appreciated that it was inferior to the breech-loaders of France and Germany. By 1880 no-one could pretend any longer that the British system was competi-tive with rival ordnance. W.H. Smith informed the House of Commons of upcoming tests of a 43-ton breech-loader, adding

> I have no doubt that it will be remarked that the Navy is again coming to the adoption of breech-loading guns; but that is nec-essary in order to insure the length of range, which cannot oth-erwise be obtained, and in order to secure a penetrating power which will put us in successful competition with other countries whose Navies possess breech-loading guns.[82]

Yet notwithstanding the conservatism manifested in Cooper Key's recommendations, the Childers Board's decision not to sanction experiments with breech-loaders in 1868, and the continued retention of the Woolwich muzzle-loading system throughout the 1870s, the Admiralty had virtually no control over the type of guns mounted in Her Majesty's ships of war.

Before 1856 the Navy's own Bureau of Ordnance was responsi-ble for designing the weapons used by the service, but that depart-ment was abolished as part of the reforms following Britain's gen-erally embarrassing performance in the Crimean War. After its elimination, sole responsibility for ordnance for both services was vested in the Ordnance Department, which answered to the War Office only. This consolidation 'may have been an early exercise in service unification [but] its consequences were disastrous for the Navy'.[83] Far from being blind to the increasing inferiority of the Navy's guns from the mid-1870s onward, the Admiralty, at least its responsible professional departments, was fully alive to the worsening situation. In June 1877 the Constructor's Department frankly admitted that 'the German 10.3 [inch] gun is much superior to our 11 [inch]-25 ton gun,' and 'that the new 17 cm [6.6 inch German gun] is weight for weight much superior to our 6 ½ ton [7 inch] gun.'[84] The following November the British naval attaché in France, Captain Nicholson, reported that 'it may be said the English are [the] stronger and much better armoured [ships], but that the French carry more powerful guns.'[85] Both the Controller, William Houston Stewart, and the D.N.C., Nathaniel Barnaby, agreed with Nicholson's assessment. The Admiralty was well aware of the worsening ordnance situation, but it could not convince the Ordnance Department to address the matter in a constructive fashion.

Among papers relating to the ironclads *Ajax* and *Agamemnon* is a remarkable paper titled 'Precis of Correspondence relative to the Armament of the *Ajax Colossus* and *Edinburgh* (late *Majestic*) class and the Manufacture &c of the 43-ton Breech-loading Gun' which illustrates vividly the tribulations endured in the process of trying to requisition a new heavy naval gun. The process took more than four years.[86] In August 1878 Sir William Armstrong approached the Admiralty with details of 'the results of some recent successful experiments with the manufacture of heavy guns at Elswick [the company's foundry] by which a considerably greater effect had been obtained with guns of reduced weight.' Armstrong's 8in breech-loader achieved a muzzle velocity of 2116ft/sec, a 'considerably greater effect' indeed, since the muzzle velocity of the 8in Woolwich gun was only 1413ft/sec.[87] Armstrong further reported that 'a 12 [inch] gun of 40 tons is . . . in progress [of manufacture] which is expected to rival the piercing power of the new 80-ton

[Service] gun,' and [t]he adoption of guns of this new type would enormously increase the power of existing ships and greatly reduce the size of future ships in relation to the power of their armament.' Finally, the armaments baron opined that '[t]he question of breech-loading is forcing itself forward,' and graciously 'offer[ed] any assistance from his firm in the investigations which may take place.'

W.H. Smith's Board expressed immediate interest. On 10 September Armstrong's firm was asked its opinion as to the possibility of altering the turrets of *Ajax* and *Agamemnon*, then under construction, 'in order to obtain some important advantage in description of ordnance, or mode of mounting and working it.'[88] Armstrong's reply was optimistic: 'they were distinctly of opinion that the armament of the *Ajax* and *Agamemnon* could be advantageously altered.'[89] But in early October, when the War Office was furnished with this correspondence, the Admiralty was informed that the Ordnance Department would undertake to supply an improved gun, 'if their Lordships will state their requirements'.[90] This offer was not well received at the Admiralty, especially when it was learned that the gun proffered by the Ordnance authorities had, according to the D.N.O. Richard Vesey Hamilton, already been rejected once before as being 'too long for naval purposes'.[91] As a consequence of these inconclusive negotiations, 'the War Department dropped the question' in late 1878.

Altering the guns of *Ajax* and *Agamemnon* was debated at the Admiralty for two months. Barnaby and Vesey Hamilton advocated testing breech-loading guns, and Houston Stewart was staunchly in favour of them, but Sir George Wellesley and Sir Arthur Hood, the First and Second Sea Lords respectively, preferred the 38-ton muzzle-loading Service gun.[92] Only on 23 December did First Lord Smith resolve the issue, deciding he was 'not prepared to delay these ships any longer' while their armament was being argued over.[93]

The change to longer guns and breech-loading, or loading outside the turret [he added] . . . involves large considerations which

---

79. Caspar F. Goodrich, *Report of the British Naval and Military Operations in Egypt, 1882* (Washington, 1885), pp33-4, 67.

80. Parkes, *British Battleships*, p287.

81. Ibid, pp288, 293. The first British ironclads to carry heavy breech-loading guns were *Edinburgh*, *Colossus*, and *Conqueror*, the first two of which were not completed until 1886 and the last a year later, although in all three instances the ships were ready for sea years prior to the delivery of their guns.

82. *Hansard*, 3d ser., 251 (1880), col. 599.

83. Sandler, *Emergence of the Modern Capital Ship*, p89.

84. Remarks of Constructor's Department on Report from Foreign Office to Admiralty, 26 June 1877, PRO: ADM1/6422.

85. Foreign Office to Admiralty, 15 November 1877, PRO: ADM1/6424.

86. Precis of Correspondence relative to the Armament of the *Ajax, Colossus* and *Edinburgh* (late *Majestic*) class and the Manufacture &c of the 43-ton Breech-loading Gun, 1882, NMM: ADM138/60, no fol.

87. Ibid; Table shewing the power of Heavy Guns with Service and Experimental Charges, 1876, PRO: ADM1/6382.

88. Precis of Correspondence relative to the Armament of the *Ajax, Colossus* and *Edinburgh* (late *Majestic*) class and the Manufacture &c of the 43-ton Breech-loading Gun, 1882, NMM: ADM138/60, no fol.

89. 12 September 1878, ibid.

90. Admiralty to War Office, 2 October 1878; War Office to Admiralty, 19 October 1878, ibid.

91. 26 October 1878, ibid.

92. 27 November, 18, 19, 20, 21 December 1878, ibid.

93. 23 December 1878, ibid.

cannot be disposed of hastily, and the long guns are not yet made and therefore untried. The ships must be completed for the service 38-ton gun, chambered as it now is.

That settled the matter regarding the ships then under construction.

But the question of what sort of ordnance to mount in future designs remained open. The same month Smith made up his mind on the *Ajax* class, a model of the proposed breech-loading armament and turret arrangements for the subsequent trio of ironclads–the *Colossus, Edinburgh,* and *Conqueror*–was forwarded to the Admiralty by Armstrong and Co. Then, in January 1879, the *Thunderer*'s gun exploded, prompting the appointment of an Ordnance Committee to consider 'the question of breech-loading guns and such other questions as may be brought before it'.[94] The Admiralty was permitted to name two members of the Committee. Admiral Henry Boys, a former D.N.O. and Captain Cyprian Bridge, a future Director of Naval Intelligence and Admiral of the Fleet, were chosen.[95]

In August, without waiting for the report of the Committee, the Admiralty arrived at its own conclusion and 'inform[ed] W[ar] O[ffice] that they incline towards Armstrong-design breech-loading guns for *Colossus, Majestic,* and *Conqueror*'.[96] But the following day the Committee on Ordnance countered by recommending the construction, not of the Armstrong-designed gun, but rather 'a 12-inch rifled breech-loading gun of 43 tons in accordance with R[oyal] G[un] F[actory]' design at Woolwich.[97] Whether by choice or necessity, the Admiralty subsequently concurred in this proposal. Its decision brought forth an anguished howl from Armstrong, however. On 8 December 1879 the company wrote the Admiralty to 'complain that it is not now proposed to treat with them for the supply of any of these guns, and they urge the special claims they possess to a more liberal treatment'.[98] Armstrong claimed credit for originating the coil principle for constructing 'built-up' guns, research and development on the principle of chambering, perfecting gas checks to provide a complete breech seal, and improving the French system of breech closure. Finally, the company 'urge[d] that their establishment should be encouraged as a reserve arsenal available to the nation in time of war'.

Whether or not the Admiralty was in favour of the strengthening of the nascent military-industrial complex explicit in the last of Armstrong's pleas, the appeal must have been persuasive as a whole, for at the end of January 1880 the firm was asked to submit a written proposal of its terms for supplying four 43-ton breech-loading guns for *Colossus*. The terms submitted were satisfactory.[99] On 20 February the Admiralty informed the War Office of its actions, and urged that,

the request of Sir William Armstrong Co. might be complied with on account of the well-known character of the firm and the excellence of the work which they produce, and the necessity for mak-

ing an immediate change in our system of artillery, owing to the rapid progress being made in the power of breech-loading guns by foreign nations.[100]

The Board added,

My L[or]ds also think that great benefit is derived from the competition of private manufacturers, as has been shown in the case of shipbuilding, and the designing and production of steam machinery, and that this principle should be extended to the production of guns for our first-class ships.

This eloquent appeal fell on deaf ears. The following month the War Office replied, 'calling attention to the inconvenience that may result from the Admiralty corresponding with and inviting tenders from firms for supplies which would in the usual course be obtained and paid for by the War Dept.'[101] Furthermore, it pointed out that Armstrong had already been contracted to supply smaller (6in) breech-loading guns, and, in an instance of blatant obstructionism, announced that it did not want to place an order with a private firm until the Royal Gun Factory's own 43-ton breech-loading gun had been tried. Armstrong promised a gun ready for testing by June 1881. The Ordnance authorities, on the other hand, informed the D.N.C. that it would be five months beyond that date before they could supply a weapon for that purpose.[102]

On 24 April 1880 the Admiralty urged the War Office to reconsider its decision, arguing that it should be allowed to draw on the experience and expertise of Armstrong's firm, especially since 'the armament of our fleet was now about to undergo a most important change, the bearing of which on our naval power can scarcely be exaggerated'.[103] In response to this appeal the War Office condescended to order a single 43-ton gun from Armstrong for testing. This concession by no means marked the end of the struggle. On 3 December 1880 Vesey Hamilton wrote to the War Office to ascertain when a 43-ton Woolwich gun would be ready for testing, and, assuming trials were successful, when the Royal Gun Factory could supply the guns for *Colossus, Edinburgh,* and *Conqueror*.[104] The War Office replied that the first production gun would be ready in six months, and an additional piece would be finished every five weeks. Even if the trials came off without a hitch, Woolwich would need a year-and-a-half to supply the ten guns needed.[105]

There were several hitches. Most of 1881 was consumed in modifying the chamber of the prototype gun to hold a larger charge.[106] And, in what must have been very close to the final straw for the Admiralty, the War Office, on 27 January 1882,

state[d] . . . there are no 43-ton guns in course of preparation for naval service, but as there are some under construction for land service there will be no objection to two [the Admiralty needing fourteen of the 12in guns by this point] being appropriated for sea service. The manufacture will be expedited, but five or six months must elapse before completion.[107]

Only in February 1882 was the Royal Gun Factory's 12in breech-loading design approved; 'the weight of the projectile was not decided upon until September; and the weight of the [powder] charge only finally determined in March 1884.' And, as Parkes succinctly summarises, 'the change-over to breech-loaders was to be marked by both danger and delay–danger because of faulty material and obsolete methods of construction, and delay which held up deliveries so that ships came to be commissioned without all their big guns aboard.'[108] The 43-ton gun originally produced by Woolwich had to be increased to 45 tons, the additional 4000lbs consisting of reinforcement after one of the earlier guns, mounted in HMS *Collingwood*, burst while undergoing trials.[109]

The anomalous method of designing, requisitioning, and supplying naval ordnance reached an acute stage after 1875, yet it had posed problems long before that point. Testifying before the Hartington Commission several years later, Naval Lord and former D.N.O. Hood elaborated on the system and its shortcomings: 'the estimates for naval ordnance stores of all descriptions, and guns, were prepared by the Director of Naval Ordnance; they were then placed before the Board, and after approval by the Board, they were sent to the War Office for execution, but the money to meet these requirements had to be found out of the army estimates, and the result was, and has been during a number of years, that these estimates were reduced considerably'.[110] Richard Vesey Hamilton cited similar problems. 'Nothing,' he stated in 1884, 'could be more unsatisfactory than the manner in which the naval gun estimates were put forward year after year to be criticised, manipulated, and reduced by the War Office.'[111]

---

94. 3 April 1879, ibid.

95. 5 May 1879, ibid.

96. 28 August 1879, ibid. The Admiralty *Digest* notes on 25 August: '*Majestic, Colossus, & Conqueror*–43 ton gun to be constructed and tried' (25 August 1879, PRO: ADM12/1042/59.4a). In the 1880 *Digest* it is stated that the Board decided to prepared the three ships for breech-loading guns on 8 December 1879 (8 December 1879, PRO: ADM12/1060/59.4a).

97. 29 August 1879, Precis of Correspondence relative to the Armament of the *Ajax, Colossus* and *Edinburgh* (late *Majestic*) class and the Manufacture &c of the 43-ton Breech-loading Gun, 1882, NMM: ADM138/60, no fol.

98. 8 December 1879, ibid.

99. 20 January 1880, ibid. The terms were four guns at £5800 each, to be rejected if inferior to Woolwich guns, and to be ready within two years of their order.

100. 20 February 1880, ibid.

101. 13 March 1880, ibid.

102. March 1880, ibid.

103. 24 April 1880, ibid.

104. 3 December 1880, ibid. In the Admiralty *Digest* for 13 December 1880 is an entry reading 'Replacement of 9 in, 10 in, 11 in, & 12 in 25 ton M.L. Guns of the Navy by 8 in, 9.2 in & 10.4 in B.L. Guns–Observations by D.N.O.–W.O. asked whether they can predict the successful issue of the new 9.2 in & 10.4 in B.L. guns with sufficient confidence to enable their L[or]d[shi]ps to determine upon a policy of replacing M.L. by B.L. guns in 81-82' (Admiralty to War Office, 13 December 1880, PRO: ADM12/1060/59.4a).

105. 14 December 1880, Precis of Correspondence relative to the Armament of the *Ajax, Colossus* and *Edinburgh* (late *Majestic*) class and the Manufacture &c of the 43-ton Breech-loading Gun, 1882, NMM: ADM138/60, no fol.

106. January, February, March, April, September 1881, ibid.

107. 27 January 1882, ibid.

108. Parkes, *British Battleships*, p287.

109. Ibid, p302.

110. *Report of the Royal Commission appointed to make Enquiry into the Civil and Professional Administration of the Naval and Military Departments and the Relationship of those Departments to each other and to the Treasury* (generally known as the Hartington Commission), Strictly Confidential, PRO: HO73/35/3, p147. As far as can be ascertained, at no point between 1866 and 1880 did the Admiralty make any attempt to rectify this clearly unsatisfactory situation. In fact, the one administrator to address the issue was Sir John Pakington, but in his guise as Secretary for War, not First Lord of the Admiralty. Furthermore, it would appear that the initiative for his effort came primarily from a desire to reduce the Army

Estimates by removing from them the cost of naval guns, rather than from the evident need to rationalise the system of naval ordnance requisition. On 17 October 1868, during the waning weeks of the first Disraeli Ministry, the Admiralty received a communiqué from the War Office in which it was stated that 'Sir John Pakington considers that the practice of making provisions in the Army Estimates for the whole of what are termed "Gunner's Stores" required for the Navy is open to the most serious objections & opposed to the principle now so generally recognised that the Dept in whose Votes the Funds are provided shall be responsible for their proper appropriation–also that the present system gives rise to great inconvenience and complications. Sir J. Pakington considers that the difficulties can be met by their Lordships making provision in future in the N[ava]l Estimates for all Guns, Carriages, Ammunition & other Warlike Stores required for Naval Service and that such stores should remain permanently in charge of the Admiralty' (War Office to Admiralty, 17 October 1868, PRO: ADM12/814/59.4a).

Henry Corry, however, responded 'that neither efficiency nor economy would be promoted by the proposed change' (Admiralty to War Office, 17 October 1868, PRO: ADM12/814/59.4a). Perhaps he was unwilling to shoulder the additional cost of naval ordnance, seeing how much trouble he had already had with Disraeli over expenditures. Anyway, the proposal came to naught when the Treasury came down on the Admiralty's side, stating that they 'are of opinion that the arrangement proposed by the War Office is opposed to the principles on which the Estimates have been framed for a long period of years and no practical convenience would result from it. Acquaint War Office that My Lords do not consider it would be either practicable or advantageous to make any change by creating separate and distinct establishments' (Treasury to Admiralty and War Office, 21 December 1868, PRO: ADM12/ 814/59.4a). Note that the Treasury's decision was rendered after the change of government, and that Robert Lowe was now Chancellor of the Exchequer.

The matter ended, although why Childers or Goschen never turned their energies to so blatantly anomalous and unsatisfactory a situation remains something of a mystery, especially since the latter, following a clash with Edward Cardwell, the Secretary for War, over the arrangements for naval guns, wrote the latter that 'I quite concur as to the inconvenience of the present arrangements about the supply of guns &c to the fleet' (Goschen to Cardwell, 22 August 1872, Cardwell Papers, PRO: PRO30/48/27, fol. 48).

Indeed, Richard Vesey Hamilton claimed that '[a]lthough the general system found some defenders among military officers, it was condemned by the naval service, and most of the high officials at the War Office utterly disapproved of it. Lord Cardwell, Sir Henry Storks, Sir G. Balfour, Sir H. Gordon, Sir H. Lafroy, Sir John Ayde, Sir F. Campbell, and many more advocated a change, and their views were shared by several Secretaries of State, notably Mr. Childers, Lord Hartington, and Mr. W.H. Smith.' (Vesey Hamilton, *Naval Administration* [London, 1896], p81.) The reference to Childers alludes to his stint as Secretary for War in the early 1880s, rather than to his days at the Admiralty.

Only after 1886 was the problem addressed, in large part due to the appointment of John Fisher as Director of Naval Ordnance that year, and the long overdue establishment of a separate Ordnance Department for the Navy (Parkes, *British Battleships*, p288).

111. Vesey Hamilton, *Naval Administration*, pp79-80.

The problem was apparent by the early 1870s. John Fisher, at the time an instructor on the gunnery ship *Excellent*, wrote to Henry Boys in 1871:

[i]t always makes my blood boil when I remember the studied and deliberate manner in which the Navy is ignored at all these places, especially at Woolwich and least at Chatham [headquarters of the Royal Engineers], and it takes its origin from the Admiralty being subordinate to and dependent on the War Office for almost any species of warlike store, from a 35-ton gun down to a boarding pike and a common shovel.[112]

Fisher knew of what he spoke. On 27 December 1871 Secretary for War Edward Cardwell wrote First Lord of the Admiralty George J. Goschen, complaining of a 'demand . . . from the Admiralty which involves an unexpected addition of about £100,000 for 9 inch guns, and the replacement of breech loading guns by muzzle loaders for shore practice.'[113] In addition, Cardwell claimed that he had understood the First Lord to have assured him previously that 'no large demand for guns would be made this year'. 'I cannot alter the Estimate without some sanction from the Cabinet.' The Secretary for War's allegations did not sit well with Goschen, for the latter replied a day later he had warned Cardwell 'from the first that for new ships building we should of course require additional guns.'[114] 'We want additional guns for additional ships,' continued the First Lord:

I do not understand you to object to new wants for future ships & for this head of expenditure I presume you have made some provision. I know the wants of the Navy have been before General [Sir John] Ayde, & . . . you assured me that we should want nothing and accordingly omitted us from your [draft] Estimate.

Having understood this to be the situation, the receipt of Cardwell's letter pushed Goschen beyond the bounds of temperance.

Before I can answer your note & and know to what extent I am expected to be content with building ships without guns to put on board of them, will you kindly let me know what part of our proposals you consider to be new and unexpected & especially what provisions you have made in the Estimates for naval purposes.

Similarly, problems involving the timely delivery of ordnance were not a novelty by the late 1870s. An entry in the 1868 Admiralty *Digest* on the state of the year's shipbuilding programme noted 'the armaments have been a great cause of delay'.[115] A year later Cardwell became embroiled in a dispute with Hugh Childers over the supply of guns for HMS *Monarch*. The War Office claimed that the delay in producing them stemmed from the Admiralty's failure to decide whether the guns should be bored to 11in or 12in.[116] Childers, however, saw only War Office footdragging:

[a]fter 2 years of correspondence the Admiralty receive information from the War Office that the 22-ton Guns for the *Monarch* cannot be supplied for a month. It is earnestly requested that they may be furnished in less time, as otherwise the *Monarch*, which is urgently required, cannot be got ready in time.[117]

Two-and-a-half weeks later Childers again wrote to Cardwell, almost pleading:

My Dear Cardwell
We are in despair about the projectiles for the '*Monarch*'s' guns. The models, recently received, we are told are only *probably* like the real projectile which has not yet been decided on.
There will be a great outcry if she is not ready by the 1st May.[118]

Nor was the Admiralty entirely happy with the quality of ordnance furnished to the Navy by Woolwich. In his testimony to the Hartington Commission Vesey Hamilton accused the Ordnance Department of supplying the Navy with shoddy guns, and later remarked 'the Admiralty itself found grave practical disadvantages, and even danger, in the system'.[119] In a remarkable petition to the House of Commons in 1880, several Fellows of the Royal Society, pioneer steel manufacturer Henry Bessemer among them, stated their 'belief that the system of heavy ordnance now in use and known as the Woolwich system is inefficient and dangerous . . .Your petitioners look with dismay upon the defects of the English heavy guns, and they are of opinion that these defects seriously endanger our naval supremacy and national safety . . .'.[120] Equally striking, in 1884 Colonel Edward Maitland, the Superintendent of the Royal Gun Factory, freely admitted to an audience at the Royal United Services Institution 'during the latter part of the seventies England fell behind in the artillery race'.[121] 'Up to 1875 or 1876,' Maitland maintained, British heavy guns were as good as anybody else's, but '[t]hen came a period of comparative stagnation, and we fell to leeward.'

Finally, the poor channels of communication between the Admiralty and those whose responsibility it was to design and produce naval ordnance was a source of additional complication, to say nothing of frustration. In April 1880 the Board was compelled, with regard to '[p]roposals in Gunnery matters made to [the] W.O. which may be considered to affect the Naval Service in any way,' to request that the military authorities 'pass all such subjects before they are disposed to My L[ords] to enable them to express opinions.'[122] Years later Vesey Hamilton bluntly informed the Hartington Commission,

[t]he only unsatisfactory work I have ever had in my career of 46 years in the Navy was in connexion with the Ordnance Department of the War Office. Nothing could be worse or more unsatisfactory than their arrangements were.[123]

Like Fisher, Vesey Hamilton knew of what he was speaking. In 1880, when D.N.O., he learned;

[i]n 1873 some experiments were made by the War Office in chambering guns, but the Director of Artillery in summing up at that time remarked 'that several complications and difficulties would apparently arise in the endeavour to obtain excessive velocities and it does not seem necessary at present to pursue the question any further'.[124]

One can sense Vesey Hamilton's incredulity at finding that '[t]hese trials appear not to have been communicated to [the] Director of Naval Ordnance, who would have probably urged their continuance'. The moral was clear to him: 'this shows the necessity for having a Naval member on the Experimental Branch at Woolwich.' That there had not been up to this point was perhaps as damning an indictment of the system as any of its more glaring shortcomings.[125]

At the same time, the flaws in naval ordnance that could not be attributed to the Navy itself should not be allowed to obscure some that could. First, divided counsels at the Admiralty played a considerable role in the delay in switching to breech-loaders at the end of the 1870s. Though he had 'no doubt as to the greatly increased power of the [new] long guns', in late 1878, Rear-Admiral Sir Arthur Hood still argued 'there are considerable structural difficulties to be overcome before such long guns can be loaded satisfactorily in turrets'.[126] Consequently, he concluded 'it would be unwise to arrive at a decision to prepare even one turret in *Ajax* for these guns, until an actual trial has fully established their satisfactory powers of endurance.' Hood's view was shared by his superiors on the Board, First Sea Lord George Wellesley and First Lord W.H. Smith, with the consequence that the *Ajax* and *Agamemnon* ended up being armed with outdated 38-ton muzzle-loading Woolwich guns.

Related to this lack of consensus was another factor which contributed to the Admiralty's lack of receptivity to innovations in naval ordnance prior to the late 1870s. The official most concerned with matters of naval gunnery was, of course, the D.N.O., and of the four men who held that post during the period 1866-80 (the position was created the former year), two – Cooper Key and Hood – were demonstrably conservative.[127] Both played major, perhaps decisive, roles in the Admiralty's decisions first not to adopt breech-loaders or even to conduct further experiments in 1868, and then resolutely to maintain that stance throughout much of the 1870s. Cooper Key was D.N.O. from 1866 to 1869, when he was replaced by Hood. He returned to the Admiralty as First Naval Lord in 1879. Hood served as D.N.O. from 1869 through 1874 and then on the Board as Second Naval Lord from 1877 to 1879. One or the other was therefore in a position to

112. Fisher to Boys, 22 August 1871, quoted in Arthur J. Marder (ed.), *Fear God and Dread Nought: The Correspondence of Admiral of the Fleet Lord Fisher of Kilverstone. Vol. 1: The Making of An Admiral 1854-1904* (London, 1952), p73.

113. Cardwell to Goschen (Copy), Private, 27 December 1871, Cardwell Papers, PRO: PRO30/48/27, fol. 46.

114. Goschen to Cardwell, 28 December 1871, Cardwell Papers, PRO: PRO30/48/27, fol. 49.

115. Controller's Department to Admiralty, 31 March 1868, PRO: ADM12/818/91.1. Similarly, a further entry about three months later states that '[d]elay in the armaments of ships–will defer the completion of the Ironclads named in the Programme' and that '25 ton Guns & 18 ton Guns urgently required for *Hercules, Monarch, Captain, Cerberus,* and *Sultan . . .*' (Admiralty Minute, 4 July 1868, PRO: ADM12/ 814/59.4a). Nineteen days later it was noted that an explanation for the delays in completing the 10in guns for *Hercules* had been received from the Ordnance Department's Colonel Campbell (Director of Naval Ordnance to Admiralty, 23 July 1868, PRO: ADM12/814/59.4a).

116. Cardwell to Childers, February-March 1869, Cardwell Papers, PRO: PRO30/48/36, fols. 53-58.

117. Childers to Cardwell, 5 March 1869, ibid., fol. 60.

118. Childers to Cardwell, 22 March 1869, ibid., fol. 62. See also ibid., fols. 87-89 for further recriminations on the subject.

119. *Report of the Royal Commission appointed to make Enquiry into the Civil and Professional Administration of the Naval and Military Departments and the Relationship of those Departments to each other and to the Treasury* (generally known as the Hartington Commission), Strictly Confidential, PRO: HO73/35/3, p238; Vesey Hamilton, *Naval Administration*, p79.

120. Quoted in Parkes, *British Battleships*, pp288-9.

121. Edward Maitland, 'The Heavy Guns of 1884', *Journal of the Royal United Services Institution* 28 (1884), pp693-4.

122. Admiralty to War Office, 5 April 1880, PRO: ADM12/1060/59.4a.

123. *Report of the Royal Commission appointed to make Enquiry into the Civil and Professional Administration of the Naval and Military Departments and the Relationship of those Departments to each other and to the Treasury* (generally known as the Hartington Commission), Strictly Confidential, PRO: HO73/35/3, p238.

124. Precis of Correspondence of Correspondence relative to the Armament of the *Ajax, Colossus,* and *Edinburgh* (late *Majestic*) class and the Manufacture, &c of the 43-ton Breech-loading gun, 1882, NMM: ADM 138/60, no fol.

125. Marder, *Fear God and Dread Nought*, Vol. 1, p73. John Fisher complained to Henry Boys on 22 August 1871 'I suppose that half the gear made at Woolwich is for naval use, and yet there is not a single Naval Officer there in authority. I know of course that the Admiralty can complain of the dilatoriness of any particular department at Woolwich or at any of the out stations but this would probably make them more dilatory by way of showing they were under the War Office and not under the Admiralty.'

126. Precis of Correspondence of Correspondence relative to the Armament of the *Ajax, Colossus,* and *Edinburgh* (late *Majestic*) class and the Manufacture, &c of the 43-ton Breech-loading gun, 1882, NMM: ADM 138/60, no fol.

127. The other two were Boys and Vesey Hamilton. Hood's entry in the *Dictionary of National Biography*, written by John Knox Laughton, goes so far as to label him 'a painstaking officer, though without the genius much needed in a period of great change, and clinging by temperament to the ideas of the past', *Dictionary of National Biography*, 2nd supplement (Oxford, 1912), p293; Bryan Ranft, 'The Protection of Britain's Seaborne Trade and the Development of Systematic Planning for War, 1860-1906,' in Bryan Ranft (ed.), *Technical Change and British Naval Policy, 1860-1939,* (London, 1977), p7. Ranft states that Hood's testimony to the Hartington Commission 'suggests an irascible if not a stupid man. . . .'.

The after 13.5in breech-loading rifled guns of HMS *Rodney*. The long-range striking power of these weapons and their muzzle-loading predecessors was ignored by senior officers obsessed with close-range *melees*. (U.S. Naval Historical Center: NH55499)

influence Admiralty decisions on gunnery matters for virtually the entire period.

In 1870 Hood reported that the Admiralty was 'quite satisfied with the Service [Woolwich] Rifled Guns'.[128] Furthermore, other than recommending that experiments be made with high-compression steel developed by Sir Joseph Whitworth – another ordnance manufacturer – Hood blandly stated '[t]he Adm[iralt]y are not desirous for any general competitive trials of guns on other patterns & by other designers'. Such an attitude was not likely to produce the best guns for the Navy, nor was it conducive to good relations between the Admiralty and private industry, regardless of the course taken by the Ordnance Department. A year later, seconded by First Sea Lord Sir Sydney Dacres and Controller Robert Hall, Hood again stated his preference for muzzle-loading guns, this time to the Director of Artillery at Woolwich.[129] The War Office was certainly not inclined to alter its system of ordnance, and neither Cooper Key nor Hood was inclined to argue the point.

Moreover, while the Royal Gun Factory extolled the virtues of its products after their inferiority had become apparent, the Woolwich system had its advocates at the Admiralty as well. In May 1875 W.H. Hall, Assistant to the Director of Naval Ordnance, produced a memorandum on 'Breech-loading v. Muzzle-loading Guns'. In it he argued the muzzleloader still had 'the advantage in facility of loading', that hydraulic loading had made it possible to use muzzleloaders of any length in turrets (!), and that, as Cooper Key had claimed seven years previously, the theoretical advantages of breech-loading were not realised in practice by any existing system. In conclusion, wrote Hall, 'I have no hesitation in stating my opinion that muzzle-loaders are superior to breech-loaders for the Naval Service.' Hall's superior, Henry Boys, agreed: 'I endorse the statements he has made, and concur in the conclusions he has arrived at. . . . '.[130]

Beyond the realms of design, research and development, there were other ordnance shortcomings for which the Admiralty bore partial responsibility. While British muzzle-loaders were equal or superior to their Continental counterparts until the mid-1870s, even at their best they had substantial limitations. Aside from the problems caused by the method of rifling, the combination of the large windage – the gap between the shell and the bore of the gun – coupled with the short barrel and high muzzle velocity diminished accuracy. As early as 1867 Controller Robert Spencer

Robinson noted the accuracy of British ordnance was 'undeniably less than that of the larger [French] projectile; the heavier charge & heavier projectile requisite for greater precision would destroy too rapidly our naval guns unless we added greatly to the weight.' Moreover, 'the highly explosive English powder causes the life of the rifled gun to be very short, and forbids a breechloader. Muzzle-loading . . . is at the foundation of the short projectile, which our naval gun adopts . . .'.[131]

Likewise, the Navy's attitude towards long-range gunnery practice was scarcely likely to encourage making the most even of the ordnance's limited capabilities. Contemporaries universally assumed that future naval battles would take place at close range; one stated 'all ideas of firing at sea in iron-cased ships at long range had been banished'. The 'Table of Charges and Projectiles allowed for [Gunnery] Practice' required firing ten rounds per gun per quarter, or forty rounds from each gun yearly.[132] The favoured target of the Channel Squadron was a rock in the Atlantic Ocean outside Vigo Bay on the Portuguese coast. In 1870 three ironclads carried out target practice against this rock, scoring twenty-three hits out of forty rounds.[133] It was not a particularly impressive accomplishment, given that the range was only 1000yds and 'the target was twice as long as any ironclad and four times its height, and conditions of sea and wind were eminently favourable'.[134]

From time to time the Admiralty made efforts to improve gunnery. In 1872 Geoffrey Phipps Hornby, commanding the Channel Squadron, was ordered to take the ships 'to sea occasionally' for target practice.[135] A more significant effort was made by Childers' Board in 1870 with the establishment of a competition for prize-firing, but even this noble attempt seems to have fallen short of satisfying the need for improved gunnery.[136] In 1879, in fact, Hornby, now in command in the Mediterranean, was informed 'no shot' in the competition 'is to be reported as a direct hit, that does not actually hit the target'.[137]

In July of 1882 the Mediterranean Squadron was ordered to bombard the Egyptian port of Alexandria in response to the per-ceived threat to the Suez Canal posed by a nationalist revolt. In the Navy's report on the action, Captain Charles Hotham stated that '[t]he accuracy of the fire when under weigh [was] very fair [and] when at anchor, very good . . .'. This appraisal was seconded by no less an ordnance authority than John Fisher who, with Arthur K. Wilson, wrote that 'we have to remark that the appearance of all the [Egyptian] batteries justifies the statement that our fire was accurate.'[138] This conclusion is somewhat difficult to reconcile with statistical data. The Mediterranean Squadron fired a total of 1632 rounds from forty-three heavy guns. Of these 1632 shells, six were direct hits on enemy guns, six dismounted enemy guns, and a further three targets were knocked out of action by falling debris. Fifteen enemy guns were silenced.[139] Visibility was excellent, and the sea calm. The fire from the shore was so desultory that evasive manoeuvres were largely unnecessary; most of the ships, in fact, were able to anchor.

When other factors are considered, however, British gunnery appears in a more favourable light. Egyptian batteries were widely dispersed around Alexandria harbour, whose mouth was more than five miles wide. The squadron could not therefore concentrate its guns on a compact target. Moreover, near-misses which would have badly damaged more sophisticated defences often buried themselves in the sand where they detonated harmlessly. Additionally, as Peter Padfield points out, the calm sea was actually a detriment to the gunnery. Had there been any swell the gun layers could have set the elevation and waited until the ship rolled the sights on target; lacking such customary help one ship at least had bodies of men moving from one side of the deck to the other to produce an artificial roll. The report of the captain of the *Monarch* illustrates some of the difficulties:

After the captain of the turret had ascertained and communicated the heel to the numbers laying the gun, the time necessarily taken to work the elevating gear, lay the guns by means of the crude wooden scales and make ready is so great that probably another gun or turret will have fired in the interim, and conse-

128. Director of Naval Ordnance to Admiralty, [1870], PRO: ADM12/852/59.4a.

129. Admiralty to War Office, 4 April 1871, PRO: ADM12/875/59.4a.

130. Memorandum by W.H. Hall, 5 May 1875, Hornby Papers, NMM: PHI/109/7/pt. 1.

131. Robinson to Admiralty, 13 June 1867, PRO: ADM1/6012.

132. Table of Charges and Projectiles allowed for Practice quarterly, 20 December 1867, PRO: ADM1/6013.

133. Philip Colomb analysed this practice shooting and other similar results in the course of his paper 'The Attack and Defence of Fleets', *Journal of the Royal United Services Institution* 22 (1871), pp405-37. He concluded that from the evidence available, 'that ten per cent of the *Monarch*'s shot will strike a *Monarch* [*ie* a target that size] in action at 1,000 yards' (p413).

134. Sandler, *Emergence of the Modern Capital Ship*, p92. The entry in the Admiralty Digest for the practice ambiguously reads: 'Report on firing at a rock at Vigo – practice was good

– but some few projectiles missed the object.' (Commander-in-Chief, Channel Squadron to Admiralty, 31 August 1870, PRO: ADM12/852/59.4a).

135. Admiralty to Commander-in-Chief, Channel Squadron, 26 May 1872, PRO: ADM12/814/50.2a.

136. Admiralty to Treasury, 6 July 1870, PRO: ADM12/852/59.4a. The idea evidently originated with Arthur Hood. Prizes amounting to £830 3s. 0d. were to be distributed yearly in the competition.

137. Admiralty to Commander-in-Chief, Mediterranean Squadron, 25 March 1879, PRO: ADM12/1042/54a.

138. Report on the Bombardment of Alexandria, 1882, PRO: ADM116/208.

139. Ibid.; Goodrich, *Report of the British Naval and Military Operations in Egypt*, p67. Fisher and Wilson, it should be noted, did admit that 'the batteries appear to have been silenced more because the men were driven from their guns than because the guns were actually disabled or the earth-works demolished'.

quently the heel of the ship will be so affected that a relay of the gun is necessary unless a bad or chance shot is purposely delivered.[140]

In sum, then, British gunnery at Alexandria was, in the words of one recent authority, 'of a high standard'.[141]

The capabilities of the Navy's ordnance notwithstanding, many of the service's officers as well as many naval designers and tacticians had, by 1876, turned away from the traditional reliance on guns and put their faith in torpedoes or, more commonly, the ancient tactic of ramming. In 1876 the D.N.O. Boys complained 'the power and accuracy of our artillery is much underestimated by the strong advocates of the ram, . . . [in] some of our best ships . . . rapidity and accuracy of fire . . . are now attained . . . while going at considerable speed.'[142] Faced with seemingly insoluble problems of effectively utilising the heavy guns of the day at sea, coupled with the as-yet undeveloped potential of the torpedo, some of the keenest and most influential minds in the Service seized on the expedient of turning the ship itself into a projectile.

140. Peter Padfield, *The Battleship Era* (New York, 1972), p100. For a scathing verdict on the Alexandria bombardment, see gunnery zealot Percy Scott's *Fifty Years in the Royal Navy* (New York, 1919), p62.

141. Andrew Lambert, 'The Shield of Empire', in J.R. Hill (ed.), *The Oxford Illustrated History of the Royal Navy* (New York, 1995), p194.

142. Minute by Boys, 17 January 1876, NMM: ADM138/66, no fol.

Anson firing one of her forward 13.5in guns. (U.S. Naval Historical Center: NH658720

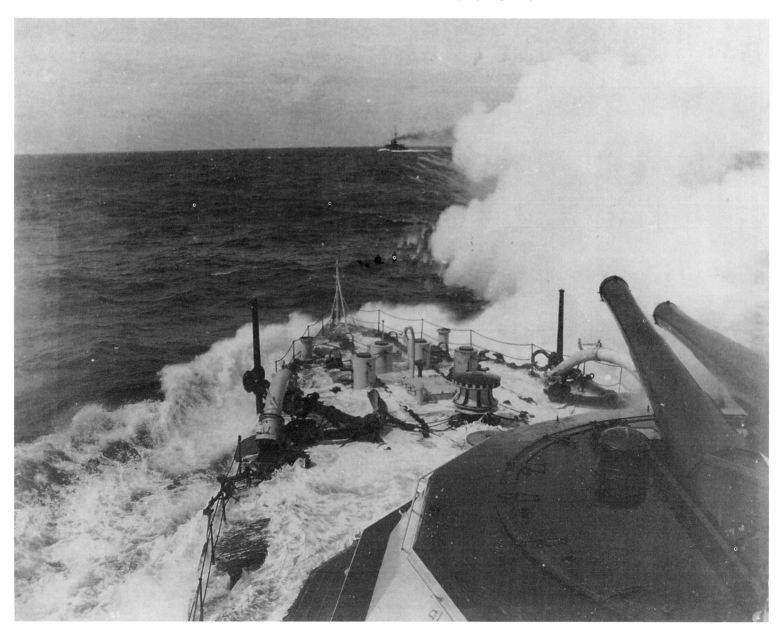

Chapter 5

Strategy, Economics, Politics, and Design Policy

'We build mighty vessels at gigantic cost, which are obsolete almost before they leave the stocks, even if we can be sure, as we cannot always be, that they will float when they get to sea.'

The Times, 31 August 1877.

WITH THE exceptions of ordnance and the substitution of steel for iron, neither of which was wholly in the Admiralty's power to influence, the allegation that the British Navy suffered from a technological lag, either *vis a vis* other powers, or in absolute terms, is difficult to sustain. Yet between 1870 and the early 1880s the Navy built a profoundly disparate collection of vessels, including a few of the most manifestly unsuccessful designs in the annals of naval architecture. There is no single, simple explanation for what went 'wrong'. Design shortcomings resulted from a host of factors–political, economic, strategic, tactical, technological and, certainly not least of all, human. The naval administrators of the period were the first to confront fully the phenomenon of unceasing rapid technological change, a revolutionary, confusing, and often unsettling situation. To convey some idea of how far adrift this situation left many observers, the *Times*, in reflecting on the development of torpedoes, wondered in 1877;

> whether our whole system of naval warfare, and perhaps naval architecture, will not have to be changed, and whether our magnificent ironclad fleet is not liable to be paralysed by means of little machines which almost any Government could afford to construct.[1]

This lack of certainty was equally evident regarding what sort of gun the Navy should employ, the type, extent, and thickness of armour, whether armour should be used at all, and whether to retain sails. Confusion was no less prominent in the sphere of naval tactics, for that matter. 'We do not know what to build,' the *Times* observed in early 1873, 'because we do not know how we shall fight our future naval battles.'[2]

> How can we lay down an efficient Navy in absolute ignorance of naval tactics? How can Naval Lords of the Admiralty direct with wisdom the Constructors of the Navy if they have hazy notions as to the use and employment of ships and their armaments?

The late 1860s, 1870s, and early 1880s, in short, were not the best of times for naval planners and designers.

The Strategic Context

The difficulties posed by rapid technological change and the concurrent reluctance of government to commit large sums to shipbuilding have been put forward as principal causes of the confusion which characterised British naval architecture during the 1860s, 1870s, and into the 1880s, confusion which was particularly pronounced after 1871. Between 1869 and 1880 the Navy built ironclads to no less than three distinct, novel designs, utilised two further designs predating 1869, and built a number of vessels which shared characteristics of more than one type. This apparent want of coherence, if not direction, in naval design policy sprang, unsurprisingly, from a want of consensus among officers, administrators and designers as to what constituted the best type of armoured ship. This want of consensus, in turn, was largely a product of the absence of any coherent, widely shared view of the future of naval warfare and tactics.[3]

A quick glance at pictures of the 'bizarre and ill-assorted designs' turned out by the Constructor's department during the 1870s seems to provide ample confirmation of this interpretation. The confusion wrought upon naval architecture by rapid technological change from the introduction of steam line-of-battle ships in the late 1840s, accelerating following the advent of the ironclad, and only ending with the emergence of a standard battleship type –the pre-dreadnought–and the return of design stability in the 1890s, caused those responsible for ship design to concentrate, it is often alleged, almost exclusively on technological and tactical considerations. Moreover, charges one critic, the Board of Admiralty, deluged by routine, often trivial, administrative duties,

---

1. *The Times*, 16 May 1877, p9.

2. Ibid, 2 January 1873, p9.

3. Sandler, *The Emergence of the Modern Capital Ship*, pp118-55.

Dreadnought's low freeboard, mandated by her intended coast-assault role, is readily evident in this picture. (U.S. Naval Historical Center: NH61004)

lacked the capacity to view naval policy in the round, a further reason the warships of the 1870s and 1880s were designed and constructed without reference to their strategic role. Indeed, the Navy 'was backward in technology and often reactionary in outlook, its ideas of strategy not so much misguided as non-existent'.[4]

To be sure, there were issues on which disagreement was paramount: the relative values of guns, torpedoes and the ram in future naval battles, the utility of armour, and whether it was best applied vertically, along the sides of a vessel, or horizontally, in the form of an armoured deck. These and many other topics generated heated debate among naval officers and designers, and led to much of the heterogeneity which characterised the mid-Victorian

battlefleet. However, far from failing to appreciate strategic roles, it is clear that as early as the 1850s Admiralty administrators were giving careful thought to the manner in which technology altered the ground rules of traditional British naval strategy. Furthermore, the ships designed and built during the period reflected their intended strategic roles as clearly as they did the prevailing tactical confusion and the limitations of contemporary technology.

To understand the situation from the perspective of contemporaries, it is first necessary briefly to survey the consequences of the technological revolution for the application of Britain's traditional naval strategy. By the mid-eighteenth century that strategy encompassed several facets, most crucially the maintenance of a blockade to prevent the enemy's battlefleet from menacing the sea lanes along which moved British trade, military expeditions, and other traffic. Ancillary to the blockade, cruisers were employed to chase down isolated enemy marauders which managed to evade the net, convoys were used to protect British trade in vital areas frequented by enemy raiders, and command of the sea was exploited through combined operations against peripheral targets. All of these missions were performed by sailing ships, whose operational radii were circumscribed only by their draught of water and the nutritional needs of their crews. The sailing navy was capable of worldwide operations without a sophisticated logistical support network, although major blockading fleets and squadrons certainly required substantial bases in close proximity.

This freedom, flexibility, and virtually unlimited strategic reach disappeared with the transition to steam power. In one respect the advent of steam was liberating, freeing ships from dependence on the wind, but in all others it was uniformly debilitating. It circumscribed operational radii, required sophisticated and expensive logistical support, increased the incidence and cost of maintenance, and, by simultaneously freeing enemy vessels from their dependence on the wind, greatly complicated the Navy's tasks of blockade and hunting down commerce raiders. Yet as soon as naval rivals – in this case France – made the transition to steam-powered line-of-battle ships the Royal Navy had to follow suit or relinquish command of the sea and the security that it engendered. Sailing ships were no defence against an enemy steam battlefleet. In other words, the strategic consequences were an inevitable side-effect of the switch from sail to steam. Subsequent technological developments further confounded the strategic picture. The advent of the steam line-of-battle ship generated doubts as to the continued efficacy of blockade as the foremost component of national and imperial strategy, and later the appearance of the locomotive torpedo raised the question of whether blockade was even possible. And if it were no longer possible, then the whole basis of security policy required overhauling, along with the Navy's *matériel*.

The commonplace assessment holds that contemporary appreciation of the inadequacy – if not the unfeasibility – of blockade led to the abandonment of Britain's traditional 'blue water policy' during the mid- and late-Victorian era. Reliance on the Navy as the first and most crucial line of defence was supplanted by land-based strategic schemes: the ascendance of military strategy – the 'brick and mortar' school – over naval. 'The purely military views of the "brick and mortar" school,' writes Arthur Marder, 'dominated

after 1860, and defensive policy was based on the assumption of a formidable lightning invasion against which the Navy alone, concentrated at home in a defensive attitude, would be ineffective.'[5] This assessment needs revision.

First, 'brick and mortar' advocates never achieved ascendancy over the 'blue water' school. Throughout the Victorian era the Navy remained the bulwark of national and imperial defence. In 1867 First Lord Henry Corry succinctly summed up the real strategic picture, while arguing for increased naval funding:

> If we cannot command the Channel and the coast of Ireland, we are open to invasion. If we cannot command the Mediterranean, we are cut off from our direct line of communication with India. . . . In addition to the force required for the maintenance of our superiority at home and in the Mediterranean, we should have to provide for the protection of our colonial, commercial and political interests, in the Baltic, in North America, the West Indies, the Pacific, the Indian, Australian and China Seas . . .[6]

Moreover, so far from meekly allowing strategic direction to pass from its hands to the Army's after 1850, the Admiralty systematically considered the logistical infrastructure required to enable the steam navy to match the strategic reach of its sailing predecessor, and – equally crucial – explored alternative strategies to blockade. In the case of the former, by 1858 'defence of the Coaling Stations and the arrangement requisite to be made for the vast supply of Coal required to kept up all over the world for the use of HM Ships' was listed by Junior Naval Lord Alexander Milne among the 'duties required of the Navy in the event of war'.[7] Coal and coaling stations were the crucial ingredients for maintaining the Navy's world-wide scope of operations after the transition to steam, and during the mid-Victorian era Britain moved towards the creation both of the logistical network and the methods and means of ensuring its security.[8]

As for the consequences of steam for the maintenance of the close blockade, instead of abdicating responsibility and allowing national security to fall back by default on 'brick and mortar' defences, the Admiralty supplanted watchful waiting with explicitly offensive operations. Rather than run the risk of enemy squadrons evading blockaders at night or in fog, the Navy's

4. N.A.M. Rodger, 'The Dark Ages of the Admiralty, 1869-1885, Part I, Business Methods, 1868-74', *Mariner's Mirror* 62/1 (1975), p331 and *The Admiralty* (Lavenham, 1979), pp99-105. For similar assessments, see Richard Millman, *British Policy and the Coming of the Franco-Prussian War* (London, 1965), p151; C.J. Bartlett, 'The Mid-Victorian Re-appraisal of Naval Policy', in Kenneth Bourne and D.C. Watts (eds.), *Studies in International History* (London, 1967), p207; and Jeffrey L. Lant, 'The Spithead Naval Review of 1887', *Mariner's Mirror* 62/1 (1975), pp67-79, especially p76.

5. Arthur J. Marder, *The Anatomy of British Sea Power: A History of British Naval Policy in the Pre-Dreadnought Era, 1880-1905* (New York, 1940), p67.

6. H.T.L. Corry, 'Memorandum for the Consideration of the Cabinet,' Printed,

Confidential, 2 December 1867, Milne Papers, NMM:MLN/143/3/10, p10 [National Maritime Museum, Greenwich].

7. Draft report in Milne's hand, in response to 'Three Questions put by the Queen to the Members of the Board of Adm[iral]ty, Early 1858' NMM:MLN/142/2 [1].

8. The principal works on coal, coaling stations, and their place in imperial defence are Donald Schurman's *Imperial Defence, 1868-1887* (ed. John Beeler, London, 2000) and W.C.B. Tunstall's essays in the *Cambridge History of the British Empire* (Cambridge, 1940, 1959): 'Imperial Defence, 1815-1870', Vol. 2, pp807-41, 'Imperial Defence, 1870-1897', Vol. 3, pp230-54, and 'Imperial Defence, 1897-1914', Vol. 3, pp563-604.

strategists planned *to destroy them before they could escape.* Milne wrote in 1858 that, in the event of war [t]he first and most important point, must be the Home defence,' but the surest manner of defending British soil and preventing 'any attempt on the part of the Enemy to land Troops,' was by having 'the Channel Fleet . . . as soon as possible put to sea, and the Cherbourgh [*sic*] and Brest Squadrons . . . watch those ports'. Moreover, he argued, the fleet should 'act offensively on the Coast of France, so as to keep the attention of the Enemy to the defence of their own Shores,' and 'attempts [should be] made not only to destroy their trade, but to attack and burn their Mercantile and other Ports.' 'Having this in view,' he concluded, 'the Hydr[ographic] Of[fice] of the Admiralty should prepare charts of the Coast of France with all requisite information of their respective defences.'[9]

Indeed, coast assault became the dominant operational doctrine for the British battlefleet between 1850 and 1889, employed prominently in the Crimea, to be sure, but also evident in contingency plans for attacking American ports following the *Trent* Affair, the bombardment of Alexandria in 1882, and in 1885 when

offensive operations against Batum were planned in anticipation of hostilities with Russia.[10] Owing to the steam warship's limited range, the frequency with which it required maintenance, and the perceived demise of blockade's utility, enemy naval arsenals and ports became the principal targets of offensive operations. In the wake of his experience in the Baltic during the Crimean War Captain Henry Codrington opined 'almost all war afloat will now be litoral [*sic*] warfare'.[11] Echoing Codrington, Captain Sherard Osborn informed an Admiralty Committee on ship design in 1871 '[t]he probabilities are, that the day for fleet actions on the high seas has gone by; and that fleets will in future be used at strategical points upon their own or their enemy's coasts'.[12] Alluding to French naval dispositions in the recently-ended Franco-German war, Osborn added, 'those fleets would have fought close in shore if an action had come off, and not upon the high seas'.

The transformation of British naval strategy after 1850 in turn affected the Admiralty's design policy, leading to the bifurcation of the ironclad battlefleet, dependent on its perceived strategic role. For coast assault the Navy needed and built heavily-armed and armoured, low-freeboard ships, capable of slugging it out with shore fortifications. But it simultaneously required battleships capable of keeping the seas and operating worldwide if need arose. For these purposes the low-freeboard coast assault vessels were not merely unsuitable, but in many cases downright danger-

The torpedo-ram *Polyphemus* breaking the boom at Berehaven in Ireland during coast-assault exercises in 1885. Attacking enemy fleets in port was the dominant British naval doctrine in this period. (U.S. Naval Historical Center: NH57868)

ous. Hence, despite the seeming design miscellany, the battlefleet was divided between two basic ship types, coast-assault ironclads and cruising ironclads. In April 1875 Milne, then serving as First Naval Lord, explicitly spelled out the reasons driving the dichotomy, at the same time underlining the centrality of coast assault to the Navy's mid-Victorian strategic doctrine: 'this country cannot,' he wrote;

> solely depend on unmasted ships for sea or Foreign Service, however great and important the power of their guns and how admirable [sic] they may be adapted for the attack of an Enemy's fleet, forts, or harbours, yet their sphere of action is limited by the means of obtaining coal nor are they adapted for ocean cruizing, hence the necessity for masted and sailing ships for blockades, convoys, or distant stations.[13]

Ordnance and mountings drove this divergence. The first British ironclad, *Warrior*, carried forty guns ranging in size from 68pdrs to 110pdrs, the latter the largest piece of naval ordnance available at the time. Within ten years of *Warrior*'s commencement *Devastation*'s design—incorporating four 12in, 35-ton guns—was approved. On the most fundamental level the growing size and weight of naval guns from 1860 through the late 1870s meant a virtually inevitable reduction in the number carried by a ship. Forty 35-ton guns would have weighed by themselves 1400 tons, to say nothing of the weight of their carriages, ammunition, and powder, an impossible burden to be carried on early British ironclads, typically of less than 10,000 tons displacement. There was, moreover, considerable debate during the 1870s and 1880s as to whether the gun had been supplanted by other weapons: torpedoes or the ram.[14]

To be sure, the gun retained numerous advocates. The D.N.O. Henry Boys stated in 1875;

> it must be taken as a maxim that the most powerful guns for their

weight must be carried in our ships, & that arrangements must be made to meet the necessary requirements for working them, in fact, that the ship must be constructed to fit the guns & not the guns to fit the ship.[15]

In the Constructor's Department, Nathaniel Barnaby was similarly emphatic as to the primacy of the gun. 'Looking at the relative distances within which the gun, the torpedo, and the ram are operative,' he informed the Institute of Naval Architects in 1876, 'and the risks of failure in striking with them, the gun occupies the first place, and the ram the last, as instruments of naval warfare.'[16] And few of ramming's most ardent devotees advocated sole reliance on the prow.

But a gun which could not be brought to bear on its target owing to a limited arc of fire was of no value at all, and the fewer the guns carried in a ship, the greater the arc each had to cover in order to be effective. The traditional broadside arrangement for a ship's armament, which had been utilised in the first-generation British ironclads, was not effective for all-around fire. Fire directly ahead and astern was restricted to one or two guns, usually of light calibre. This shortcoming had been of little consequence during the age of sail, when the dominant tactical formation, line ahead, rendered broadside fire all-important. But with the advent of steam, the strategic switch from blockade to coast assault, and a concurrent revival of ramming, the broadside arrangement became a weakness rather than a strength. In order to assault an enemy harbour or to ram a ship had to steam bows-on towards its target, rendering its own main battery ineffectual.

By the late 1860s, therefore, numerous naval officers and tacticians were stressing the importance of end-on fire: the ability to fire ahead and astern, especially the former. In his evidence to the Committee on Designs Milne emphasised the necessity for end-on fire.[17] The sentiment was echoed by Rear-Admiral George Randolph, who maintained 'fire ahead' was 'of the very first importance' and whatever design 'admits of most is *pro tanto*

9. Draft report in Milne's hand, in response to 'Three Questions put by the Queen to the Members of the Board of Adm[iral]ty, Early 1858' MLN/142/2 [1].

10. See 'List of the Chief Ports on the Federal Coast of the United States, showing the Shipping, Population, Dockyards, and Defences, as far as known; also how far accessible or vulnerable to an Attack, as far as can be gathered from the Charts. With an approximate Estimate of the Number of vessels required to blockade the several Ports and Rivers,' Confidential Admiralty Print, December 1861, NMM: MLN114/8; Barbara Jelavich, 'British Means of Offense Against Russia in the Nineteenth Century', *Russian History/Histoire Russe* 1, pt. 2 (1974), pp119-35; also George Ballard, 'British Gunvessels of 1875: The Larger Twin-Screw Type', *Mariner's Mirror* 26 (1940), p15. '[A]fter the work that fell on the Fleet during our war with Russia in the fifties, many naval officers of rising prominence formed the conviction that the principal duty of the British Navy—or of any great navy—in the wars of the future, would be the attack of coastal fortresses, requiring ships of special design. They said as much in giving official evidence before Parliamentary Commissions. . . . Moreover, as the blockade an attack of southern ports forming the chief feature of the American Civil War, coming later, seemed to confirm this novel theory that coastal bombardment was to be the chief function of fleets thenceforward, it found enough agreement at the Admiralty for ten or twelve years after the war

to cause the building of a certain proportion of vessels suitable for such work, of various sizes and armament, but with the one feature regarded as indispensable common to all, of an abnormally light draft in proportion to other dimensions.' Ballard, it should be stressed, had first-hand knowledge of the situation, having entered the Navy in the 1870s.

11. Codrington to Rear-Admiral Peter Richards, 7 July 1855, cited in C.I. Hamilton, *Anglo-French Naval Rivalry, 1840-1870* (London, 1994), p78.

12. Evidence of Sherard Osborn, printed in 'Report of the Committee appointed by the Lords Commissioners of the Admiralty to examine the Designs upon which Ships of War have recently been constructed, with Analysis of Evidence,' *Parl. Papers*, 1872, Vol. 18, p83.

13. Draft memorandum by Milne, April 1875, NMM: MLN/144/5 [2].

14. Sandler, *Emergence of the Modern Capital Ship*, pp118-55.

15. Boys to Barnaby, 31 March 1875, NMM: ADM138/49, fol. 210.

16. Nathaniel Barnaby, 'On Ships of War,' *Transactions of the Institute of Naval Architects* 17 (1876), p2.

17. Milne to Committee on Designs, 11 April 1871, Hornby Papers, NMM: PHI/110/2.

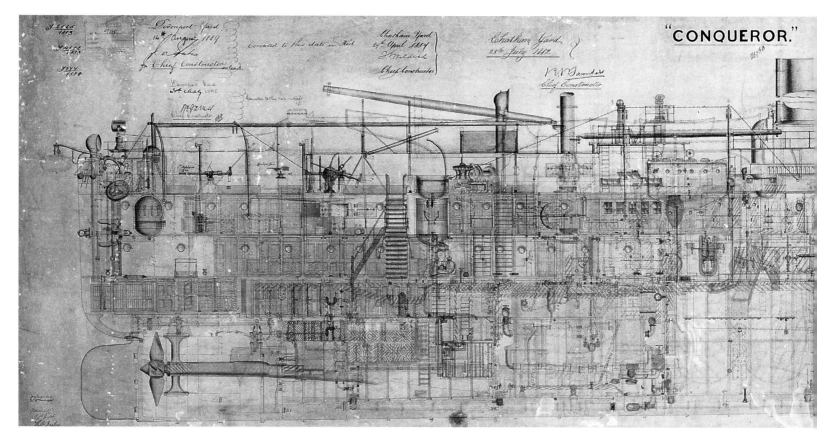

"CONQUEROR."

The layout of *Conqueror* (launched 1881) and similar shallow-draft ironclads – low freeboard and a single turret incapable of firing astern – illustrates the aggressive intentions of the designers. (National Maritime Museum, London: 9118)

The turrets of HMS *Edinburgh*, shown while she was fitting-out. (U.S. Naval Historical Center: NH61027)

superior . . .'.[18] Similarly emphatic statements were proffered by Captains William Armytage and L.G. Heath.[19]

Various design expedients were brought forward in the course of the 1860s to achieve powerful end-on fire, the two most important being Edward Reed's 'box-battery' and Cowper Coles' turret. The former placed the heavy guns in a central battery which projected beyond the ship's sides, enabling the guns to be trained ahead and astern, as well as on the beam, without impediment from superstructure, masts, or rigging. The turret, in theory, could be trained a full 360 degrees. In practice, however, the arc was likely to be circumscribed – often substantially – by other parts of the ship, especially masts and shrouds. Turrets, therefore, were ill-suited to ocean-going ironclads fitted with full rigs and with the exception of *Monarch*, the ill-fated *Captain*, and *Inflexible*, the British Navy demurred from building the type.[20]

Aside from restricted arc of fire, turrets posed another difficulty for designers: weight. Apart from the gun and its carriage, naval architects had also to consider the burden of complete armour protection around, above, and below – Coles' turret armour extended downward to protect the rotating machinery – the gun, plus the weight of machinery. Each of *Inflexible*'s turrets, for instance, weighed 750 tons, exclusive of ammunition and loading machinery, both of which were disposed externally, owing to constraints of space. Even so, the two turrets by themselves accounted for more than 13 per cent of the ship's 11,000-ton displacement. When mounted as much as 15 or 20ft above the waterline this con-

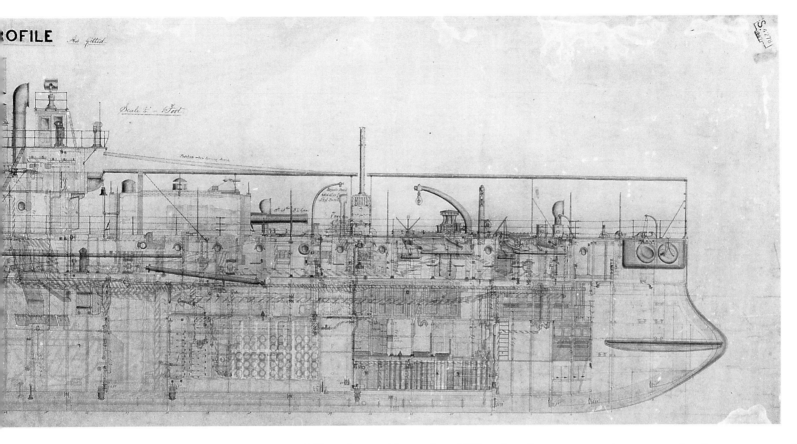

centration of weight could compromise the stability of most ships of moderate dimensions. As Reed maintained, '[t]he great weight of armour needed for the turrets would demand low freeboard.'[21] Low freeboard, in turn, was detrimental in a seagoing ship. Stability was not a problem in a properly designed low-freeboard vessel—even one of moderate dimensions—but lack of seaworthiness was. The deck would be immersed in heavy seas. Coast assault ships, designed for tangling with shore fortifications, required both the heaviest armour and ordnance. These vessels were without exception turret ships. 'Cruising' ironclads, on the other hand, were generally box-battery designs. They mounted lighter ordnance and carried thinner armour, liabilities if employed against shore fortifications, but of less significance on the high seas, where they would likely encounter few ships more heavily armed and protected than themselves. The lighter guns and thinner armour were requisites for the sails and high freeboard which enabled these ships to function as cruisers.

Differences between the two types were accentuated after the late 1860s, when improvements in steam technology—compound engines, surface condensers, and cylindrical boilers—made it possible to design and build mastless capital ships *for service in European waters* where the logistical support for such vessels—coaling stations and colliers, and repair and dry-docking facilities for iron steamships, whose engines and boilers required frequent maintenance and whose hulls necessitated equally frequent cleaning and scraping—existed. The savings of weight and space, in turn meant such ships could carry still heavier armour and guns. The battle advantage thereby gained was too important to pass up for the sake of retaining sails, and thus the British began to build mastless capital ships with the *Devastation*, approved and laid down in 1869. The intended operational theatre for the vessel was explicitly stated in the opening paragraph of Reed's memorandum of 2 March 1869:

[t]he object of the Admiralty in the preparation of this design has been to produce a warship of great offensive and defensive

18. Remarks of George Randolph, 11 April 1873, ibid.

19. Remarks of Armytage, 10 April 1871; and Heath, 14 April 1871, ibid. As a sidelight illustrative of the tactical quagmire and the utter lack of consensus, in 1878 Philip Colomb wrote '[T]o me it is an astonishing question which is commonly put—"whether is the bow or the broadside the most important fire?" because I have never heard a serious argument in favour of the bow fire. I know than an opinion in its favour exists, or is supposed to exist, because in a great many ships the broadside is weakened, and very many terrible inconveniences, and dangers, submitted to in order to supply bow fire. But I have only heard it asserted in support of this policy, that as a ship must not expose herself to be rammed, she must be prepared to fight an end-on battle. But unless she is pretty close to her enemy, and in a particular relative position, there is no objection in life to her presenting her broadside, and an end-on battles must become a broadside one after the lapse of a very few minutes.' (Philip Colomb, 'Great Britain's Maritime Power: How Best Developed as Regards Fighting Ships, etc,' *Journal of the Royal United Services Institution* 22 [1878], pp28-9.)

20. The *Neptune*, a full-rigged turret ship, was purchased in 1878.

21. Sandler, *Emergence of the Modern Capital Ship*, p180.

"AUDACIOUS" "INVINCIBLE" AND "IRON DUKE"

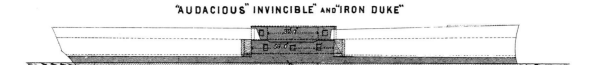

"SWIFTSURE" "TRIUMPH"

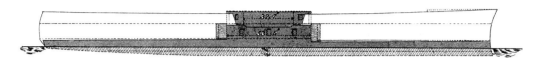

"ALEXANDRA".

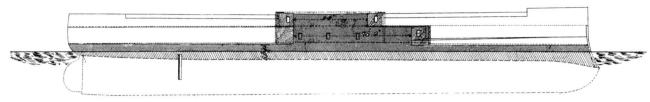

"TÈMÈRAIRE" WITH BARBETTE TOWERS

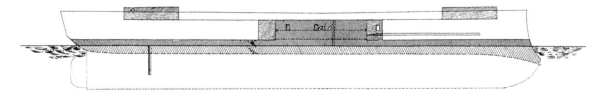

"SHANNON"

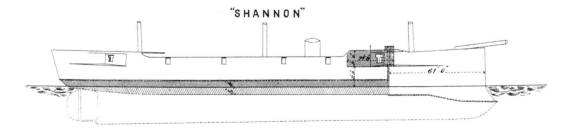

"NELSON & NORTHAMPTON"

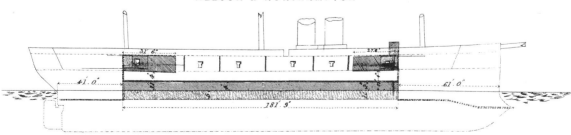

Cruising ironclads. The upper four designs illustrate the central-battery concept championed by Edward Reed, in which both the main armament and much of the armour protection was confined to a small area amidships to save weight. The bottom two show Nathaniel Barnaby's preference for armoured bulkheads across the ends.

powers, well adapted for naval warfare in Europe. The capability of the ship to cross the Atlantic has also been considered; but the primary object, and that in view of which the qualities of the design have been regulated, is that of fitness for engaging the enemy's ships and squadrons in the British channel, the Mediterranean, and other European seas.[22]

Devastation's construction and subsequent success, albeit within the confines of the theatre for which she was designed, has led several historians to conclude that the technological means for creating a wholly steam-powered navy existed by 1870, and that the Admiralty's failure to do so owed to the obstructive influence of

conservative, if not outright reactionary, naval lords at Whitehall, administrative weakness, and a Chief Constructor 'unsuited for his post' during the subsequent decade.[23] After the breakthrough of *Devastation*, Stanley Sandler, for instance, terms the 1870s a decade of stagnation in British warship design.[24] But this conclusion is not sustainable when either the world-wide demands made of the Navy or the remaining limitations of boilers and engines are considered.

Coast assault ironclads could not perform every envisioned strategic role; most importantly they could not fight on the high seas, so the Navy also designed and built cruising ironclads. These 'cruising' ironclads required for service beyond Europe operated within different logistical and strategic parameters than their coast-assault counterparts. Given the existing state of maritime steam technology, the paucity of overseas coaling stations and

22. Edward Reed, 'Considerations entering into *Devastation* design', 2 March 1869 NMM: ADM/138/23.

23. N.A.M. Rodger, 'The Dark Ages of the Admiralty, 1869-1885, Part 2,' *Mariner's Mirror* 62/1 (1976), pp43-6; Sandler, *Emergence of the Modern Capital Ship*, pp248-9; Parkes, *British Battleships*, pp204-5.

24. Sandler, *Emergence of the Modern Capital Ship*, pp248-9.

The French armoured cruiser *Bayard* (launched 1880). (U.S. Naval Historical Center: courtesy of Rear-Admiral Ammen C. Farenholt, USN (MC) 1931; NH32)

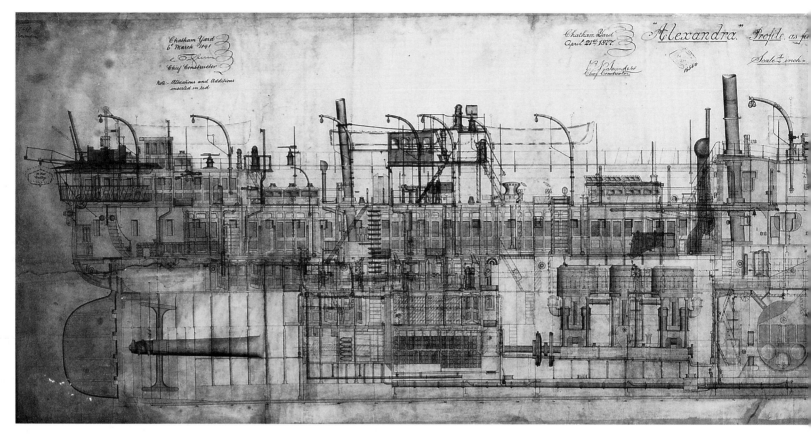

Despite the greater efficiency under steam afforded by HMS *Alexandra*'s oval boilers and compound engines – clearly visible here – possible service outside European waters mandated the retention of a full sailing rig. (National Maritime Museum, London: 17617)

repair facilities, the rapid deterioration of boilers, and the possibility that the services of warships overseas would require extended operations beyond the reach of a convenient coal depot (unlike trans-oceanic merchant steamships operating on regular schedules), the Navy could not dispense with sails on 'cruising vessels', whether armoured or not, before the early 1880s at the earliest, and arguably only when the next generation of steam technology – water-tube boilers and triple-expansion engines – made their appearance in the Navy's vessels after 1885. A wholly steam-powered navy could only be realised in the age of steel, rather than the age of iron.

Thus, the bifurcation of the battlefleet was the necessary consequence of the state of technology during the 1870s. It was also, contrary to allegations to the opposite, explicit testimony to the consideration given intended strategic roles by professional advisors and ship designers. The coast-assault vessels were designed for one specific strategic role, the 'cruising ironclads' for another. Doubtless the Admiralty would have liked the simplicity – and the savings – which would have accrued from designing and building one type rather than two, but it could not be done. The features of the coast-assault vessel – especially its freeboard – were irreconcilable with seaworthiness outside confined waters; the high freeboard, modest protection, and weak armament of the cruising ironclads made them ill-suited for attacking shore installations.

The Economic Context

The division of the battlefleet into coast assault and cruising vessels was largely the consequence of technological limitations and strategic factors. A further set of considerations influenced overall design policy and in particular a division between first- and second-class vessels of both types. Some were tactical, some economic. Faced with the unpleasant necessity of dividing the limited funds available for the Navy's *matériel* between repairs, which regularly consumed more time and money than anticipated, a 'non-fighting' fleet which continued to account for almost half the tonnage constructed despite the enthusiastic efforts of Hugh Childers and others to curb the size of the forces overseas, a battlefleet in which increasing technological sophistication went hand-in-hand with increasing cost, and, most significantly, rapid technological change and uncertainty which condemned expensive ships to virtually instantaneous obsolescence and raised serious doubts as to their value in the first place, the response of naval administrators

25. John Beeler, *British Naval Policy in the Gladstone-Disraeli Era, 1866-1880* (Stanford, 1997), pp83-96, 151-70, 244-49.

26. Spencer Robinson to Admiralty (Copy), 3 February 1869, PRO: ADM1/6138.

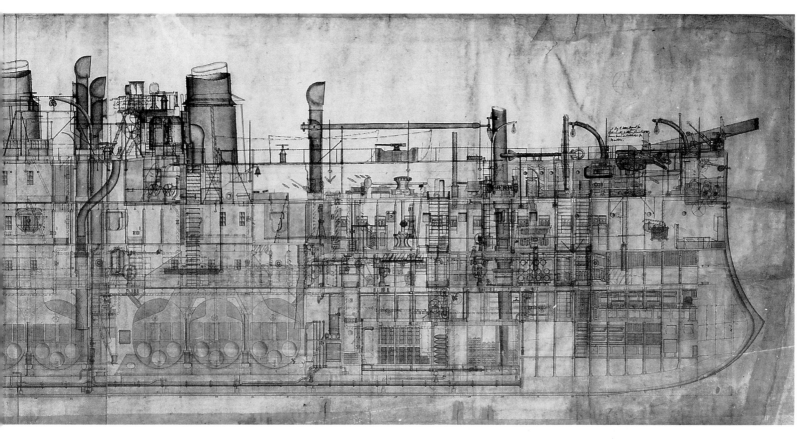

was predictable. One of the most significant factors governing ironclad design policy from the early 1860s through most of the 1880s was expense.[25] The Admiralty tried to get more for less, while simultaneously attempting to guard against risky investments.

Several strategies were pursued in this quest for economy. One was the practice, increasingly common as the 1870s progressed, of modifying vessels in the course of construction in order to improve machinery, protection, or especially ordnance with the most recent technological developments at home or overseas. There was a direct correlation between the number of vessels under construction and the tendency to modify them. This tendency in turn produced an inverse correlation between the number of vessels under construction and the amount of time they took to build. The fewer the ironclads being built, the greater the concern of the Admiralty to embody cutting-edge technology in each of them, and thus maintain a qualitative advantage over rivals without resorting to the even more expensive alternative of laying down further ships. Hence, the fewer the ships under construction, the longer they ordinarily took to build.

Most of the expedients for conserving expenditure revolved around saving money on the hull, rather than on scrimping on machinery, weapons, or protection. The methods employed to achieve this end fell under three headings, although there was considerable overlap between them. Two of the three also imposed substantial limitations on the ships which resulted.

'MODERATE DIMENSIONS'

The first, and most obvious, policy was a general insistence on 'moderate dimensions', in large part as a means of saving money. Childers' instructions to the Controller's Department in early 1869, for instance, asked Robert Spencer Robinson and Reed to produce a ship design carrying two guns 'of the largest size', enough coal to cross the Atlantic at cruising speed, 'limited sail power', and 'as much . . . armour defence . . . as can be obtained,' all on a ship 'not to exceed 3,000 tons'. These guidelines prompted from Reed the unusually temperate observation that;

> [i]t will be obvious on a moment's reflection that this outline comprises conditions which have never yet been fulfilled in any actual ship . . .[T]he limitation of the size of a ship to 3,000 tons precludes the possibility of her being an efficient first-class war-vessel.

Spencer Robinson, was equally emphatic: 'it is tolerably certain that no modifications of such a design, without an essential departure, especially as to tonnage, from the conditions given can make a good fighting vessel fit for service with a fleet of the present day.'[26] In this particular instance Reed and Spencer Robinson carried the day, winning approval for a somewhat larger (4400 builder's tons, 9500 tons displacement) design in which one of the requirements set forth by Childers—sails—was dropped. The resulting design, the *Devastation*, was in some crucial respects the forerunner of the modern capital ship.

But the general insistence on moderate dimensions outlived this setback, and continued to exercise a large degree of influence on the characteristics of capital ships built during the 1870s and 1880s. The preference was evident in the instructions from the Board for the design of HMS *Shannon*, which was 'to cost about half as much as the *Superb*', a first-class sea-going ship laid down in 1873 (and later renamed *Alexandra*).[27] It manifested itself again in 1878 with the Board's refusal to accede completely to D.N.C. Barnaby's argument that two ironclads, *Colossus* and *Edinburgh*, be lengthened to 350ft to secure greater speed.[28] The following year, the First Sea Lord, George Wellesley, insisted that the design of *Collingwood* not exceed 10,000 tons displacement.[29] Of the eighteen sea-going British ironclads laid down by the Navy between 1870 and 1883, only two–*Dreadnought* and *Inflexible*–did not labour under tonnage and size restrictions.[30]

When asked by the Hartington Commission about the factors dictating warship design, Rear-Admiral George Tryon replied 'the only influence I have known in that way has been with reference to the limitations imposed as to the size of ships . . .'.[31] The primary consideration, he added, was cost.

Like most other British capital ships of the 1870s and early 1880s, *Camperdown*'s displacement was circumscribed by the insistence on moderate dimensions. (U.S. Naval Historical Center: NH75972)

I have known decisions in reference to the construction of ships considered from the point of view that we can get five ships instead of four for a certain sum of money, and that there is some objection to building a few ships of very high tonnage in lieu of more ships of less tonnage.

Barnaby made much the same observation in early 1881, when the Board was considering designs for future ironclads. Noting although *Inflexible* was not much larger than *Dreadnought*, 'she has been popularly regarded as a monster far too large & costly to be repeated'.[32] Hence, he added, '[i]t has been considered to be good policy to produce ships of 8,500 tons to 9,100 tons. . .'. A few years later Director of Naval Intelligence Captain Reginald Custance observed that the 'question [of cost] has been answered by the Admiralty; they have to consider whether they should build six *Inflexibles* or a larger number of slightly smaller vessels. Instead of going to 11,000 tons they have taken a displacement of 8,500 in the *Ajax*, costing £350,000, which will given them for £3,000,000 nine ships instead of six.'[33]

But if cost was the major factor impelling adherence to moderate dimensions, it was by no means the only one. As Milne wrote in the early 1870s, '[t]here has always been an anxiousness at the Admiralty to keep down the large dimensions of our Iron Clad ships, not only from the very large expense but also from their being so unwieldy and drawing so much water.'[34] In his study of nineteenth-century naval architecture (1902), Barnaby listed the

98

advantages of moderate dimensions: 'to secure handiness, and to diminish the first cost and the upkeep of individual ships, and to avoid large crews'.[35] To add to these justifications, it was argued the smaller the ship, the smaller the target, and the easier it would be to provide adequate armour protection.

The emphasis contemporary designers and, especially naval officers, placed on manoeuvrability cannot be gainsaid. The first-generation British ironclads, several of them 340ft or more long, were notoriously unhandy. Their clumsiness, coupled with the impossibility of providing sufficient armour protection for such long ships against the escalating power of guns, originally informed the Admiralty's adoption of moderate dimensions in the early 1860s.[36] The resulting design was Reed's 'box-battery,' based on the premise 'that in armoured ships as the extent and thickness of the armour are increased, the proportion of length to breadth should be diminished'.[37] The stubbier form of the resulting vessel would, Reed admitted, require 'a little greater horsepower' to be driven at the same speed as a fine-lined hull, but

> the benefits in point of first cost, handiness, and maintenance, resulting from moderate proportions, are tangible facts, far outweighing in importance the small economy of steam-power resulting from the adoption of greater proportion and fineness of form.

The premium attached to handiness rested in turn on the widespread perception that ramming would become, as one contemporary put it, 'the prominent feature of future naval victories.'[38] The advantages possessed by small, handy ships over large clumsy vessels in a ramming encounter scarcely needs elaboration.[39] Cost, important though it was in the calculations of the Board, was not the only factor which drove the Navy to adopt the policy of moderate dimensions.

Yet whether from considerations of cost or handiness, it is plain that the policy was, as contemporaries termed it, one of 'false economy', although this situation was not fully evident at the time. The conflicting imperatives of incorporating heavy guns and thick armour into ships while at the same time reducing or at least restricting tonnage were not capable of satisfactory resolution. The problem was not apparent in the early box-battery ships, which were generally judged successful vessels, but became acute after 1870, when gun weight escalated from 12 to 35 to 81 tons and armour thickness increased from 8 to 10 to 12 to 24ins. The *Bellerophon*–the first full-sized box battery ironclad–and its successors had moderate thicknesses of armour–6 to 9in– and modest-sized guns (9in and 10in) loaded on their moderate displacement; their successors after 1870 suffered from attempts to increase weight of armour and ordnance while maintaining moderate displacement. The result was a series of ships with drawbacks in terms of seaworthiness, speed, and, ironically, even handiness.

An ancillary to the general insistence on moderate dimensions was the practice of repeating accepted designs with reduced dimensions in subsequent versions. This practice had been employed in ironclad designs as early as 1859, hard on the heels of laying-down *Warrior*. The idea belonged to Secretary to the Admiralty Lord Clarence Paget and was subsequently taken up by both the First Lord, the Duke of Somerset, and Lord Palmerston. The latter wrote Chancellor of the Exchequer William Gladstone on 25 November 1859 'I think the Duke right in proposing to build iron-plated ships of a smaller size and therefore less expensive than the two which were begun by the late Government.'[40] The results were disappointing. Surveyor Baldwin Wake Walker predicted as much, and objected to the idea from the start.[41] The diminutive versions of the *Warrior* 'cost at least two-thirds as much as the larger [ship] . . . but offered only a quarter to half the value.

27. Barnaby to Constructor's Department, 11 March 1873, NMM: ADM138/43, fol. 1.

28. Considerations put forward by the Director of Naval Construction to the Preparation of the Designs of *Colossus* and *Imperiuse*, Spring 1878, NMM: ADM138/60, no fol.

29. Parkes, *British Battleships*, p297.

30. This calculation does not take into account the two large ironclads purchased in 1878, and also omits *Alexandra*, for which the Ship's Cover is missing. It is possible that the latter's design was not circumscribed by the requirement for moderate dimensions but it, unlike *Dreadnought* and *Inflexible*, did not exceed 10,000 tons which was generally the outside limit for British ironclads throughout the 1870s.

31. *Report of the Royal Commission appointed to Enquire into the Civil and Professional Administration of the Naval and Military Departments and the Relationship of those Departments to each other and to the Treasury* (generally known as the Hartington Commission), Strictly Confidential, PRO: HO73/35/3, p133.

32. Barnaby to Admiralty, 7 April 1881, PRO: ADM1/6608.

33. Custance quoted in Thomas Brassey, *The British Navy: Its Strengths, Resources, and Administration* (London, 1882), Vol. 3, p14.

34. Minute by Milne, 3 April 1873, NMM: ADM138/43 fol. 19.

35. Nathaniel Barnaby, *Naval Development in the Century* (London, 1902), p65.

36. Sandler, *Emergence of the Modern Capital Ship*, p20. 'To protect such a lengthy gun deck with six-inch plates would destroy the ship's stability or raise its waterline to an alarming height. Obviously, new design concepts were needed.'

37. Edward J. Reed, 'On Long and Short Ironclads', *Transactions of the Institute of Naval Architects* 10 (1869), pp39-91.

38. George Elliot, 'The Ram: The Prominent Feature of Future Naval Victories', *Journal of the Royal United Services Institution* 28 (1884), p357.

39. One of the most tireless advocates of moderate dimensions in the late 1870s was the ardent navalist M.P. and future Civil Lord and Parliamentary Secretary of the Admiralty, Thomas Brassey. In a letter to the *Times* in September 1875 he asserted that '[a] survey of the proceedings of foreign constructors fails . . . to establish the necessity for spending large sums on monster ironclads for the English Navy. Does not an examination of the actual and prospective conditions of naval warfare point to a very different policy? Would not the ingenuity of our naval architects be most fitly exercised in the construction of swift, handy, and unsinkable rams?' (*The Times*, 22 September 1875, p8). Similar letters to the 'leading journal' appeared on 13 July 1875, p11, and 25 December 1877, p5. Brassey frequently spoke in the same vein during naval debates in the House of Commons.

40. Palmerston quoted in Lambert, *Warrior*, p30. Also printed in Guedalla, *Gladstone and Palmerston*, p113.

41. Lambert, *Warrior*, p31.

HMS *Ajax*, which with her sister-ship *Agamemnon* was considered by Oscar Parkes to be 'the worst examples' of the 'futile economy' of building scaled-down versions of earlier vessels. (U.S. Naval Historical Center: NH64209)

Later even smaller ironclads were built. They were all failures, unable to combine the speed, endurance, protection, and firepower required for a front rank ship'.[42]

Despite repeated failures the tactic was revived in the 1870s, using *Inflexible*'s design as the model. Before its completion – and hence prior to any opportunity to ascertain the design's merits and shortcomings – the Admiralty concluded the ship represented 'the model upon which future types of battleship were to be based'. Among the four reduced versions were the hapless *Ajax*

and *Agamemnon*, which 'had all of the larger ship's defects and none of her alleged virtues', forming the 'worst examples of this particular form of futile economy'.[43] Fortunately, the tonnage restrictions were not so draconian in the subsequent two central-citadel types, *Colossus* and *Edinburgh*, but generally the practice, like the overall adherence to moderate dimensions, was one of false economy. The savings in cost did not outweigh drawbacks in performance imposed by the reduction of scale.

SECOND-CLASS IRONCLADS

The second major method of saving money on shipbuilding – the division of the battlefleet, both cruising and coast-assault iron-clads, into first- and second-class vessels – correlated conveniently

42. Ibid, pp31-2.

43. It persisted for another twenty years beyond the 1870s, for that matter. See Parkes, *British Battleships*, p262.

44. Augmentation of the Naval Force, in Ships and Stores (Copy), 9 August 1870, PRO: ADM1/6159.

45. *Hansard's Parliamentary Debates*, 3d ser., 166 (1862), col. 265.

46. Ibid., cols. 580-630.

47. Ibid., col. 597. The resolution was passed in modified form 74 to 13. The text read:

'That it is expedient to suspend the construction of the proposed Forts at Spithead until the value of iron-roofed [*ie* turreted or otherwise covered] gunboats for the defence of our Ports and Roadsteads shall have been fully considered; and that this House will, on Tuesday the first day of May, resolve itself into a Committee, to consider of authorizing the application of any portion of the monies which have been voted for the construction of forts, and not already expended or appropriated, to the construction of iron-sheathed vessels, or to the conversion of wooden vessels into iron-sheathed vessels.'(col. 630) The forts were subsequently completed, but several small wooden vessels were also converted to carry armour.

48. Ibid., 3d ser., 193 (1868), col. 1112.

with tactical and deployment considerations. A fleet of large coast-assault and cruising ironclads was necessary to uphold British naval hegemony, but there were also roles for which large vessels were ill-suited or unnecessarily expensive, which could be filled by smaller and cheaper ironclads. Driven by these considerations, Britain built several 'second-class' coast-assault vessels between 1866 and 1886, and likewise constructed a number of small cruising ironclads, most of them during the late 1860s.

For second-class coast-assault vessels–the so-called coast-defence types–small size, so far from being a shortcoming, was a boon. Several arguments were advanced for their construction. From a purely naval standpoint, ships built specifically for operations in coastal waters actually fulfilled a particular want of the service–shallow-draught armoured ships. Spencer Robinson first advocated building them in 1866 on that very ground: 'there is no doubt we are deficient in a class wholly adapted for harbour and coast defence.'[44] First-class ironclads–even the coast-assault vessels –were incapable of operating in shallow coastal waters owing to their draught–typically 24ft or more. 'Coast-defence' ships generally drew about 10ft less.

An additional factor in favour of building 'coast-defence' vessels was their popularity amongst Liberal and Radical politicians like Gladstone and Richard Cobden, who maintained the Navy should be purely defensive, and who furthermore saw in such ironclads an inexpensive alternative to both seagoing vessels (with their offensive capabilities), and to expensive land fortification projects. Nor were Liberals and Radicals alone in their advocacy of coast defence. In 1862, Conservative M.P. Sir Frederic Smith, alluding to

the *Monitor-Virginia* engagement, asked the House of Commons '[w]hat danger would there be of a foreign fleet anchoring in the Solent if they had a fleet of twenty or thirty Ericsson *Monitors* in Portsmouth harbour, which could be constructed at one-tenth the cost of the forts?'[45] Later in the session, Bernal Osborne brought forward and Sir Morton Peto (Radicals both) seconded a resolution calling for the suspension of work on the forts.[46] Six harbour-defence ironclads would, claimed the latter, 'offer more effectual defence than the construction of any of the permanent forts'.[47] In 1868 another Radical, Charles Seely, moved a resolution calling for the appointment of a committee to consider designs of future ships. He pointed out that the government planned to spend £700,000 building ironclads that year and wanted to know;

> why such haste to build ships of doubtful utility, when we had resolved on non-intervention, and were in no fear of attack? Why, then, not take breathing time? He asked the Admiralty to pause before spending vast sums of money on ships which after all might prove utter failures.[48]

'But,' continued Seely, 'if they were resolved to build, let them at least build ships respecting which there was no controversy.' He

HMS *Hero* (launched 1885) and other heavily armed and armoured shallow-draft warships were designed, in the words of Robert Spencer Robinson, to attack small enemy ports 'not assailable by large ships'. (U.S. Naval Historical Center: NH88844)

meant 'coast-defence' ships: '[i]t would be far better to spend in protecting our coasts and harbours than in increasing the number of our cruising vessels.'[49]

Just as well for the consciences of economic Radicals who so enthusiastically advocated building 'coast-defence' ironclads, the Admiralty did not publicise the primary, unmistakably offensive role for small, shallow-draught ironclads. Yet there can be no doubt that they were crucial for the implementation of the Navy's coast-assault strategy, to operate in tandem with the first-class breastwork monitors, the latter advancing in the main channel, the former covering the shallows to ensure that no enemy ships escaped, or employed alone in attacks on shallow-water ports.[50] In pressing for construction of such vessels in 1866, Spencer Robinson described the design as 'being intended either for coast defences, or the attack of shipping in an enemy harbour'.[51] Several years later, in testifying to the Admiralty's Committee on Designs of Recent Ships of War, he unequivocally stated that the *Glatton* was designed specifically 'for attack of first-class ports and fortresses', and the *Cyclops* class 'for defending harbours and attacking shallow-water ports not assailable by the larger ships'.[52] Of especial concern in the minds of naval men was the need to have coast-assault ironclads capable of operating safely in the Baltic in the event of war with Russia. In 1873 D.N.O. Sir Arthur Hood sent a memorandum to First Naval Lord Milne warning that if the Navy faced hostilities with Russia at that instant operations in the Baltic would be virtually impossible. 'We are utterly deficient in the class of vessels for service in those waters,' he informed his superior; 'such vessels should not exceed a draught of 16 feet.'[53] The need for shallow-draft ironclads had been rendered more acute, so it seemed to Navy men, by the example of the French Fleet in the Franco-German War. It had been dispatched to the North Sea to conduct offensive operations against the German coast, only to find that it lacked vessels capable of inshore work. Consequently the fleet had to content itself with instituting a blockade, which, although cutting off sea traffic to and from Germany, did nothing to redeem the French war effort.

Last but not least among the arguments for building coast-defence ironclads was the matter of cost. Small armoured ships could be built for less than their first-class counterparts, a fact lost neither on economy-minded M.P.s nor Admiralty administrators agitating for more ships. In 1871, Thomas Brassey argued suspending *Devastation*'s construction could 'provide, by the end of three years, without any addition to the present Vote for shipbuilding, 36 vessels of a [monitor] type admirably adapted for coast defence.'[54] Spencer Robinson, urging the construction of four small coast-defence ironclads in 1870 as a response to the war on the Continent, stressed they would cost only £115,000 each, for a total of £460,000, whereas building two new seagoing ironclads would run £589,000 and, of course, 'we should get four ships instead of two'.[55]

Hence, the need both for 'coast-defence' vessels to defend home waters and for shallow-draught ironclads to carry out offensive operations in confined waters overseas–needs which could be neatly met by building a single type of vessel–plus the desire to stretch the construction budget as far as possible, prompted the Admiralty to turn its attention to the construction of small, low-freeboard, shallow-draught ironclads, usually along monitor lines. Between 1866 and 1880 eleven small and two considerably larger ships ostensibly intended for coast or home defence were laid down and another two were purchased during the 'war-scare' in early 1878. These fifteen ironclads amounted to more than a third of the thirty-nine armoured ships commenced or bought during the period.

In retrospect, the blessings accruing from the policy were mixed. The coast defence vessels would have been quite adequate for protecting harbours, but the freeboard of many was so low that proceeding from one port to another was attended with risk, even danger. In assessing the seaworthiness of one such ship, HMS *Glatton*, in late 1871, Controller Robert Hall and First Naval Lord Sir Sydney Dacres criticised the design's shortcomings. 'The calculations of the Constructors,' Hall wrote, 'show that this ship will not be fit for general service at sea and that she is only safe for passages from Port to Port in favourable weather. She is not fit for trial at sea. . . . '.[56] Dacres was even more critical.

> This report nearly confines the services of the *Glatton* to the Defence of our harbours . . . for favourable weather is far too uncertain in this latitude for any one to risk a fatal accident by ordering the ship from port to port unless under convoy during summer or to meet emergency in that when all risk must be run . . . The ship only half meets the purposes for which she was ordered for she could hardly be trusted across the Channel to attack an Enemy's port–much less venture to the Baltic.[57]

Yet not all 'coast-defence' vessels were as vulnerable as *Glatton*, and not all appraisers as pessimistic as Dacres. Shortly after his appointment as First Lord, and obviously unversed in the business of his department, George J. Goschen observed 'he sees it constantly assumed that foreign monitors can make ocean voyages to attack us, but that our turret ships and monitors are fit only for coast defence . . .'. Not surprisingly, he wanted 'to know if this were really so'. Barnaby's response was carefully worded: 'while it is prudent to assume that foreign monitors which can, at a certain risk, cross the ocean may do so, it would not be wise to claim for the English vessels, designed exclusively for coast defence, that they are suitable for ocean service.'[58] 'But,' he continued, 'it may be taken for granted, that if the services of the coast defence vessels, even in their present condition,' without temporary superstructures installed to improve their seaworthiness, 'were required on the other side of the English Channel, of the North Sea, or of the

Bay of Biscay in a time of war, they would be got there.'[59] In short, the coast-assault vessels could have played the role assigned to them in the Admiralty's strategic plans.[60]

Second-class cruising ironclads were, at least until the early 1870s, similarly utilitarian, effectively filling a niche more economically than could first-class vessels. Goschen spelt out the rationale for such ships in April 1873. 'It would be a wrong policy,' he avowed,

> to build ideal ships of enormous strength and cost if other countries were building vessels so inferior that we could meet them with ships very short of the ideal. The commonsense view to take was this. What was the service which our ironclad ships would have to perform, and what was the class of ships they would have to encounter?[61]

Ironclad ships on distant stations generally undertook the same duties as the 'peacetime navy', albeit in places, such as North America, the Pacific and China, where foreign powers maintained armoured ships. They were unlikely to encounter first-class vessels. Instead, they would probably be facing ships such as the French *Alma* class, which, in Goschen's words, 'were small and not very

powerful ships, but they were useful and efficient'.[62] Moreover, on distant stations modest size could itself be a virtue, as well as a means to economy. It was extremely desirable, Goschen added, 'that there should be some small ironclads capable of going through the Suez Canal and into ports and regions where ships of heavy draft could not go.'

Second-class seagoing ironclads were a class of vessel in which sail power was a requisite, rather than a luxury or an adjunct. The successful-second class ironclad was, therefore, of moderate size, with guns and armour commensurate to the scale of the ship, and carried a good spread of canvas to enable it to cover the vast expanses of the Pacific or the North Atlantic. They carried no more than 8-10ins of armour, and in many places considerably less, and 18- to 25-ton ordnance. The Conservative Board laid down six such vessels in 1867 and 1868, and a further three were constructed during the 1870s.[63] The first six, as it turned out, were capable of fulfilling roles beyond those for which they had been designed. These *Audacious* and *Swiftsure* class vessels were virtually as large as the first-generation first-class French ironclads and were more heavily armoured. Moreover, they had iron hulls, internally subdivided into watertight compartments. They were, in other words, superior to most of the French battlefleet, and ended up

---

49. Ibid. The cry in favour of building coast defence ships also rang loud in Parliament in the early 1870s, triggered by alarm over the Franco-German War, and the British Government's decision to build four small monitors in response. See *Hansard*, 3d ser., 205 (1871), cols. 663-80. The occasion was a resolution by Conservative M.P. and shipowner Samuel Robert Graves, stating that 'in the opinion of this House, it is desirable to make additional provision for the defence of the Commercial Harbours of this Country, by building, without delay, gun vessels of a light draught, armed with heavy guns, which may, in case of emergency, be manned by any existing local or other force.'(col. 671) See especially the comments of Graves (cols. 663-68), Brassey (cols. 668-71), Liddell (col. 676), Laird (col. 677), and Eastwick (cols. 677-80). Brassey, in particular, stated that '[h]e should be sorry to advocate increased expenditure, and he would suggest that we ought to substitute for the costly vessels of deep draught now in contemplation vessels of more moderate cost and lesser size, and better adapted to the defence of our coasts'(col. 669). He envisioned, by re-appropriating shipbuilding moneys in this manner, building a coast defence fleet of no less than thirty-six monitors and 100 iron gunboats within three years, at no more cost than current spending. Construction on the proto-battleship *Devastation* would, in this scenario, be suspended.

50. I am indebted to Dr. Andrew Lambert for pointing out this tactical scenario.

51. Augmentation of the Naval Force, in Ships and Stores (Copy), 9 August 1870, PRO: ADM1/6159.

52. 'Report of the Committee appointed by the Lords Commissioners of the Admiralty to examine the Designs upon which Ships of War have recently been constructed, with Analysis of Evidence', *Parl. Papers*, 1872, Vol. 14, pp351, 355.

53. Hood to Milne, 5 February, 1873 Milne Papers, NMM: MLN/144/1/3. Hood was undoubtedly exaggerating British weakness on this score. There were actually several vessels of the type available, most notably the four ships of the *Cyclops* class which had been laid down in 1870. Although none of them had been technically completed at this point, all were capable of being quickly made ready for active service.

54. *Hansard*, 3d ser., 205 (1871), col. 670.

55. Augmentation of the Naval Force in Ships and Stores (Copy), 9 August 1870, PRO: ADM1/6159.

56. Minute by Hall, 13 October 1871, NMM: ADM138/64.

57. Remarks of Dacres, 12 December 1871, ibid. The choice of name for *Glatton*

occasioned one of the few humorous exchanges in the Commons' naval debates, when, in May 1868, M.P. Captain MacKinnon referred to the ship as the '*Glutton*'. In response First Lord Henry Corry 'said that he might venture to avail himself of this opportunity to make an explanation with reference to the name of one of the vessels which, as it stood in the Question of the hon. and gallant Member, was not very creditable to the good taste of the Admiralty in naval nomenclature. They might hope that if the ship in question should ever be engaged with an enemy she would prove a '*Glutton*' in the metaphorical sense of the word; but, in fact, her name was not the '*Glutton*,' but the *Glatton*.' (*Hansard*, 3d ser., 192 [1868], cols. 651-52.)

58. Remarks of Barnaby on Captain Goodenough's Reports on the Russian Navy, 30 October 1871, PRO: ADM1/6198.

59. The reference to 'their present condition' alludes to a recommendation made by the Committee on Designs that some of these ships be fitted with additional temporary superstructures to increase their freeboard and render them more seaworthy for ocean voyages.

60. Stanley Sandler surveys the 'coast defence' policy in 'The Royal Navy's Coastal Craze: Technological Results of Strategic Confusion in the Early Ironclad Era', *American Neptune* 51/3 (1991), pp165-72, yet almost completely ignores the offensive dimension despite citing explicit evidence of it. He quotes Palmerston, for instance, to the effect that the ships were 'for defence of coasts and harbours [and] for attacking forts, or invading squadrons'.

61. *Hansard*, 3d ser., 218 (1873), col. 53.

62. Ibid., col. 56. See also his comments on the design of the *Shannon*, NMM: ADM138/43, fols. 20-1. Noting '[i]t would be a waste of power (even if it were possible) to send ships of the class of the . . . to look after ships of the *Alma* class' [small French ironclads], Goschen concluded '[t]hese & similar considerations have weighed for some time so strongly with me, that I have urged in concert with the Senior Naval Lord [Milne] very strongly on the Controller & the Chief Naval Architect the propriety of preparing designs for a second class ironclad of moderate dimensions & light draft of water, ships which should be more than a match for the second class ironclad [*sic*] of foreign powers, but of a character which could be multiplied in a shorter time & at less cost than first class ironclads.'

63. One of the latter was not completed until 1882.

providing valuable service on stations much closer to home than China or the Pacific, forming a significant portion of British armoured strength in the Mediterranean and the Channel throughout the 1870s, although the Navy persisted in labelling them 'second-class' ships.[64]

DESIGN MODIFICATION

The cost-containment policy most visible to contemporaries was modifying vessels during their construction, in order to upgrade weapons, machinery, or protection. By staving off obsolescence, albeit temporarily, the number of replacement vessels needed to uphold Britain's naval position would be reduced. In practice, however, the policy was an across-the-board failure. First, vessels so treated invariably suffered from cost overruns, which partially undermined the fiscal rationale. Barnaby's original estimate for *Ajax* and *Agamemnon*, for instance, calculated cost at £420,000 per ship. *Ajax* ultimately cost £548,393, *Agamemnon* £530,015.[65] *Inflexible*, originally pegged at about £500,000, ultimately cost £812,485.[66] Cost overrun was only one among several drawbacks, however. More seriously, as far as British naval strength was concerned, design modification often caused increased weight and reduced performance, usually the consequence of fitting a ship with larger guns or heavier armour and machinery than originally designed. *Inflexible*'s original specifications called for 60-ton guns. As constructed the ship carried 81-ton guns, and drew a foot more water than planned.[67] *Imperiuse* and *Warspite*, two armoured cruisers laid down in 1881, furnished further examples of the pitfalls of design modification. Owing to increases of weight caused by enlarging the coal bunkerage and adding heavier guns while under construction, the armour belt designed to protect the waterline was, 'with a full complement of fuel aboard . . . practically submerged . . .'.[68]

In addition to higher cost and diminished performance, a third major consequence of modifying designs was construction delays. *Ajax* and *Agamemnon* were authorised by the Admiralty in late 1875 and laid down the following spring. During the course of construction they were subjected to no less than seven major alterations which interrupted progress on them.[69] On 14 September

1878, for instance, the Dockyards were 'informed that [the] question of alteration of armament was under consideration & that progress of Turrets and deck over citadel was to be stopped.' Similarly, the decision in 1881 to enlarge the charges used in the ships' heavy guns 'necessitated partial reconstruction of the magazines'. Alterations, delays, and stoppages meant that the pair were not completed until early 1883, having been almost eight years in construction. This pace was not extraordinary for British capital ships in the late 1870s and early 1880s.

Some contemporaries realised the futility of the policy. In 1878 Thomas Brassey levelled a biting critique at the practice of design modification:

> Continued alterations in ships in construction in the vain hope of bringing the designs of past years to the level of the latest ideas in a time of rapid transition, have contributed with other causes to that delay in the production of fighting ships which . . . is so exceedingly unsatisfactory to the British taxpayer.[70]

But the temptation to 'bring the designs of past years' up to date proved impossible for the Admiralty to resist, and this policy, like that of circumscribing the size of the Navy's ships, was a significant contributor to the drawbacks displayed by many of the resulting ships of war.

The Tactical Morass

Although in broad terms the mid-Victorian battlefleet consisted of only two basic vessel types, divided between first- and second-class vessels, given the diversity of detail – alternative gun-mounting schemes, hull-layouts, and armour arrangements – it is often difficult to appreciate overarching classifications. This diversity was the direct consequence of technological developments coupled with tactical bewilderment. Accumulated centuries of tactical experience under sail went by the board when the fruits of industrialisation were applied to warship designs in the middle of the nineteenth century.[71] The advent of steam, first of all, meant that ships were no longer at the mercy of the wind. A squadron of steamships,

64. Sandler, *Emergence of the Modern Capital Ship*, p164. They were of decreasing utility as the 1870s progressed as other powers, in particular Russia, turned to building cruisers with greater speed and far larger coal capacity. They were very much inferior to the British ironclads on the counts of armour and guns, but could easily stay out of harm's way thanks to their superiority in other respects. See N.A.M. Rodger, 'British Belted Cruisers', *Mariner's Mirror* 64/1 (1978), pp23-8.

65. Ship's Cover for HMS *Ajax* and *Agamemnon*, [1875], NMM: ADM138/60, fol. 51; Parkes, *British Battleships*, p262.

66. Parkes, *British Battleships*, p252.

67. Ibid, p252.

68. Ibid, p311.

69. *Ajax* and *Agamemnon*, major alterations affecting the rate of Construction, 20 January

1879, NMM: ADM138/60, no fol.

70. *The Times*, 12 January 1878, p6.

71. Sandler, *Emergence of the Modern Capital Ship*, pp118-55. Sandler devotes an entire chapter to a comprehensive treatment of naval tactics and ramming, which is recommended to those who wish to learn more about the subject.

72. Parkes, *British Battleships*, p252. Among prominent adherents of the gun were Arthur Hood and Henry Boys.

73. Boys' Minute, 17 January 1876, S.1320/1878, 'Reports and Correspondence relative to the design of the Torpedo Ram (now *Polyphemus*) to be built at Chatham Dockyard,' NMM: ADM138/66, no fol.

74. Neither ship was able to damage the other significantly. On a strategic level it was a Union victory, since it stymied the Confederate attempt to raise the blockade.

therefore, did not have some sort of tactical unity imposed upon them by shared reliance on the same source of motive power, as had fleets in the days of sail. The appearance of the turret and box-battery designs meant that ships were no longer subject to unanswered fire when steaming bows-on at an enemy ship.

Concurrently, armour, along with the problems which plagued the Woolwich muzzleloaders, gave rise to a widespread loss of regard for guns, the traditional weapon of the sailing ship era. The guns of the era fired slowly and their rate of fire, coupled with the likelihood that armour would stop many, if not all projectiles, suggested ordnance would be of limited value in future naval warfare. Even prior to the advent of armour, guns had not by themselves ordinarily caused the destruction of wooden ships unless they happened to catch fire as well. More often they surrendered or were taken by boarding, albeit after having been pounded by gunfire. Armour made it appear unlikely that the situation would change, although the ever-more powerful guns of the period attest to the fascination of ordnance exponents – and there were several even at the height of the ramming craze – with delivering a single 'knock-out' blow which would render an enemy *hors de combat*.[72]

Considered solely in terms of muzzle velocity, the Navy's guns of the 1870s were extremely powerful. Throughout the period the service possessed pieces of sufficient 'battering' strength to have caused grave damage to all except the most heavily armoured ships. True, the stubby Woolwich muzzleloaders were not particularly distinguished for their accuracy, but it, to say nothing of their range and power, far exceeded that of their smoothbore predecessors. 'I believe the power and accuracy of our artillery is much underestimated by the strong advocates of the ram,' wrote Henry Boys in February 1876, adding that even arch-rammer Sir George Sartorius 'would hesitate before entirely ignoring it if he had witnessed the rapidity and accuracy of fire which are now attained in some of our best ships while going at considerable speed.'[73] The bombardment of Alexandria suggests the damage that could be done by them. Of course, practice against an enemy ship under way would doubtless have been less impressive, and it is perhaps scarcely surprising that naval officers and theoreticians in search of that 'knock-out' blow cast about for other, more effective, offensive weapons. Thus, the 1860s witnessed the enthusiastic revival of interest in the ancient tactic of ramming, a revival which lasted for the better part of two decades and still claimed its share of exponents as late as the early 1890s. Given the perceived shortcomings of ordnance, the ram was to many a far more potent offensive weapon and seemed destined to become the 'prominent feature of future naval victories'.

The period of unbroken general peace between 1856 and the end of the century provided few practical examples on which to base speculations about future naval warfare. The Crimean War witnessed the introduction of armoured floating batteries and mines, thus providing some pointers for future warship construc-tion and coastal assault tactics. In other respects the conflict was quite typical of previous warfare at sea, consisting largely of blockade and shore bombardment. Within the following decade, however, two naval engagements were seized upon by the tacticians of the day: the Battle of Hampton Roads (1862) during the American Civil War, and Lissa (1866), a contest between Italian and Austrian forces during the Austro-Prussian War.

Hampton Roads was a two-day action, fought on a modest scale. On the first day the Confederate ironclad *Virginia* played havoc with Union blockading forces – all wooden ships – in the roadstead, sinking the *Cumberland*, burning the *Congress*, and forcing the *Minnesota* aground. The following day witnessed the famous *Virginia-Monitor* duel: the first battle between ironclads. Despite the attention given it, the second day's battle was tactically a stand-off.[74] It convincingly demonstrated the value of armour but was

Inflexible's ram, the weapon of preference of many tactical theoreticians of the 1870s and 1880s. (U.S. Naval Historical Center: NH65956)

otherwise devoid of novelties. The first day's battle was a different affair. The *Congress* was dispatched by gunfire, with red-hot shot heated in the *Virginia*'s stokehold. The *Cumberland* was sunk by ramming, victim of the Confederate vessel's iron beak. In the wake of the battle the tactics of ramming, dormant since the days of the galley, began to attract notice.[75]

The Battle of Lissa, in the Adriatic Sea four years later, strengthened ramming sentiment. During this small-scale fleet action, the Italian ironclad *Re d'Italia* was rammed and sunk by Austria's *Erzherzog Ferdinand Max*. The contest transformed interest in ramming into a craze. By 1870 most British naval officers who recorded their opinions on the subject thought the ram a potent offensive weapon: many argued it would supersede guns as the principal means of attack. Gerard Noel entered the Royal United Services Institution essay contest in 1874 with an effort entitled 'The Gun, Ram and Torpedo', in which he boldly maintained '[i]n a general action I do not hold that the guns will be the principal weapon'.[76]

Another ram, this being HMS *Howe*'s. All British capital ships up to the *Dreadnought* in 1906 were built with ram bows. (U.S. Naval Historical Center: NH75916)

Instead, wrote Noel, 'there can be little doubt of the prominent part that "Rams" will play in the next naval battle.'[77] The contest's judges agreed to the point of awarding him the prize. Testifying to the Committee on Designs, Captain L.G. Heath stated '[u]nder any circumstances, I think Nelson's maxim, slightly modified, should be instilled into the minds of all officers in command – "no captain can do very wrong who succeeds in ramming an enemy's ship".'[78] Captain William Armytage declined to invoke the memory of Nelson, but was no less emphatic: 'I consider ramming of the utmost importance. No captain should lose an opportunity of using the stem against an opponent.'[79] Even Philip Colomb, among the era's most thoughtful tacticians, opined in 1868 'I have no doubt whatever in my own mind that the "ram" is to be the weapon of the future for naval attack and defence.'[80]

More importantly, ramming attracted enthusiastic adherents in the Controller's Department. Though an early doubter, Reed was by 1870 convinced of its efficacy: 'it is the ram – and with it the sea torpedo – that will henceforth work the greatest destruction in a naval action.'[81] Controller Spencer Robinson was more ambivalent, but while urging the acceptance of the *Devastation* design in early 1869, he set forth the crucial qualities for ships of the battlefleet: 'the means of carrying and defending a formidable artillery, combined with the greatest facility in making use of the power of impact . . .'.[82] Reed's successor, Barnaby, was also initially a staunch proponent of the ram, proudly recalling in 1902 that one of his 'greatest personal efforts was to endeavour to get the ram recognized as a proper weapon of war and to secure its introduction into every ship of war.'[83]

From the start there were also doubters. Curiously, the *Times* expressed reservations in 1870:

> if the ship attacked has the same or nearly the same speed of the attacking ship, and is equally handy and equally well handled, it can always elude or reduce to insignificance the assault of the Ram. Any one who has seen a race on the Cam will understand at once how easily with plenty of sea room the charge of the enemy's ram could be avoided.[84]

The lesson of Lissa was not that ramming was an effective method of attack. Instead, the 'battle only proves that now, as in former times, good seamanship is required to do justice to the fighting qualities of any fleet. If the Italian fleet had been better handled, the *Ferdinand Max* of the Austrian Squadron would never have rammed the *Re d'Italia*'.

Another sceptic was First Lord of the Admiralty the Duke of Somerset who, immediately following Hampton Roads, acknowledged the *Virginia* had dispatched the *Cumberland* with its prow, but added 'it would not be so easy to run down a steamer in motion, which would be able to avoid a collision'.[85]

The officer corps also contained a few doubters before 1880, although very few indeed earlier than 1870. In 1873 Commander W.B. Hardy noted 'although both sides made continual, desperate attempts to ram' at Lissa, only one blow actually went home.[86] Hence, concluded Hardy, the battle, 'which is so often quoted by the advocates of the ram as an instance of its success, is, on the contrary, the best illustration of its possible failure'. Another sceptic, one near the top of the officer list, was Admiral Frederick Warden, who by 1868 had come to a conclusion similar to the *Times*'. 'It is as clear as anything can be,' he stated,

> that so long as a ship has good way [speed] on her, and a good command of steam to increase her speed at pleasure, that ship cannot be what is called 'rammed'; she cannot even be struck to any purpose so long as she has room and is properly handled.[87]

Until the 1880s, however, the few doubting voices were drowned out in an enthusiastic din extolling the potency of the new/old weapon.

The use of the ram, of course, signalled the end of the sacrosanct line-ahead formation. A concerted ramming attack could not be made in a single column. In addition, line ahead was itself highly vulnerable to a ramming attack. So tactical thought therefore centred on line-abreast, angular, and indented formations, the latter two placing the ships *en echelon*. Equally evident, the abandonment of line ahead furnished a further reason for the demise of the broadside ship, with its concentration of guns on the beam. The ordnance of the day certainly had its limitations, but few (Sartorius was one) argued that the gun was entirely *passé*, and gunfire might still play an important supporting role in a ramming attack by confusing or distracting the attention of an enemy captain. This could not be done to any effective degree by a broadside

ship, and thus provided an impetus for the development of 'box-battery' and turret designs.

In no other instance was the confusion wrought by technological change more evident. The advent of armour, coupled with the shortcomings of the service's heavy ordnance, suggested the gun had lost its primacy at sea. The realisation left tacticians adrift. Into the tactical vacuum came the lessons of Hampton Roads and Lissa. At best they were ambiguous lessons, but they seemed better than nothing at all. And with no practical, inexpensive, and safe way to test the feasibility of ramming (Russia conducted experiments with gunboats, but they did not reflect likely combat circumstances), the difficulties and dangers could not be easily revealed. Ramming tactics remained largely theoretical. Men like Admirals George Elliot and Sartorius worked out elaborate schemes and tactical diagrams to utilise the ram, but they were never tested. On paper ramming looked feasible, but naval battles are not fought on paper. Even ships of moderate dimensions could not turn in an instant to strike an enemy ship nor stop instantaneously to avoid hitting a friend. In time such impossibilities would become all too apparent.

The officers, administrators, and designers of the late 1860s and 1870s were not blessed with foresight, however, and the tactical tangle created by the competing, sometimes conflicting, theories and claims put forward by the advocates of one or another of the means of attack exercised a large, none-too-beneficial, influence on the Admiralty's design policy from 1870 onwards. In 1877, without a trace of irony, Barnaby acknowledged an 'absence of any authoritative tactical system', and this profoundly confused situation inevitably had serious ramifications for warship design.[88] The Admiralty often fell victim to divided counsels during the 1870s, and when it did not, there remained no guarantee that the consensus reached produced a satisfactory design.

---

75. Sandler, *Emergence of the Modern Capital Ship*, pp130-1. Sandler points out that revived interest in the ram actually predated the Battle of Hampton Roads. In Britain both Admiral George Sartorius and Douglas Campbell proposed the construction of steam rams during the 1850s, and in Russia Admiral Gregori Boutakov began a theoretical investigation of ramming tactics late in the same decade. But the wholesale reawakening, it is safe to say, took place only after 1862.

76. Gerard Noel, *The Gun, Ram, and Torpedo* (London, 1874), p5. Originally an essay, Noel's work was subsequently published in book form.

77. Ibid, p74.

78. Heath to Committee on Designs, 14 April 1871, Hornby Papers, NMM: PHI110/2. Nelson's maxim had originally run 'no captain can do very wrong who places himself alongside an enemy'.

79. Armytage to Committee on Designs, 10 April 1871, ibid.

80. E.A. Inglefield, 'Naval Tactics, with some Remarks on the Recent Experimental Cruising of the Mediterranean Squadron', *Journal of the Royal United Services Institution* 12 (1868), p498. Colomb's remarks were made in the course of the discussion which followed the paper. These are by no means the only examples from which to choose. Pownall Pellew called rams 'the arm of naval warfare to which I attach the chief importance.' (Pownall Pellew, 'Fleet Maneuvering,' *Journal of the Royal United Services Institution* 11 [1867], p538. A Captain Dawson stated '[u]nder many conditions of battle, as ships are at present equipped, the stem, whether employed to run into high-sided, or to run

over low free-board vessels, would occupy the foremost position' (quoted in Noel, *Gun, Ram, and Torpedo*, p75). In 1884 Admiral George Elliot delivered a paper to the Royal United Services Institution entitled 'The Ram – The Prominent Feature of Future Naval Victories.' (*Journal of the Royal United Services Institution* 28 [1884], p357.) Added to these examples were similar pronouncements from Admirals George Sartorius, A.P. Ryder, and George Randolph, Captain Vanisttart, and naval architect John Scott Russell, who went so far as to publish an imagined account of a ramming duel (Scott Russell quoted in Thomas Brassey, *The British Navy: Its Strengths, Resources, and Administration* [London, 1882], Vol. 3, pp68-9).

81. Reed to the *Times*, 8 August 1870, p10; Sandler, *Emergence of the Modern Capital Ship*, pp141-2. Sandler notes that in 1863 Reed had maintained that 'the wholesale destruction of ships by ramming them will never be a favourite system of warfare among European navies . . .'.

82. Robinson to Admiralty (Copy), 3 February 1869 PRO: ADM1/6138.

83. Barnaby, *Naval Development in the Century*, p163.

84. *The Times*, 1 August 1870, p9.

85. *Hansard*, 3d ser., 166 (1862), cols. 440-41.

86. Quoted in Sandler, *Emergence of the Modern Capital Ship*, pp150-1.

87. Quoted in Brassey, *British Navy*, Vol. 3, p430.

88. Barnaby to Houston Stewart, 8 January 1876, ADM138/66.

Chapter 6

DESIGN BY COMMITTEE

'The activity of modern invention, and the constant competition between the makers of the weapon and the makers of the armour, have kept the Admiralties of Europe in the same perplexed and tormented condition as that inflicted by a tyrannical dictator of fashion upon the gilded youths in one of Mr. Disraeli's earlier novels, who never know whether they may not have to effect an entire change of costume before noon.'

The Daily News, 27 February 1873

'[A]t this moment those who are charged with the important duty of providing this country with a sufficient and an adequate naval force, are so entirely at sea as to what is the right style of ship to construct, that they are meditating appealing from their professional advisers to a Royal Commission, well or ill constituted . . .'

Robert Spencer Robinson to the Institute of Naval Architects, 1876

THE MULTIPLICITY of design details which gave rise to the 'fleet of samples' during the 1870s and 1880s was due largely to tactical and technological considerations. The Admiralty generally had a good conception of the strategic roles of the ships it built, but beyond clear strategic intent there was often little consensus between the members of the Board, the D.N.O., the Controller, and the D.N.C. as to the ideal features of a particular design. Moreover, although the dichotomy between coast-assault and cruising vessels was preserved up to the *Alexandra* and *Temeraire* (both commenced 1873), after those two designs no further masted first-class cruising ironclads were laid down, a testimony to contemporary realisation of their limited fighting power. But from that point onward, policy makers were tempted, sometimes irresistibly, to improve the high-seas capabilities of what were essentially coast-assault vessels. Simultaneously, designers and administrators were continually tempted to get the most 'bang for the pound' by grafting first-class fighting capabilities onto second-class displacement.

Until 1869 all of the Navy's first-class ironclads were cruising vessels, fitted with three, and sometimes four, masts and square-rigged. *Devastation* thus marked the emergence of the cruising/coast-assault dichotomy as it pertained to first-class vessels. By this point cruising vessels were clearly divided between first- and second-class types, and although the first-class coast-assault vessel appeared only with *Devastation* and its sister *Thunderer*, the Admiralty had been building second-class 'coast-defence' ironclads since the early 1860s. Indeed, *Devastation* itself was an enlarged version of the 'coast-defence' breastwork monitor *Cerberus*, whose construction marked 'the beginnings of practical turret ship design in Britain'.[1]

The Admiralty's Committee on Designs of Ships of War (1871) subsequently recommended that the Navy abandon building cruising vessels and concentrate on the mastless breastwork monitor type, touted as representing 'in its broad features the first-class fighting ship of the immediate future', and indeed the disposition was repeated in *Dreadnought*, designed and begun in 1870, but substantially redesigned in 1871-2 following the Committee's recom-

mendations.[2] Even at the latter point, however, the prototype breastwork monitor had yet to be tested at sea. When it was, the following year, widespread contemporary misgivings about *Devastation*'s seaworthiness were quickly proved groundless. Battleworthiness was another matter, though. *Devastation*'s minimal freeboard – 8½ft forward, 4ft aft – posed no danger of another disaster as had befallen HMS *Captain*, owing to lack of masts and sails but it markedly impaired fighting efficiency. Alexander Milne's 'grave doubts' as to the ability of the ship to use its guns in any circumstances other than 'moderately smooth waters' were borne out by its trials.[3] The report of one cruise in moderate conditions noted '[a]s the seas met the ship they rose at the stem, forming occasionally a wall-like heap of water to a height of 6 or 8 feet up the graduations at the jackstaff. The heap then broke as a wave and fell on the forward deck covering it to an average depth of 6 to 10 inches.'[4] With the main battery a mere 12ft above the water, the ship's gunners could not aim their weapons in even a gentle Atlantic swell. Moreover, the low bow greatly impeded steaming into a head sea, and allowed copious quantities of water into the quarters below. Hence the breastwork monitors, although designed to carry 'sufficient fuel for a passage to America' were 'limited to Home waters and the Mediterranean', the theatres for which, as Edward Reed stated, they had been designed.[5] The *Devastation* fulfilled service requirements as far as fighting efficiency went, but only in Europe's relatively sheltered waters. Moreover, it lacked the operational range requisite for service beyond that theatre. The same was true of its half-sister, *Dreadnought*, which, as Nathaniel Barnaby noted in 1872, following the vessel's redesign, represented 'as efficient an engine of war for naval actions in the Channel, Mediterranean, and Black Seas, as can be contrived in the present state of our knowledge'.[6]

Under the circumstances, George J. Goschen's decision to defy the Committee of Design's recommendation and build *Alexandra* and *Temeraire* with high freeboard and full sailing rig was more logical than first appears. World-wide strategic reach was beyond the capabilities of wholly steam vessels for at least another decade. Moreover, as Goschen noted in Parliament, other powers – most

The quintessential first-class cruising ironclad with masts and sails, *Temeraire* (launched 1876) was authorised by G.J. Goschen's Board despite the Committee on Designs' recommendation that the Navy cease building such vessels. (U.S. Naval Historical Center: NH75995)

notably France and Prussia—were still building cruising ironclads; to ensure command of the sea Britain had to follow suit.[7] As of 1872, therefore, the Navy appeared reconciled, if not firmly committed, to the necessity of building two different capital ship types to fulfil the diverging strategic roles of command of the coast and command of the sea.

Within a year, however, the Admiralty confronted additional problems which further complicated the task of designing capital ships. The heaviest naval ordnance could by 1873 penetrate armour less than 24ins thick.[8] *Alexandra* carried a maximum of only 12ins, *Temeraire* an inch less. The weight of the sailing rig and exposed side carried by the box-battery and broadside types—necessary though they were for operating on the high-seas—precluded the possibility of carrying armour thick enough to withstand the biggest guns. This weakness was not critical to second-class cruising ironclads, which in the ordinary course of duties would not encounter front-line units, but it was of such gravity for first-class cruising ironclads that no such vessels were designed after *Alexandra* and *Temeraire*.[9] The strategic imperative impelling the

1. Chesneau and Kolesnik (eds.), *Conway's All the World's Fighting Ships, 1860-1905*, p21.

2. 'Report of the Committee appointed by the Lords Commissioners of the Admiralty to examine the Designs upon which Ships of War have recently been constructed, with Analysis of Evidence', *Parl. Papers*, 1872, Vol. 14, ppxii-xiii, xxx-xxxii.

3. Milne to Committee on Designs, 11 April 1871, Hornby Papers, PHI/110/2. For unknown reasons, possibly related to his subsequent appointment as First Naval Lord, Milne's evidence was not printed in the published Report. A printed copy can be found in Hornby's papers.

4. 'Account of Voyage of H.M.S. *Devastation*,' *Parl. Papers*, 1876, Vol. 40, p515.

5. Parkes, *British Battleships*, p201.

6. Barnaby to Houston Stewart, 26 July 1872 NMM: ADM/138/46, fol. 114.

7. *Hansard's Parliamentary Debates*, 3d ser., 210 (1872), cols. 452-53.

8. Parkes, *British Battleships*, p204.

9. Two 'cruising ironclads,' one of them a full-rigged turret ship, were purchased in 1878.

The Liberal Board justified building HMS *Alexandra* (launched 1875), despite her relatively thin armour, on the grounds that the Navy needed such ships to meet equivalent foreign vessels on the high seas. (U.S. Naval Historical Center: NH63154)

retention of masts and sails was ultimately irreconcilable with the tactical imperative of fighting efficiency.

From Devastation *to* Inflexible

Equally alarming, *Devastation* and *Thunderer*'s armour was no thicker than *Alexandra*'s, and *Dreadnought*'s only 2ins more. Again, the consequences of rapid technological change and rapid escalation of ordnance size and power created ultimately insoluble problems for naval architects and ship designers. It was clear by 1873 that the effectiveness of armoured protection was temporary, often fleetingly so. Reed, indeed, had reached this conclusion no later than 1870. 'A glance at the rapid strides which have been made in the

manufacture of heavy guns' over the past decade, he wrote in a departmental memorandum that year, 'will be a sufficient incitement to consider carefully what we are likely to reach within the next ten years.'[10]

A year after the *Devastation* was laid down–three years before her completion–her armour was already 'inadequate'. Thicker armour on subsequent ships would merely goad ordnance designers and founders to build still bigger guns, and their moment of invulnerability would likely be as short as *Devastation*'s. Not only was it clear that no warship could carry impenetrable armour; one of moderate size could not carry a complete swath much thicker than *Devastation*'s. Its low freeboard restricted the area which needed coverage, allowing Reed to provide virtually complete vertical plating between 8½ and 12ins thick, only to see its protection quickly derided as 'pie crust'.[11] *Alexandra*'s 'crust' was just as thin, of course, and did not even cover the whole pie.

The quandary was unquestionably apparent to Reed by the time the *Dreadnought* was initially laid down (1870), for among the

10. 'Papers and legends relating to Mr. Reed's plan of Central Citadel Iron-clads, delivered over to the Chief Draughtsman by Mr. John in 1872 . . . ,' nd., NMM: ADM138/49, no fol.

11. Parkes, *British Battleships*, p195. Only the forecastle lacked protection.

12. 'Papers and legends relating to Mr. Reed's plan of Central Citadel Iron-clads, deliv-

ered over to the Chief Draughtsman by Mr. John in 1872 . . . ,' nd., NMM: ADM138/49, no fol. In the second volume of *Inflexible*'s 'ship's cover', William White provides a chronological frame for this memorandum, referring to 'the papers and drawing herewith representing the work done in this office in 1868-69 on designs for Central Citadel Iron-clads on Mr. Reed's plan . . .'. See White to Barnaby, 28 August 1874, NMM: ADM138/50, no fol.

papers relative to *Inflexible*'s design is a lengthy memorandum of his, undated, but written when 8ins was the maximum armour thickness capable of being pierced.[12] 'In our latest ships,' he began, 'we have adopted 12 and 14 inches of armour plating, but it is only too probable that in the course of a very few years we shall be driven to armour even considerably thicker than above.' Hence, he maintained, the 'imperative necessity of reducing the space which it is necessary to protect with such armour must . . . be obvious.' The choice faced by the naval architect, he argued, was between protecting a ship's buoyancy and its offensive power. For Reed the answer could only be the former, and he revealed his overriding *desideratum* for warship design in proposing the optimum way in reducing the armour coverage. 'The question which will have to be solved,' he argued, 'is how to make a ship unsinkable with the least amount of armoured surface.' The answer which he sketched out may be taken as the genesis of *Inflexible*. The proposed design featured an armoured 'citadel', 'extending for a length of about 200 feet along the side, and from 6 feet below the water to 6 feet above it, and two bulkheads across the ship of the same thickness.' This citadel 'is just long enough to ensure the ship having a steady platform and being perfectly safe when the parts before and abaft this belt are perforated with shot and filled with water to a depth of 6 feet below the waterline.' Put another way, a ship so designed would have sufficient buoyancy from the 200 or so feet of the midships portion covered with armour, that even were both ends flooded it would continue to float.

To do so would require would require a much wider hull than any previous seagoing British ironclad. Reed himself acknowl-

France's continued construction of masted ironclads such as *Bayard* through the 1870s exerted strong pressure on the British to follow suit. (U.S. Naval Historical Center: NH74931)

By the time of her launch in 1875, *Dreadnought*'s armour was penetrable by current heavy ordnance, spurring naval designers to turn away from providing ships with a complete waterline belt like she had. (U.S. Naval Historical Center: NH61003)

edged that 'in order to get sufficient stability amidships with as short a length of armour as possible, it is desirable that the ship should have a good beam'. Moreover, that beam would have to be carried 'as far forward and aft as is necessary for stab[ility]'. Finally, Reed envisioned flooding the ends intentionally prior to battle, to prevent fuel stowed there from being ignited by an enemy shell, thus it was also 'desirable' that the bow and stern 'be fined away as much as possible in order to reduce the w[eight] of water to be carried there,–this also tends to reduce their resistance'. That the resulting vessel would be unprecedentedly broad and stubby was evidently of little concern to him.

Not surprisingly, the Admiralty Committee on Designs acknowledged the increasing difficulty of providing adequate protection to waterline, guns, and machinery, and endorsed Reed's solution.[13] Indeed, the Committee's Report sketched out the design of such a ship in terms which might have come from the former Chief Constructor himself, 'compris[ing] a very strongly plated central citadel', mounted on an 'unarmoured raft' subdivided into numerous watertight compartments. The Committee furthermore recommended that such a design be built for experimental purposes. And with such advice, coupled with the obvious shortcomings of the breastwork monitor type, and equally significantly, a challenge from Italy, which was constructing two very powerful ironclads on the central-citadel principle, the decision of Goschen, Milne, and the remainder of the Board to embark on the construction of *Inflexible* made considerable sense. Yet the evolution of the vessel's design was anything but straightforward, and a synopsis of it serves as a useful introduction to the 'design by committee' approach which the Admiralty used throughout the 1870s and early 1880s.

First, Reed's sketch was nothing more than a rough outline. It

13. Report of the Committee appointed by the Lords Commissioners of the Admiralty to examine the Designs upon which Ships of War have recently been constructed, with Analysis of Evidence', *Parl. Papers*, 1872, Vol. 14, px.

14. White to Barnaby, 28 August 1874, NMM: ADM138/50, no fol.

15. 'New *Fury*,' January 1873, NMM: ADM138/49, fol. 1.

16. Ibid. 'Take the *Fury* as she stands', the Constructor's instructions stated, 'and make the following changes: 1. Remove the armour, backing &c (leaving only sufficient for a thin side) from about 32 station to the stem and from about 134 station to the stern; and complete the belt protection by armoured bulkheads worked across the ship at these stations.'

17. 'S.7104/1873: From the Director of Naval Construction to the Controller, for Consideration while the Design is in progress, 3rd June 1873, Report of the Committee on the '*Inflexible*,' with Appendix, *Parl. Papers*, 1878, Vol. 14, Appendix 1, p1 (p163 in microprint ed.).

was, in the words of future D.N.C. William White, 'mainly restricted to the investigation of the forms and proportions most suitable for ships protected in the way proposed'.[14] Consequently, in examining the papers left at the Admiralty by Reed, White found 'no trace of any of the designs having been pushed beyond the preliminary stage. No internal arrangements, or stowage of hold, seemed to have been planned.' Moreover, although the basic arrangement of protection was solved by the central citadel type, Reed evidently reached no decision on disposition of the armament, and his papers sketched out a variety of options including an unprotected battery, a central-battery design in which the waterline citadel extended upwards to cover the guns, and a turret design.

We know also that the Constructor's department consulted Reed's papers when undertaking preliminary work for the design of the 'new *Fury*' (*ie Dreadnought*) which was to be laid down in the 1873 shipbuilding programme. In January of that year, before the 'new *Fury*'s' design was actually begun 'it was considered desirable to look into the heavily armoured designs prepared . . . for Mr. Reed embodying the principle of unarmoured ends'. On this foundation, the Constructor's department undertook various calculations as to 'the effect of water entering the unarmoured ends of a *Fury*-type vessel' before beginning work on the new *Fury* proper on 18 January 1873.[15] Calculations for the dimensions of the vessel were to be made on the basis of *Fury*'s hull with the armour and backing removed from the bow and stern and an armoured bulkhead across the hull at the point the midships armour ended.[16] These unarmoured ends were to carry 'patent fuel', but for the sake of calculating stability, the department was ordered to '[a]scertain how much the ship's breadth must be increased beyond the *Fury*'s in order that she may preserve the same vanish-

ing angle [of stability] as that ship (56½ degrees)', *if* the fuel in the ends had been exhausted, 'the side so damaged that water from the outside can freely take its place,' and 'the buoyancy and righting power of the superstructures are lost'. The answer was 'about 11 feet' to *Fury*'s breadth of slightly more than 63ft.

On 27 January D.N.C. Barnaby, supplied other vital statistics: a speed of 13kts and a draught of 25ft forward and 25½ft aft. The coal capacity was to be identical to *Dreadnought*'s 1200 tons. At this point the department was also working with a beam of only 70ft, mandated by the width of existing dock facilities, rather than the 74ft + which its earlier calculations had shown would be requisite to match *Fury*'s angle of vanishing stability. Not surprisingly, further calculations showed that with the 'coal out of the ends, the water flowing into the ship at these parts [*sic*] and including for purposes of stability the part of the after superstructure standing upon the protective plating of the upper deck, the ship would have a range of 50½ degrees,' or 6 degrees less than *Fury*'s.

Working within those constraints, the department set about preparing sketches and estimating weights in early May 'for a Turret ship 320 ft long and 70 ft broad, with a mean draught of 25¼ft'. By this point other features of the design had been decided upon, for Barnaby's instructions called for 24ins of armour on a 70ft long citadel, four 15in, 60-ton guns in turrets covered by 14ins of armour, a 3in horizontal armoured deck, and stowage for 1200 tons of coal. Both the armament and the armour posed confounding problems for the Constructor's department.

A month later, when the design was passed on to the Controller and D.N.O. for their comments, Barnaby addressed the armament predicament. 'In deciding upon the power of the guns,' he reminded Houston Stewart, 'it is necessary to remember that, as it will take about four years to build the ship, great advances may be made in power of naval guns by the time she is completed . . .'[17] At that point, a 15in, 60-ton gun was 'already being spoken of, both at Woolwich and Elswick, as being within the present powers of the factories; and when the gun is once constructed it is quite certain

Although a later and somewhat longer ship than *Inflexible*, *Benbow*'s breadth and stubbiness are clearly evident in this overhead shot. (U.S. Naval Historical Center: NH61511)

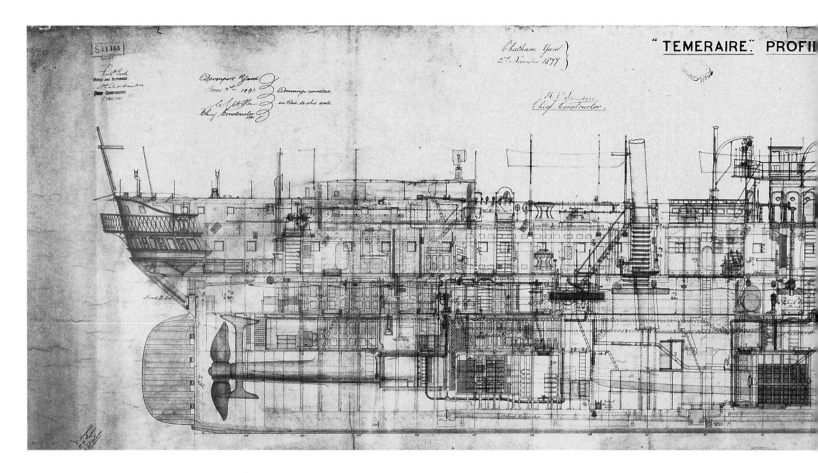

"TEMERAIRE" PROFII

Profile of HMS *Temeraire*, with *Alexandra* one of the last first-class cruising ironclads laid down by the Royal Navy. (National Maritime Museum, London: 17390)

that machinery may devised to control and work it.' The predicament arose because, as Barnaby admitted, 'a still heavier gun may be in the process of manufacture . . . before the ship is completed.'

The escalation in armament size and power had two direct consequences. First, with increase in size came the concomitant increase in weight, and if on a ship of given displacement, the guns weighed more, then weight had to be subtracted from something else, in all probability the armour. Secondly, and more critically, the bigger the gun the greater, in all likelihood, its 'smashing power', and the thicker the armour necessary to keep out its projectiles. As Reed had noted three years earlier, there was little telling how far ordnance might advance in the ensuing decade, and if armour was to keep pace, it would thicken beyond *Inflexible*'s 24ins.

But within the confines of moderate dimensions, even within the confines of the 11,000 tons the *Inflexible* was to displace, it was impossible to have it both ways: to have both the heaviest guns of the day and armour capable of resisting them. Faced with a choice between the two options, Reed no doubt would have opted for invulnerability, for an 'unsinkable' ship, even at the cost of severe-

ly reduced powers of offence. Barnaby chose the other. 'We do not consider it essential to the efficiency of the English Navy,' he informed the Controller, D.N.O., and Board, 'that it should always have ships impregnable to the heaviest existing guns . . .' On the other hand, he steadfastly maintained 'we . . . think it essential that the English ship would have guns of the most powerful description which can be made and worked, even up to hundreds of tons, if such masses of material can ever be wrought.' Hence, although '[w]e propose . . . that the new design should carry 60-ton guns,' Barnaby added that the vessel 'should be capable of receiving much heavier guns hereafter.'

The divergence in design philosophy between Barnaby and his brother-in-law is worth emphasising for the light it sheds on their respective attitudes towards the role of the Victorian battlefleet. Reed's was essentially a defensive mentality: indeed, Oscar Parkes dubs Reed's designs 'you can't sink mine and I can't sink yours' ships. Barnaby, on the other hand, was prepared to sacrifice floating power for fighting efficiency. Reed's ships were, above all, 'a fleet in being', even if their powers of commanding the seas were circumscribed; Barnaby's ships accorded far better with Nelsonian offensive traditions which were the touchstone for British naval tactics in the century following Trafalgar.

Not that the D.N.C. was prepared wholly to sacrifice defence to offence in 1873. That would come later. The 24ins of armour covering *Inflexible*'s citadel was impenetrable by any gun then existing.

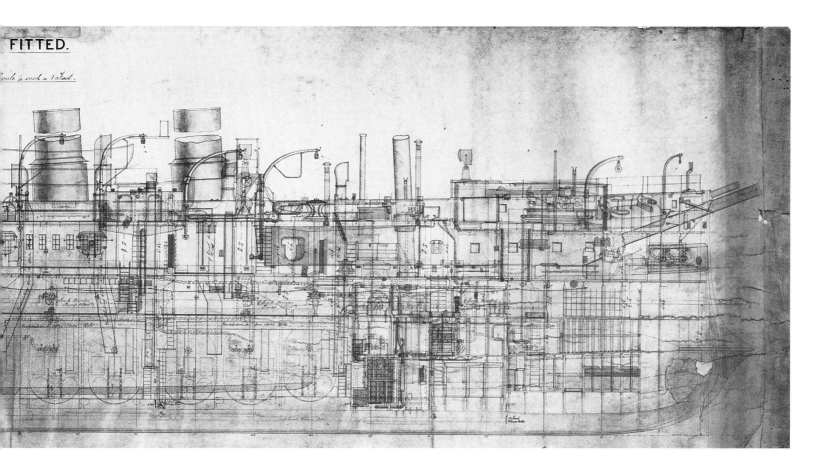

FITTED.

Moreover, the armoured deck was designed to supplement vertical protection. Since it was universally assumed that future naval battles would be close-range affairs, the trajectory of gunfire would, of course, be near-horizontal. That being the case, horizontal protection, in the form of an armoured deck, was a much more efficient (and lightweight) means of protecting buoyancy than was vertical armour, since it would be subject only to glancing blows. Under these conditions even the heaviest shells would ricochet off relatively thin armour. For the vitals of the 'new *Fury*' – the armoured midships section which contained the guns, engines, and boilers – the thickest possible vertical armour was deemed a necessity. Beyond the citadel, however, the armoured deck 'at a depth of 6ft below the waterline' was designed to protect the buoyancy of the otherwise unprotected ends, even if the hull above the deck were completely flooded, by keeping enemy fire from penetrating the lower reaches of the hull.

Barnaby's memorandum accompanying the design as forwarded to the Controller on 3 June 1873 contained a synopsis of the premises guiding the department's labours. 'In considering the matter,' he informed Houston Stewart, 'we have taken the conditions of a ship of the *Fury* type to be those laid down by Sir Spencer Robinson in February 1869, when the design of the *Devastation* and *Thunderer* was decided on . . . .'[18] The principal criteria laid down by the former Controller were, not surprisingly, 'heavy guns, thick armour, and great handiness'. Beyond those crucial features, how-

ever, were a number of others which go far in explaining the chief aims of the Admiralty in designing *Inflexible*:

> The greatest speed that could be obtained, coal enough to provided for the necessities of warfare in the Channel, Mediterranean, or Baltic, such seagoing qualities as will enable operations in those seas to be performed with safety, good arrangements for officers and men, and as little sail-power as is consistent with the use to be made of a fleet in time of peace.

In other words, the ship was unequivocally designed as a first-class vessel for service in European waters.

Yet having arrived at the overriding design features solely on the basis of fighting efficiency, the Admiralty complicated and ultimately reduced their effectiveness by simultaneously attempting to improve seaworthiness. There are explicit references in Barnaby's memorandum to envisioned service beyond European waters. He submitted a list of twelve conditions dictating the shape of the design, one of which was that it be 'capable of passing through the Suez Canal when lightened of coal' and another of which mandated the maximum beam and draught, to permit the vessel to 'enter the docks at Portsmouth, Chatham, [and] Malta', which were in

---

18. Ibid.

keeping with the intended theatre of operations, 'and the lift dock at Bombay', which unquestionably was not. Moreover, the vessel's original sketch called for '[t]wo masts to carry a moderate spread of canvas', and further evidence indicates plans, subsequently dropped, to sheath its hull with wood and copper, presumably in anticipation of its operation beyond ready access to graving docks.[19]

Who at the Admiralty in 1873 foresaw an extra-European role for *Inflexible*, and on what grounds was his or their assumption based? The surviving papers, alas, offer few clues. In the cases of the closest contemporary vessels for which unequivocal evidence remains – *Shannon* and *Temeraire* – the overall features of the designs, including gun layout in the latter instance, were clearly dictated to the Constructor's department by the Board, the D.N.O., and Controller.[20] No such evidence of Board direction exists with regard to *Inflexible*, however, and the wording of Barnaby's memorandum of 3 June hints that his office was acting on its own initiative: '[w]e [*ie* the Constructor's department] . . . lay down the following conditions for the design.' Yet there are other indications that Barnaby and his colleagues were acting on Board directives, and considerable circumstantial evidence to suggest that the decision to 'improve' the sea-keeping qualities of the design – to combine the features of coast-assault and cruising vessels – originated outside the Constructor's department. There are, in other words, grounds for informed speculation, in the absence of explicit evidence.

First, the Constructor editorialised on the requirement restricting beam and draught in a manner which suggests that it did not originate with his department:

it is to be observed that to make the ship capable of entering the Devonport, Malta [subsequently crossed out], and Bermuda Docks, it will be necessary to reduce her breadth so much as to deprive her of stability when the ends are so perforated and injured as to add nothing to it, and we do not think this sacrifice should be made.

Moreover, there is clear evidence elsewhere that Barnaby himself was no unswerving advocate of masting and rigging ironclads.

In his remarks on the Admiralty's copy of the Committee to examine the Designs upon which of Ships of War have recently been constructed, he acknowledged that sailing ironclads like *Monarch* and *Hercules* 'would be able to economise coal to a very large extent when preceding to distant stations', but added that mastless ironclads could carry 50 per cent thicker armour than a masted ship of the same displacement, required only half the crew, and suffered less wear and tear to the hull. He concluded that sailing power was 'practically unattainable' on the most powerful ironclads (undoubtedly including *Inflexible*) and that the Navy required no sailing ironclads larger than second-class vessels of the *Audacious* class.[21] Moreover, Reed's short-lived but entertaining journal, *Naval Science*, noted the Committee on Designs' recommendation 'that no more rigged first class armour-clads shall be built' was supported by the Admiralty's 'President of the Council of Construction, Mr. Barnaby', and the Admiralty's decision to ignore the Committee's advice, signalled by *Alexandra* and *Temeraire*, did 'Mr. Barnaby the more credit' as they were ships 'of which he, curiously enough, disapproves'.[22] If Barnaby's own opinions, plus those of his fellow naval architect and brother-in-law are reliable indicators, we may safely conclude that he was not the driving force behind the decision to mast *Inflexible*.

On the other hand, there were at the Admiralty at least two staunch sail advocates: First Naval Lord Milne and Controller Houston Stewart. Milne gave evidence to the Admiralty Committee on Designs in which he maintained 'the scope of Naval requirements in all parts of the world' made it impossible to design a fleet suited only for service in European waters. Hence, the Navy 'should embrace both turret and broadside [*ie* box battery] types . . .'.[23] He did not mean turret ships like *Devastation*, but rather Reed's *Monarch* and the ill-fated *Captain*, for he maintained sails were '[a] necessity for the above foregoing ships for cruising and passage purposes, and to enable ships to work to windward.' Houston Stewart, a member of the Committee on Designs, dissented from the majority recommendation that no more first-class sailing ironclads be built. He, the D.N.O. Arthur Hood, and Dr. Joseph Woolley argued 'it will always be necessary that this country should possess very powerful iron-clad ships with a sufficient amount of sail power', since 'these types would in time of war be of very great value, especially in distant seas, where there would probably be great difficulty in sending more heavily armed mastless ves-

19. Ibid.; '*Inflexible*,' 7 May 1873, NMM: ADM138/49, fol. 7.

20. See Chapter 10.

21. S.9847; Barnaby's comments on the *Report of the Committee appointed by the Lords Commissioners of the Admiralty to examine the Designs upon which Ships of War have recently been constructed, with Analysis of Evidence*, 26 July 1871 PRO: ADM1/6212.

22. [Edward Reed], 'The Late Admiralty Committee on Designs', *Naval Science: A Quarterly Magazine for Promoting the Improvement of Naval Architecture, Marine Engineering, Steam Navigation, and Seamanship* 1 (1872), p305.

23. Milne to Committee on Designs, 11 April 1871, Hornby Papers, NMM: PHI/110/2.

24. 'Report of the Committee appointed by the Lords Commissioners of the Admiralty to examine the Designs upon which Ships of War have recently been constructed, with Analysis of Evidence,' *Parl. Papers*, 1872, Vol. 14, pxiv.

25. Memo by Milne 'New Class of Ship to be laid down to add to the Iron clad Fleet', March 1875 PRO: MLN/144/5 [2].

26. 'Report of the Committee on the '*Inflexible*,' with Appendix,' *Parl. Papers*, 1878, Vol. 19, Appendix 1, p3.

27. Precis titled '*Inflexible* Sail Power,' 1875, NMM: ADM138/49, fol 279.

sels.'[24] The evidence may be circumstantial, but it is also considerable. Two of the three men with the largest say in matters of Admiralty design policy, three if Hood is included, were proponents of masting ironclads. Milne, indeed, advocated providing the subsequent *Ajax* and *Agamemnon* with 'two masts with topsails as a steadying sail' even though they were explicitly designed for coastal service.[25] The desire to extend *Inflexible*'s intended operational range through dictates about draught, freeboard, and sails, came, in all likelihood, from the Board, rather than from the Constructor's department.

In retrospect, the decision to mast *Inflexible* was clearly a mistake. Yet it is also easy to appreciate probable motives for the Board's action. With the realisation that masted ironclads of the *Alexandra* type could not hope to match the fighting power of the Navy's breastwork monitors, to say nothing of the recently-designed Italian central-citadel ironclads *Duilio* and *Dandolo*, the Admiralty had sensibly concluded that building further such vessels was of doubtful utility. Yet while the Italians could build vessels intended solely for Mediterranean service, the British had to address the need for vessels to serve beyond Europe as well. There was, therefore, doubtless a strong temptation, having abandoned cruising ironclads so recently, to attempt to graft some of their valuable qualities—range and sea-keeping—onto a ship otherwise designed strictly for European waters.

It is, moreover, clear that the decision was not one to which the Board was inflexibly wedded. In fact, opposition to the design put forward in May 1873 came from Hood who, despite agreeing with Houston Stewart's dissentient Committee on Designs report, 'strongly recommend[ed] that the idea of having masts in such a vessel . . . be abandoned . . . .' Hood argued, accurately enough, 'the small amount of sail which could be carried on the proposed masts would be of very slight value in . . . the remote contingency of both sets of engines being totally disabled', plus they were a potential liability to the ship's fighting qualities: 'in action the fall of the masts might interfere considerably with the delivery of fire . . .'.[26] Instead, he advocated using the weight saved by elimination of masts and sails for increasing armour protection for the turrets and waterline belt along the citadel. Hood carried his point; the masts were subsequently dropped from the design approved by the Board. Battleworthiness took precedence over seaworthiness.

However, on 9 September 1875, dockyard officers at Portsmouth, where the *Inflexible* was building, forwarded a sketch 'showing masts, sails, boats, &c,' a move which prompted Barnaby to remind Houston Stewart 'it has never been decided whether the ship shall carry canvas' and that 'it is possible to work about 18,500 sq ft', which 'would give her steerage way in case of breakdown of engines, improve her behaviour with a beam sea, &c.'[27] Barnaby added that the weight could be accommodated, and the Board approved his suggestion on 13 October 1875, more than two years after the initial design was approved. The desire to improve sea-

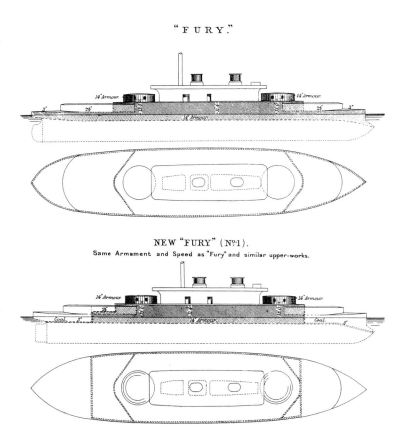

Of the designs mooted for *Inflexible* ('New *Fury*'), the first was a near repeat of *Fury/Dreadnought*.

worthiness was finally too much to resist, although 18,500 sq ft of canvas was of little use in moving a vessel of over 11,000 tons displacement. The sails were removed within five years of her completion.

The most important aspect of *Inflexible*'s design—the number and disposition of her guns—has yet to be considered. As seen, Barnaby maintained that the vessel should mount the heaviest guns possible, and his credo was echoed by the D.N.O. and Board, but there still remained the questions of how many guns she was to carry and how they were to be arranged. The Constructor's department sketched out several possible designs during the early months of 1873.

Five of these were submitted to the Controller and Board in June 1873, along with the design finally selected. The first—new *Fury* (no. 1)—was a virtual repeat of *Fury/Dreadnought* itself, save for the restriction of the armoured protection: a turret on the centreline at either end of a fore-and-aft superstructure. It otherwise had the 'same Armament and Speed as *Fury*, and similar upperworks' and as such it is difficult to see how it met Barnaby's insistence on mounting the heaviest possible guns. The second design, new *Fury* (no. 2), provided one possible answer. It too had the same two-turret layout as *Fury/Dreadnought*, but in addition to the four 12in, 35-ton guns they carried (two per turret), the second

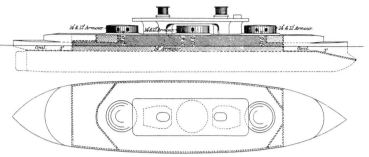

NEW "FURY" (N°2)

With One 50 Ton Gun and Four 35 Ton Guns in Turrets. Speed 13 knots.

Concerned about escalating ordnance size and *Fury/Dreadnought*'s relatively feeble guns, the Constructor's Department provided a possible solution in 'New *Fury* No. 2', which carried a single 50-ton gun in a turret amidships in addition to the 35-ton guns in the fore and aft turrets.

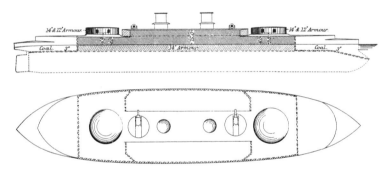

NEW "FURY" (N°3).

With 4_35 Ton Turret Guns, and 4_18 Ton Guns, Mounted en barbette.
Speed 13 knots.

Barnaby's third 'New *Fury*' design added barbette guns to the turrets of *Fury/Dreadnought*, although the 18-ton guns mounted would have had little value against heavily-armoured opponents.

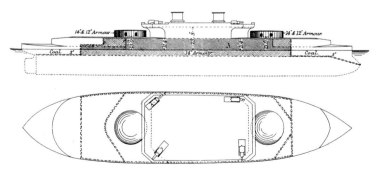

NEW "FURY."

With 4_35 Ton Turret Guns, and 4_12 Ton unprotected Guns on the Flying Deck.
Speed same as "Fury."

The fourth (albeit unnumbered) variation on *Fury/Dreadnought* supplemented the 35-ton turret guns with four 12-ton guns on the flying deck. These, like the 18-ton guns in Design No. 3, were incapable of penetrating heavy armour.

design included a third turret mounted amidships, carrying one 50-ton gun capable of firing on either broadside. The third design, new *Fury* (No. 3), was a curious amalgam of turret and barbette features. Like designs 1 and 2 it featured two of the former mounted on the centreline, each carrying four 35-ton guns. An additional four 18-ton guns were mounted *en barbette*, however, the barbettes themselves rising above the superstructure, fore and aft of the funnels. As depicted in the Constructor's rendering, the barbette guns would be capable of firing over the turrets—not unlike the superfiring barbette/turret design adopted by the United States Navy and later copied by other powers in the early twentieth century. Again, though, the *desideratum* of carrying the heaviest possible guns would hardly be met by the addition of four 18-ton guns to *Fury*'s armament. Along with sketches of these three departures from the *Fury* design, Barnaby also provided a straight repeat of *Fury*, (no design number), with a full waterline armour belt and four 12-ton guns mounted—without protection—on the flying deck.[28]

Finally, the D.N.C.'s memorandum provided a sketch of a fifth potential gun arrangement, which had been 'prepared by Mr. Hounsom of this office for the late Emperor Napoleon III'.[29] What business a member of the Constructor's department had preparing designs for the former French Emperor Barnaby did not explain, nor did he specify why this design was included along with those based on the *Fury* for the Board's perusal. Parkes rightly terms it a 'radical departure from all previous capital ship designs', consisting as it did of an open-topped armoured citadel-cum-barbette in which were mounted no less than ten 35-ton guns, a pair on turntables at either end of the massive, elongated barbette, the others on pivots, three to each broadside.[30] There was no doubt something to be said for the volume of fire such a ship would produce, but unless it was decided to substitute a smaller number of heavier guns for the ten 35-ton pieces, this design came no closer to meeting Barnaby's criterion that the Navy must design ships with 'guns of the most powerful description which can be made and worked', than did any of the previous four sketches. Other designs were mooted during the spring of 1873 as well. At the end of April Barnaby requested one of his assistants calculate the weights for a vessel of 14kts speed, '& four guns 2 of 50 or 60 tons & 2 of 35 tons each in a single 14 in [armoured] turret of 2/3 the weight of the existing turrets of *Fury*'. The turrets Barnaby envisioned were in fact barbettes; they were 'to be open at the top so that the guns may be used as barbette guns for distant firing'.[31]

It is not clear when the Constructor's department decided to adopt the *en echelon* turret arrangement employed by Italian naval architect Benedetto Brin in the design of *Duilio* and *Dandolo*. Certainly, however, the crucial decision to widen the ship's beam, which made the arrangement possible, was taken very late in the process. On 20 May, barely two weeks before the design was presented to the Controller, Barnaby 'decided to increase the

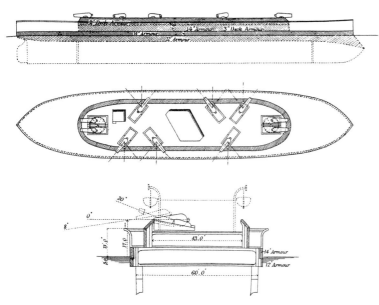

Twin Screw Iron Clad Vessel to carry 10-35 Ton Guns, Mounted en barbette.

Easily the most unorthodox of the design sketches submitted for *Inflexible* was this proposal originally prepared for the exiled French Emperor Napoleon III. The huge barbette would have housed no less than ten 35-ton guns.

beam'.[32] Acting on information 'with reference to dock accommodation at home and abroad . . . the beam was fixed at 75 ft.' Having made this alteration 'mainly for the purpose of obtaining stability after perforation of the unarmoured parts,' the Constructors found themselves 'able to place the turrets so far apart laterally as to obtain direct fire right ahead and astern in conjunction with a high deck forward and aft . . .'.[33] With both turrets placed amidships, where the ship's buoyancy was greatest, rather than at either end of the superstructure, the heaviest possible guns could be carried with the least threat to stability and, for that matter, seaworthiness, since heavy guns mounted closer to the ends exacerbated rise and plunge in a seaway. Moreover, as

Barnaby suggested, the *en echelon* arrangement permitted all four guns to fire on either beam, and, theoretically, ahead and astern also, the latter of great perceived import, given the ramming frenzy. Thus, also, the drawbacks to a fixed-battery arrangement such as that sketched in Hounsom's design – in which only seven of ten guns could fire on both broadsides and, worse still, only two could fire right ahead and astern – were surmounted. Certainly *Inflexible*'s design appears directly modelled on that of Brin's vessels, although Barnaby never explicitly admitted as much. Indeed, years later he claimed the *en echelon* arrangement was dictated not by the Italian model, but by domestic public and political opinion.[34] '[I]t was held in Parliament and the Press,' he stated, that *Devastation*'s low freeboard fore and aft 'were dangerous features in a sea-going ship', and although there was no foundation to these fears, 'they were very influential in determining the form of upper works of the *Inflexible*, and high hatchway freeboard was given to her from stem to stern.' With a high superstructure dominating the centreline fore and aft – probably another manifestation of the desire to improve sea-keeping – placing the turrets *en echelon* was mandated, unless a fixed broadside battery design was chosen in its stead. Barnaby's retrospective writings are, however, suspect. Many passages in his *Naval Development of the Century* betray a mind prone to wandering, if not outright memory lapses, and certainly developments in Italy influenced the deliberations of the D.N.C. and his colleagues in the early months of 1872. Barnaby himself informed the Institute of Naval Architects, relative to *Inflexible*'s design, '[t]here could be no question that we could not allow Foreign seamen to have guns afloat more powerful than any of our own, however ready we might have been to allow them to defend themselves with thicker armour.'[35]

Whatever the impetus for adopting the basic layout of *Duilio* and *Dandolo*, Barnaby forwarded the recommended design to the

Inflexible's design as approved by the Board. The *en echelon* turret arrangement was made possible by the decision to increase the ship's breadth from 70 to 75ft.

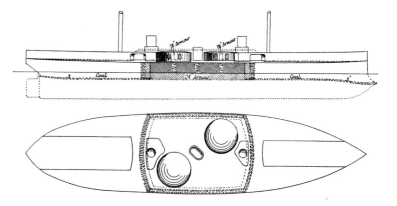

"INFLEXIBLE".

4-60 Ton Guns.

28. 'Report of the Committee on the *Inflexible*', *Parl. Papers*, 1878, Vol. 19, plates 1-3 (pp203, 205, 207 in microprint ed.)

29. 'S.7104/1873: From the Director of Naval Construction to the Controller, for Consideration while the Design is in progress, 3rd June 1873, Report of the Committee on the '*Inflexible*,' with Appendix,' *Parl. Papers*, 1878, Vol. 19, Appendix 1, pp2-3 (p164-5 in microprint ed.).

30. Parkes, *British Battleships*, p248.

31. Barnaby to Dunn, 29 April 1873, NMM: ADM138/49, fol. 16.

32. Minute of 20 May 1873, NMM: ADM138/49, fol. 7.

33. 'S.7104/1873: From the Director of Naval Construction to the Controller, for Consideration while the design is in progress, 3rd June 1873,' 'Report of the Committee on the '*Inflexible*' with Appendix, Parl. Papers, 1878, Vol. 19, Appendix 1, p2 (p164 in microprint ed.).

34. Nathaniel Barnaby, *Naval Development in the Century*, p75.

35. Nathaniel Barnaby, 'On some Recent Designs for Ships of War for the British Navy, Armoured and Unarmoured', *Transaction of the Institute of Naval Architects*, 15 (1874), p8.

Controller, D.N.O. and Board with a ringing endorsement. 'This design,' he averred, 'is so much superior to those which we had under consideration previously, that we only present these former designs to show what might be done were the principle of sinking the ship one foot on going into action, and incurring a risk of as much as another foot of immersion while in action objected to.'[36] Houston Stewart passed Barnaby's memorandum on to D.N.O. Hood without remark. Hood, however, produced his own commentary on the design. Like Barnaby, he alluded to the general naval situation. Admitting that the *Devastation, Thunderer,* and *Fury* (*Dreadnought*) were 'by far the most powerful fighting machines in the world for service in European waters,' with the sole exception of Russia's *Peter the Great* (still far from completion in 1873), he stressed 'it is known that in Italy two double turret vessels are to be built' with 22in armour over the vitals and 60-ton guns. In addition, 'Mr. Reed has . . . (I have been informed) received instructions to prepare the design of a vessel for the Prussians, protected over the vital parts with a similar thickness of armour.'[37]

If Hood's intelligence was correct, Prussia never ordered such a ship be built. The Italian ironclads, however, were unquestionably real, and in light of their construction, the D.N.O. concluded that within a few years 'other European powers will construct vessels protected . . . with the thickest armour which can be carried and armed with far heavier guns than have yet to be contemplated for the armament of ships . . .' Against such foes the guns of the British breastwork monitors 'would be powerless' and even *Fury/Dreadnought*'s 14in armour 'could be penetrated easily, at very considerable ranges, by 60-ton guns'. Hood therefore maintained it 'imperative' that since the new ironclad 'will take probably between three and four years to complete' (she took seven-and-a-half), contingency plans to provide for 'a very considerable increase in the thickness of the armour protection, and the power of the guns, should be made; in order to ensure that when completed, the powers of offence and defence of this vessel may, in so far as can at present [be] foreseen, meet the requirements of that date'. If concrete corroboration of the urge to modify designs in the course of construction in order to keep their armament and protection on the cutting edge were wanted, Hood's statement could not be bettered.

On the whole, the D.N.O. found the new design 'satisfactory', assuming the necessity of building a warship that 'shall possess, at all events, equal powers of offence and defence with any vessel as yet contemplated by other European powers . . .'. Yet objections were raised to details of the design. As seen, he strongly demurred on the question of masts and sails, preferring the weight they represented be used in thickening the protection. Moreover, he expressed displeasure with the turret arrangement, since it 'limits considerably the bearing which can be commanded by the fire of all four guns, and the superstructures interfere considerably with the delivery of fire upon an enemy's vessel when crossing the bow or stern . . .'. Yet rather than cut down the superstructure to obtain a wider arc of fire, Hood regarded it as a necessity, again illuminating the desire to combine battleworthiness and seaworthiness in a single vessel: 'it is absolutely necessary to have superstructures forward and aft' of the height proposed, for stowing boats and working anchors. More to the point, the 'height of freeboard forward thus obtained will also enable the vessel to steam against a head sea'.

Instead, the D.N.O. advocated reducing the *width* of the forward superstructure by 5ft to obtain 'a better right-ahead fire', and the ends of both superstructures nearest the turrets 'should be altered in shape, to lessen the effect of the concussion of firing, and increase the angle of training of the after turret'. Furthermore, Hood found the Constructors' placement of the funnels, between the two turrets, 'decidedly unsatisfactory, and recommended they 'be placed in the centre line, one before the foremost turret, the other abaft of the after turret'. Finally, he requested more particulars about the armoured deck, specifically its thickness and placement relative to the waterline.[38]

From the D.N.O. the design went back to Houston Stewart on 9 June, and the following day the Controller forwarded Hood's comments to Barnaby 'for your consideration and report'. In early July the D.N.C. replied that the preliminary design debated the previous month 'has now been worked out so far as to admit of its being laid before their Lordships.' In so doing, various of Hood's recommendations had been incorporated; the turret, breastwork, and underwater armour belt along the citadel were thickened, and the masts and sails disappeared–albeit temporarily–to be replaced by two pole masts for signalling.[39] The Constructors themselves also lengthened the citadel 'to give more space for uptake and downcast shafts within it, and to increase the amount of stability in the event of the entire destruction of the parts of the ship lying before and abaft it'. These alterations in turn necessitated reducing the number of rounds per gun carried from 170 to 100 to compensate for increased weight elsewhere. Furthermore, Hood's recommendations regarding the width of the forward superstructure and the placement of the funnels were incorporated in the subsequent re-design.

Simultaneously, a sheer drawing of the design, complete with underwater hull lines, 'accompanied by those of the *Fury*, were sent to Mr. Froude for the purpose of having the resistance of the two ships at given speeds compared'.[40] William Froude had pioneered the study of hull shapes and resistance, and had a test tank for models at Torquay.[41] He also played an important role in the discovery that water resistance–drag–was largely a function of surface of hull rather than of the fineness of its lines, thus encouraging both Reed and Barnaby to design the short, beamy British ironclads of the late 1860s and early 1870s. The *Inflexible* model bore out his earlier research, for Froude reported back 'that at 14 knots speed' the *Inflexible*'s 'resistance was not greater than that of the *Fury*,' despite being 12ft wider. Hence, the Constructors decided that 8000 indicated horse power, the same as *Fury*, 'be taken' for the new design.

Thus modified, Barnaby provided a synopsis of the design for the instruction of their Lordships, dated 4 July and approved by the Council of Construction (Constructor's Dept.) the following day. 'As compared with the '*Fury*,' he wrote, 'the ship will stand as follows':

1. Same size, cost [!], speed, and coal endurance

2. Three feet less draught of water.

3. Sixty-ton guns instead of thirty-five tons.

4. From 8 inches to 10 inches thicker armour on the central citadel.

5. The ends of the ship made impregnable by an under-water shot-proof deck, instead of being protected by armour of 10 to 8 inches.

6. An upper deck 17 to 20 feet out of water, instead of a low fore-castle and after deck, and a central hurricane deck.

7. Both turrets can fire right ahead and right astern, with one gun each.

8. Much greater bulk out of water and range of stability.[42]

In such light the new design appeared a paragon of fighting qualities, and regardless of how much retrospective doubt has been cast on, as David K. Brown put it, what *Inflexible*'s designers intended her for, informed contemporaries expressed no such uncertainty.[43] U.S. Navy Chief Engineer James W. King, for instance, succinctly summed up the rationale for British capital ship design in the 1870s in terms which echo those of Spencer Robinson, Barnaby, and Hood. 'It is to the production of the most powerful seagoing fighting-ships,' he wrote, 'that the resources of the navy are first directed; ships sufficiently armoured to resist projectiles of any ordinary kind, sufficiently armed to silence forts or meet the enemy under any conditions proffered, sufficiently fast to choose the time and place to fight, and sufficiently buoyant to carry coal and stores into any ocean.'[44]

At the same time that the Constructors forwarded the modified design, Barnaby was directing still further changes be made. On 4 July, 'after consultation with Mr. Crossland', he 'directed that a 4 ft belt of cork be placed at the ships side throughout the length of the coal space.'[45] The cork was to assist floatation in the event of shell holes in the unarmoured ends, since any spaces occupied by cork could not be filled with water. From the Controller, Barnaby's memorandum and the accompanying sketches went to the Board, along with Hood's remarks on the first design, since First Naval Lord Milne thought them 'very full and satisfactory' and should therefore be considered along with the modified design.[46] The Board approved the design on 23 July 1873; slightly less than a month later 'a perspective drawing . . . was forwarded to Portsmouth,' where *Inflexible* was to be built, 'for guidance'. From start to Board approval, excluding Reed's preliminary calculations, the process had taken almost seven months.

36. 'S.7104/1873: From the Director of Naval Construction to the Controller, for Consideration while the design is in progress, 3rd June 1873; Subsequently corrected, to show the modifications made to meet the views of Captain Hood, the directions of the Controller, and the exigencies of the design as it progressed,' 'Report of the Committee on the '*Inflexible*,' with Appendix,' *Parl. Papers*, 1878, Vol. 19, Appendix 1, p2 (p164 in microprint ed.). Reed's initial premises called for the ship to be immersed a foot deeper than its load draft prior to going into battle by flooding the ends. Such a procedure would increase stability markedly and would obviate the danger of fire from coal ignited by shellfire.

37. Ibid, Vol. 19, Appendix 1, p3 (p165 in microprint ed.).

38. Ibid., Appendix 1, p2-3 (pp164-5 in microprint ed.)

39. Ibid 'Subsequently [to 30 May], and in conformity with Capt. Hood's proposal, the Turret armour was made 18 [inches], and the *upper* protective deck plating 3 [inches] thick. The proposal for the jury rig was therefore abandoned and the weight of 30 tons allowed for two pole masts, for signalling, &c.'

40. 'New *Fury*', 19 June 1873, NMM: ADM138/49, 8.

41. On Froude, see David K. Brown, 'William Froude', *Warship* 1 (1979), pp212-13.

42. 'S.7104/1873: From the Director of Naval Construction to the Controller, for Consideration while the design is in progress, 3rd June 1873,' 'Report of the Committee on the '*Inflexible*,' with Appendix', *Parl. Papers*, 1878, Vol. 19, Appendix 1, p4 (p166 in microprint ed.).

43. David K. Brown, 'The Design of H.M.S. *Inflexible*,' *Warship* 4 (1980), pp146-52, especially p152.

44. James W. King, *The Warships and Navies of the World* (Boston, 1881), p63.

45. 'New *Fury*,' 4 July 1873, NMM: ADM138/49, fol. 8.

46 Memorandum by Milne, 21 July 1873, printed in 'S.7104/1873: From the Director of Naval Construction to the Controller, for Consideration while the Design is in progress, 3rd June 1873, Subsequently corrected, to show the modifications made to meet the views of Captain Hood, the directions of the Controller, and the exigencies of the design as it progressed,' 'Report of the Committee on the *Inflexible*, with Appendix,' *Parl. Papers*, 1878, Vol. 19, Appendix 1, p4 (p166 in microprint ed.).

Chapter 7

THE *INFLEXIBLE* AND MR REED

BARNABY EVINCED pride in his department's handiwork when speaking to the Institute of Naval Architects the following year. 'Imagine,' he asked his audience, 'a floating castle 110 feet long and 75 feet wide rising 10 feet out of the water,' with two guns in each turret of the most powerful description 'capable of firing all four together at an enemy ahead or on either beam, and in pairs towards every point of the compass', a 'powerful ram bow', and far thicker armour than on any previous ship.[1] Moreover, 'no pains have been spared to protect her against underwater attack,' for in addition to the armoured deck, the hull was 'divided into 127 water-tight compartments,' and all of these engineering marvels had been accomplished 'without an increase in cost . . .'.

Yet despite the attention paid and labours devoted to the design in early 1873, and despite Barnaby's unmistakable sense of accomplishment, virtually every assumption regarding *Inflexible* made by those responsible for her turned out to be wrong. Instead the £619,000 which *Dreadnought* eventually cost, *Inflexible* ran to £812,000, more than 30 per cent higher. Instead of taking 'three or four years' to complete, she was under construction from February 1874 – more than a year after her design was first mooted – to October 1881. And instead of setting a standard for the future shape of capital ships, she was obsolescent upon completion and obsolete outright within a decade of her commissioning. For the first two shortcomings contemporary circumstances, in part technological, in part personal, were responsible. For the last, technology again was a factor, but it worked in concert with changing perceptions of the future of naval warfare.

Of all the ships subject to construction delays as the Admiralty struggled to keep abreast of rapidly changing technology, none was more plagued than *Inflexible*, and her unhappy construction history goes far to explain why she was so long on the stocks. The first and biggest hurdle was the question of armament. The ship was originally approved with 60-ton guns, but both Barnaby and Hood had emphasised the desirability of designing her to accommodate heavier guns if foreign developments required a British response. They quickly did. The Italian *Duilio* and *Dandolo* had been originally designed to carry 35-ton guns, but the Admiralty's decision to design *Inflexible* around 60-ton guns spurred the Italians to a escalation of ordnance size, and after the two vessels were laid down (June 1873), the decision was taken to mount guns of the same size in them.[2] Given the avowed premise that the Royal Navy's ships should carry 'guns of the most powerful description which can be made and worked', there was little question that the Admiralty would respond in turn. In April 1874 *The Engineer* published a lengthy account on 'a series of monstrous successors' to the 35-ton gun, to be built by the Royal Ordnance Factory, the first of them 'intended to form the armament of the future ironclad *Inflexible*'.[3] This gun, the journal reported, 'will . . . be of a weight slightly over or slightly under eighty-one tons,' and, after experimentation, had its bore enlarged from 14in to 15in, and finally 16.25in. In retaliation, the Italians contracted with William Armstrong to furnish 17in, 100-ton muzzle-loading rifles for *Duilio* and *Dandolo*.[4] During March 1875 the Admiralty, in turn, debated a further escalation in the size of *Inflexible*'s guns, but eventually decided to retain the 81-ton weapons.

---

1. Nathaniel Barnaby, 'On Some Recent Designs for Ships of War for the British Navy, Armoured and Unarmoured', *Transactions of the Institution of Naval Architects*, 15 (1874), pp8-9.

2. Chesneau and Kolesnik (eds.), *Conway's All the World's Fighting Ships, 1860-1905*, p340; Parkes, *British Battleships*, p244. *Conway's* states 35-ton guns, Parkes claims 38-ton.

3. Excerpt from *The Engineer*, 24 April 1874, bound in NMM: ADM138/49, fol. 77.

4. In so doing, the fighting qualities, to say nothing of the structural integrity, of the Italian ships was seriously compromised. See Parkes, *British Battleships*, p244.

5. Ibid, p250. Parkes maintains that the Navy was restricted by the Ordnance Department

to purchasing Woolwich guns, and that the 81-ton gun was the largest gun 'contemplated' by the Royal factory. No doubt the Ordnance Department exercised a restrictive influence on the Navy's sources of *matériel*, yet Parkes himself notes in the following sentence that the Navy did buy four of Armstrong's 100-ton guns, which were installed at Gibraltar and Malta.

6. 'S.639: 1875, "Precis of Correspondence on 'Proposed alterations in *Inflexible* to enable her to carry 80 or 100 ton guns'", NMM: ADM138/49, fol. 207.

7. Remarks of Boys, 24 March 1875, ibid, fol. 213.

8. Barnaby to Crossland and Dunn, 4 April 1875, ibid, fol. 219.

The Italian ironclad *Dandolo*'s 17.72in, 100-ton guns. The Admiralty was prevented from matching them on *Inflexible* by space limitations. (U.S. Naval Historical Center: NH88685)

Why did the Admiralty not match the Armstrong guns ton-for-ton? The answer was space limitations.[5] In late March 1875, Barnaby informed Houston Stewart '[i]t appears to me to be idle to attempt to provide for such a length of gun as that assigned for the 100 ton gun', then still in the course of construction.[6] Moreover, stated the D.N.C., if his view was correct, the true factor limiting the power of shipboard ordnance was size, rather than the 'weight of the guns or . . . projectiles'. Even so, upgrading from 60 to 81 tons generated a whole host of subsidiary modifications to enable the guns to be worked within the cramped confines of *Inflexible*'s citadel. It was discovered, for instance, that the length of the larger pieces – 27ft – prohibited each turret from being trained around to the opposite broadside, with the guns run out in firing position, since the muzzles would collide with the ship's superstructure. The D.N.O., Captain Henry Boys, who had replaced Hood, reported himself,

strongly of opinion modifications must be made in the construction of the uptakes and ventilators to enable the turrets to revolve freely round with the guns out ready for firing; & that the constructors department should at once take this into consideration.[7]

Barnaby deprecated Boys' criticism, maintaining he 'was disposed to think . . . that the importance of training the turrets to opposite broadsides with the guns run out is greatly overrated' by the D.N.O.[8] As it was, however, the 81-ton guns were so long that they could not be loaded inside the turrets. Instead, hydraulic loading machinery – a necessity given the 1700lbs each common shell weighed, to say nothing of the muzzle-loading system still employed by Woolwich – was located under an armoured glacis outside the turret. To load the gun required swivelling the turret around and depressing the guns to line them up with the rammer. To fire them, in turn, required rotating the turret back around to

The paradox of low freeboard and high superstructure on the central citadel ironclads is clearly shown in this photograph of HMS *Colossus*. (U.S. Naval Historical Center: NH65876)

Prior to his attack on *Inflexible*'s stability, Reed had attempted to create similar controversy around the Italian *Duilio* (shown here) and *Dandolo*. (U.S. Naval Historical Center: NH88710)

face the target and elevating the guns for the correct range. Little wonder, therefore, that the rate of fire was a round every eleven minutes. Barnaby had it right when opposing Boys' wish that turrets be capable of rotating with the guns run out: '[r]apid firing from her guns is not a thing to be provided for or encouraged.'

The biggest obstacle to completion of *Inflexible*, however, came not from the 'pernicious' habit of modifying the vessel in course of

construction, but from Edward Reed. Progress on the vessel was completely halted in 1877-8 – and work on *Ajax* and *Agamemnon* suspended also – after Reed, by this point an M.P., alleged that she lacked adequate stability. Reed initiated his campaign with an attack on *Duilio* and *Dandolo*, an attack which the Italians met by stonewalling his charges, claiming that he could 'not possibly prove any such statements', and that his 'approximate calculations were inexact'. He then turned his attention to the *Inflexible*, informing Barnaby in late March that 'he was about to make public' calculations which 'made him suspect that the *Inflexible*, and probably also the *Ajax* and *Agamemnon*, did not possess that final reserve of stability, after a severe and protracted engagement, which he considered necessary'.[9]

To understand Reed's objections, the principles on which *Inflexible* was designed must be further examined. Reed himself envisioned a ship whose buoyancy and stability would be wholly guaranteed by the length of the hull covered by the citadel. In other words, his ideal vessel would have had a citadel about 200ft long, or almost two-thirds its total length. Even were the whole of the unarmoured ends waterlogged to the armoured deck, 6ft below the waterline (below which the ship was not likely to be struck, and compartmentalisation would prevent extensive flooding), the ship would remain buoyant and stable. The Admiralty Committee on Designs, however, advocated departing from Reed's ideal, suggesting 'some method may . . . be devised of securing the requisite reserve of buoyancy by other means than armour plating'. In Barnaby's words, the Committee 'did not agree with Mr. Reed's view as to the necessary dependence of the ship upon her armoured citadel for her floating power'. Instead, 'they were prepared to trust the floating power of the ship to the unarmoured raft constructed in cells and containing buoyant substances'. The Italians, who, again in Barnaby's words, were 'fully and keenly alive to all the conditions of the problem', had followed the recommendation of the Committee to the letter, and 'trust[ed] for both buoyancy and stability to their unarmoured raft.' Hence, regardless of their denials, Reed's charges were fundamentally correct: were *Duilio* or *Dandolo* to have their unarmoured ends completely riddled, the central citadel portion lacked the buoyancy to keep them afloat.

But Barnaby and his colleagues did not trust entirely to the raft hull for *Inflexible*'s floating power and stability. To be sure, they made full use of both of the Committee's recommendations, and the design as approved called for those 127 watertight compartments, plus a belt of cork to keep water out should the unarmoured ends be perforated. Yet, 'we did not,' Barnaby stated, 'go so far as the committee indicated, but we made the citadel so wide and long, that there was armoured buoyancy without any aid from the raft, and sufficient stability, both transverse and longitudinal, when it was completely riddled.' Foreseeing the possibility that the ends might be perforated repeatedly in a protracted engagement,

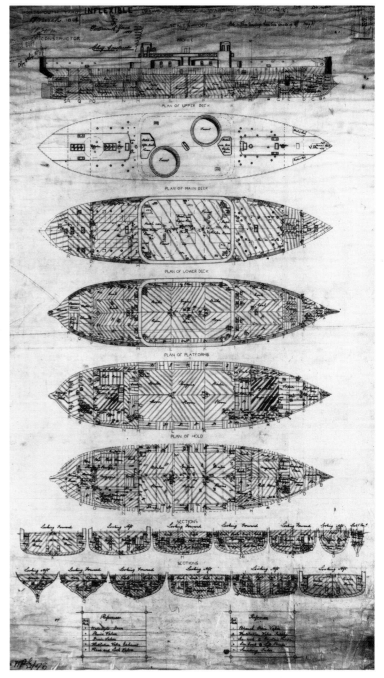

Inflexible's extensive watertight compartmentalisation can be seen, deck by deck, in this series of plans. (National Maritime Museum, London: 7712)

the Constructors 'therefore, laid down the proposition that when completely riddled under water and every single compartment thrown open to the sea, the cork walls perforated, and the cofferdams destroyed, she should still be safe and able to fight'. Under such conditions the ship would still have a range of transverse stability of 30 degrees.

---

9. '"Correspondence between Mr. E. Reed, M.P., and the Admiralty, in connexion with the stability of the *Inflexible*", Report of the Committee on the *Inflexible*, with Appendix', *Parl. Papers*, 1878, Vol. 19, Appendix 1, pp4-11 (pp166-73 in microprint ed.). The quotation comes from p7.

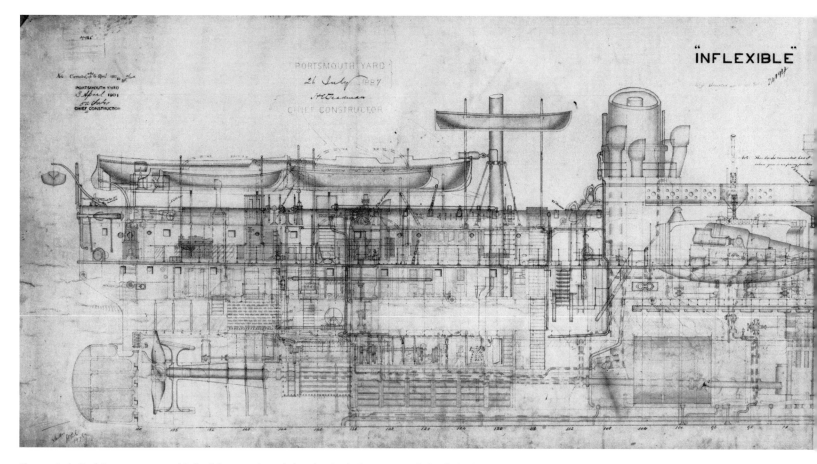

The central-citadel arrangement of *Inflexible* necessitated situating both the boilers and the engines, as well as the turrets, in the heavily-armoured amidships section. (National Maritime Museum, London: 7725)

The design approved by the Admiralty thus represented a compromise between Reed's views on the one hand, and the Admiralty Committee's on the other. It called for an armoured citadel 110ft long, and rather than relying solely upon the armoured portion of the ship to secure buoyancy and stability, Barnaby and his colleagues had designed *Inflexible* so that a variety of means were utilised: the citadel coupled with extensive subdivision of the hull into watertight compartments, plus the armoured deck which, it was expected, would keep water out of the ends below the armour. Yet even if the latter should fail, the ship would retain a reasonable reserve of stability. Moreover, Barnaby blunted stated 'I regard the possibility of the ship ever being reduced to this state as being infinitely remote, although not utterly impossible.'

Under the circumstances, the D.N.C., who pointed out that he could have followed the Italian example and simply denied Reed's allegations out of hand, 'thought it best to be perfectly frank, and open in the matter . . .'. Hence, the former Chief Constructor was invited to examine the Admiralty's model of the vessel, with it 'expressly [understood] that there was nothing . . . to consider as confidential . . .'. Barnaby was confident Reed 'would have seen that . . . no possible improvement could have been made in the

original design, in the sense desired by him, without either building a larger ship, or leaving the ship in guns and armour considerably inferior to the Italian ships . . .'.

This was a crucial observation, and one which has generally been overlooked in assessing the respective merits of the two designers' positions. To have acceded to Reed's insistence that the central citadel alone provide ample stability – to fit the ship with a citadel 200ft rather than 110ft long – would have necessarily involved either a large increase in displacement, or a sharp reduction in the weight of other features, obtainable only through reducing the size of the guns and the thickness of armour. Given Reed's insistence on armoured invulnerability, the latter strategy was hardly credible, and it must be concluded that his demands, if met, would have resulted in a far bigger and more expensive ship.[10]

Barnaby's assumption that Reed would find 'the features of the design . . . wisely balanced' was sadly misplaced. Instead, he summarised the former C.N.A.'s stance:

either the design should comply with his dictum that the . . . ship should have stability from her protected structure alone sufficient to meet certain unspecified contingencies of wind and sea, without receiving any benefit whatever from the unarmoured parts of the ship, or, this condition not being satisfied, she is badly designed.

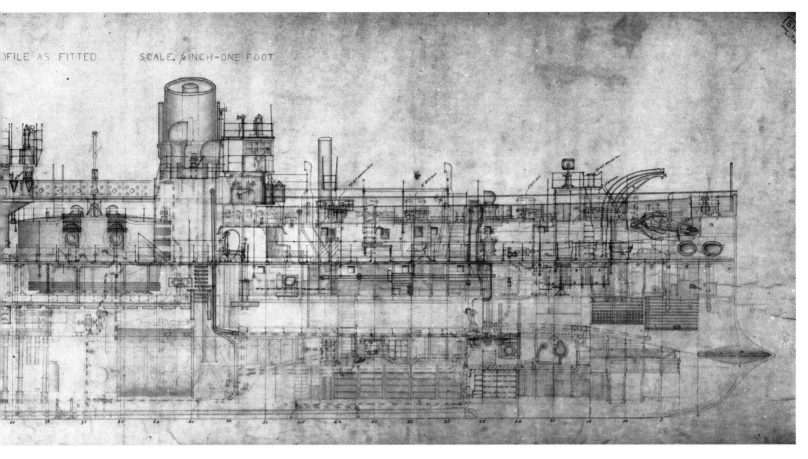

OFILE AS FITTED   SCALE, ¼ INCH-ONE FOOT

In response, Barnaby drafted a lengthy memorandum (16 April 1877) defending the design against Reed's charges, citing the report of the Admiralty Committee on designs, comparing *Inflexible* to *Devastation*, and maintaining, among other things, that;

> [i]n order to justify Mr. Reed's objection, it is necessary to assume . . . that every atom of solid material excluding water in the cellular storerooms and in the cork walls has been blown out of the ship, and that only the battered iron shell remains . . .

He added derisively, 'no heavily armoured ship ever has been designed to comply with such a condition', not least among them Reed's *Devastation*, which risked the same 'fatal damage' should its 'pie crust armour' be perforated. Moreover, not only had no ship been designed to meet such criteria: 'it would be wrong to attempt to do it'. He further noted that Reed's criticisms turned solely 'on the power of the ship to resist the attacks [*sic*] of artillery', and 'we have also to consider the underwater attack'. The D.N.C. then mimicked his brother-in-law's *modus operandi*: '[i]t would be easy, following Mr. Reed's course, to lay down some principle with regard to these attacks, and to say that no ship is well designed which is not so subdivided as to satisfy certain conditions.' Barnaby added that through 'such an unfair method of criticism' few ships beyond *Inflexible*, *Ajax*, and *Agamemnon* would be deemed safe, implicitly condemning all of Reed's creations on this score.

Finally, he remarked pointedly '[l]arge ironclad ships, costing nearly as much as the *Inflexible* [*ie Ajax* and *Agamemnon*] and not yet complete, might in this way have their reputations severely damaged.'

Fighting fire with fire, however, was not the best tactical approach to take in arguing with Reed, who relished controversy as most do food and sleep. His response to Barnaby's defence of *Inflexible* was thus predictable. On 16 May he asked the D.N.C. 'to communicate my objection to the Controller and the Board, with any remarks you may please to make upon it'.[11] Yet even as he made this request, he changed the angle of attack on *Inflexible*. He had initially charged that the ship would lack stability should the unarmoured ends be perforated and filled with water. Barnaby's response that the combination of extensive subdivision, coffer

---

10. Ibid, p7 (p169 in microprint ed.) Reed responded (18 May) 'I cannot admit Mr. Barnaby's proposition that no improvement could have been made in the sense desired by me without either building a larger ship or leaving the ship in guns and armour inferior to the Italian ships. On the contrary, I believe that perfectly safe ships, with equal protection, might have been designed on the dimensions of the *Inflexible*. 'Yet, as Barnaby pointed out the following day, for all of his grandiose claims, 'Mr. Reed does not say how he would propose to remedy what he considers a defect in this class of ship; as he has such a detailed account of the ship that he has been able to estimate the position of the centre of gravity, he must be able to indicate those modifications which in his view would make a better ship'.

11. Ibid. Barnaby had (16 April) requested Reed take this step rather than air the subject in public.

dams to prevent water from filling coal stowage spaces even if the sides were perforated, and cork 'to preserve the solidity of the side walls', coupled with his assumption that the cork and other solid materials in the ends would, in the event of a prolonged battle, only be 'blown out' by 'slow degrees' precipitated an abrupt shift in Reed's tactics. 'After what has passed between us,' he wrote,

> I need hardly say that my objection is confined strictly to the point that whereas you believe the cork chambers . . . would remain more or less intact during a protracted action, I fear and believe that exposed as they are to the full attack of the enemy's shell fire, they would be speedily and completely gone.

That being the case, alleged Reed, 'she would capsize'. Nothing in his initial letter to Barnaby (11 April) alluded to the claim that the cork would be 'speedily blown out' of the chambers, and though he might have thought he hardly needed to state his specific objections, Barnaby probably saw matters quite differently.[12]

Moreover, Reed presented a lengthy memorandum of his own, which purported to refute the D.N.C.'s arguments point by point. In so doing he revealed his talents as a polemicist. Barnaby's memorandum, he alleged, 'in no way meets the case', that is to say, answered Reed's charges. The D.N.C. was accused of contradicting himself regarding Reed's calculations of *Inflexible*'s curve of stability, and of basing his defence on irrelevancies. Reed furthermore claimed that the Committee on Designs did not depart from his stated views, 'nor does the extract from their Report, which Mr. Barnaby appends to his memorandum, convey anything of the kind. If carefully read, their remarks bear an opposite construction'. Like much else in his attack, it is difficult to lend credence to this last charge. The Committee on Designs had speculated that 'some method may . . . be devised of securing the requisite reserve of buoyancy by means other than armour plating', and sketched out the principle of not only the armoured citadel, but also the unarmoured raft 'constructed on a cellular system, or containing some buoyant substance such as cork, which, without offering any material resistance to the passage of projectiles, would not be deprived of its buoyancy by penetration'. How Reed squared these observations with his claim that the Committee report in no way supported Barnaby's argument he did not bother to explain.[13]

Likewise, he denied Barnaby's charge that to follow his dicta would result in a far larger vessel or a less well protected one. But rather than produce a sketch for such a design, he abruptly changed the subject: 'that is not a question I wish to raise'. Instead, he claimed to be motivated solely by 'the dangerous character of the *Inflexible* as designed . . .'. The allegation that the cork would be apt to be quickly blown out of the chambers by shellfire was frequently repeated; in response to one of Barnaby's points he alleged the vessel 'is without stability when the cork is blown out of the chambers by shells, a result which I fear might occur very early in action.' A few sentences later he reiterated the charge: 'I regard [it] as likely to occur very early in an action.' He moreover claimed, without bothering to cite its source, '[t]he only information which has been made public respecting the use of cork in enclosed chambers as a means of safety for ships tends, in my opinion, to confirm my fears that when exposed to heavy shellfire it will speedily disappear.'

Other elements of his screed were more disingenuous. As for Barnaby's observation that were the *Devastation*'s thin armour perforated, she would be even less stable than *Inflexible*, Reed argued '*Inflexible* can be destroyed without her armour being either penetrated or touched'. In consequence, he maintained he could not 'understand how this question can be met by an intimation that the *Devastation* and other ships may be destroyed by the *piercing* of their armour'. This line of reasoning ignored the fact that *Devastation*'s armour was much more likely to be pierced than were both *Inflexible*'s ends to be riddled by shellfire and deprived of their water-excluding contents. He continued in a similar vein for more than two columns of small print.

In closing, Reed disclaimed 'any desire to unfairly criticise *Inflexible*', and that even his strictures – to his eyes no doubt fair – caused him 'no little pain and distress of mind', but he avowed himself unable to 'neglect what I feel to be the duty of inviting the reconsideration of the Admiralty' to his charges, since his correspondence with Barnaby 'had no useful result'. In perhaps the most honest statement of his memorandum, he acknowledged that the dispute was 'almost entirely a matter of opinion', and deprecated any 'wish to set my judgment as superior to that of Mr. Barnaby', yet it is difficult to see how his action in appealing to the latter's superiors could be interpreted in any other light.

Nonetheless, Barnaby dutifully forwarded Reed's request and memorandum to the Controller on 18 May, providing a brief explanation of both for the latter's information. He too acknowledged that the dispute turned on differences in opinion, and admitted that the decision to fit *Inflexible* with larger ordnance left the vessel 'more dependent upon the integrity' of its unarmoured

---

12. Reed to Barnaby, 16 May 1877, 'Report of the Committee on the *Inflexible*, with Appendix,' *Parl. Papers*, 1878, Vol. 19, Appendix 1, p7 (p169 in microprint ed.).

13. Reed to Houston Stewart, 18 May 1877, ibid, pp7-8 (p169-70 in microprint ed.).

14. Barnaby to Houston Stewart, 19 May 1877, ibid, p8 (p170 in microprint ed.).

15. Ibid. Barnaby also accused Reed of springing his objections to the ship on him out of the blue: 'the first intimation I had . . . that he was dissatisfied with the ship was on the

evening preceding the day when he was to read a paper at the last session of [the Institute] of Naval Architects. He then informed me that he had designed very carefully an approximate *Inflexible*, and proposed to describe her publicly the next day, and say that if the *Inflexible* were like her she would capsize in action.'

'Only a few days before,' Barnaby finished, 'he was vigorously contending that she was of a novel type proposed by himself,' an echo of similar claims by Reed regarding *Captain*, prior, of course, to her loss.

portions than 'when the ship was first designed'. He added unequivocally, however, that were he and his colleagues given the task of re-designing the ship, 'we should make no changes in the direction indicated by' Reed. Barnaby also warned Houston Stewart that Reed 'has made no secret of his views'; indeed, 'several eminent public men' had passed along statements from him 'most damaging to the character of the ships in question'. Unfortunately, the task of defending the design from those charges was not simple. The D.N.C. acknowledged it was 'very easy to understand the nature of Mr. Reed's objections, and not at all easy to communicate to unskilled persons a knowledge of the real strength of the answer to it'.[14]

Barnaby, too, could not resist rebutting some of Reed's allegations, despite claiming he had 'nothing to add' to the latter's memorandum. The former Chief Constructor, he stressed, did 'not say how he would propose to remedy what he considers a defect in this class of ship', although he had such detailed information regarding its centre of gravity that 'he must be able', assuming he had any idea, 'to indicate those modifications which in his view would make a better ship'. Reed, in other words, should put up or shut up. Were he to do so, Barnaby promised 'I shall be prepared to submit to be judged by the comparison', assuming Reed's ship were bound to the same terms of displacement and speed as *Inflexible* as approved. Until Reed did, 'we are fighting a shadow', quite possibly a reference to his tendency to alter arguments and objections as each was countered. Barnaby then reiterated the 'singular nature' of the engagement which Reed envisioned, in which no torpedoes, ramming, or armour-shattering guns would figure, yet the *Inflexible* would 'be struck by many shells, exploding at and below the waterline, in her unarmoured ends'.[15]

Houston Stewart passed the papers to the D.N.O., Henry Boys, who composed a memorandum to be forwarded to the Board. Boys minced no words in deriding Reed's alleged fears: 'I cannot conceive,' he wrote the Controller, 'that the conditions on which Mr. Reed bases his argument can be brought about in a naval engagement.' Boys advanced a number of supporting reasons for his view: it would be very difficult to strike *Inflexible* at or below the waterline as the ship would roll very little, the armour-shattering shells likely to be used against the ship would probably pass through the light ends unexploded, thus leaving the buoyant cork largely intact, and, certainly not least, it was most improbable that the ship could be struck enough times in the right places to do the damage envisioned by Reed. 'Considering the few guns that are likely to be carried by any ship engaging the *Inflexible*, and the ever-varying distance and bearing that must exist in any future naval action,' he argued, 'it is next to impossible that any number of

Inflexible under construction in Portsmouth Dockyard, about a year before Reed's attack halted work on her. (U.S. Naval Historical Center: NH71228)

shells could be planted in a ship in such an exact position (even supposing them to burst) as to "blow out the cork" from the chambers in which it will be fixed.' Moreover, Boys pointed out that Reed's scenario presupposed that those on board the *Inflexible* could not effect repairs during action 'to prevent the unarmoured ends . . . from being waterlogged' or, 'supposing the water to come in, to allow it to run into the bilge, to be pumped out by the engines'. Of course, '[n]aval fighting cannot be undertaken without risk,' but he perceived no threat from the danger apprehended by Reed happening ' "very early in action," as I do not believe it can occur.' Boys pointed out that simple means existed for correcting a list, and thus concluded 'I have no hesitation in saying that I do not share for one moment Mr. Reed's anxiety for the safety of the *Inflexible* in action from the effect of artillery fire . . .'.

Houston Stewart was similarly emphatic. Reed's assertion that the ship was 'so designed that she would not float upright in action without the assistance of cork chambers', was, he scoffed, 'opposed to the obvious facts of the case'. 'After the most careful study' of the correspondence relative to Reed's charges, 'I cannot find anything which has not been fully anticipated and considered by all of us who are responsible since the design was first undertaken . . .'. The fate sketched by Reed 'could, in my opinion, only be arrived at if we can suppose the ship lying perfectly helpless and immovable, and allowing herself to be attacked by an indefinite number of guns'. In such circumstances, he admitted, 'it is possible that a large portion of the unarmoured structure above the water might be destroyed,' but even in that eventuality he professed himself unable

> to see how it is possible to destroy or remove entirely all material, timber, cork, stores, coal, or other articles which, while remaining in any portion of the structure, must exclude water or prevent water from taking their place.

Reed's scenario, in short, 'represent[ed] an exaggerated state of circumstances which could never occur in real warfare.'[16]

Like Barnaby, the Controller deprecated Reed's charge that *Devastation*'s armour made it less susceptible to capsizing than *Inflexible*'s raft ends: '[p]lace any other ironclads defended with what is now very weak armour at the extremities', he challenged, 'in this assumed position, and where would these ships be after a course of such treatment as we are asked to consider likely to occur during an action to the *Inflexible* . . .'. In a direct attack on Reed, he noted that the Brazilian ironclad *Independencia*, designed by the former C.N.A. (and later purchased by Britain), had no more than 9in armour – 'easily penetrable by the 12-ton gun' – not merely at the ends, but covering the vitals.[17] The same was true of the recently completed German *Kaiser* class battleships, also designed by Reed, whose 'powder magazines and engines are protected by not more than the eight inches of armour which is perforable by the

9-ton gun'.[18] 'A few well-delivered rounds from these guns, or even much larger guns, could have but small effect on the unarmoured ends of the *Inflexible*, whereas they would be fatal to the existence of the above and most other ironclads of their type.'

Finally, Houston Stewart alluded to an earlier attack by Reed on the safety of the *Minotaur* class broadside ironclads which, he alleged, lacked adequate structural integrity to withstand the strains caused by heavy seas, going so far as to claim that 'the breaking in two of any such ships would probably result in her immediate and total loss', a reasonable enough conclusion were the class actually in peril of coming apart. They were not. The Controller pointed out to the Board that Barnaby had investigated Reed's allegations and found that he had incorrectly ascertained the ships' strength. Moreover, during Reed's tenure as Chief Constructor he had 'raised no objection to the continual and constant employment of those ships at sea'. Reed had not been in the House of Commons in 1871, when those charges were made, so he could not bring forward his allegations in that forum, but he did make them 'the subject of a statement in public' and of 'an official letter to the Admiralty'. Now he was an M.P. and Houston Stewart plainly foresaw his capacity to make mischief, although he himself dismissed charges regarding *Inflexible* as 'equally groundless' to those made against the *Minotaur*s.[19]

With its three leading technical advisors – Barnaby, Boys and Houston Stewart – arrayed against Reed, the response of the Board was predictable. On 5 June Reed was informed confidentially that the 'subject has been fully investigated' by the responsible officials at the Admiralty, 'who are unanimously of opinion that the effects anticipated by you could not occur under the conditions of a naval action'. Moreover, their Lordships 'differed from' Reed and reiterated their conviction that *Inflexible* was 'a safe and most formidable fighting vessel', charging that Reed himself 'appear[ed] to have overlooked certain facts in connexion with the condition of the ship under the circumstances supposed by you, which if taken into consideration would remove all apprehension of their being any risk that she would turn over'.[20]

This rather brusque dismissal was certainly not the best tack to take with someone of Reed's temperament, and his response, too, might have been anticipated. Within four days he answered the Admiralty's letter, admitting that standing against the unanimous opinion of the Board's 'very able and experienced' technical advisors did not lead him to expect his opinions 'would be sufficient to deter their Lordships from adopting the views of such advisors . . .'.[21] Not surprisingly, though, Reed found that his 'conviction remain[ed] unaltered', and although he deprecated the idea of 'further press[ing] the matter upon their Lordships', he also 'reserve[d] . . . the liberty of considering of considering what steps it may be my duty to take in Parliament with reference to the new ship of this type' mentioned in the year's Navy Estimates.

Reed's conviction may have remained unaltered: his objections to *Inflexible*, however, did not. First he had alleged that the ship lacked an adequate reserve of buoyancy; when that argument was countered he had switched tacks and claimed that the cork meant to exclude water from the unarmoured ends would be 'speedily blown out' in an engagement, leaving her prone to capsizing. Now he informed the Board that 'I have hitherto refrained from mentioning the whole extent of my apprehensions, for, in truth [!], I fear that even with a considerable portion of the cork chambers intact, the *Inflexible* would nevertheless be seriously deficient in stability.' This wording must be stressed, for Reed, in the face of the unanimous opinion of Barnaby, Boys, and Houston Stewart that the cork would remain intact, abandoned that line of argument and instead reverted to the general charge that the ship was unsafe with it in place. Yet he did not explicitly restate the original allegation that, as Barnaby put it, '*Inflexible* did not possess that final reserve of stability, after a severe and protracted engagement, which he considered necessary'. Instead, he contented himself with the nebulous claim that the ship was 'seriously deficient in stability'.

To this letter Barnaby advised 'their Lordships will not, probably, desire to send any response', although he assured them 'it should not be supposed that Mr. Reed's hints, that he knows more than he has revealed, have any foundation'.[22] Moreover, his wrath at Reed's behaviour finally surfaced. 'The whole question,' he informed the Board, 'relates to an estimate of six inches, one way or the other, in the position of the centre of gravity of the completed ship, and if I had not confirmed his assumption as to where it was likely to be, his criticism would be pointless.' Thus, rued the D.N.C., having had

> nothing to conceal in the matter . . . I gave him the weapon he is now using. . . . I know therefore, its exact value; and I say that not only has he not scrupled to use it to the full extent of his power, but also that he has used it unfairly.

Reed's calculation of the centre of gravity was, Barnaby bluntly stated, 'wrong', and if his curve of stability 'had been rightly calculated he would have seen why the model still has stability in the condition assumed by him, and why the ship should have also'.

The D.N.C. also reminded the Board that his department had 'had to defend many of the designs for which Mr. Reed was responsible', against similarly partial views. Moreover, he, like Houston Stewart, alluded to Reed's charges regarding the *Minotaur*s, but, 'Mr. Reed's view is not only partial: it is unwise.' To lengthen the citadel to secure armoured buoyancy, as Reed had explicitly advocated in his letter of 9 June, would, notwithstanding his blithe claims to the contrary, involve enlarging the ship or 'thinning the armour . . .'. The former course was impossible, the latter, Barnaby maintained 'is to sacrifice the greater for the less: it is to sacrifice the vital for that which is not vital', since 'a single shell through the armour may disable the ship but no single shell in the armoured structure could possibly do so'. Finally, concluded the harassed Chief Constructor, '[i]f the unarmoured ends . . . were completely swept away, the stability protected by armour would give her a range of nearly 50 degrees', and, even worse, were the ends intact but devoid of water-excluding materials so that they reduced rather increased buoyancy, she 'would still have a large range of stability'.

The lengthy exchange between Reed and the Admiralty was, however, but the opening salvo in the conflict. As the former intimated in his letter of 9 June, having failed to carry his views by attacking *Inflexible* privately, he made his charges public. On the morning of 18 June the *Times* printed a lengthy unsigned article detailing his allegations along with an editorial on the subject. The former reviewed the genesis and evolution of the central-citadel principle, professing that it was 'with the greatest surprise we now learn that, notwithstanding the consideration which has been given to this point [*ie* securing floatation and stability] . . . it has either been lost sight of or misapplied at our own Admiralty'.[23] Thus, it appeared, stated the journal, that '*Inflexible* and other ships of her type have been designed and are being built so as to have no stability whatever, independent of the unarmoured ends', and if the ends were flooded 'any one of these ships would inevitably capsize'. This charge was, of course, crude, alarmist, and false. It was also just what Reed was after, for the *Times* followed it with a demand for immediate experiments on *Inflexible* and the two *Ajax* class ships to ascertain their safety and what alterations should be made to secure it. If the Admiralty were satisfied with their designs, surely then they could have no objection to coming clean in public.

The editorial was similarly alarmist and misinformed: '[i]t is said that the unarmoured ends are, in fact, the corks on which she

16. Boys to Houston Stewart, 22 May 1977, 'Report of the Committee on the *Inflexible*, with Appendix,' *Parl. Papers*, 1878, Vol. 19, Appendix 1, p9 (p171 in microprint ed.). Boys' comments appear on pp8-9, Houston Stewart's on p9.

17. *Independencia* actually had a waterline belt of 12ins maximum thickness and citadel armour of 10ins. The general thrust of Houston Stewart's argument was accurate despite these errors. See *Conway's 1860-1905*, p25.

18. The *Kaiser*s had a waterline belt of 10ins maximum thickness; the casemate armour was 8ins, and it was presumably this to which Houston Stewart referred. See *Conway's 1860-1905*, p245.

19. Houston Stewart to Board, 22 May 1977, in 'Report of the Committee on the *Inflexible*, with Appendix,' *Parl. Papers*, 1878, Vol. 19, Appendix 1, p9 (p171 in microprint ed.).

20. Robert Hall to Reed, 5 June 1877, ibid.

21. Reed to Hall, 9 June 1877, ibid, pp9-10 (pp171-2 in microprint ed.).

22. Barnaby memorandum to Board, 12 June 1877, ibid, p10 (p172 in microprint ed.).

23. *The Times*, 18 June 1877, p5.

floats; that she cannot swim without them, and it would appear that if she lost one she would capsize.'[24] Admitting that Reed's charges were speculative, it nonetheless demanded 'some enquiry . . . entrusted to . . . persons . . . in whom Parliament and the country can confide', since the Constructors passed judgement on the merits of their own designs, with no supervisory body to detect errors:

> There is no one in the Department to whom we can with confidence appeal. If an inquiry is needed, it must be made to some independent tribunal, with all the attendant disadvantages of needless publicity and inconvenient interruption of business.

By the time Parliament met that evening the issue was already one of public notoriety. Former First Lord George J. Goschen, whose Board had authorised the design, alluded to a statement appearing in 'the leading journal with regard to the *Inflexible* which was calculated to alarm the public as much as those . . . which had been made respecting that most efficient ship the *Devastation*'.[25] George Ward Hunt attempted to dismiss the *Times*' charges: the Admiralty, he avowed, 'were satisfied that it was impossible' that 'a destruction of the unarmoured ends could happen in battle' and that even were 'the unarmoured ends blown out, she would not capsize'.[26] Reed, piously claiming he had 'been doing his best for some weeks to keep the discussion . . . out of the newspapers', immediately disputed the First Lord, however. Barnaby's memorandum to the Board, already attacked privately, was denounced as 'wrong in almost every paragraph, and was of a nature to mislead the minds of civilians and naval officers'.[27] Of Houston Stewart's and Boy's unequivocal rejection of his charges, Reed said nothing, but reiterated the claim that if *Inflexible* 'was attacked by a shell fire [*sic*] and her unarmoured ends were destroyed, she would be left without stability, and would then capsize'.[28]

Barnaby attempted a rebuttal in a letter to the *Times* the following day, branding Reed's allegations 'not true', but his defence, which took the same lines as his earlier private exchanges, was drowned out in the furore which the former C.N.A. had ignited and now stoked with evident relish. Reed immediately and derisively replied to Barnaby's letter, claiming that he 'did not even touch on the essential part of the question'.[29] His old ally Rear-Admiral Robert Spencer Robinson, Controller from 1861 to 1871, also pitched into the fray on 20 June, terming Reed the 'master' and Barnaby his 'pupil' in matters of naval architecture, and demanding the appointment of an examining Board to pass judgement on the Admiralty's recent designs.[30] 'It seems incredible,' he declaimed,

> that no steps should yet have been taken, by calling a properly constituted and independent tribunal, to verify the probability or

otherwise of the designs of ships corresponding to the intentions of those who ordered them, to check the calculations presented to them, and to watch the progress and alterations made in those designs before the ship is completed.

For those with long memories, this demand was shot through with irony, since Spencer Robinson himself had violently opposed just that course of action in 1870 when, in the wake of the *Captain* disaster, the Gladstone government appointed the Committee on Designs to reassure public opinion. His stance in 1877 was therefore inconsistent, if not downright hypocritical.

Not that such facts had any bearing on the state of public and press opinion. Barnaby's follow-up letter of 21 June, which disputed Spencer Robinson's assertions and disclaimed any intent of further arguing the matter with Reed, was overshadowed by another editorial in the *Times*' best thundering mode.[31] The journal evinced satisfaction of the ruckus it had helped stir up, and reiterated the demand for an investigative tribunal in the form of a Royal Commission or Parliamentary Select Committee.[32] Further letters from Reed and Spencer Robinson followed on 25 June.[33] A day later the eminent Dr. Joseph Woolley, a member of the 1871 Committee on Designs (and a crony of Reed), expressed his own fears that the scenario envisioned by Reed was 'only too probable' and seconded the call for 'a competent, unbiased, and impartial tribunal' to consider the issue.[34] On 9 July the *Times* printed yet another editorial which railed against Admiralty and government alike. The former did not, it claimed, possess Parliament's or the nation's confidence to pass judgement on *Inflexible*.[35] Only an examining board along the lines Spencer Robinson had demanded would do. 'As matters now stand, the Constructive Department constitute a Court of Design, from which there is no appeal, either for the Government or the public, without resorting to some external advice.' Moreover, all the old charges of Admiralty obstructionism and conservatism, largely quiescent since the *Captain* controversy the previous decade, resurfaced in the wake of Reed's charges. 'The reason of this general demand for independent investigation,' the *Times* alleged, 'is that the Admiralty is not trusted. They have not heretofore kept abreast with the progress of the times.' Again, the whole litany of supposed defects and shortcomings was trotted out: the Board had been slow to adopt steam, had clung blindly to masts and sails, and had 'disregarded the ram and the torpedo, while concentrating all their attention on resistance to shot and shell'. 'Of all the great Departments,' in short, 'the Admiralty is the one in which the Government have experienced the most frequent failures and risen the least to the exigencies of the day.'

For the observant, the *Times*' broadside involved more irony, for the controversy swirling around *Inflexible* involved anything but the Admiralty's refusal to stay abreast of the latest technological developments. Indeed, the ship was controversial precisely because she was experimental rather than retrograde. Reed was conservatism's advocate: Barnaby, Hood, and Houston Stewart had boldly broken with the past. Moreover, to anyone familiar with Reed's private attacks and Barnaby's rebuttals, the charge that the Constructor's Department had ignored the threats posed by ram and torpedoes for obsessive concentration on gunfire must have appeared ludicrous. Again, the exact opposite was the case: Reed had monomaniacally focused on ordnance, whereas Barnaby had stressed cellular subdivision and watertight compartmentalisation which would provide defence against underwater weapons. Such subtleties, however, were lost on the *Times* and presumably much of the public as well. 'Is Parliament content to leave this question in the hands of the Department,' the paper spluttered cholerically, 'the administration of which has been crowned with so much disaster?'

Reed must have been gratified by the result his onslaught produced. A week after the *Times*' latest editorial–during which time Reed published two additional letters, one of which alleged that the Admiralty had released a false curve of stability–the government bowed to pressure and appointed an independent Committee, consisting of Admiral James Hope and three civilian authorities, William Froude, George Rendel of Armstrong's, and the same Dr. Woolley who had expressed his doubts about *Inflexible* in print a few days earlier. This distinguished panel was asked to answer a number of questions raised by Reed's allegations, three of which were of particular significance:

[1.] As to the possibility or probability of the occurrence of the contingencies contemplated by Mr. Reed as being likely to happen very early in an engagement, namely, the complete penetration and water-logging of the unprotected ends of the ship, and the blowing out of the whole of the stores and cork by the action of shellfire.

[2, clause 1.] As to whether their would be any risk of the ship capsizing if she were placed under the conditions mentioned in the previous paragraph, supposing that the water ballast were admitted into the double bottom of the armoured citadel.

[3, clause 1.] Whether, all points considered in so far as can be

ascertained from the designs and calculations, the '*Inflexible*' is a safe sea-going vessel.[36]

If Reed was gratified with the success of his campaign, he must have been disappointed at the outcome of the Committee's investigation, for its report amounted to a solid endorsement of *Inflexible* and an exoneration of Barnaby and his superiors. 'We are of opinion,' it concluded,

that 'the complete penetration and water-logging of the unprotected ends of the ship', coupled with 'the blowing out of the whole of the stores and the cork by the action of shell fire', is not likely 'to happen very early in an engagement;' further, that it is in a very high degree improbable, even in an engagement protracted to any extent which can be reasonably anticipated.

Moreover, the Committee did not even envision the possibility of such an eventuality, save 'in the event of her being attacked by enemies of such preponderating force as to render her entering into any engagement in the highest degree imprudent'.

As for the likelihood of *Inflexible*'s capsizing were Reed's far-fetched scenario realised, the findings were somewhat more equivocal:

We find that under the extreme conditions assumed the ship, even without water ballast, would yet have stability, and would therefore float upright in still water, and we are of opinion that the stability that she would have in that condition, though small, is, in consequence of the remarkable effects of free internal water in extinguishing rolling, sufficient to enable her to encounter with safety waves of considerable magnitude.

True, the ship would have to be manoeuvred and fought with extreme caution were she battered to such an extent–'we should consider the ship in a very critical state if reduced to this condition in the presence of a still powerful enemy'–but, the panellists reiterated, 'it is in a very high degree improbable that the ship would be reduced to this condition, even in a protracted engagement.' Was the ship therefore 'a safe, sea-going vessel?'. With ends intact,

24. Ibid, p11.

25. *Hansard's Parliamentary Debates*, 3d ser., 234 (1877), col. 1990.

26. Ibid, col. 1992.

27. Ibid, col. 1996.

28. Ibid, col. 2010.

29. *The Times*, 20 June 1877, p10.

30. Ibid.

31. *The Times*, 21 June 1877, p8.

32. Ibid, p9.

33. *The Times*, 25 June 1877, p5.

34. *The Times*, 26 June 1877, p8.

35. *The Times*, 9 July 1877, p9.

36. 'Report of the Committee on the *Inflexible*, with Appendix', *Parl. Papers*, 1878, Vol. 19, piii-iv (pp145-6 in microprint ed.). The ensuing findings, quoted in the following three paragraphs, are found on ppv-xv (pp147-57 in microprint ed.). The remaining questions were: 2. clause 2. 'Whether she would retain a sufficient amount of stability to enable such temporary repairs to be executed as would enable her to reach a port.' 3, clause 2. 'Whether, when the amount of damage to which her unprotected ends would be exposed in action is borne in mind, sufficient provision has been made to ensure in all human probability her safety under such conditions.'

unquestionably. In the event that the ends were perforated and awash, and the coal – but not the cork – out of the ends,

> the ship would possess both buoyancy and stability enough to enable her to face all contingencies of weather, and to exercise all her powers, subject, however, to the limitations of speed which may be imposed by the character and position of the wounds in the ends . . . .

The actual range of stability in that condition would be, they determined, 35 degrees at minimum, less, it was admitted, than the standard set down by the Committee on Designs in 1871, but that criterion, they added, 'requires revision' owing to subsequent investigations of rolling, and was in any case inapplicable in this instance, since 'the water-logging of the ends . . . has a most remarkable effect in preventing rolling . . .'.

As for the central element of Reed's attack, that the cork which prevented water from filling the chambers would be quickly 'blown out' by shellfire, the Committee displayed no such equivocation. Shot penetrating the unarmoured side, unless fired at a very oblique angle, would be through the outer wall of the hull before exploding. This factor, coupled with the shell's explosion, which would radiate 'forward in a cone of dispersion', led them to conclude that the cork wall and coffer dam, being only 6ft thick in all, would not be quickly destroyed, as Reed alleged. 'We think . . . that although the riddling of all the compartments is a possibility to be recognised and taken into account, this cannot be said of the blowing out of all the cork and materials.'

If Disraeli's government and the Admiralty expected the report to silence Reed and his partisans, they, too must have been sorely disappointed. Published accounts of the Committee's proceedings drew Reed's ire in mid-September, but he and the *Times* conserved the bulk of their considerable wrath until December, when the report was made public.[37] Reed immediately denounced it as a whitewash, manipulated by the Admiralty to cover its mistakes.[38] The summary of the Committee's findings had been, he alleged, 'so drawn, by some evil and deceptive pen', as to lead the reader to believe that it approved of *Inflexible*'s design. In his closing words Reed passed well beyond the bounds of criticism into outright alarmism, expressing the hope that the Admiralty would not pro-

ceed with the ship, for 'terrible will be the responsibilities which rest upon them if, in the face of the Committee's concluding facts and adjurations, they send our seamen to sea in such a ship'. The following day the *Times* itself weighed in with a long article which concluded that the Committee's findings amounted to an admission 'that, if the *Inflexible* is not unsafe, it is because naval gunnery is very fallible'.[39]

The Committee had its defenders, too. Thomas Brassey praised its report and assured his 'countrymen . . . that they may place undoubting confidence in the Constructive Department of the Admiralty'.[40] Yet this defence only provoked further paroxysms from the *Times*, which, on the final day of the year, denounced much of the report as being of 'a speculative and questionable character'.[41] It, furthermore,

> establish[ed] beyond question the truth of the main proposition originally advanced by us and confirmed by Mr. Reed, that if the unarmoured ends were to be so injured as to be unable to retain any buoyancy or stability, the *Inflexible* must inevitably capsize.

The vituperative campaign spilled over into 1878, its fury unabated: Spencer Robinson rejoined the fray on New Year's Day, strongly supporting Reed and the *Times* and renewing his call for a independent council to pass judgement on Admiralty designs. This missive was answered by future D.N.O. and Naval Lord Richard Vesey Hamilton, who opined that the vessel, 'like any other work of human hands, may be destroyed by overwhelming force; but against any force she ought, or is likely to engage under present conditions of artillery armaments I believe her almost indestructible'.[42] Reed followed this apparent affront in a speech to his constituents at Pembroke (Wales) on 10 January in which he depicted himself as a martyr for his selfless pursuit of the truth, a quest in which he had been courageously supported by the *Times*.[43] Brassey's rebuttal on 12 January – 'we are assured by naval officers that the risk to the *Inflexible* is minimal' – was followed by one final blast from Reed, who seems to have obsessively desired to get the last word in.[44] He now claimed that he had been the victim of personal attacks by the First Lord of the Admiralty, W.H. Smith, and the rest of the Board to undercut his reputation and influence. He likewise savaged Admiral Charles Hope, who had voiced

---

37. *The Times*, 4 September 1877, p9; 15 September 1877, p11; 18 September 1877, p11; 19 September 1877, p6.

38. Ibid, 13 December 1877, p10.

39. Ibid, 14 December 1877, p4.

40. Ibid, 25 December 1877, p5.

41. Ibid, 31 December 1877, p11.

42. Ibid, 8 January 1878, p7.

43. Ibid, 10 January 1878, p11.

44. Ibid, 12 January 1878, p6; 18 January 1878, p4.

45. For the *Captain* fracas, see Sandler, *The Emergence of the Modern Capital Ship*, pp177-233.

46. It might be noted, also, that the *Captain* was less unsafe for the reasons her detractors (Reed and Spencer Robinson) claimed – *ie* masting a low-freeboard turret ship – than from other factors: excessive weight of hull which reduced her freeboard still further, the rigidity of her iron tripod masts, and the unswerving determination of her designer, Cowper Phipps Coles, and Captain, John Burgoyne, to outsail her consorts.

47. Parkes, *British Battleships*, p396.

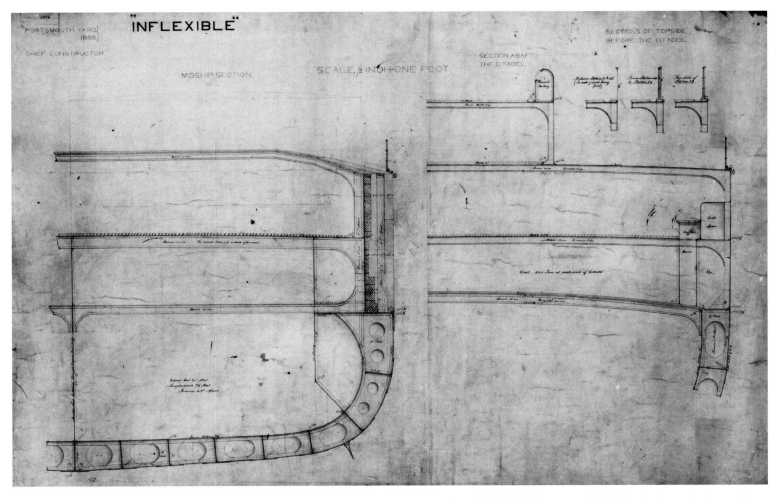

Cross-sections of *Inflexible*. The one on the left clearly shows the heavy side armour of the central citadel; that on the right displays the absence of such armour at the ends. The slightly curved armoured deck can also be seen. (National Maritime Museum, London: 7706)

a defence of *Inflexible* which Reed termed rife with 'monstrous defects'. The ship, although still far short of completion, was written off as 'a hopeless and terrible failure'.

Making sense of this mudslinging contest more than a century after the event is, like the fracas a decade earlier over HMS *Captain*, a difficult task owing to the partisanship which enveloped the fray. Assessing the merits of the two sides in the *Inflexible* squabble is compounded by the fact that, as both admitted, it was largely a matter of conjecture and opinion.[45] Yet in other respects it is easier to get to the bottom of the matter than is the case with *Captain*. First, as revealed by her service career, *Inflexible* was unquestionably a seaworthy ship while in an intact condition, as the Committee reported. No tragedy overtook her as did the *Captain*.[46] Moreover, the unarmoured ends, so far from being discarded following this seemingly fatal verbal assault, became a fixture in British capital ship design for the subsequent two decades, and when a forward waterline belt was finally reintroduced in the *Canopus* class (authorised 1896-97), it was 2in thick–designed to stop tertiary, rather than main or secondary shellfire. 'There was,' Parkes unequivocally states,

no question of any public agitation against 'soft-enders' having been responsible for this additional plating in the hope that it

might be fobbed off as 'a complete belt forward'. . . It would, of course, have been useless against medium guns except at very long range.[47]

The 'soft ends,' in short, became a standard feature of British pre-dreadnought design, Reed's alarmism notwithstanding.

Finally, the likelihood of the ends being riddled in action and deprived of their buoyancy was equally insignificant, as subsequent events demonstrated. *Inflexible* never received enemy fire save at Alexandria in 1882, and was not struck enough times to test Reed's assertions, but during the Sino-Japanese War two very similar ships were. The Chinese *Ting Yuen* class central-citadel turret ships with 'soft ends,' were hit by concentrated enemy fire at the Battle of the Yalu (17 September 1894). *Ting Yuen* herself was struck almost 200 times and her sister *Chen Yuen* nearly as often, but, as Parkes notes, 'in neither case were the unarmoured ends blown to pieces'. *Inflexible*, if similarly attacked, 'would hardly have become a sitting and almost helpless target as was the case with the Chinese ships'.[48] Furthermore, in 1908 HMS *Edinburgh*, last of Britain's central-citadel battleships, with the same 'soft ends' as *Inflexible*, served as a gunnery practice target for the fleet 'without her unarmoured ends being blown away or extensively damaged, after enduring a more devastating fire than she would have experienced in possible action during her active life'.[49] Reed's charges, from the available evidence, were as specious as his tone was alarmist.

Another dissimilarity with the *Captain* episode was the availability of assessments by qualified and detached observers from whom press and public could draw reliable conclusions. Only after *Captain* capsized did the government appoint a qualified committee to pass judgement on the safety and seaworthiness of the Navy's battlefleet. It was, perhaps, a measure of the lingering influence of that ship's horrifying fate that when charges about *Inflexible*'s safety and doubts about the Admiralty's integrity and competence were aired by one who presumably spoke with authority, the government quickly responded just as Gladstone's had in late 1870. That both ministries aimed at 'damage control' need not be doubted, but it is also beyond argument that the panel appointed – like the Committee on Designs – was not lacking the professional and scientific expertise needed to pass qualified judgement. Indeed, there was no greater authority on hull forms than William Froude. Moreover, Froude, although routinely employed by the Admiralty to test models of its own design, was not an employee of the service, while his fellow Committee member, Joseph Woolley, it will be recalled, publicly stated his misgivings about *Inflexible*'s stability prior to being appointed. This was not a committee of whitewashers, in other words, and even had its members been so inclined, the fate Reed alleged threatened *Inflexible* was so terrible, and *Captain*'s capsizing so recent, it is most unlikely that any member would have risked his reputation for the sake of covering up Admiralty mistakes.

The *Inflexible* was, practically speaking, perfectly safe. It was not unsinkable; no warship before or since has been, and nobody with any understanding of naval warfare or, indeed, of the risks of going to sea, could envision such a vessel. Certainly Reed's desiderata in this regard should have been tempered by his professional knowledge. That they were not reflects poorly on his honesty and integrity. Yet Reed neither ceased his agitation against 'soft-enders' nor, for that matter, curbed his dishonesty, as subsequent events revealed. In 1885 John Knox Laughton, the pioneer of methodologically-rigorous naval history and, at that time, the foremost authority on the history of the Navy, took notice in the pages of the august *Edinburgh Review* of Reed's public utterances. Laughton's chief aim was deprecating the panic unleashed by W.T. Stead's 'Truth about the Navy' articles in the *Pall Mall Gazette* the previous fall, but he found space to spare three pages for savaging Reed, a man

who, at different periods of his unofficial life, has publicly testi-

fied his admiration and approval of almost every possible type of ships of war except those which, at the particular time, happen to be accepted by the Admiralty.[50]

Reed, continued Laughton, had furthermore taken a comment of Nathaniel Barnaby's from the *Encyclopaedia Britannica*, which, out of context, could be misunderstood and misrepresented, and had 'chosen to avail himself of this possibility; he has misrepresented it, and he has done so deliberately . . .'. To use Barnaby's words out of context, as part of a polemic against Admiralty design policy, 'in the language which Sir Edward Reed has used,' Laughton wrote, required 'a very full measure of effrontery and virulence'. Yet this was not the worst of Reed's transgressions.

Laughton adduced other instances of Reed's invective, describing one as his 'very disagreeable way of saying that just at present his views on certain points of naval construction differ from those of Mr. Barnaby', before concluding with the former Chief Constructor's crowning outrage.[51] Laughton noted that Reed refused to take up the cudgels before a professional audience; he

> has always avoided the discussion of [Admiralty policy] before a competent tribunal . . . but in the columns of a newspaper, or before an audience ignorant of his technicalities, he has accustomed himself to an unrestrained indulgence in flowers of rhetoric, in flights of imagination, and, we are compelled to add, in disingenuous presentation of facts and illegitimate distortion of evidence.[52]

There followed the most damning indictment printed against Reed, one which certainly would have produced a libel suit had it not been so thoroughly documented in Laughton's characteristic fashion.

> It is painful to have to say this, but it is necessary to point out that, in writing to the 'Times' the gross and vehement letter to which we have . . . referred, he did not scruple, by omission of some words and the alteration or insertion of others, to give a widely different colour to a remaak [*sic*] made by Admiral Wilson, the present superintendent of the dockyard at Devonport. The charge is so grave that it is incumbent on us to substantiate it by repeating the passage, marking in italics the words which Sir Edward Reed omitted, and by brackets the words which he inserted.
>
> 'I do not like these soft ends at all; they may *not* [all] be breached and *have* a *big* hole knocked into *their deck* [you] big enough to drive a coach and four through; *but* [even] if one or two shots *penetrate* [get in], *and* water gets in, the ship *will get* [gets] down by the nose, she won't steer, she cannot steam, [and] she is thrown out altogether *and you* [. You] lose confidence in *the* [your] ship. [And] What is the result? Your are at a [great] disadvantage, and you are [soon] knocked into a cocked hat.'[53]

Aside from the damage done to the Admiralty's and Barnaby's public standings by Reed's irresponsible denunciations, *Inflexible*'s progress suffered as well. Construction ceased for virtually a year.[54] When the delays caused by upgrading the armament and its fitting, along with those caused by other modifications are added to this hiatus, the reasons for her painfully slow rate of construction are readily apparent. In 1877 George Ward Hunt presumed she would be ready for sea sometime in 1878.[55] In 1878 she was among four first-class ironclads W.H. Smith hoped 'to complete within the coming financial year'.[56] The following year, noting the delays consequent upon switching from wrought iron to compound armour on the ship's turrets, Smith wisely refrained from predicting a completion date. But in 1880 George John Shaw-Lefevre asserted 'the *Inflexible* would be completed in the course of the year'.[57] She was finally finished in October 1881.

By the time *Inflexible* entered her first commission, moreover, the currents of strategic and tactical thought were beginning to shift. Changing professional perspectives, along with the more evident switch over to long-barrelled breech-loading ordnance which, thanks to improved powder, could provide increased velocity and impact with reduced weight of gun, meant that *Inflexible* was outmoded. Even had the ship's ordnance been exchanged for more modern guns – a problematic switch given the greater length of breech-loaders and *Inflexible*'s space limitations – her unwieldiness (of little import in her originally envisioned role of coastal assault) was a telling shortcoming with the advent and development of the torpedo boat. Indeed, the strategy of the *Jeune Ecole*, which surfaced in mid-decade, was explicitly aimed at negating Britain's superiority in precisely this sort of vessel. Handiness, speed, and manoeuvrability became increasingly valued over protection and smashing power. Indeed (as will be examined in greater detail in Chapter 9), from the late 1870s through most of the subsequent decade, considerable debate raged as to whether the day of the heavily armed and armoured ironclad had come and gone. By 1876 the *Times* wondered in print whether it might be better to abandon armour. As noted, there were opinions of great weight – William Armstrong's and Joseph Woolley's among them – to lend support to the idea.[58] Even the Admiralty succumbed to doubts, the Parliamentary Secretary boldly prophesying in 1886 – following the lead of First Naval Lord Sir Astley Cooper Key – that the heavily armed and armoured turret ships *Nile* and *Trafalgar* 'will probably be the last ironclads of this type that will ever be built in this or any other country'.[59] By the time this opinion was quashed, owing to the continuation of foreign battleship building, the Admiralty was looking for a very different type of warship from *Inflexible* and her coast-assault descendants: thus the decision to build the high-freeboard (and much larger) barbette ships of the *Royal Sovereign* class: the first first-class, high-seas, cruising battleships since *Alexandra* and *Temeraire*.

48. Ibid, p259; see also *Conway's 1860-1905*, p395.

49. Parkes, *British Battleships*, p291.

50. [J. K. Laughton], 'Past and Present State of the Navy', *Edinburgh Review* (April 1885), pp501-02. Laughton's allusion to Reed's approbation for 'almost every possible type of ships of warfare' probably refers, at least in part, to an 1875 series of letters to the *Times* (later published in pamphlet form) extolling the manoeuvrability and seaworthiness of two curious circular coast-defence monitors built for the Russian Black Sea fleet. Reed appears to have been their sole English-speaking advocate.

51. Ibid, p503.

52. Ibid, p504.

53. Ibid. Wilson's remark appeared in the *Journal of the Royal United Services Institution*, 28: p1039; Reed's 'paraphrase' of it in *The Times*, 19 February 1885.

54. Parkes, *British Battleships*, pp258-9.

55. *Hansard*, 3d ser., 232 (1877), col. 1814.

56. Ibid., 3d ser., 238 (1878), col. 1411.

57. Ibid., 3rd ser., 252 (1880), col. 1385.

58. *The Times*, 25 February 1876, p4.

59. Cited in Parkes, *British Battleships*, p342.

Chapter 8

FROM *INFLEXIBLE* TO *COLOSSUS*

THE SUBSEQUENT four coast assault ironclads – *Ajax*, *Agamemnon*, *Colossus*, and *Edinburgh* (originally named *Majestic*) – followed the general layout of *Inflexible*, and thus are grouped with the prototype under the rubric 'Central Citadel' battleships. Yet it is clear from the surviving papers that this course was anything but a foregone conclusion. Indeed, the Constructor's Department lobbied hard in both the case of the *Ajax* and *Colossus* classes to design and build ships very different from *Inflexible*, based partly on its evaluation of foreign designs and partly as a consequence of Nathaniel Barnaby's shifting views on the relative utility of guns, torpedoes and rams, on the value of armour, and certainly not least of all, on the nature of future sea battles. Not

A diminutive repeat of *Inflexible*, *Ajax* and her sister-ship *Agamemnon* suffered from several drawbacks as a consequence of attempting to marry first-class armament and protection with second-class displacement, draft and length. (National Maritime Museum, London: 7618)

coincidentally, the period encompassing these ships' genesis – 1875-9 – witnessed the greatest ferment in the tactical sphere. Thus the design histories of the two classes, along with that of the unique armoured ram *Polyphemus* warrant careful scrutiny. This was, after all, the deepest night of Parkes' 'Dark Ages', although when illuminated and clearly examined the rationale for building some of the most criticised designs in the annals of the Navy are readily apparent.

Ajax *and* Agamemnon

The history of *Ajax* and *Agamemnon* began, prosaically enough, with a note from Barnaby to his subordinate Henry Dunn, asking him to 'prepare a sketch for an *Inflexible* with four 38-ton barbette guns, 18in armour, 600 tons of coal, 20 feet draught of water, and 13 knots speed.'[1] The barbette was a French innovation, popular for mounting heavy guns in the ironclads of that navy. Compared

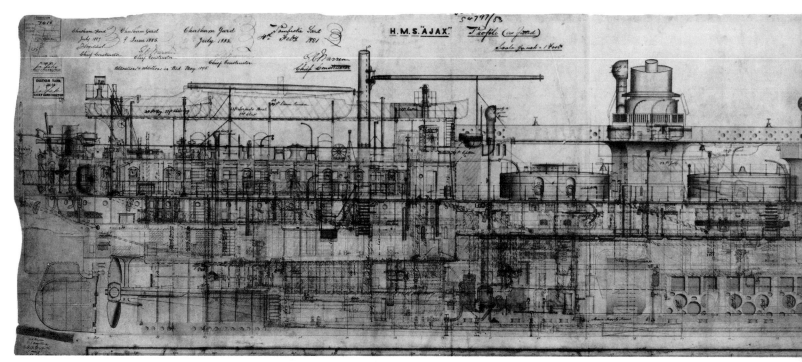

to the turret it was a paragon of simplicity. Rather than a heavily armoured shell enclosing a gun, mounted on a turntable, the barbette was an armoured tube or tower. Only the gun was mounted on a turntable. The tower offered little protection for the gun crew, but the absence of the heavy turret, as well as the fact that the barbette's turntable and machinery were lighter and more compact, meant a considerable saving of weight, a matter of no small importance for guns mounted high above the waterline where they could seriously compromise the stability of a ship of moderate dimensions.

Yet upon first reading Barnaby's instructions appeared contradictory; *Inflexible* was not, after all, a barbette ship, and indeed a few sentences later the D.N.C. referred to 'turrets' rather than barbettes. The context, however, leaves no doubt that he meant barbettes to be mounted on a central-citadel, raft hull like that of *Inflexible*: 'the turrets [*ie* barbettes] to be four in number [each mounting a single gun] fixed like those in the [barbette ship] *Temeraire* and standing only 6 feet above the deck.' Perhaps most crucially, Barnaby informed Dunn, the ship was to be designed for 'Home Defence' and 'the displacement not to exceed 7000 tons'.

Barnaby's note leaves no clue as to whether he was acting on his own volition or at the instigation of Controller William Houston Stewart, although standard Admiralty procedure would certainly point to the latter.[2] Either way, it is clear from other papers that the Board–First Lord George Ward Hunt, First Naval Lord Alexander Milne, Second Naval Lord Geoffrey Phipps 'Uncle Geoff' Hornby, and Junior Naval Lord Gilford–had not yet aired its views on the design. It is likewise obvious that whether it was his or the Controller's, the design Barnaby described was radically different from *Inflexible*, even if it was to mount turrets rather than

barbettes. There were to be four such gun platforms rather than two, each positioned at a corner of the citadel. The layout was, in fact, strikingly similar to the French *Océan* class central battery ships, laid down in the mid-1860s and completed between 1870 and 1875. D.N.O. Astley Cooper Key had provided the Board with a description of the French design in June 1867, noting '[t]he principal feature of this ship consists in the four towers on the upper deck–two on each side–before and abaft the mainmast–each partially projecting over the ship's side' for axial fire.[3] The chief difference between the French ships and that described by Barnaby was that the former were high-freeboard cruising ships rather than home defence types. However, they were not successful as such; Barnaby's stress on the height of the barbette towers (6ft was very low, low enough in fact to expose the crews to plunging fire if such a ship were to be used against shore fortifications), was probably related to the deficient stability of the French ships, one of which had been complete for five years by 1875. The *Océan*s' metacentric height was less than 2½ft and their barbette armour was eventually removed to reduce top weight and improve stability.[4]

But Barnaby's ideas never got beyond the drawing board. The following month Milne composed the first of two memoranda detailing his conceptions of how *Ajax* should be built. Milne used the size of the ship's intended armament as the central criterion around which he sketched out his design. Indeed, he forthrightly stated that 'the type of Ship will be dependent on the size of the gun, which should possess the greatest penetrating power'.[5] The First Naval Lord assumed the heaviest such gun available to be that of 38 tons (12.5in bore), 'and as this can only be worked in a revolving turret, it becomes necessary to adopt a Turret ship as the new type to be laid down.' Strictly speaking, Milne was incorrect; there was no compelling reason why 38-ton guns could not be mounted in barbettes as well as turrets, assuming that the barbette was large enough to house a disappearing mount. Yet even were this technical point conceded, he nonetheless envisioned the type of ship for which turrets were much preferable to open-topped barbettes: 'for Home defence,' he concluded, 'and Mediterranean operations as well as Special Service, the power of the . . . Ship from having the heaviest guns', plus armoured 'plating . . . as heavy as can be determined by the Constructors' mandated the turret. Hence, he suggested, the new ship should 'somewhat

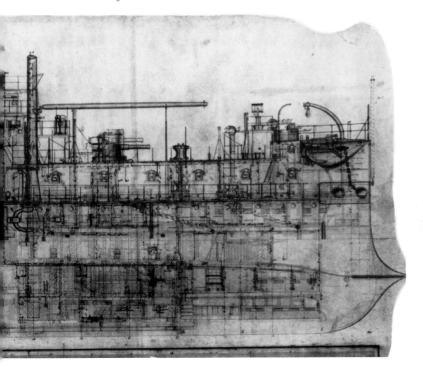

1. Barnaby to Dunn, *Ship for Home Defence*, 9 February 1875, NMM: ADM138/60, fol. 1 (Ship's Cover for *Ajax* and *Agamemnon*).

2. For confirmation, see Richard Vesey Hamilton, *Naval Administration. The Constitution, Character, and Functions of the Board of Admiralty, and of the Civil Departments it Directs* (London, 1896), pp170-1.

3. Cooper Key, 'Report on Foreign and English Guns', 13 June 1867, PRO: ADM1/6012.

4. Chesneau and Kolesnik (eds.), *Conway's All the World's Fighting Ships, 1860-1905*, p288.

5. Milne, 'New Class of Ship to be laid down to add to the Iron clad Fleet', March 1875, NMM: MLN/144/5 [2].

resembl[e] the *Fury* [*ie Dreadnought*] or *Inflexible*'. Likewise, Milne left no doubt that this design was intended for coastal operations, whether offensive or defensive, by stipulating that 'the Draft of water should not exceed 22 feet [and] less would be advisable if this could be practically carried out'.

Several other recommendations followed. 'The speed,' the First Lord stated, 'should not be below 13 knots' and a large coal capacity was 'a necessity', although he also maintained that the vessel should 'have two masts with topsails as a steadying sail in a heavy sea to check excessive motion'. Last, but certainly not least, Milne opined that '[t]he shorter the ship the more satisfactory it would be, for every purpose of naval warfare'.

It is evident from the surviving evidence that two designs were prepared following Milne's memorandum. It is not clear who, aside from Houston Stewart, advocated the barbette ship, but the idea was kept alive, and in June the Constructor's department furnished Barnaby with sketches and particulars of two designs, matched up against *Temeraire* for comparison. Again, both were explicitly termed 'Home Defence Ships'.[6]

Although a damaged print, *Ocean*'s after barbette is clearly visible abeam of the mainmast. (U.S. Naval Historical Center: NH74922)

	Temeraire	Barbette	Turret
Length (ft-in)	285-0	280-0	280-0
Breadth (ft)	62	65	65
Extreme draught (ft)	27	21	21
	(8400 tons)	(7840 tons)	(7800 tons)
I.H.P.	7000	5500	5500
Speed (kts)	14	13	13
Coal (tons)	400	600	600
Thickest armour (in)	11	18	18
Deck Plating (in)	½	3	3
Armament	4 25-ton	4 38-ton	4 38-ton
	4 18-ton		
Right ahead fire	3 25-ton	2 38-ton	4 38-ton
Right astern fire	1 25-ton	2 38-ton	4 38-ton
Broadside	3 25-ton	2 38-ton	4 38-ton
	2 18-ton		

The barbette arrangement of four singly-mounted guns at the corners of the superstructure put it at a substantial disadvantage both in weight of broadside and of end-on fire; the offset turrets of *Inflexible*'s disposition theoretically allowed all four heavy guns to

140

Ajax and *Agamemnon*'s low freeboard, consistent with their 'home defence' role, is clearly evident in this photograph of the latter. (U.S. Naval Historical Center: NH64207)

be used both directly ahead and astern as well as on the beam. Only half of the barbette ship's guns could be worked in each direction, although three guns could be worked on the quarters, as opposed to two of *Inflexible*'s. This disparity, coupled with the Constructor's estimates of £361,000 for the turret ship and £369,000 for the barbette vessel (£383,700 if masts and sails were added), along with the First Naval Lord's unequivocal preference, presumably dictated the Board's decision in June 1875 to select the turret design. The Constructor's department was ordered to work up a full sketch and details, which were approved by the Board on 13 October. The design departed from some of the criteria first laid down in February; the displacement, most notably, had swelled from 7000 to almost 9000 tons.[7] Yet the fundamental intent–a 'Home Defence' ship–had not altered.

---

6. Constructor's Dept to DNC, nd, NMM: ADM138/60, fol. 29. An accompanying paper (fol.23) comparing the estimated costs of the two designs and that of *Temeraire* is dated 3 June 1875; it seems reasonable to conclude that the statement of particulars dates from the same period. Regrettably, the accompanying sketches have not been preserved.

7. Barnaby to Houston Stewart, 8 October 1875, NMM: ADM138/60.
'Controller
 The outline design for the two new ironclads to be commenced this financial year was approved by their Lordships in June last.
 It has now been worked out and the plans and specifications are ready to go to the yards.
To be of 8492 tons
6000 H.P.
13 knots
Maximum armour: 18"
4-38 ton guns'

Agamemnon, seen here from the stern, is the most criticised of Barnaby's designs. Her 'tray-like' hull form (as Parkes put it), can clearly be seen here. (U.S. Naval Historical Center: NH64208)

The resulting ships, *Ajax* and *Agamemnon*, are the most criticised of all the designs which Barnaby oversaw. In these vessels, Oscar Parkes observes, the Navy was 'burdened . . . with a couple of unreliable steamers which ranked with that handful of designs that never evoked a good word even from the men who had the responsibility of handling them'. So pronounced was their unhandiness that at Queen Victoria's 1887 Jubilee Naval Review at Spithead the *Standard* reported '[t]he erratic *Ajax* . . . would dart out of line at times, making a wide sweep'. In 'thick weather they came to be regarded as no fit company for a squadron at sea and were directed accordingly; "take station on the horizon" being the reputed signal'.[8]

For Parkes and other critics, there is no question as to who to blame for this unhappy outcome. Barnaby has been held largely responsible for designing 'two of the most unsatisfactory battleships ever built for the Royal Navy'.[9] Yet it is clear that the D.N.C. originally envisioned a very different ship from that which eventually emerged. The *Ajax* and *Agamemnon* were not his creations, but rather Milne's. The chief drawback of the ships as constructed, their unhandiness, was the direct consequence of their dimensions: '[b]eing of great proportionate beam and moderate draught, also very flat-bottomed and of full lines, they were apt to behave more like trays than ships.' These features were the inevitable result of Milne's insistence that the draught 'should not exceed 22 feet' and 'the shorter the ship the more satisfactory it would be, for every purpose of naval warfare'. The outlines of the ships were generally in accordance with the specifics sketched out in his memoranda of March and April 1875. It is likewise clear that a ship carrying 38-ton guns in turrets and protected by 'plating as heavy as can be determined by the Constructors' would of necessity have great beam and full lines and bottom to secure the requisite stability in order to carry such a burden, especially on such a short and shallow hull.[10] *Ajax* and *Agamemnon* were, moreover, explicit attempts to cram first-class ordnance and protection onto coast-defence hulls, and this attempt contributed much to their unsatisfactory performance. Squeezing the essential features of *Inflexible* onto a ship over 3000 tons smaller, 40ft shorter, and drawing 2½ft less water was all but guaranteed to result in a design with numerous shortcomings. Barnaby's barbette ship might have proved no more successful, if weighed down by the same burdens, but it at least would have been his. As matters stand, he has been excoriated for a design over which he had little control.

The End of the Ironclad Era?

By the time the Board came to consider *Ajax* and *Agamemnon*'s design, doubts about the continued utility of heavily armed and armoured battleships were beginning to manifest themselves. In his April 1875 memorandum Milne noted 'the Italian Government or Admiralty have . . . decided that no more Iron clad Ships are to be built', a reference to that navy's decision to abandon a thick vertical waterline belt on *Italia* and *Lepanto* in favour of an armoured deck.[11] The reason was the locomotive torpedo which, the First Lord observed 'is . . . becoming a most formidable engine of war and may be so used to destroy the largest ships . . .'. He maintained that Britain's obligation 'to replace defective Ships to maintain our [naval] position' prohibited following Italy's lead, but his recognition of the problem signalled the advent of the most perplexed and confounded period of Admiralty design poli-cy during the nineteenth century. As early as 1871 the Admiralty Committee on Designs had admitted doubts about the continuing efficacy of armour.[12] By 1875 Milne could point to the additional menace of torpedoes, whose potential, based on tests at Portsmouth, he took very seriously.[13] Two years later the *Times* matter-of-factly termed the Whitehead torpedo 'the most formidable modern enemy of our men-of-war', and wondered if a half-dozen torpedo boats, which could be constructed for an 'expense quite trifling compared with great ships of war' might not 'prove a more formidable enemy to the *Devastation*' than the cutting-edge Italian ironclads *Duilio* and *Dandolo* together.[14] In sum,

[i]t is naturally, at the present time, a matter of great anxiety . . . to have to decide on any form of ironclad construction; and it is, perhaps, a still greater anxiety to the Government, not only to have to make up its mind what sort of ironclads to build, but to have to decide whether or not to build ironclads at all.[15]

Nor were torpedoes and guns the only menaces to lumbering, heavily armoured vessels. Exponents of the ram, led by the ageing Admiral Sir George Sartorius, touted their pet weapon as a threat to which no ironclad could stand up without fear of speedy destruction. It was in consideration of the latter weapon that in 1876 Barnaby gave extensive thought to the shape of future naval warfare. Sartorius had long lobbied for the creation of a ramming force consisting of vessels of '15 or 16 knots speed, without armour, with a light rig and with bow and stern guns', claiming;

I think I can satisfactorily show that the efficient Ram can combine all the qualities most necessary for a war vessel and be suited for every kind of warfare coast and ocean, offensive and defensive, that it can combine in itself the perfect Ram, the perfect gun carrier and the perfect torpedo vessel, possessing at the same time the greatest speed and handiness.[16]

Small, fast, and handy rams, he grandiosely claimed, 'will be undisputed master[s] against any floating machine in the world and no fleet or warships or convoy of troops could be protected from [their] attacks'.[17]

---

8. Parkes, *British Battleships*, p266. All quotations in this paragraph are drawn from Parkes.

9. Ibid, p262.

10. Milne, 'New Class of ship to be laid down to add to the Iron Clad Fleet', March, 1875, Milne Papers, NMM: MLN/ 144/5/2. It was probably just as well that the Board never sanctioned another of Milne's recommendations: '[s]hip to have two masts with topsails as a steadying sail in a heavy sea to check excessive motion'.

11. Milne Memorandum, April 1875, NMM: MLN/144/5 [2]

12. 'Report of the Committee appointed by the Lords Commissioners of the Admiralty to examine the Designs upon which Ships of War have recently been constructed, with Analysis of Evidence' (Hereafter Admiralty Committee on Designs), *Parl. Papers*, 1872, Vol. 14, ppix-x.

13. Milne Memorandum, April 1875, NMM: MLN/144/5 [2].

14. *The Times*, 4 January 1877, p3; 22 March 1877, p9.

15. *The Times*, 8 September 1876, p3.

16. Barnaby to Houston Stewart, 8 January 1876, NMM: ADM138/66, no fol. (Ship's Cover for *Polyphemus*); Sartorius to Admiralty, 27 June 1876, PRO: ADM1/6400. *Polyphemus*'s Ship's Cover contains no folio numbers. Thus, neither this citation nor those from ADM138/66 that follow have folio references.

17. Sartorius to Admiralty, 27 June 1876, PRO: ADM1/6400.

Sartorius initially met rebuffs in attempts to convince the Admiralty of the wisdom of his ways. As early as December 1867 he had forwarded a 'Letter . . . with pamphlet suggesting the building of armed and unarmed rams'. This address generated a memorandum 'from Sir S. Robinson unfavourably criticising Sir Geo. Sartorius' proposal'. A further missive from Sartorius in 1869 'condemning *Warrior, Black Prince*, &c, and advocating the building of small Rams' met with Spencer Robinson's curt reply 'that the suggestions are crude & ill defined and are refuted by letter D.I. 22/68'.[18]

By 1874, however, Barnaby and his staff had independently worked out a design for 'a ship to use torpedoes at a high speed . . . capable of operating wherever an Armourclad could, and to be able to maintain speed equal to that of the fastest ironclad for 8 or 10 hours, and to be armoured at waterline'.[19] This design also fea-

tured a ram prow, but it was first and foremost a torpedo vessel.[20] Neither the D.N.O., Captain Henry Boys, nor Controller Houston Stewart was impressed with the concept, however, and on 9 December 1874 Barnaby sent a note to the latter acknowledging that his department's design was not 'viewed favourably by D.N.O. [or] Controller' and since neither France nor Italy was proceeding in that direction 'he [was] disposed to give up especial torpedo vessels, and to fit all the fastest of the armoured and unarmoured ships with Whitehead torpedo gear'.[21]

By 1876, however, Houston Stewart had undergone a change of heart, remarking of Sartorius' most recent solicitation, 'I do not hesitate to express my firm conviction that were we now in possession of 2 of the 1st Class of these armoured monitor torpedo Rams' and four of a larger type with guns in addition to the prow, 'the Admiral in command of them might attack the . . . existing Ironclads of Europe even if combined with every prospect of being the Victor'.[22] Barnaby was more dubious. First, mindful of the financial exigencies of the peacetime navy, he pointed out that

Benbow with anti-torpedo booms and nets partially deployed. As Barnaby noted, such defences would foul the screws if deployed on a vessel under way. (U.S. Naval Historical Center: NH61616)

Sartorius' envisioned ram 'would require to be as large as the [unarmoured corvette] *Rover* [280ft x 43ft 6in x 22ft, 3460 tons displacement] and would cost at least £170,000'. Moreover, such a vessel would 'be of no use in a time of peace except for torpedo practice. She could not be commissioned and sent to a foreign station'. In peacetime she would float uncommissioned and idle, and the D.N.C. thought this a wasteful way to invest the service's limited construction funds. In addition, he expressed serious doubts as to the utility of such a warship: '[s]he would be crowded with machinery throughout two-thirds of her length, and she could only escape destruction by a miracle if she ventured to use the ram against a properly defended ironclad by daylight'. Indeed, given such vulnerability Barnaby baldly observed that the same attacks envisioned by Sartorius could be carried out by components of the already-existing unarmoured fleet: 'I do not know in what respects we could improve upon the *Rover* for the service contemplated by the Admiral, except in reducing the rig, the complement, and the armament, and taking in a corresponding larger supply of coals.'

Yet he was willing to acknowledge that under certain circumstances a ram might be a very dangerous vessel indeed: 'no ironclad, however powerful, could hope to escape from the simultaneous attack of three or four such vessels if she were unsupported in fighting the action and depended only upon her artillery for her defence'. Such being the case, the implications for future sea battles were ominous, and Barnaby found little in contemporary tactical thought to guide him in meeting the theoretical challenge posed by rams and torpedoes. 'In the absence of any authoritative tactical system,' therefore, 'I am obliged to devise one to satisfy myself . . . .' He did so in unprecedented fashion:

I reflect that our ironclads can have light flanking vessels associated with them for their defence against the rams and torpedo vessels. Without active supports they will, it appears to me, be liable to become the prey of such vessels as Admiral Sartorius

describes. They might be able to sink one or two of their assailants, but numbers would I fear carry the day, provided the attacking vessels had speed.[23]

Barnaby added that the mode of defence then under consideration for capital ships from torpedoes was 'a cordon or enclosure of nets and spars'. Such defensive measures, he speculated,

would be a very valuable defence . . . in a vessel *at rest* . . . but I consider that no such device is possible in a ship in motion, propelled by screws. The propellers would inevitably be disabled by the wreck of her own defences, before such defences had rendered her any service.

Hence, '[t]he proper defence of such a ship against small active assailants is, it appears to me, a cordon or service of vessels capable themselves of employing torpedoes, guns, and the ram.'

In this remarkable piece of speculation Barnaby had sketched out the essentials of future clashes at sea, and had done so without any examples on which to draw. A light screening force would protect the capital ships from the attacks of smaller assailants. In the days of sail, such screening forces kept out of harm's way during the clash of the main fleets for fear of speedy destruction. Barnaby seems to have divined that circumstances had changed: in future encounters capital ships would reserve their gunfire for each other, rather than concentrating on enemy screening vessels, for to do so while the enemy's big guns were trained on them would increase the risk of suffering hits and perhaps destruction for paltry gains. Such, again, had not been the case in days of sail, when capital ships' hulls had been relatively impervious to enemy ordnance. This 'combined fleet', as the D.N.C. explicitly termed it, should 'also have fast despatch vessels of superior speed . . . which could keep themselves acquainted with, and could report' on the position of enemy forces.

18. 'Correspondence Concerning a New Torpedo Ram', nd., NMM: ADM138/66.

19. 'Minute from Mr. Barnaby to Controller', 26 September 1874, cited in 'Correspondence Concerning a New Torpedo Ram', nd., NMM: ADM138/66.

20. Ibid. The surviving papers in *Polyphemus*'s Ship's Cover leave no room for doubt on this score, as the following excerpts demonstrate:
26/9/74: 'Minute from Mr. Barnaby to Controller says:- that a design has been prepared for a ship to use torpedoes at a high speed. In the '*Vesuvius*' [Britain's first torpedo boat] noiselessness & comparative invisibility were depended upon. The present design is for a ship capable of operating wherever an Armourclad could, and to be able to maintain speed equal to that of the fastest ironclad for 8 or 10 hours, and to be armoured at waterline. Submitted that Messrs Penn & Co and Messrs Humphrey be called upon to prepare a design for suitable engines.'
8/10/74: 'Minute from Capt Boys to Controller says:—swift torpedo boats are now necessary. He suggests that arrangements should be made to project torpedoes from side as well as right ahead, and also for the use of Harvey's torpedo.'
22/12/74: 'Minute from D.N.O. to Controller urging the desirability of having a few fast torpedo vessels as Experiments have proved that the Whitehead torpedo can be used with almost certainty of effect at night & have also shewn the difficulty of using the spar torpedo. Concurs with C.N.A. as to fitting present ships with torpedo gear.'

26/12/74: 'Minute from C.N.A. to Controller submitting that he may confer with Captain Singer & Torpedo Committee and forwarding design (with model) of a corvette (for 20 miles speed) and in which Whitehead Torpedoes can be used.'
13 December 1875: Barnaby to Dunn: Ram design:
'Mr. Dunn
   It is desired to transform the smaller torpedo ship of high speed into a Ram of the same general form and distribution of armour but having fuel enough to steam at 10 knots to Gibraltar with say 50 tons to spare.
   I should like to know what max speed we might expect with the present engines if the ship is being lengthened to take this fuel and widened correspondingly so as to keep present fineness of entrance and run. She should have a broadside Whitehead torpedo arrangement. There should be provisions for six weeks for her complement of 75 men.
   N.B.'

21. 'Minute from C.N.A. to Controller', 9 December 1874, ibid. Both Houston Stewart and Boys soon changed their minds on the subject of purpose-built torpedo boats. See previous note.

22. Houston Stewart Minute, ibid.

23. Barnaby's quotations in the previous two paragraphs and those in the following four are all taken from Barnaby to Stewart, 8 January 1876, NMM: ADM138/66.

Sister-ship to HMS *Conqueror, Hero* was laid down in 1883. Her anti-torpedo net booms are stowed against the hull. (U.S. Naval Historical Center: NH60582)

However, having come to this prescient conclusion, Barnaby then undermined much of the force of his argument by maintaining that the Navy could use existing vessels to fulfil the screening role:

> We possess to some extent the means of forming such flank supports for our ironclads, in the classes of gunvessels of 9 to 10 knots speed, costing from £15,000 to £35,000 each. These vessels now perform consular service only, and are incapable of operating alone in War. On the outbreak of war they might be grouped with the ironclads.

His over-solicitous desire to keep costs down coupled with his failure to appreciate fully the crucial value of speed led him astray after his unerring opening premises. He was right: in future no battlefleets would operate without supporting vessels to screen them. The screening vessels would, however, be faster than the vessels they supported. Likewise, although quite correct 'that the grouping of *ironclads only* together into squadrons in a time of war, would be dangerous, and wasteful policy' and that 'each powerful ironclad operating independently with smaller vessels of the kind indicated, would, except in very heavy weather, have her power multiplied by two or three', he missed the mark in asserting that such groups 'might of course operate in company, but the four or five ships constituting the squadron [*ie* the ironclad and its escorts] would, according to my view, be worked as a unit'. In future naval warfare the battlefleet would operate as a unit, as would the screen around it, rather than each capital ship operat-

24. See in particular N.A.M. Rodger, 'The Dark Ages of the Admiralty, 1869-85 Part II: Change and Decay, 1874-80', *Mariner's Mirror* 62/1 (1976), p44.

ing in conjunction with its own escorts. Still, it was an impressive and imaginative bit of speculation.

In regard to the idea of using slow and poorly-protected gunvessels as escorts, Barnaby added,

> that the 10-knot peace vessels could, in a few days, be made fairly shot-proof for end-on attack, by iron on the transverse bulkhead between decks, and by plates upon the fore deck at the waterline. They could also be readily strengthened for a ram if there should be on the part of their Lordships any acceptance of the views indicated herein.

Moreover, should it be found desirable

> to increase the mobility of one of these units, it could be done by associating with the 14-knot ironclad, two 13 or 14-knot unarmoured vessels, which need not cost more than £90,000 each, and they could carry fast steam launches to be lowered to aid in resisting an attack by numerous ram or torpedo vessels of speed higher than that of the Ironclad and her consorts.

Speed was not quite as much of a blind spot as it first appeared, and certainly not as much of one as some of his critics have alleged.[24] Finally, it is crucial to stress the circumstances in which Barnaby found himself formulating these arguments. 'I am aware how presumptuous it must seem for me to venture at all into the question of the probable tactics of the next naval war,' he stated apologetically to the Board, 'but I found myself unable to meet the arguments of Sir Geo. Sartorius and other advocates of small vessels in preference to armour clads, without forming some idea of the way in which their imaginary navy could be met and overcome by our actual Navy.'

As for the particular question at hand – whether or not to build an experimental vessel designed solely for ramming – Barnaby was not encouraging. A squadron of one powerful ironclad and three escorting vessels could be built for £475,000. For the same sum 'we could build only four of the armoured rams, or if we take [Sartorius' proposed] armed unarmoured larger rams, there would be only three of them for this money'. 'The four fast armoured rams,' he acknowledged,

> might be formidable competitors if they were worked well together, but it is by no means certain that they would not be beaten off, or sunk, by the ironclad and her consorts, and it is to be borne in mind that they could perform no other service as they would be unarmed.

He was more dismissive of Sartorius' other type:

> [t]he three unarmoured, but armed, vessels do not appear to me to be likely to stand the least chance of escape from utter destruction against such a squadron. For independent service as cruisers the three unarmoured rams would do good service, but as they could not compete even in groups with the squadrons; I cannot see that any advantage would be gained by building such vessels as substitutes for Ironclads.

Moreover, for cruising purposes the unarmoured rams appeared to possess no significant advantages over the service's existing cruisers. Hence, 'I do not strongly advocate the building of such a vessel as that which I have referred to for special ram and torpedo

The torpedo-ram *Polyphemus*, launched in 1881. She displaced 2640 tons and had a top speed of 17.85kts. (U.S. Naval Historical Center: NH88868)

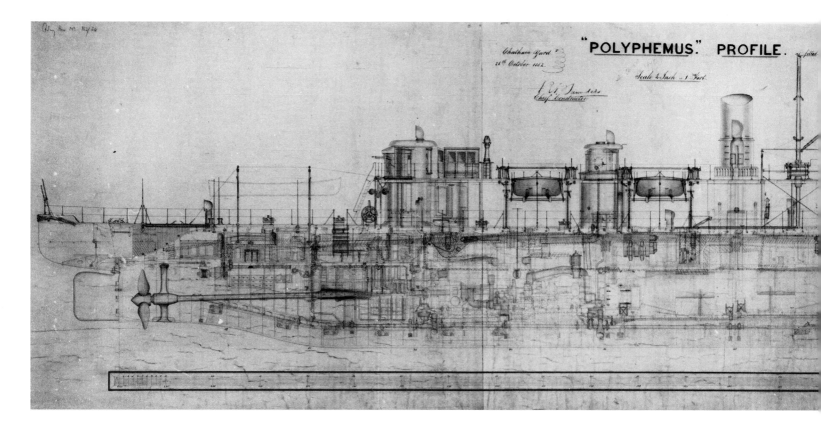

"POLYPHEMUS." PROFILE.

Polyphemus was designed with speed and stealth as her foremost features. Her hull, crammed full of steam machinery, was practically submerged at high speed. (National Maritime Museum, London: 7618)

service.' If the Board were determined to build such a vessel, Barnaby was 'confident that no such efficient ram and torpedo vessel has yet been designed as that which is here submitted', but furthermore warned that '[t]he design is now two years old, and has not been kept secret, and I should not be surprised if some Foreign Power were to commence building one on the principle on which it is designed . . .'.

From the Constructor's Department Barnaby's paper circulated through the Admiralty, first to the D.N.O., then to the Controller, and finally to the members of the Board. The differing responses to the D.N.C.'s vision of future naval warfare could not be bettered as evidence of how little consensus existed within the service on the chief object of its business. Henry Boys, the D.N.O., saw no value in Barnaby's tactical vision. 'I must entirely dissent,' he wrote, 'from [the] idea of attaching to every Iron-clad three or four unarmoured nine or ten knot gun-vessels, as rams . . .' The grounds for objection were numerous:

they would in my opinion simply hamper the Iron-clad in all her movements, if out of range of her guns in action they would be useless, if within range and sufficiently near to operate against an opposing ram, the Iron-clad would be obstructed in the use of her guns, and her own manoeuvring power materially affected,

so that instead of being free to act offensively her first object would be to protect her attendant vessels.

Controller Houston Stewart agreed, confessing himself unable to see 'how the extemporised sloops to act as attendant Rams on [for] Ironclads could be worked with advantage'. So did First Naval Lord Milne, who praised the D.N.O.'s paper for the 'clear view of this question and the many complicated difficulties which surround the present state of naval warfare'. Significantly, however, the Second Naval Lord, Vice-Admiral Geoffrey Phipps Hornby, widely viewed by contemporaries as the foremost tactician in the mid-Victorian Navy, saw much merit in the D.N.C.'s proposal. He maintained that any escorting vessels would have to match the speed of the vessels they accompanied, but with this one proviso stated emphatically that such escorts 'might, if used as Mr. Barnaby suggests afford [an ironclad's] best chance of foiling the attack of similar vessels on an Ironclad fleet'. Future events would vindicate Barnaby and Hornby on this score, though at the time they stood in a minority at the Admiralty.

As for *Polyphemus* in particular, Boys took an even more dismissive view of Sartorius' premises than did Barnaby, producing a lengthy minute, the chief thrust of which was 'the idea of unarmoured rams attacking armourclads ought not to be entertained or encouraged, the chances of a successful result being so remote that it would certainly lead to disappointment and disaster. With but very moderate gunnery an unarmoured ram ought to be sunk before she could strike any armoured adversary'.[25] He elaborated

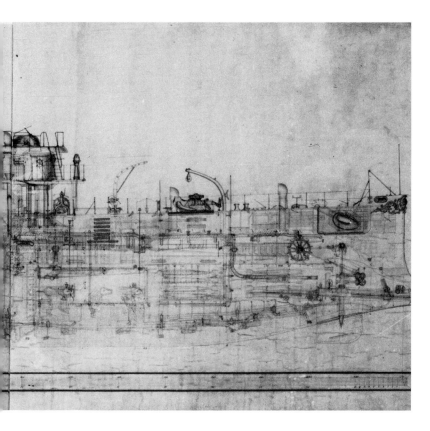

fire would come into play, or the effect of the blow be so lessened as to reduce it to a glance, the armour of armour-clad vessels being more especially serviceable as a protection against a ram.

Yet the vessel put forward by the Constructors might have its uses. It 'should be kept aloof till after the first mêlée, in order to dispose of disabled enemies, to take an opportunity to apply her [*sic*] torpedoes or rush into an enemy's port'. Such a ship would have to be 'fast, and as far as possible protected by armour'. Barnaby's design therefore received Boys' qualified approval, although more on the strength of being 'a torpedo vessel as well as a ram'. Nonetheless, he added 'I should still prefer her [more] could she be made available for [*ie* capable of] carrying one heavy gun'. Finally, he concluded, there was little to be gained by rushing headlong into the construction of a large fleet of rams until their value was demonstrated under wartime conditions; '[i]n building one or two such rams as Mr. Barnaby now proposes, we shall be going quite far enough in the direction of special ram vessels.'

Houston Stewart largely agreed with Boys on the potential for ramming. 'Except under the special circumstances of surprising an enemy or taking advantage of neglect or mismanagement on his part,' the Controller minuted, 'I cannot understand how unarmoured Rams or Torpedo vessels can attack armoured ships without incurring destruction either by sinking or exploding under their gunfire.'[26] He adduced a number of historical examples to demonstrate the point – Boys had done the same – and added that fitting torpedoes to existing 'fast unarmoured cruisers – including the *Opal* class' would make purpose-built unarmoured rams redundant. Yet '[t]o my mind the protected Monitor-Ram-Torpedo vessel designed in this department is the most formidable vessel of the sort which has yet been proposed, and *I strongly advocate the construction of such a vessel.*'

First Naval Lord Milne agreed 'that we ought to have Several small vessels fitted as Rams,' but found several features of the proposed design objectionable.[27] Like Boys he preferred a vessel with guns in addition to underwater weapons, and like Barnaby he was keenly aware of its purely wartime utility in light of funding constraints: '[t]he crew could not live in her and she is not suited for any service except as a Ram and Torpedo Vessel.' Moreover, Milne's vision of a proper ramming vessel was one 'somewhat resembling' the small ironclads *Pallas* or *Research*, which 'might be so fitted as to fulfil all necessary conditions lightly rigged but with good stowage of coal and two or four guns. Tonnage about 2000 to 2500 tons'.

on his reasoning, based on 'experiments with the *Glatton* attacked by a tug of superior speed'. His observations led him to argue that it was anything but 'a foregone conclusion, that a moderately fast ironclad is to succumb to the attack of three or four rams without guns; on the contrary, if the Iron-clad can only get them abaft of her beam so that she can manoeuvre to prolong [*ie* avoid] a collision, she would detain them under the fire of her guns a sufficient time to destroy them in detail before they could get the chance to use their rams . . .'. If so, 'even the vessel now proposed by Mr. Barnaby is not sufficiently armoured to resist a close fire of very heavy guns.' As for the possibility of ramming by night, Boys was similarly derisive: against a moving target it was 'almost impracticable, this was fully elucidated in the attacks of a gunboat on the *Glatton* at Spithead, where it was found impossible to judge the relative distance of the two vessels from each other.' Most fundamentally, however, Boys doubted the efficacy of ramming under any circumstances:

> If a ram attacks from the bow or broadside [of] a ship going at speed, it is simply a matter of chance which ship gets rammed, or even of a collision taking place at all, the slightest error in the estimation of relative speed, or even of faltering or hesitating on the part of one might turn the 'rammer' into the 'rammee' or the ships would miss each other altogether. If the ram attacks from astern, or abaft the beam with less speed than the vessel attacked, of course the ram could be avoided altogether, if with more speed [*ie* even if the ram has greater speed] as before stated the artillery

---

25. S.1320/1878, Minute by DNO on Barnaby's memorandum, 17 January 1876, in S2001/1878, 'Reports and Correspondence relative to the design of the Torpedo Ram (now *Polyphemus*) to be built at Chatham Dockyard', nd., NMM: ADM138/66.

26. Houston Stewart minute, 8 February 1876, ibid.

27. Milne minute, 29 February 1876, ibid.

Hornby disagreed with Boys' conclusions on ramming as well as those on tactics, maintaining 'that at night' even unarmoured rams 'might easily destroy an Ironclads [*sic*] . . .'.[28] Moreover, he deprecated constructing the vessel put forward by the Constructor's department. She would, he acknowledged, 'be formidable for offence, so long as her coal lasted. But the *Ajax* will be nearly as strong as a ram – may be made her equal as a torpedo ship – and will be much stronger in artillery'. Finally, noting the sluggish pace of construction, he objected 'to the adoption of designs a year before any progress is to be made with them. If the proposed vessel were now laid down Ironclads now building would be delayed.'

Left: Polyphemus under way. Her hull was designed so that water would flow over it when steaming at high speed. (U.S. Naval Historical Center: NH65967)

Below: This photograph clearly shows *Polyphemus*'s separate superstructure, designed to float off if the hull sank. (U.S. Naval Historical Center: NH57867)

Nothing was done in the immediate wake of this exchange of views. First Lord George Ward Hunt blandly noted 'A very interesting paper & minutes. The programme being settled for 76-7 no decision appears to be required on this subject at present'.[29] Only in the following fiscal year was it decided to construct an experimental vessel based on Barnaby's design. At that point it became necessary to undertake 'minute and laborious calculation' to divine 'the dimensions of the ship' and what hull form and engine power would be required 'to get a speed of 17 knots', since 'when the subject was last under the consideration of their Lordships that it was only a sketch design which had been prepared . . .'.[30]

The particulars of the resulting vessel are worth detailing, owning to its uniqueness. It was 'to be capable of making a passage in any weather from Plymouth to Gibraltar, or from Gibraltar to Malta at 10 knots without assistance' and of 'making 17 knots in smooth water'. It was to carry, in addition to the ram prow, twenty-five torpedoes, capable of being discharged from three tubes, right ahead or on either beam. To armour such a vessel heavily enough with vertical protection sufficient to stop heavy ordnance at close range would have burdened it impossibly; Barnaby and his colleagues instead relied on 3in sloping deck armour, which most projectiles would, it was hoped, glance off. Hence, *Polyphemus*, as the torpedo ram was dubbed, had 'a turtle back four feet out of water at the Crown', a design feature which also permitted water to rush smoothly *over* the hull at moderate and high speeds and gave her a markedly low profile. Above the turtle back was a flying deck which housed the steering and navigating arrangements, boats, anchors, and two Gatling guns. The flying deck was also designed 'to be formed of two rafts, each of them seaworthy and capable of floating the whole crew in an emergency. Each raft so fitted as to float away from the ship automatically if she should be sunk by an enemy.' The crew consisted of 80 men and officers, 'for whom accommodation is provided for such passages as may be necessary but not for permanent habitation as a commissioned ship'. Below the turtle back the hull was to 'be so divided that any compartment may be filled without danger to the ship', and as an additional safety feature it was to 'have the means of rapidly relieving the ship by discharging ballast should their be a sudden and heavy leak which the pumps cannot control'. 'To fulfil these conditions,' Barnaby informed the Board,

& produce a torpedo-ram capable of encountering at a speed superior to their own in any weather in which an action could be fought any existing ironclad with but little risk to itself, the following dimensions are required: Length–250' 0"; Breadth–37' 0"; Draft of Water–24' 0"; Displacement–2340 tons; Ind[icated] Horse Power–5000.

Two hundred tons of coal was normal bunkerage, 300 tons the maximum. Finally, the estimated cost was £142,000, far more than that of the vessels that Barnaby himself advocated building. As he stressed, this sum was more than a third of that of a first-class ironclad, for a vessel of much less power, one which, in addition, could perform no peacetime function. Moreover, the D.N.C. admitted that much of the new design rested on theory rather than experience. Thus, and doubtless in light of the *Inflexible* controversy then unfolding, he warned the Board;

if the probable results of shell fire in action upon the ends of the *Inflexible* is [*sic*] capable of raising doubt which neither the designers nor their Lordships can satisfy this new design will certainly be found capable of raising grave doubts which cannot be met except by an expression of opinion.

By way of example he explained that

it would be impossible to prove from experience or by any calculations what would happen if it were attempted to force the ram with her fine lines and low freeboard against a sea. At full speed the water even in smooth water will sweep completely over the turtle back and only experience can gradually give confidence & shew how the vessel should be used in heavy weather.

Small wonder that the Board authorised only one experimental version.[31]

The Lords were well advised to be cautious. By 1882, when *Polyphemus* was completed, the pace of technological change had begun to undermine the premises on which her design was based. With the growing size and range of quick-firing, armour-piercing ordnance the ship was increasingly vulnerable, especially at the close ranges at which she would have to operate. She also had more than her share of technical problems at the outset, in partic-

---

28. Hornby minute, 8 March 1876, ibid.

29. Ward Hunt minute, 11 March 1876, ibid.

30. Barnaby to Controller, "State of designs," 16 July 1877, S.14223, ibid.

31. Barnaby also informed the Board that since the design had been made public he had been contacted by Sir George Sartorius, with a reiteration 'of the conditions he laid down for a Ram. They differ very widely from those taken here. They are:

1. A ship without armour
2. With "full jury" rig

3. To have both ends alike & to be able to ram with either end.
4. To have two screws at each end.
5. To be able to steam for at least 12 days at 16 or 17 knots without taking in fuel.
6. To have 64 pdrs for chase at both bow and stern.
7. Engines to be 6 feet under water [*ie* below the water line].
8. To carry a torpedo boat.

   I would submit that Sir Geo Sartorius be informed of the conditions accepted by their Lordships for a Torpedo-Ram and informed also that the vessel indicated by him would not be accepted. She would require to be larger than the *Shah*.
   N.B.'

Quick-firing ordnance such as this 6-pounder in the foreground of this photograph of *Rodney*'s forward barbette rendered *Polyphemus* too vulnerable for her ramming role by the time she was completed. (U.S. Naval Historical Center: NH55490)

ular with her boilers.[32] Yet she should not be dismissed out of hand. At the time her design was drawn up, and even when authorised, as one recent authority notes, 'guns heavy enough to pierce her armour were too slow firing and difficult to train to stand much of a chance of hitting so fast a ship'. Thus, although widely '[r]egarded as a freak intended mainly for ramming, she was in fact a well thought out and combat-worthy design intended chiefly

for torpedo attack'.[33] She was, however, like *Inflexible*, designed for the envisioned combat of the 1870s; by the time both vessels were completed conditions were changing and both fell victim to the inexorable march of technology.

Speed versus Handiness: Colossus *and* Edinburgh

The next class of ironclads were not circumscribed by coast defence limitations, a situation which doubtless made Barnaby's work easier. Yet new complicating factors took the place of the earlier one. As early as 1876, when mooting *Polyphemus*'s design, he questioned the tactical assumptions on which most professional

32. 'Report on Boilers of *Polyphemus* by J. Wright', 8 September 1882, NMM: ADM138/66.
'I very much regret to be obliged to report that the working of the boilers of the *Polyphemus* continues to give unsatisfactory results after all that has been done in the endeavour to render them efficient. In fact, the more they are worked the less reliable they become, and all those who have had to manage them and watch their performance are losing hope of ever getting them reasonably efficient for service, even at considerably

reduced power'. A new set of boilers was subsequently ordered, at a cost of £13,000.

33. *Conway's 1860-1905*, p88.

34. Barnaby to Board of Admiralty, Spring, 1878, NMM: ADM/138/60, no fol. These papers, relative to both the *Colossus* and *Imperiuse* classes, were for some reason bound in the Cover for *Ajax* and *Agamemnon*. The quotations in the following six paragraphs are all drawn from this source.

visions of future naval battles were based. By the time he was called on to consider the next class of ironclads to be laid down – *Colossus* and *Edinburgh* (originally *Majestic*) – he had concluded that the circumstances dictating future combat at sea had changed, and that new ships should be thus designed with new premises in mind. To that end he prepared a lengthy synopsis in the spring of 1878 summarising the 'considerations' which he thought the Board should consider 'preliminary to the preparation of Designs' for the next generation of ironclads.[34] First of all, Barnaby took explicit exception to the Admiralty's general insistence on handiness over speed, since in order to use either the ram or the torpedo, the first requisite was to 'get up to [*ie* close with] her adversary', a necessity which rendered 'speed more valuable than handiness'. Only if the ship could 'get up to her adversary' could she 'be sure of being able to employ one of the . . . weapons against her'. Moreover, with the development of torpedoes capable of being fired on either beam as well as directly ahead, the importance of speed over handiness was further enhanced, since the powers of turning were not necessary for using the Whitehead. Hence, Barnaby stated, this 'consideration makes speed more important than handiness, as a means of *defence* as well as of offence'.

On the basis of this fundamental premise, the D.N.C. next turned to the matter of obtaining speed. Again he took exception to the previously expressed opinions of the Board, especially those of Milne, who maintained shortness was high on the list of desirable design attributes. 'So far as an opinion can be formed from the performances of actual ships,' Barnaby stated, 'speed cannot be obtained in short ships without large engine power.' Therefore, '[t]o economise power, i.e., to reduce the size and cost of machinery, and the consumption of fuel, long ships have an advantage over short ships.'

Of course, lengthening a ship created its own set of problems, especially that of providing adequate protection. 'When there is armour from end to end, either complete or as a belt, long ships are wasteful of armour', Barnaby acknowledged, but with the central citadel principle, coupled with extensive watertight subdivision and an armoured deck, the difficulty was solved. 'When it is designed to defend the stability and buoyancy by armour, short ships have the advantage', the D.N.C. admitted, but when armour was 'designed to protect only vital parts by an underwater deck and a citadel, this is not so'. Thus, he concluded, the '*Ajax* class may be increased to 350 feet with advantage, if by doing so the speed can be increased to 14½ knots instead of 13 knots, and the coal endurance raised to that of the *Devastation*'. By so doing, the Navy would have a class of vessels 'suitable not only for European warfare' but also for stations abroad, where they could operate from the 'naval centres' advocated six years previously by the Committee on Designs.

Edinburgh fitting out. (U.S. Naval Historical Center: NH61026)

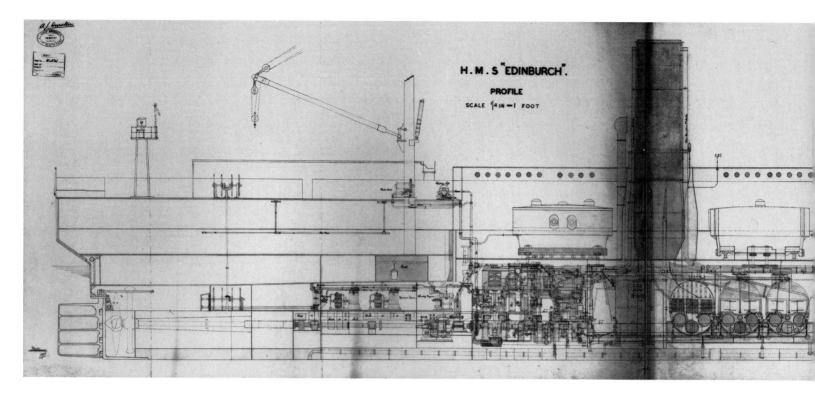

The last of the central-citadel ironclads, *Edinburgh* and her sister-ship *Colossus* were also the first British capital ships to be routinely called 'battleships'. (National Maritime Museum, London: 10021)

Barnaby's logic failed to impress the Board, which, on 6 June 1878 decided that 'the recommendation of the Controller and the Director of Naval Construction to adopt a length of 350 feet in a new first-class battle ship . . . could not be accepted'. Indeed, the Board, even after Milne's retirement, took fundamental issue with Barnaby's tactical priorities: 'It was considered that 325 feet . . . was as great as could be admitted in view to the necessity for handiness and good manoeuvring qualities.'

Whatever the D.N.C. may have lacked, it was not persistence. This rebuff prompted a more detailed summary of his reasoning. He admitted that their Lordships' decision was 'in accordance with the principles which have guided the construction of first-class fighting ships throughout Europe for the last 15 or 20 years', adding that he concurred in this view. Yet, he maintained, 'during the last year or two a new factor has appeared in the elements of naval warfare, and that when it receives due consideration we shall be prepared to accept greater length in our first-class ships'. 'That new factor,' Barnaby stated, 'is the Whitehead torpedo projected from either broadside.' Only if two conditions held would 'shortness and facility to turn' be of extreme importance 'in first class battleships'. These conditions were (1) that the ram would be the principal means of attack in future naval battles and (2) that 'if the ram misses there are no means of attack from the broadside except the gun'. These conditions were no longer valid with the appearance of the torpedo mounted on the beam, since it would give 'the ship three rams, one in the stem, and one on either side, inclined to it at some angle, either fixed or adjustable'.

Under these circumstances, Barnaby argued, extreme shortness and handiness were of no advantage unless it could 'be shown, which I doubt, that the short handy ship can deliver its Whiteheads as well as its ram more surely than the long ship . . .'. He acknowledged that the long ship would necessarily present a larger target for torpedoes, but the risk of a torpedo hit would be of such gravity that no captain, whether in a long ship or a short one, would 'expose themselves to it, if they can avoid it'.

This pronouncement is worth stressing, for it clearly shows that Barnaby had by mid-1878 reached the conclusion not only that speed was more important than handiness, but that the *mêlée* tactical concepts thought by many, if not most, naval officers to be the future direction of battle at sea, were dead in the water. Three years earlier he had maintained publicly that the gun held first place among the weapons of war at sea because of its effective range, and the ram last. Now he explicitly stated;

I believe . . . that the ram will not be employed as a means of attack by and against first-class battle ships when naval officers truly realise the value of these three co-ordinate powers [*ie* torpedoes fired ahead and abeam], and when disasters and successes in a great naval war have established the relative values of different modes of attack and defence.

As of 1876 his tactical vision had been half-baked. Within three years, as the *Colossus* memoranda unequivocally demonstrate, it was a golden brown. *Mêlées* between capital ships – using rams and

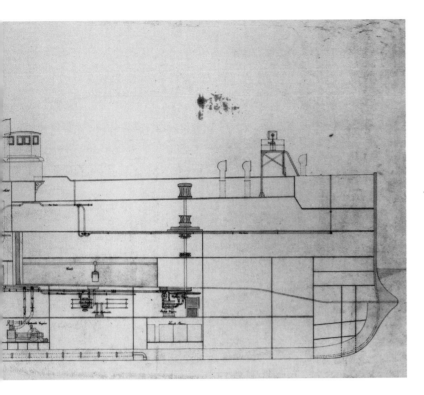

Draft 23 ft fow[ard]: 25 ft aft (but may be increased a little). As good an entrance & run as she [*ie Warrior*] Twin Screws.

Ram. Torpedoes on broadside on each bow. 15 knots speed. 1000 tons of coal. Signal poles. 100 tons for unarmoured guns and ammu[nition].[35]

Such a ship would have been, in terms of steaming qualities and speed, a vast improvement on previous ironclads stretching back at least to the late 1860s. Thwarted in his efforts to design it, by late June the D.N.C. had settled for 'the same length as the *Sultan, Alexandra* & *Dreadnought,* and *Inflexible* [*ie* 320ft]; much wider than the three former but narrower than the *Inflexible*. It will have considerably less engine power than any of them but will be designed for a 14 knot speed ie one knot faster than the *Ajax* class'.

Drawing up the particulars of this design was delayed by correspondence with William Armstrong relative to mounting long breech-loaders instead of Woolwich guns in order to gain '50% greater penetrative power'.[36] So involved was the process—as detailed in Chapter 4—that the Constructor's Department finally went ahead with the issue still unresolved, and 'provision . . . [was] made to receive [breech-loaders] should it be decided hereafter to introduce them.'

Barnaby then made a lengthy comparison of the new design first with the masted central battery ironclad *Sultan* and then *Devastation*. This exercise is worth summarising to illustrate how quickly technology had advanced in the decade since the former was laid down. 'The displacement . . . is rather less than that of the *Sultan*,' the D.N.C. informed the Board, 'and the indicated horsepower 2,600 less, yet we are looking for the same speed . . . coal endurance at 13 knots 120% greater . . . armour of twice the thickness; and guns of twice the power, throwing a broadside of 60% to 70% greater weight', and all of this with barely one-half the number of crew, since, of course, *Colossus* lacked sails. Moreover, the armour would, if the example of *Ajax* were followed, be almost twice as thick, or armour could be sacrificed slightly to increase the armament by four 6in armour-piercing weapons. 'As compared with the *Devastation*', the standard by which fighting efficiency had been judged by the Admiralty Committee on designs and most subsequent commentators, Barnaby enumerated the advances; *Colossus* would be slightly lighter yet '40 ft. longer, nearly 6 ft. wider, 9 to 12 ins less draught of water, ¼ knot higher estimated speed, 10% more coal endurance . . . 50% thicker hull armour and 38 ton instead of 35 ton guns.' Furthermore, owing to the *en echelon* turret arrangement 'the right ahead, and the right astern fire, and the horizontal range of the guns is much increased'. Were those improvements not enough to win the

torpedoes against *each other*—were not going to happen, no matter what had taken place at Lissa; future fleet actions would be fought with the gun. Coupled with the realisation that speed *was* more important than handiness for capital ships, and the concept of a screening force to cover the capital ships from either ramming or torpedo attacks, Barnaby's vision foreshadowed the re-emergence of the gun's predominance and thus pointed to the return to line-ahead tactics. He had, in short, predicted the future of naval warfare much more accurately than did the most prominent contemporary professional tactical thinkers, and was far in advance of many officers who continued to extol the power of the ram until the accidental loss of HMS *Victoria* in 1893—the victim of HMS *Camperdown*'s prow—sealed its fate. Moreover, by arriving at the realisation that the citadel principle coupled with extensive watertight subdivision made it possible to build adequately-protected, battleworthy ships of great length, Barnaby pointed to the post *Royal Sovereign* era. This was the hull form on which the entire line of British pre-dreadnought battleships was based, and he seems to have divined its possibilities before anyone else.

On the more immediate level, the results of the wrangle between Barnaby and the Board was little more successful from the former's perspective than its immediate predecessors. Barnaby wishfully instructed his subordinate William White on 28 May 1878 'I want a new *Ajax* worked out as follows.'

The present citadel and armour and turrets & guns, and the present engines and boilers.

The ship lengthened to 350 feet with underwater deck and raft body. About 9500 tons displacement & about same midsection as

35. Barnaby to White, 31 May 1878, NMM: ADM138/67, fol. 5.

36. Particulars of *Colossus* and *Majestic*, S.15,182, 20 December 1878, NMM: ADM138/60 (*Ajax* and *Agamemnon*), no fol.

Board's assent, the new design also featured 'much superior accommodation in the living spaces; and boats and anchors are carried higher out of the water'. With such an impressive recitation the Board's concurrence was unsurprising.

In terms of British capital ship design *Colossus* and *Edinburgh* represented even greater steps forward than Barnaby's comparisons indicated. They were the first British capital ships to benefit from the large-scale incorporation of steel, rather than iron, for the hull and fixtures; only the largest and heaviest pieces – such as the stem and stern posts – remained of iron. Likewise, they were the first such vessels extensively to utilise compound, rather than wrought iron, armour; both belt and turret protection were compound, unlike the *Ajax* class, which had compound armour on only the latter. The *Colossus* class also sported an effective armour-piercing secondary armament and, certainly not least of all, marked a permanent return to breech-loading main armament after the abortive experiment with Armstrong guns in the early 1860s.

But the two final central-citadel ships were ultimately judged in little more charitable terms than their immediate predecessors. Some of this verdict can be attributed to their shortcomings:

HMS *Colossus*. With their breech-loading guns and steel hull, she and *Edinburgh* were an important step forward, but their low-freeboard design – intended for coast assault – was losing favour when they were completed in 1886 and 1887 respectively. (U.S. Naval Historical Center: NH65875)

although both exceeded speed expectations, logging 16kts + on their trials, they rolled badly – the consequence of the high metacentre required to ensure stability if the ends were damaged – and manoeuvred only marginally better than the *Ajax* class. More to the point, however, both were victims of changing contemporary perceptions of war at sea in much the same fashion as the other central-citadel ships. By the time they were completed in the late 1880s the rationale for building low-freeboard coast-assault ships appeared to be fading. The Admiralty had veered away from the type – as will be noted at length – with the decision to build the *Collingwood* and its half-sisters, the immediate successors to *Colossus* and *Edinburgh*, only to return to it in the first half of the 1880s. By 1887, however, when the ships came into service, coastal assault was a dying doctrine; only one of the eight battleships authorised by the Naval Defence Act of 1889 was a low-freeboard turret design. By the time they were finished *Colossus* and *Edinburgh*, like *Inflexible*, *Ajax*, and *Agamemnon*, were ships without a perceived wartime mission, and this factor, at least as much as their more obvious shortcomings, accounts for their lack of success. In every respect save manoeuvrability and steadiness they were marked improvements on *Devastation*, and for the role of coastal assault in sheltered waters the latter drawback was of marginal consequence. Yet they were not judged by the same standards as the earlier vessel had been: it was an unequivocal success; they were equivocal failures. The strategic/operational paradigm had shifted.

Chapter 9

THE COAST ASSAULT PARADIGM SHAKEN: *COLLINGWOOD* AND THE 'ADMIRAL' CLASS, 1879-81

The Paralysis of Admiralty Capital Shipbuilding Policy

IN CHARTING the course of design policy steered by the Admiralty at the end of the 1870s and the beginning of the 1880s, several extraneous factors contributing to confusion and the sluggish pace of construction need to be noted. Part of the latter feature was due to ambitious unarmoured shipbuilding programmes begun by Ward Hunt's Board in 1876 – carried out at the expense of armoured construction – and some was unquestionably due to the Conservative government's preference for maintaining the existing fleet for any short-term contingency over building programmes to augment the future fleet.[1] Equal emphasis, however, must be given to the Admiralty's paralysis as to what sorts of armoured ships it should have been building, if indeed it should have been building them at all, coupled with a rapid turnover of Board membership in the late 1870s.

Doubts about the continued utility of building heavily armed and armoured ironclads – 'battleships' as they were increasingly termed from *Colossus* onward – apparent by the mid-1870s, continued to grow for the remainder of the decade and through much of the 1880s, fuelled, it might be added, by the emergence of the French *Jeune Ecole* midway through the latter decade. On top of such nagging professional, not to mention strategic, tactical, and national security, doubts, the Board itself experienced debilitatingly rapid personnel turnover in the late 1870s. Between 1876, when Milne retired, and 1879 no fewer than three men – four if Milne is included – occupied the First Naval Lord's seat. Two of them, Hastings Yelverton and George Wellesley, brought with them little experience of either administration or technological issues. Yelverton, in addition, was in poor health for the majority of his 1876-7 tenure. Only with Astley Cooper Key's appointment (1879-85) did a measure of continuity return to the professional decision-making process, and even then the blessings were mixed, since he, although noted for his technical expertise, especially on ordnance questions, was an innately cautious man, one who moreover tended to immerse himself in details to the detriment of comprehending the big picture.[2] The turnover was less pronounced among the junior Naval Lords but nonetheless significant.

The most visible consequence of this combination of factors was

markedly slower capital ship construction during the late 1870s. The 1866-8 Conservative ministry had laid down thirteen ironclads, the 1868-4 Liberal government contributed eleven more, while the 1874-80 Conservative ministry initiated only nine armoured vessels – ten if *Polyphemus* is counted – of which five (*Inflexible, Nelson, Northampton, Ajax* and *Agamemnon*) were underway by 1876. During the final four years of the administration, in other words, only *Colossus, Edinburgh, Polyphemus*, the small coast assault ram *Conqueror*, and *Collingwood*, first of the 'Admiral' class, were begun. And as the number under construction dwindled, so did the pace of work, as the temptation to modify designs to incorporate updated weaponry, protection, and other technology became irresistible. *Inflexible* was seven-and-a-half years in construction, *Ajax* seven, *Agamemnon* almost seven, *Colossus* over seven, and *Edinburgh* over eight, although the latter two were complete save for their armament within five years. Even *Polyphemus*, a small ship regardless of its novelty, took four years to build.

In the meantime, the French were pushing ahead with an ambitious programme of naval reconstruction, which had been underway since 1872, but was not a matter of priority in the immediate wake of the Franco-German War. Between 1875 and 1880 they laid down thirteen seagoing or station battleships and another four coast defence/assault vessels, more than double the total number – seven – begun by Britain during those years. By 1877 Houston Stewart warned ominously that the French 'are rapidly going ahead of us, and unless it is decided to lay down 12 Armoured Battle Ships to be completed by the end of 1881, that year will find the Navy of France decidedly superior to that of Great Britain in ships and guns'.[3] This sentiment was echoed by Second Naval Lord Arthur Hood, who calculated the relative numbers of iron-

---

1. For a general survey of the course of Admiralty policy during the late 1870s, see John Beeler, *British Naval Policy in the Gladstone-Disraeli Era, 1866-1880* (Stanford, 1997), pp150-70. For specifics of Conservative shipbuilding policy, see pp154-6.

2. N.A.M. Rodger, 'The Dark Ages of the Admiralty, 1869-1885: Part 2', *Mariner's Mirror* 62/1 (1976), p40.

3. Comments of Houston Stewart on Captain Nicolson's Report #18, 'The comparative strength of the English and French Fleets', 15 November 1877, PRO: ADM1/6424.

Collingwood's 9500 tons mean displacement was a product of Admiralty insistence on 'moderate dimensions'. (U.S. Naval Historical Center: NH61397)

clads built and building at fifty-one for Britain to fifty-five for France, and First Naval Lord Wellesley who warned that France's building programme would 'give her a very considerable superiority . . . unless steps are taken in this country to keep pace with her'.[4] To these alarming accounts, however, First Lord W.H. Smith merely noted '[a] very interesting paper'.[5] The Board neither increased the pace of construction on existing ships nor authorised new ones in the wake of this exchange of views.

Yet it is misleading to attribute this apparent sloth solely to the Admiralty's political masters: it was at least as much a consequence of the technological uncertainty which engulfed the Board after 1875. There were cogent arguments to delay the start of new ironclads until some idea of the utility of *Polyphemus*-type vessels had been established (although how its battleworthiness was to be judged without the coincidence of a war was a problem that the Admiralty seems resolutely to have ignored). It was hoped, as Barnaby put it, 'that the *Polyphemus* might prove a formidable assailant' to such ships as Italy and France were then building without having to go to the expense of 'putting into one ship the three qualities of high speed, great defensive power in armour, and great effective power of guns'. The torpedo-ram was not, of course, ready for trials until 1882, so as of 1879 or 1880 her potential could only be speculated upon.

But even if the need for more capital ships was conceded,

Polyphemus or no, there was an utter want of consensus at the Admiralty as to what sort of ship should be built. The Controller and the D.N.C. generally advocated emulating the Italians by abandoning side armour in favour of greater speed and firepower. Barnaby sketched out the essentials of his vision to the Board in 1880:

> If the *Polyphemus* is *not* deemed a viable opponent for 1st class ironclads . . . and 1st Class Battle Ships are required at once, we should recommend the adoption of the high rate of speed, the newest, of course, heavy guns of great power, say of 60 tons, protected by thick armour 18' or 20' steel faced, but we should recommend the abandonment of armour on the sides, and the adoption of an underwater protecting deck. . . .[6]

Such a vessel, however, would require a large increase to the displacement, to say nothing of the horsepower, traditionally favoured by British policy-makers; the Italian models for the design were some 14,000 tons, or almost 50 per cent larger than *Colossus*. The D.N.O. Richard Vesey Hamilton disagreed, pushing

---

4. Comments of Hood and Wellesley, ibid.

5. Comment of Smith, ibid.

6. Barnaby to Houston Stewart, 6 November 1880; Houston Stewart minute, n.d., in bound papers relative to decision to build 'Admiral' class, Surveyor's Branch, 1 August 1881, PRO: ADM1/6608.

7. Parkes, *British Battleships*, p297.

instead for barbette ships along the lines of the French second-class station battleships *Vauban* and *Duguesclin* (6112 tons). Were that divergence of opinion not enough, Hood wanted something else entirely, based on the Austrian casemate/central battery ship *Tegetthoff* (7600 tons). And Wellesley, so long as he was a member of the Board (1877-9) expressed no explicit views on his preference of ship-type, but did make clear his opposition to designs of larger than 10,000 tons displacement.[7] Under the circumstances it is remarkable that the Admiralty was able to settle on any design at all, much less one that in many respects pointed the way to the standardised pre-dreadnought classes of the post-1889 era.

Collingwood

The design history of *Collingwood* has not been recounted in detail. Parkes' account is unreliable, based in large part on Admiralty discussions that led up to the decision to repeat the design in the subsequent 'Admiral' class. From the Ship's Cover it appears that the initial impetus was furnished by the pressing need to build *some-*

One of the preliminary sketches for HMS *Collingwood*. This design called for two 80-ton guns mounted *en barbette* rather than the four 43-ton pieces eventually approved. (National Maritime Museum, London: E2281)

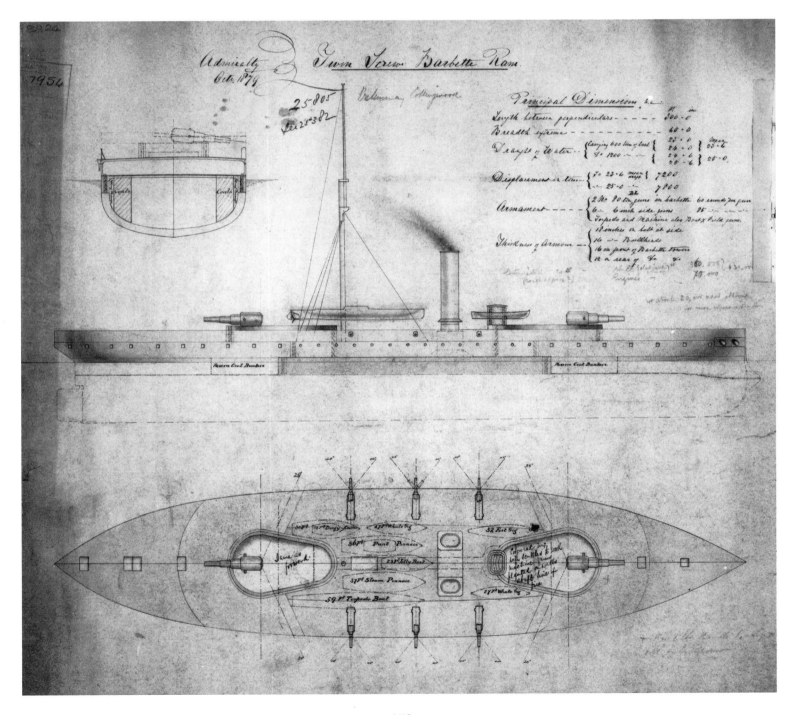

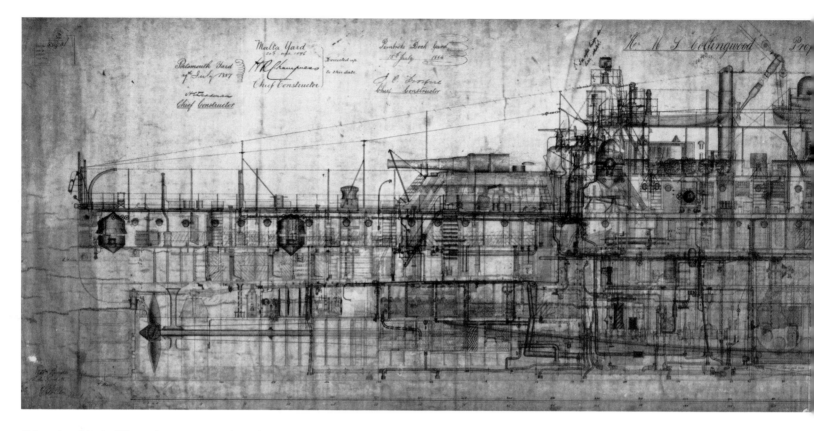

Although strikingly different in appearance above the waterline, the form and dimensions of *Collingwood*'s hull were virtually identical to those of *Colossus*. (National Maritime Museum, London: 8003)

thing, since other powers, in particular France, were pushing ahead with armoured ships. This pressure, however, was simultaneously undercut by the desire to hedge bets by keeping risky investment to a minimum. Thus the first reference to the ship which would become *Collingwood* came from none other than First Lord W.H. Smith who, on 20 August 1879 instructed the Controller 'When you have time I should like to have a *confidential memorandum* from you and one from Barnaby as to what you each consider to by our greatest want now in the matter of shipbuilding, and what description of ship you yourself would like to take in hand.'[8] Barnaby responded first, apprising Houston Stewart on 9 September that '[i]f the Dockyards needed more new work for 1880-1', which he doubted, he was 'prepared to submit a design for coast warfare about 1000 tons smaller than the *Agamemnon* with 14 knots speed & 2-80 ton guns on turntables protected by armour as thick as in the *Agamemnon*, unmasted and with rams [*sic*]'.[9] However, the D.N.C. thought 'that the most pressing need was to finish the four ships of the *Ajax* class and the *Inflexible*'.

Before proffering this design Barnaby had taken stock of the current balance between French and British battlefleets, judging the ships of the latter to be considerably 'more efficient' than those of the former, although he neglected to mention the basis on which he determined efficiency. He added that half of the eigh-

teen French ironclads under construction were designed for coast defence: '[b]y sacrificing cruising power on hulls of about the same size as *Nelson* and *Northampton* and with their speed they had put 18" to 20" of armour and 2-17" guns en barbette'. The D.N.C. was dubious as to the fighting value of such ships, anticipating the arguments of the *Jeune Ecole* by more than half a decade in suggesting that 'numerous gunboats with a heavy gun in each and torpedo boats were better for this service than the French ships'.

Two implicit contradictions were evident in Barnaby's vision, however. First, if 'numerous gun and torpedo boats' would better serve the purposes of coast defence for the French, why did he propose for the same purpose a design so similar to that which he had barely finished criticising? And if the British vessel were to be, like its predecessors, built for the dual role of coast defence and assault – a situation which would certainly explain why he preferred a battleship to torpedo boats – it merely led to another perplexing logical inconsistency. Barbette mountings were far more vulnerable to plunging fire than were turrets, and plunging fire was far more likely to be encountered in the business of assaulting shore positions than in fighting at sea. Moreover, why, if Barnaby had the previous year reached the conclusion that ramming would not play a major part in future naval battles, did he explicitly propose a ram bow?[10] As best as can be judged, his views seem to have been driven largely by financial considerations rather than suitability for a designed role. At the end of 1879 he informed Houston Stewart that by adopting the barbette 'a given thickness of armour and weight of gun could be obtained in a much smaller ship than was

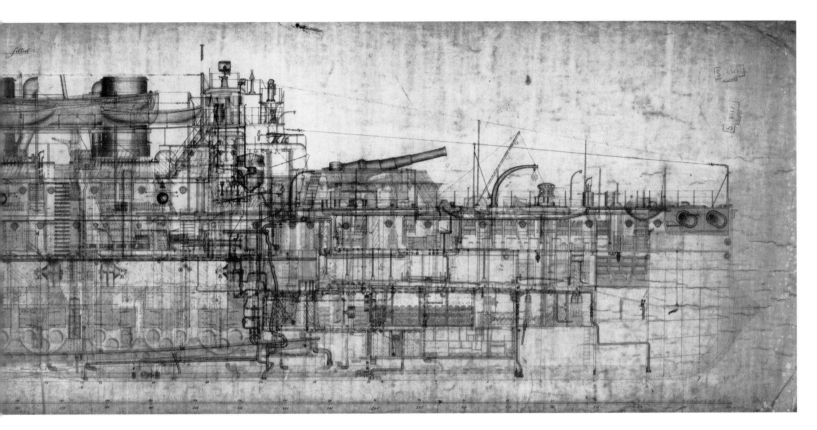

required for turret armament . . .'.[11] Additionally, of course, Admiralty consensus held that the ram would be valuable in 'mopping-up' operations against disabled enemy ships following the 'real' battle.

Shortly after the design was proposed, however, Barnaby provided an additional incentive for switching to barbettes. His initial suggestion, he admitted, 'represented rather a current of thought than a clear statement of opinion . . .'. Since then, however, 'he had received outline sketches of the latest [French] design'. Of the nine French ships under construction, four 'were of the *Requin* class designed to all appearance with a view to heavy fighting in the Mediterranean, the Channel, or the Baltic, [rather] than for purely coastal work'. If the intended foes were ships rather than forts, much, although as will be seen, not all, objection to employing barbettes receded. The *Requin* (*Terrible* or *Caiman*) class French battleships described by the D.N.C., were intermediate types laid down in 1877-8, with freeboards higher than purely coast-defence ships, but not as high as those of other contemporary French battleships.[12] In other respects they were notably similar to the design Barnaby proposed, with displacements of 7530 tons and two centre-line barbettes, one at either end of the superstructure, each mounting a single 16.5in breech-loader. As such the French design formed the basis for *Collingwood*.

While awaiting a reply from the Board during the first half of October 1879, Barnaby had his department work out details of the design, calculating the length, breadth, and draft and the engine power required to produce 'a good 14 knots speed', as well as the

disposition of guns and armour.[13] In the meantime his superior, Houston Stewart, produced his answer to Smith in the form of an assessment of Britain's naval situation. The comparison was as gloomy as that of 1877, bringing the Controller to urge that 'we must have more ironclads, and he was inclined to agree with the D.N.C. and follow the French designs. He was in favour of the barbette guns but depended on their Lordships decision which should be as soon as possible'.[14] Yet he disagreed with Barnaby as to which French model should be adopted, drawing 'their Lordships' attention to the 4 second class battle ships building in France which would be formidable cruizers for distant stations'. These four were not the quasi-coast defence *Requin*s, but rather

---

8. Smith to Houston Stewart, 20 August 1879, NMM: SWT/102. Smith had no intention of leaving the Board out of the consideration process; he simply wanted 'to have the Controllers and Constructors views altogether apart from and irrespective of the views of the Naval Lords . . .'.

9. 'Precis of Correspondence relating to design of *New Barbette Ship*', Barnaby memorandum, 9 September 1879, NMM: ADM138/68 (Ship's Cover for Collingwood), fol. 24/1.

10. See Parkes, *British Battleships*, p299.

11. Barnaby to Houston Stewart, 29 December 1879, NMM: ADM138/68, fol. 7/1.

12. Barnaby to Houston Stewart, 11 October 1879, ibid. Chesneau and Kolesnik (eds.), *Conway's All the World's Fighting Ships, 1860-1905*, pp290-1. *Conway's* terms them 'of moderately low freeboard'.

13. Barnaby memorandum, 'Principles of New Design for Coast Warfare,' nd., and Barnaby to Wright, 14 October 1879, NMM: ADM138/68, fols. 1, 4, 5.

14. Comments of Houston Stewart, 15 October 1879, 'Precis of Correspondence relating to design of New Barbette Ship', ibid., fol. 24/2.

two similar classes of French station battleships, the *Bayard* and *Vauban* barbette ships. They, unlike the *Requin*s, were fully rigged. They were also smaller (5900-6100 tons) and more lightly armed and armoured. Indeed, the ordnance disposition (but not the intended role) of both classes was similar to that which Barnaby had originally proposed for *Ajax* and *Agamemnon*. Houston Stewart explained this divergence with Barnaby's views on the grounds that 'our great want in case of war would be efficient steam cruizers that could go anywhere', rather than battleships: 'we should require to protect our commerce and look after the Russian Volunteer Navy of long steaming and fast steamers.'[15]

The conflicting views, especially Barnaby's observation that the French might be better off building gun and torpedo boats in preference to battleships, produced a predictable response from Smith, who, on 17 October 1879, 'after reading the D.N.C.'s memorandum imagined that he saw from it doubt whether armour was desirable for any part of a first-class fighting ship and he thus solicited the D.N.C.'s opinion on the best form of fighting ship irrespective of any public or other opinion on the subject'.[16] He was aware that 'a considerable portion of the armour is abandoned' in Barnaby's proposed design, 'and the Gun's crew must therefore be exposed to machine gun and rifle fire'. Since 'he

anticipated a very strong expression of opinion everywhere [in public] for smaller ships with great speed and carrying one gun', he wanted to know the professionals' views on 'the expediency and possibility of building fast and small (comparatively) vessels armed with one [big] gun and two or three lighter ones for the purpose of dealing with the larger and heavily armoured first-class line of battle ships in actual warfare'.

No reply to Smith's query survives, but it can be surmised that the professional consensus deprecated the possibility of opposing foreign battleships with such vessels as he proposed. The theories which had led to *Polyphemus*'s construction suggest the general views of the Board, Controller, and Constructor's department. Moreover, the type envisioned by the First Lord must necessarily have sacrificed protection for gun power and speed, and the sentiment within the Admiralty in favour of retaining protection was unanimous, even if opinions differed over how much armour should be retained, or where it was best applied.

If there was general agreement that some type of large armoured vessel was necessary to counter similar foreign designs, such agreement vanished when it came to the form such a vessel should take. In early December Hood produced a memorandum on '*the relative value of guns mounted en barbette, and in turrets, in sea-going battleships*'.[17] In comparing the French barbette ship *Amiral Duperré* (11,030 tons) with the *Colossus* class, the Second Naval Lord left little doubt as to his views. The latter, even though of '1350 tons less displacement,' was 'the most formidable fighting ship.' The reasons were numerous:

The French barbette ship *Requin* (launched 1885) with 16.5in guns and an armour belt with a maximum thickness of 20ins. She and her sister-ships were the direct inspiration for the design of *Collingwood*. (U.S. Naval Historical Center: NH64451)

the *Duperré*'s guns were entirely unprotected, the slides and revolving platforms on which the guns worked protected by armour of a thickness which the guns of the *Colossus* would penetrate at 2000 yards and over. She can only fire three guns on either side & three guns right ahead whereas the *Colossus* could fire four guns on either side & three guns right ahead. Also her men were more exposed to machine guns [and] top riflemen at close quarters.

Moreover;

he believed that all future naval wars would be decided at close quarters and therefore turrets efficiently protected would have a decided advantage over ships armed *en barbette* where the guns & men are unprotected and where the guns would be disabled when engaged with land batteries where the guns are mounted at considerable height above water.

Smith was clearly intrigued by the barbette question, probably on grounds of potential savings, for on 13 December he asked the Controller 'whether there is any foreign treatise or paper . . . as to the relative merits of the Turret and the barbette tower', and a day later advising him to 'ventilate the question of Turret v. Barbette' while inspecting Pembroke Dockyard.[18] He also solicited the opinion of George W. Rendel, a prominent engineer and naval architect at Armstrong's, one of the leading contemporary authorities on ordnance, and a member of the *Inflexible* Committee.

Rendel provided a ringing endorsement of Hood's position. His paper listed the advantages and drawbacks of each system, but left no question as to his own opinion.[19] After 'a general review of the relative merits of the two systems', he concluded, 'the balance would appear to be distinctly in favour of the turret ships of the English system so long as the use of armour on the waterline is continued'. Only if some other system of guaranteeing stability were employed, 'and the armour confined entirely to the protection of the gun mechanism or if great importance is attached to rigging' would it 'be necessary to reconsider the question'.[20]

Barnaby noted a further critical assessment of barbettes, this based on less theoretical analysis than those of Hood and Rendel. On 29 December 1879 he produced his own paper on the relative

merits of the rival systems. Although he opened by avowing that he 'had not intended to express any opinion on this mode of armament', since it was a 'question of principle in naval gunnery', rather than naval architecture, he evidently found the question inescapable owing to Captain George Willes Watson's report on *Temeraire*'s guns.[21] That vessel had been commissioned two years earlier, so there had been ample opportunity to evaluate its performance during gunnery practice. Watson's report was unequivocally critical. He did acknowledge that the gunnery was 'perfect at long ranges', but that was his sole positive comment. Otherwise, reported Barnaby, 'he says that the open surface of the barbettes in that ship could not well be missed up to 1500 yards, and he clearly means to refer to the *heavy guns* of the enemy . . .'. Hence, Watson maintained that 'these barbette guns would not be in action 5 minutes in a well-fought engagement'. The ramifications for the design proposed by Barnaby were even more pronounced than would first appear, since *Temeraire*'s guns were mounted on 'disappearing' carriages which swung down below the rim of the barbette, allowing the crew to reload the pieces without exposing themselves directly to horizontal enemy fire. The French models the D.N.C. advocated emulating had fixed carriages, which would necessitate the crews' exposure in the reloading process. Of course, with the return to breech-loaders the risk of being hit would be much less than would have been the case with muzzle-loaders, but even so, Barnaby matter-of-factly acknowledged that such a ship 'must soon be '*hors de combat*' if Captn Watson's view is correct'.

Barnaby himself took exception to such views, asking first how the barbette could be 'fired into' by a turret-mounted gun several feet lower than its target (he did not address the question of plunging fire from a shore battery). At close ranges, moreover, the D.N.C. maintained that barbette crews 'could be kept under cover and the broadside guns worked, if cover were found to be a necessity, or [the barbette guns] could be laid and fired down into an enemy without the exposure of men when passing him'. 'This looks so reasonable,' he professed, 'that one is staggered by Captn Watson's emphatic condemnation of barbette batteries in the ship.' Barnaby admitted that the barbette guns would quickly be silenced 'if Captn Watson's view is correct,' but refused to accept it:

15. He was also wrong in asserting that this type would be suitable for such duties. Both classes were too slow to function effectively as commerce protectors. Theodore Ropp provides a pointed criticism of the design in *Development of a Modern Navy: French Naval Policy 1871-1904* (ed. Stephen Roberts, Annapolis, 1987), p37.

16. Comments of Smith, 17 October 1879, 'Precis of Correspondence relating to design of *New Barbette Ship*', NMM: ADM138/68, fols. 24/2-3.

17. Comments of Hood, 8 December 1879, ibid, fols. 24/3-4.

18. Smith to Houston Stewart, 13 December 1879, 14 December [1879], NMM: SWT/102.

19. Smith to Houston Stewart, *Private*, 29 December 1879, NMM: SWT/102.

'My Dear Controller

I wrote to Mr Rendel a few days ago and asked him to give me the benefit of his own experience and observations on the question of Turret or Barbette and you will see from this that he is preparing a memorandum on the subject. . . . I thought you would be glad to have Mr Rendel's views, and that it w[oul]d be wise to wait for them before coming to any decision.'

20. G.W. Rendel memorandum comparing the turret and barbette systems, 5 January 1880, NMM: ADM 138/68, fols. 1-10. This was not official but was written for the Board's information. Rendel's memorandum is bound at the front of ADM1/38/68 and numbered separately from the pages that follow.

21. Memo from Barnaby to Houston Stewart, 29 December 1879, ibid.

I would put such a ship as has been sketched out confidently into the hands of English sailors. They can always see what they are firing at, and in a small ship they will have weapons of the highest power, with perfect defence of their machinery for propelling and manoeuvring and a magnificent coal supply.

Houston Stewart agreed with his subordinate (6 January 1880), endorsing the barbette system with a testimonial which transcended the realm of logical argument.[22] Claiming that he had discussed 'the relative merits of the Barbette and Turret systems' with French and German officers, 'he was of their opinion that the latter system [turret] would very likely weaken the morale of a crews [sic] whose courage and spirit in action will be more excited and better sustained in the Barbette Tower where they will have a sight of the enemy and are fighting under the eye and voice of the Captain and can to some extent see and know what is going on than when they are cooped up in a Turret enveloped in smoke and darkness whilst projectiles might enter through the armour of the citadel and possibly disable the machinery'.

This appeal to the fighting qualities and *élan* of the gun crew rested of course on unquantifiable factors and was more than a little reminiscent of similar arguments in favour of retaining masts and sails for the qualities of pluck, courage, and resourcefulness they allegedly instilled in sailors. Moreover, the Controller did not bother to address the objection that the barbette gun's mounting and machinery could be similarly disabled without an enemy shell even having to penetrate armour. Instead, he listed several ancillary advantages of the barbette system: removing the dead and wounded from a pierced turret, his foreign sources were reported to have said 'would be a slow and trying operation and the Turret would most probably be out of action'. On a more practical level, 'the weight required for armour around the citadel could be better used in increasing the speed and coal endurance and increasing the thickness of armour on vital parts.' And like the D.N.C. he maintained that the barbette crews could be protected from machine gun and rifle fire 'by corresponding fire in opposition'.

He also pointed out that existing turret guns required training around to line up with an external mechanism in order to reload. This objection, however, was of no consequence if a breech-loader, rather than a muzzle-loader, were employed, and one wonders if the Controller thoroughly considered this line of argument before putting it forward. It hinged on external loading, used only

for large muzzle-loaders. If breech-loaders were to be used in a turret this objection vanished, And if muzzle-loaders were to be used in barbettes, either the barbettes themselves would have had to have been huge, so that the guns could be mounted as in *Temeraire* and reloaded under cover of the barbette tower, or a similar system of external loading from behind an armoured glacis would have to have been used.[23] The only other alternative would have been exposing the crews to enemy fire *outside* the barbette as they reloaded the gun, and Houston Stewart did not go so far as to advance the claim that the last possibility would also 'excite and sustain' the 'courage and spirit' of the crew.

Yet having argued unreservedly for the basic type, the Controller then took pointed objection to the small 'coast-defence' design advanced by the Constructor's department. Instead, he maintained, 'at least a knot more speed should be insisted upon and if practicable 3 Barbette towers giving 2 more heavy guns than the turret ship[,] also a battery of 8 or 10 Unarmoured Breech-loading guns so mounted as to require but 3 [men] at each gun[,] a powerful supply of machine guns & steel protected crows nests aloft[,] and he would prefer a design so arranged to any he had yet seen'. Hence, the 'Controller recommended to adopt for one design the Barbette ship proposed by the D.N.C. with 25 feet added to the length[,] raising the engine power from 5000 to 7000 Horses which would give 15 knots speed and increase the cost from £430,000 to £500,000 for Hull and Machinery at the same time raising the fore part of the ship & the foremost Barbette tower higher from the water'. If the Board decided against the barbette design, Houston Stewart 'recommend[ed] . . . two armoured Battleships of the *Colossus* type but lengthened so as to give 15 knots speed.'

First Naval Lord Astley Cooper Key disagreed with both Controller and D.N.C. (7 January 1880), siding with Hood 'as to the exposed nature of the guns mounted en barbette'. He therefore 'could not consider a ship thus armed a 1st class fighting ship unless she possessed other qualities which would counterbalance this disadvantage'. Yet instead of advocating a turret ship, Cooper Key displayed unmistakable lack of resolution as to what actually should be built. He stated that he 'would like to see a ship built to carry 6-43 ton guns in 3 barbette towers with 14 ¾ knots speed and very little larger than *Majestic* . . .'. Barnaby's proposed design, 'a ship with 2-80 ton guns *en barbette*-14 knot speed & 2000 tons less dispt than *Majestic* was not,' he stated emphatically, 'a 1st class

22. Comments of Houston Stewart, 6 January 1880, ibid.

23. *Temeraire* carried 10in, 25-ton guns in its barbettes. Mounting a single 12.5in, 38-ton muzzle-loader such as carried by *Ajax* would have increased weight by over 50 per cent. How two such guns might have been mounted in a *Temeraire*-style barbette on 'disappearing' carriages seems, not surprisingly, never to have been considered.

24. Cooper Key to Houston Stewart, 7 January 1880, 'Precis of Correspondence relating to design of *New Barbette Ship*', NMM: ADM138/68, fols. 24/4-5.

25. Ibid., fol. 24/5.

26. Comments of Clanwilliam, 16 January 1880, ibid, fol. 24/7.

27. Barnaby to White on proposed modifications to barbette ship design, 13 January 1880, ibid, fol. 18.

28. Barnaby memorandum, 15 January 1880, ibid, fol.9.

29. *Warrior*'s engines produced over 5000 IHP, making her employment as a basis of comparison even more sensible.

fighting ship', but since he 'would . . . separate the armament more rather than concentrate it', he proposed still another arrangement to add to those of Barnaby, Houston Stewart, and that which he himself had proposed a few lines earlier: 'a ship of equal size and speed carrying 4-60 ton guns in four barbette towers'.[24] Whether he meant a ship equal to Barnaby's 7000-ton, 14kt design, Houston Stewart's larger version, or the first type he suggested is unclear from the wording. Four 60-ton guns in separate barbettes would certainly have necessitated a larger hull than Barnaby suggested, however.

As if this difference of opinion was not already serious enough, the D.N.O., Hamilton, also weighed in (8 January 1880), siding with Barnaby and Houston Stewart in deprecating Watson's objections to barbettes: 'as the French, Germans, and Italians had adopted the Barbette system and thought very highly of it', he argued, 'a case had been made out for a thorough consideration' of the system.[25] He also touched on the crucial matter of cost: 'for the same money a more powerful armament could be carried or what was more important more ships could be built for the same money.' Hence, he recommended, '[m]ore detailed plans should be prepared . . .'.

Turrets, however, had one more advocate at the Admiralty: Junior Naval Lord the Earl of Clanwilliam, who, on 16 January 1880, emphatically stated his preference for 'the turret system', but 'recommended the two 40 ton guns in lieu of (as a principle) one 80 ton gun, the former having sufficient penetration for a naval action'.[26] Moreover, Clanwilliam's memorandum cited the opinion of Vice-Admiral Sir John Edmund Commerell, who 'considered the barbette system in its infancy' and who agreed with Watson 'that the Hotchkiss [gun] which now penetrates 4 inches of iron and the accuracy and celerity of all machine guns at 6 hundred yards would very soon quell the fire of barbette guns'.

While this debate was being carried on by the members of the Board, Barnaby, presumably acting on Houston Stewart's recommendations, asked William White on 13 January to 'look into' the 'modifications we should need on the Barbette Ship to ensure a speed of 15 knots'.[27] To achieve this speed, Barnaby added, '[t]he length may go up to 380 feet (as an outside length), and the length of the citadel [central armoured portion, protecting the vitals] increased in proportion, I should think, to the displacement; preserving the breadth of 65 feet'. White quickly produced the requested information, for two days later Barnaby penned a memorandum reporting that '[i]f the barbette ship is lengthened 25 feet and her engine power raised from 5000 to 7000 horses we should increase the speed by one knot. Her cost would be increased from £430,000 to £500,000 for hull and engines.'[28] The same day, White produced a side-by-side comparison of potential barbette designs, one based on *Colossus*'s hull form, the other, interestingly, on *Warrior*'s. Reverting to the first ironclad's design appears a retrograde move, at least superficially, but *Warrior*'s

Collingwood's after barbette, mounting two 12in breech-loaders. The lack of protection for the gun crew is obvious.(U.S. Naval Historical Center: NH61342)

length–340ft–accorded well with that proposed by Barnaby in order to attain 15kts, and she was notably fleet under steam, even with an 1860-vintage power plant.[29]

	Colossus (as barbette ship)	*Warrior* (as barbette ship)
Length (ft)	325	350
Breadth (ft)	68	65
Draught (ft)	25	25
Displacement (tons)	9000	9000
I.H.P.	7000	7000
Speed (kts)	15	15
Weight of hull (tons)	2900	3000
Approx cost of hull armoured and fitted	£400,000	£410,000
Approx cost of engines	£98,000	£98,000

The crucial specifications of the two designs–speed, required horsepower, and cost–were strikingly similar despite the differences in length and breadth, and Barnaby (whether on his own initiative, Houston Stewart's, or the Board's is unknown), instructed his subordinate that beyond preparing a sheer drawing of *Warrior*'s hull in order that William Froude might make resistance

The authorisation of *Collingwood* on 23 February 1880 by First Lord W.H. Smith can be seen as the birth of the pre-Dreadnought battleship. (U.S. Naval Historical Center: NH88838)

calculations on it, 'no more work [was] to be done on the swifter barbette ship for the present'.[30]

On 6 February 1880 White furnished the Constructor's department with the mandated changes in the design Barnaby had originally put forth back in the autumn. *Colossus*'s hull form was indeed accepted as the basis for the new ship; the speed, as per Houston Stewart's insistence, was to be '15 knots on measured mile, with *all* bunkers full, or at fighting-line', and the armament to consist of four 43-ton breech-loaders, two per barbette.[31] The armoured belt surrounding the vitals was 'to be of such length as to secure stability and buoyancy as fully as was done in first design'. Aside from the demand for 15kts, the only other significant departure from the design put forward by Barnaby was the directive that, as Houston Stewart recommended, the '[u]pper deck and barbette – to be *3 feet higher* . . . at least the deck before fore barbette to be so raised', presumably to secure a better field of fire and to meet some of the objections raised by turret advocates regarding the gun crews' vulnerability. Finally, the Board requested that armoured bulkheads running the breadth of the ship be fitted 'if possible, to prevent raking fire sweeping through' the secondary battery of six 6in breech-loaders mounted along the broadside.

The Admiralty's deliberations over the relative merits of barbettes and turrets were finally settled in favour of the latter's advocates. At the same time, however, W.H. Smith's subsequent memorandum authorising *Collingwood* conveys the hesitancy with which the Board approached the question. '[A]fter frequent deliberations at the Board and very careful consideration,' Smith wrote on 23 February, 'it had been decided to build one ship of the Barbette principle.'[32] But at least the decision had been made.

On 30 April White forwarded 'a picture drawing, model, and legend for the "New Barbette Ship"' based on the Board's criteria to Barnaby. Adopting the *Colossus*'s hull form and increasing the indicated horsepower to 7000 resulted an increase in displacement from the 7000-ton design originally proffered to that of *Colossus*, or about 9500 tons.[33] To ensure buoyancy and stability, moreover, the waterline belt/citadel was lengthened from *Colossus*'s 123ft to 140ft. This design drew from Cooper Key the grudging admission that he 'preferred this ship to the *Colossus* but thought the 6 [inch] Bulkd unnecessary'.[34] Notwithstanding the First Naval Lord's caveat, by March 14 Barnaby 'submitted the sheer drawing, midship section and specifications for [their] Lordships signatures and name of ship', and the following day '[t]he Board approved the design', now designated *Collingwood*. The information was 'sent to Pembroke', where the battleship was to be built, 'for information and guidance'.[35]

Having made the decision to build a single, experimental barbette ship, the Board found that it could not rest comfortably and await the fruit of its labours. Within six months of *Collingwood*'s authorisation, a fresh headache confronted it in the form of a memorandum from the D.N.C. accompanying the proposed design for the ship's barbette gun mountings. Although Barnaby assured Cooper Key that the mountings would avoid 'the difficulty attending the use of two heavy guns from the same turntable in a barbette', he also bore grim news. '*Collingwood*,' he related, was 'far inferior in size to the 1st Class French ships' then under construction.[36] Moreover, the D.N.O. had ascertained that the 12in, 43-ton guns approved for the vessel could penetrate no more than 17in of compound armour at 1000yds range, and 21½in belts protected the latest French ships. 'Seeing that if the guns in the *Collingwood* can only be worked in pairs', Barnaby concluded, 'there is only a very small advantage in the second gun [and] it becomes a question whether a heavier & more powerful gun should not be substituted for the 2-43 ton guns in that ship.' He himself proposed a possible compromise solution: '[i]t might be considered to be wise to do this in the Fore barbette and keep the two 43 ton guns in the after barbette.' This opinion was seconded by Houston Stewart, who emphatically recommended 'that *Collingwood* should be armed with a gun capable of perforating armour of ships now being built such as [the] French ships named by [the] D.N.C., at 1000 yards'.

Surprisingly, the champion of *Collingwood*'s originally authorised armament was none other than the D.N.O. himself. Barnaby's view, he argued, was based on the assumption that the 43-ton guns were 'armour-piercers only, which cannot pierce the armour they attack . . .'.[37] Vesey Hamilton acknowledged 'perhaps it is so,' but added that the D.N.C. 'should remember that common shell, shrapnel, & case shot have each their special functions'. In the D.N.O.'s view, '[f]or general naval purposes [the] gun should possess maximum armour piercing power combined with efficient use of its other projectiles'. Reasoning along those lines, he concluded that '[f]or every purpose for which [the] 43 ton gun is *efficient*, two guns are double the value of one'. Were the Board to succumb to the argument that 'since the '43 ton gun cannot penetrate 21½ inches of compound armour, 2 gun barbettes of [the] *Collingwood* have only [a] small advantage over one gun', Vesey Hamilton warned that the price paid would be 'a loss of general efficiency . . .'. His arguments carried the day: *Collingwood*'s originally authorised armament remained unaltered.

Collingwood is often judged the most successful of Nathaniel Barnaby's creations, although, characteristically, her success is almost as often attributed to William White, whom, it is stressed, worked out the details of the design.[38] Yet the history of her genesis reveals far more disagreement over not only the ship's intended shape, but also her intended role, than had characterised most of the preceding decade's armoured designs. Parkes maintains that '[i]n the *Collingwood* provision was made for the acceptance of new tactical ideas—the discarding of end-on methods of fighting with the recognition that battleships would have to operate in line ahead while concentrating their fire on the beam'. The numerous explicit references to the design as a 'barbette ram', however, along with the provision of armoured bulkheads to protect against raking fire undercut his argument. Furthermore, *Collingwood* lacked the heavy protection requisite for a coast-assault vessel but simultaneously lacked the high freeboard necessary for a successful cruising battleship, as was revealed early in her service career.[39] In short, the first of the barbette ships was designed with neither a clear tactical intent nor a clear strategic one, unless it was that which Barnaby attributed to the French *Requin* class: 'designed to all appearance with a view to heavy fighting in the Mediterranean, the Channel, or the Baltic, [rather] than for purely coastal work.'

Thus we are confronted with a curious irony. The central-citadel ships, which were designed for very specific strategic purposes, and which would, by all indications, have been well suited for them, Woolwich guns aside, are retrospectively judged failures because conceptions of naval warfare changed between the time their designs were approved and the point at which they came into service, coupled with the fact that the first three were fitted with obsolescent guns—a shortcoming for which the Navy certainly bore little responsibility—guns which could not practically be exchanged for long-barrelled breech-loaders, given the constraints of space. *Collingwood*, and the subsequent 'Admiral' class, on the other hand, which were unmistakably the products of divided counsels at the Admiralty, and which represented no clear strategic or tactical vision—rather, only the desire to emulate foreign designs, coupled with the overriding concern not to squander too much money in so doing (Smith's prominent role in fostering the turret *versus* barbette debate is difficult to explain on any other grounds)—are retrospectively seen as successes. That success is obviously not attributable to Admiralty intentions, nor even to the ships' own merits, but simply because they seem to point towards the *Royal Sovereign*s and the standardised pre-Dreadnought design of the 1890s. But the coincidence is nothing other than that. The

30. White to Chief Draughtsman, Constructor's Dept. 'Not pushing ahead with barbette design, *now called Warrior type (as barbette ship)*', 15 January 1880, NMM: ADM138/68, fol. 14. The table in the following paragraph comes from the same memorandum.

31. 'Memoranda for new Barbette Ship' in White's hand, 6 February 1880, ibid. To facilitate rate of fire, the Board also specified 'an attempt [was] to be made to load by *hand* or hydraulic in any position over the whole arc of training of the gun.'

32. Comments of Smith, 23 February 1880, 'Precis of Correspondence relating to design of *New Barbette Ship*, ibid., fols. 24/7-8.

33. White memorandum, 30 March 1880, 'Precis of Correspondence relating to design of *New Barbette Ship*', ibid., fol. 24/8.

34. Comments of Cooper Key, 2 April 1880, ibid.

35. Barnaby memorandum, 14 April 1880, ibid.

36. Barnaby to Houston Stewart, n.d., and Houston Stewart to Vesey Hamilton, 6 October 1880, '*Collingwood*'s Armament, Precis of Correspondence', n.d., but about October 1880, ibid., fols. 26/1-2.

37. D.N.O. to Controller, 8 October 1880, ibid.

38. See Parkes, *British Battleships*, p299, for instance.

39. See ibid, p303.

Collingwood under construction. . (U.S. Naval Historical Center: NH61368)

tleships begun since 1875.[40] This news prompted several Board members, among them Parliamentary Secretary George John Shaw Lefevre, to produce comparative assessments of the two battlefleets. Shaw Lefevre noted that the previous Conservative Board had access to earlier assessments rendered by Barnaby and Houston Stewart, but had failed to alter 'their policy or . . . make any special exertions to increase the armour clad fleet. On the contrary the estimates for 1880-81 prepared by the late Board provided for a smaller amount of tonnage of ironclad building than in any of the past 12 years – viz. 7200 tons as compared with an average of 11000 tons for the previous 11 years'.[41]

Shaw-Lefevre refused to accept the alarmism of Houston Stewart uncritically, however, pointing instead to the views of U.S. Navy Engineer-in-Chief James W. King, whose recently published work on Europe's navies had estimated the British fleet to be 'superior to that of France by about 60 [per cent]'. He admitted, though, that King counted vessels in both cases which were far short of completion, prompting him to undertake his own calculations. These largely agreed with King as regards existing ships, but the Parliamentary Secretary then moved to the heart of the issue:

> [t]here remains the fact that the French have a much larger number of vessels in course of construction, and that the actual tonnage of ironclads built in each of the last 2 years has been considerably in excess of what has been done by England in the same time.

However, he still refused to bow to the temptation of panic. Noting that the French had done little to keep up their fleet in the immediate wake of the Franco-German War – concentrating instead on army reform and reconstruction – they now faced the need not only to replace many obsolescent ironclads which dated back to the Second Empire, but to counter the emergence of Germany and Italy as naval powers, albeit powers of limited ambition. Yet, he concluded, if the French completed their stated naval construction goals while Britain failed to respond, 'there cannot be a doubt that the strength of the French Fleet would by [1885] equal if not exceed our own, unless considerable additions be made to the latter in the interval'. And even if the French failed to meet their goals, if the British did not accelerate their own building programs, 'the time must arrive when the two fleets will closely approximate'. Shaw Lefevre thus concluded his survey emphatically:

muddled vision at the Admiralty which produced *Collingwood* and the 'Admirals' lurched back towards heavily armoured coast-assault vessels for its next two battleship designs, the *Victoria* and *Trafalgar* classes, further confirmation, were any needed, of how far at sea the Board was. Moreover, despite the superficial resemblance – Parkes presents the *Royal Sovereign*s as little more than 'Admirals' enlarged by 4000 tons – the two classes were very different. The *Royal Sovereign*s were unequivocally high-seas cruising ships (made possible not only by the large increase in displacement, but also by much improved steam technology), while the 'Admirals' were neither fish nor fowl, lacking the high freeboards (to say nothing of the advanced steam plant) which would have made high seas operations feasible, but simultaneously featuring open barbettes which were a potentially fatal liability in a coast-assault vessel. What vision drove their authorisation? The best available answer was furnished by Vesey Hamilton in the course of the debate over *Collingwood*: they could get more ships for the money.

The Decision to Build the 'Admiral' Class

The Liberal Ministry which entered office in early 1880 was acutely aware of the narrowing numerical gap between the British and French ironclad fleets. A June 1880 report submitted by the naval *attaché* in Paris, Captain Rice, informed the Board that the French Ministry of Marine had 'definitely decided to build four more [battleships] of 10,300 tons load displacement, armed with four 34 c.m.(13.4") Guns mounted *en barbette*', in addition to the nine battleships, two coast defence ships, and four cruising or 'station' bat-

40. Rice to F.O, 18 June 1880, bound papers relative to decision to build 'Admiral' class, Surveyor's Branch, 1 August 1881, PRO: ADM1/6608. This lengthy compendium lacks page numbers.

41. Shaw Lefevre memorandums 'Ironclads in the First Reserve', 16 October 1880, and 'Programme of works for building of Armoured Vessels, 1881-2. Comparison between English and French Armoured Fleets', 29 October 1880, ibid.

42. Shaw Lefevre on arrangements re: dockyards and new construction, 11 November 1880, ibid.

The drawbacks of the low freeboard of the 'Admiral' class is seen in this sequence of photographs of *Anson*'s bow. The sea in all of these is relatively smooth.

Top: Anson at 10kts. (U.S. Naval Historical Center: NH82702)

Middle: Anson at 12kts. (U.S. Naval Historical Center: NH82703)

Bottom: Anson at 14kts. (U.S. Naval Historical Center: NH65873)

[i]t appears that it will not be safe to maintain for the next 5 years the rate of construction of iron clads of the last 6 years, namely 8000 tons a year . . . and that in order to maintain a reasonable superiority over the French fleet we must considerably increase the construction of iron clads during the next few years, and so long as the French maintain their present rate of progress.

The Liberal administration clearly recognised what W.H. Smith and the Conservatives seem to have ignored, despite the urgings of Houston Stewart and Wellesley.

Yet having quickly ascertained that the Navy needed more battleships, the Liberal Board faced the same problem which had bedevilled its predecessor and contributed so largely to the sluggish pace of construction which had enabled the French to narrow the gap: what sort of ships should be built? Again, Shaw Lefevre appears to have seized the initiative, producing another memorandum in early November. The French, he observed, were not only committed to continued building of first-class battleships; they had 'altered their program *to increase* the number of' such vessels under construction.[42] Hence, they would be building seven such vessels, plus the four smaller *Requin*s, to Britain's four: *Inflexible, Colossus, Edinburgh* and *Collingwood*. 'We also have to consider the fact,' he added, 'that the Italian Government is building 2 vessels, the *Italia* and *Lepanto*, far superior in size and speed to any of our own or the French vessels', although the Italians displayed no inclination to build any further such ships.

In view of these facts it seems to be impossible for us to give up building armoured vessels of the 1st class; even if we should believe that for many reasons vessels of a smaller class would be more valuable, we must I think be guided by a certain extent by the policy of our rivals.

Yet at the same time the Parliamentary Secretary acknowledged that Britain, with its world-wide empire and unparalleled merchant marine, had a greater reason for building second-class battleships than France or any other power, and that this need could not be gainsaid. He therefore proposed a compromise, recommending that four armoured ships quickly be laid down:

I think 2 should be 1st Class Battle Ships, superior to any of the vessels now being constructed by the French, and which should

also be able to meet the Italian vessels on fairly equal terms, and 2 should be smaller vessels, of the 2nd class, of not more than 6000 tons displacement at the outside, and even smaller, if possible.[43]

The Admiralty considered the latter type first. In November and December 1880 the Board initially approved a design distinctly smaller than *Collingwood*–dimensions of 300ft x 61ft x 24ft 3in, 7000 tons displacement, yet larger (8000 IHP) engines, costing £400,000–but the Constructor's department was directed to refrain from producing a detailed design 'as long as possible in order that we might take advantage of the improvements being made' in ordnance, armour, boilers, engines, and the substitution of horizontal for vertical armour.[44] The period was on the cusp of important developments in all three fields; France had made the switchover to compound armour with the *Requins* (laid down 1877-8) and would, with the subsequent *Amiral Baudin* class battleships, begin to experiment with steel armour as well.[45] Likewise, steam machinery witnessed steady improvement, from the *Ajax*'s tubular boilers operating at 60 psi, to *Colossus*'s 64 psi, to *Collingwood*'s locomotive (cylindrical) boilers which generated steam at ninety psi (at least when new). The switch from compound to triple-expansion engines was on the horizon (it would occur with *Victoria* and *Sans Pareil*, begun in 1885), although not until the changeover from fire tube to water tube boilers (*Canopus* class, 1896-8)–possible only when metallurgical techniques could produce consistent,

high-quality steel–would enough steam pressure be generated to drive such powerplants efficiently. And yet boiler pressures crept upward through the 1880s, from the norm of 90 psi at the beginning of the decade, to 135 psi in *Victoria*, and 155 psi in the *Royal Sovereign*s. Likewise, the Italians had virtually discarded vertical armour along the waterline in their huge and fast *Lepanto* class battleships. The gun situation was, if anything, even more baffling. Barnaby expressed envy of the French, who could 'decide for new [ship] types without further delay', since they had 'the advantage of a settled form of gun concerning which they have long experience' and could design their ships around it. The Royal Navy, on the other hand, 'are not in a position to assume that we can adopt barbette batteries or even that we can take B.L. guns as a rule for new designs', thanks largely to the unhelpful attitude of the Ordnance Department. The Board could justifiably advocate holding off 'as long as possible' to capitalize on such improvements or to await the trials of novel ships like *Lepanto* and *Polyphemus*.

Were issues of technology and weapons systems not enough to cause gridlock in the decision-making process, the disagreement over ship types was no less marked than it had been in 1879 and early 1880, as the muddle over *Collingwood* so clearly illustrates. It was in December 1880 that Vesey Hamilton expressed his preference for emulating the French *Duguesclin* station ironclad design, a possible explanation for the dimensions and horsepower of Barnaby's proposed vessel. Moreover, the D.N.C. alluded to the understanding 'that something should be undertaken which would match the *Italia* and *Lepanto* . . .'. But building a battleship with the requisite 16kts speed to match the Italian vessels, plus 'heavy guns *and side armour* approximately proof to such guns'

The Italian battleship *Lepanto* was some 4100 tons heavier and a knot faster than *Collingwood*, which contributed to the Board's lengthy deliberations in 1880-1 over future capital ship designs. (U.S. Naval Historical Center: NH88712)

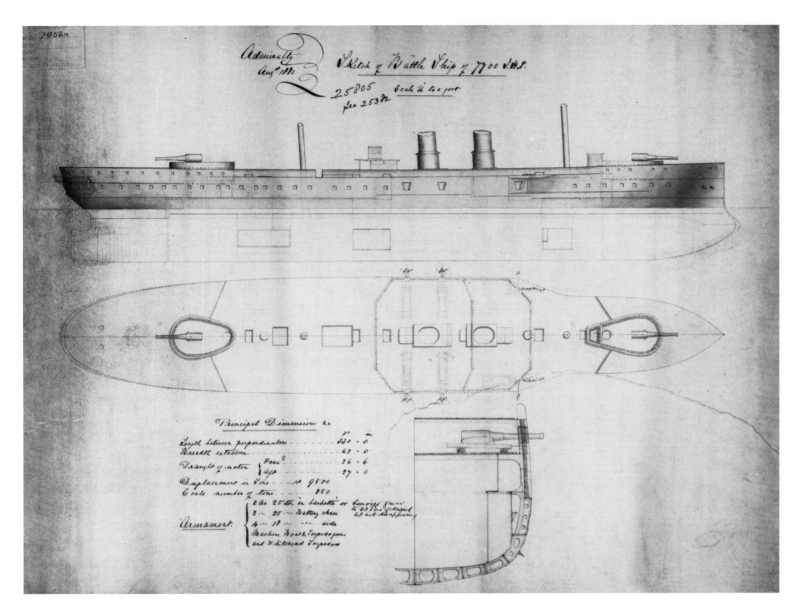

Among the first designs mooted in the lengthy deliberations leading to the authorisation of the 'Admiral' class was this, similar in size and displacement to *Collingwood*. (National Maritime Museum, London: E2280)

could not be done, Barnaby warned, 'unless we were prepared to invest more that a million of money in a single ship'. Even so, he added, 'the ship would remain vulnerable to the Torpedo and Ram, although less so than smaller ships'.[46]

The hope had been that with *Polyphemus* the Navy would find a cheap counter to the large Italian and French ironclads, but of course that vessel's potential was still untested, and would remain so for another two years. If *Polyphemus* was not considered 'a viable opponent for 1st class ironclads' and if it was instead decided to build the latter type immediately, Barnaby unequivocally advocat-

ed the Italian model, but to do so would require breaching the tonnage restrictions advocated by the 'moderate dimensions' school, to say nothing of accepting the 12-14,000 IHP necessary to drive the battleship at high speed. Mindful of the potential opposition to such a course, Barnaby added that he was 'not willing to put such a design forward until we are expressly ordered to do so

43. Ibid. Barnaby submitted a memorandum on the proposed design on 6 November 1880. No drawing appears to have survived, nor any detail on the disposition and size of guns, thickness of armour, etc. beyond the reference in the text. The Board considered it on 1 December and passed it along to the D.N.O. The initial design was approved on 14 December. This was unquestionably *Imperieuse*, for which no specific design was adopted at this point. See Chapter 10.

44. *Conway's 1860-1905*, p291.

45. Barnaby to Houston Stewart, 6 November 1880, Houston Stewart to Board, n.d., bound papers relative to decision to build 'Admiral' class, Surveyor's Branch, 1 August 1881, PRO: ADM1/6608. The quotations from Barnaby and Houston Stewart in this and the following three paragraphs come from these papers; that of Vesey Hamilton is summarised in Barnaby's memorandum.

46. Brassey memorandum, 26 November 1880, ibid.

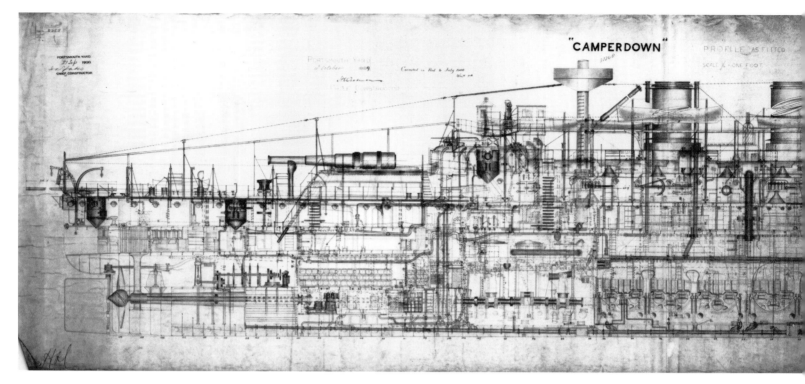

Above: A near-repeat of *Collingwood*, *Camperdown*, her sister-ships *Rodney*, *Howe* and *Anson*, and their half-sister *Benbow*, constituted the first class of more than two British armourclads since the *Audacious* class cruising ironclads laid down in the late 1860s. (National Maritime Museum, London: 8255)

Below: Rodney and her sister *Howe* were the second and third of the 'Admiral' class to be authorised. They were some 800 tons greater displacement than *Collingwood*. (U.S. Naval Historical Center: NH75951)

but our minds are made up as to all the features of the hull and engines of such a ship'.

Houston Stewart sided with his subordinate. If the Board were not prepared to accept 'the principle of abandoning side armour' and insisted on mounting guns in turrets, the Controller recommended:

a Citadel Ship with 20 inches of Steel Armour, 4-60 ton guns, 14 knot speed, and coal stowage equal to what was intended in the original design of *Devastation.* – the turrets to be placed as in the *Dreadnought* and not en echelon as in the *Inflexible.*

If the barbette system was to be accepted, however, *Collingwood* 'would constitute a first class Battle Ship' although;

[i]n what directions the increase of power should be developed, whether in guns or in Armour, would be a matter for

Below: Howe, Rodney, Anson and *Camperdown* were armed with 13.5 in guns, rather than the 12in weapons of *Collingwood*. (U.S. Naval Historical Center: NH75959)

The fourth, fifth and sixth units of the 'Admiral' class, *Camperdown* (pictured), *Anson* and *Benbow* were authorised by Lord Northbrook's board in late 1882. (U.S. Naval Historical Center: NH61394)

investigation and report by the Director of Naval Construction when their Lordships views on these points were decided and communicated for guidance.

But if Barnaby's proposal to abandon side armour was to be approved, 'then the design indicated by the D.N.C. . . . for a First Class Battle Ship on these principles should be proceeded with and matured for their Lordships' final consideration when complete in all its details'. Houston Stewart preferred the last course: 'My own opinion is in favour of adopting this design for First-Class Battle Ships'. To these opinions Thomas Brassey, the Civil Lord,

added his own thoughts, revealing a good deal of enthusiasm for, but little understanding of the subject. His muddled synopsis, however, concluded on an unmistakable note: 'I concur with Mr. Shaw Lefevre that the building of first-class vessels must be continued.'[47]

The Board concerned itself first with cruiser and second-class battleship designs in late 1880 and early 1881, only returning to the subject of first-class capital ship designs in April, when Barnaby submitted a lengthy memorandum with four possible designs, along with the rationale for each. He first considered the latest developments, both domestic and foreign. *Inflexible*, he noted, had been laid down in response to ships of more than 11,000 tons dis-

---

47. Barnaby, 'Sketch Designs for new First Class Armourclads,' 7 April 1881, ibid. The quotations in the following four paragraphs are drawn from this memorandum.

48. Observations by Houston Stewart, 3 May 1881, ibid.

placement, yet although 'only 6 or 7 per cent larger than the *Minotaur* and *Dreadnought* . . . she has been popularly regarded as a monster far too large and costly to be repeated'.[48] Instead, successive Boards had considered it 'good policy to produce ships of 8,500 tons to 9,100 tons with 43-ton guns, and armour superior to all the ships preceding the *Inflexible*'. Barnaby also noted that despite her 10,000-ton displacement, *Dreadnought* was clearly inferior even to *Ajax* and *Agamemnon* in offensive and defensive power: '[h]er comparatively feeble guns and thin armour certainly reduce her effective size to that of one of the modern ships of 9,000 tons.' Likewise, the last of the first-class masted cruising ironclads could not 'be regarded as up to the efficiency for fighting' of even the smallest of the central-citadel types.

Yet both the French and the Italians had been building ships well in excess of 10,000 tons, and if it were assumed that the power of these ships was 'fairly represented by tonnage, we shall find in France nine ships averaging over 10,000 English tons, i.e., more than 14 per cent superior, ship for ship', to the five central citadel ships and *Collingwood*, to say nothing of the three ocean-going breastwork monitors.

Two of them, the *Admiral Baudin* and the *Formidable*, are each

nearly the tonnage of the *Inflexible*. This superiority practically gives to France nine ships in a first class to which we may oppose one, viz., the *Inflexible*.

Likewise, although the Italians had lately 'recoil[ed] from the excessive size of 14,000 tons and 18,000 horses-power [*sic*] of the *Italia* and *Lepanto*', preferring instead to stick to the 10,000 ton limit, 'even this means a superiority of 14 per cent over our ships except the *Inflexible*'. Bearing foreign practice in mind, therefore, Barnaby concluded;

[W]e must . . . regard the first-class ironclad as a ship of at least 10,000 tons, as being of 11,000 tons according to French views expressed in two or three ships, and as being of over 14,000 tons if we accept the reasonings of the Italian architects and the expression of their ideas in the *Italia* and *Lepanto*.

Using these figures as the parameters for British designs, he then submitted four proposals 'of about the mean tonnage [*ie* 12,000 tons], two being 500 tons below the mean, and two 800 tons

Anson (launched 1886). (U.S. Naval Historical Center: NH63023)

175

Above: The delays in arming warships owing to Woolwich's shortcomings prompted *Benbow*'s arming with two massive 16.25in breech-loaders from Armstrong's Elswick foundry. (U.S. Naval Historical Center: NH000447)

Below: Of the designs brought forward during the 1880-1 deliberations, this was the one preferred by Barnaby and Houston Stewart. It emulated the Italian *Lepanto* class in the abandonment of side armour.

Admiralty 8. April. 1881. } SKETCH DESIGN FOR A 1ST CLASS BATTLE-SHIP. **(A)** .

ELEVATION .

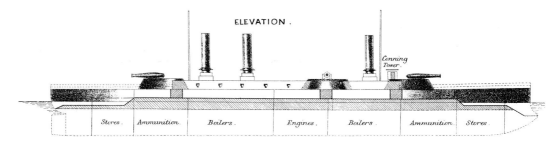

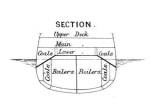

PLAN .

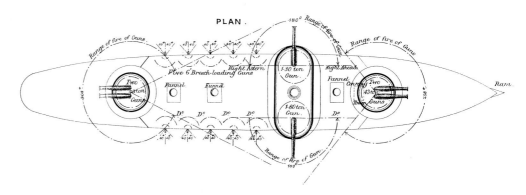

REFERENCE .

	Ft ins
Length between the perpendiculars .	420 . 0
Breadth extreme .	75 . 0
Mean draught of Water .	28 . 6
Displacement in tons .	12,850
I.H.P. (estimated)	14,000
Speed (do) knots .	18

Scale 1/40th Inch = 1 Foot .

Note . The unarmoured Guns may be made powerful machine Guns instead of Armour piercing Guns and the thickness of armour increased 3 per cent .

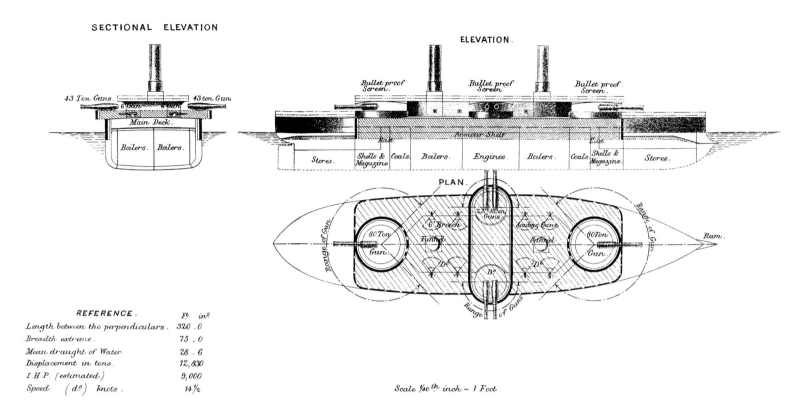

SECTIONAL ELEVATION

43 Ton Guns · 43 ton Gun

Main Deck.

Boilers. · Boilers.

ELEVATION.

Bullet proof Screen. · Bullet proof Screen. · Bullet proof Screen.

Armour Shelf

Stores · Shells & Magazine · Coals · Boilers. · Engines. · Boilers. · Coals · Shells & Magazine · Stores.

PLAN.

Range of Gun · 80 Ton Gun · 6" Breech · Funnel · L Nᵗ 80on Guns · Loading Guns · Funnel · Admiral · 80Ton Gun · Range of Gun · Ram. · Range of Guns

REFERENCE.	Ft	in⁵
Length between the perpendiculars .	320 .	0
Breadth extreme .	75 .	0
Mean draught of Water .	28 .	6
Displacement in tons .	12,830	
I.H.P. (estimated.)	9,000	
Speed (do.) knots .	14½	

Scale 1/40ᵗʰ inch = 1 Foot

This proposed design conformed to Edward Reed's opinion that buoyancy and stability should be protected by armour.

above it'. The first, '[a]n 18-knot barbette ship without side armour and of 12,800 tons', represented the previously-stated preference of both Barnaby and Houston Stewart. The second, '[a] 14½-knot barbette ship with side armour protecting buoyancy and transverse and longitudinal stability', of the same tonnage, was designed to satisfy those demanding vertical protection. For turret advocates, Barnaby also included two designs: 'a 15-knot turret ship, as *Inflexible*, with side armour of the same defensive power as in that ship, and of 11,500 tons', and a '15-knot turret ship, with the turrets in the middle of the ship, and of 11,500 tons'. The first three would cost about £800,000, the last would run about £60,000 higher. All were designed on the assumption 'that there are four 80-ton guns of greater length than those of the *Inflexible*, or that for two of them four 43-ton guns are substituted in the barbette ships'.

The D.N.C. apparently sought to have a design to appeal to everybody. His preferred design 'aim[ed] at the same conditions of excellence as the larger Italian ships; but there is, we think, a much better protection for buoyancy and trim. Reduction in size is effected by employing a different type of machinery, thinner armour, and a smaller unarmoured battery'. Yet it was, he admitted, less stable than *Inflexible* with the soft ends waterlogged, and on the chance that this was found objectionable, Barnaby could point to the alternative barbette design, 'in which speed is sacrificed for protection and stability'. It was, he bluntly acknowledged, 'a ship embodying the principle advocated by Sir E. Reed, viz., that

the armour should protect the trim, stability, and the speed; and that the ship should go into action with the ends already water-logged, if the armour is omitted from them'.

The third design was a 'new *Inflexible*,' the fourth a 'new *Dreadnought*, 700 tons larger than the present ship, but elevated into the position of a first-class ship by having the armour and the guns brought up to the power of the *Inflexible*, the only sacrifice being the abandonment of the thin armour belt, and such protection as it can afford to the trim buoyancy, and stability in a protracted engagement'. Barnaby again minced no words in his advocacy of the design without vertical waterline protection:

[L]ooking to the possible growth of the gun and the certainty in that case that all armoured walls will sooner or later be perforable, or to the alternative proposal that heavy guns and armour will be abandoned because of the advance of the submarine attack, in either case we think Design (A.) represents the arrangement of protection towards which we are advancing.

Inflexible had been, he opined, 'a large step towards' such a vessel, and design 'C' marked a distinct advance on *Inflexible* thanks to the substitution of compound for wrought iron armour and 'the partial use of locomotive boilers,' which, together, 'enable[d] us to produce a better *Inflexible* on the same dimensions'. Yet, he concluded;

it is in Design A., with its high speed and distributed batteries, that we think there is the greatest promise of permanence of type

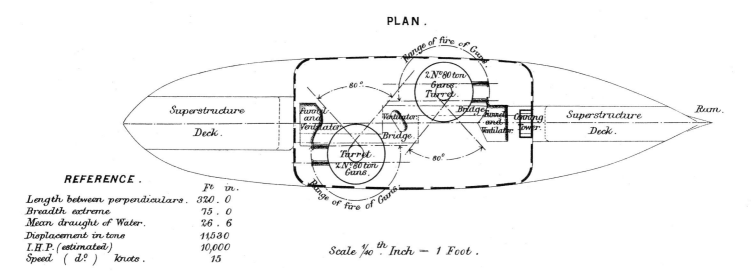

Admiralty 8 April.1881. } SKETCH DESIGN FOR A 1ST CLASS BATTLE-SHIP (C).

PROFILE.

PLAN.

REFERENCE.

	Ft in.
Length between perpendiculars.	320 . 0
Breadth extreme	75 . 0
Mean draught of Water.	26 . 6
Displacement in tons	11,530
I.H.P. (estimated)	10,000
Speed (d°.) knots.	15

Scale 1/40th Inch = 1 Foot.

The third design proffered to the Board in 1881 was an improved *Inflexible*, with higher speed and more powerful guns

for the few first-class ships designed to form flagships for powerful squadrons; and we see no reason why a similar disposition of the protecting material made not be made in battle ships of lower speed and less size.

Houston Stewart added his own words to Barnaby's memorandum, using the opportunity to provide another gloomy comparative assessment of the British and French navies. '[O]ur existing Navy, completed and completing,' he warned, 'is inferior to that of France in powerful ships and guns, and possesses no ship equal in power to the four latest additions to the Italian Fleet. If to have a decidedly superior Navy to that of any other power is a necessity for Great Britain we undoubtedly do not possess it either in Armoured or Unarmoured ships, in Guns or in Trained Seamen.' He continued in a similar vein for several paragraphs, before concluding with a ringing endorsement of Barnaby's first proposal.[49]

If Barnaby had anticipated offering 'something for everybody' with the four designs put forward, he must have been disappointed at their reception. The Board met to consider them on 19 May

1881, but adjourned without reaching a decision. Indeed, so far from being happy with any of the options, the First Naval Lord asked the Controller's Department 'to ascertain the size and cost of a ship having 25in of steelfaced armour on hull and turrets; two turrets for four 80 ton guns, and 16 knots speed'. This request, and particularly Barnaby's response to it, are noteworthy in light of the eventual decision to build the *Royal Sovereign*s at the end of the decade. Such a vessel, he replied on 23 May, 'would cost apart from guns and stores over a million of money of which about £400,000 would be required for armour. The displacement of the ship would not be less than 14,000 tons'. Leaving aside the matters of turrets *versus* barbettes and, more importantly, freeboard, Barnaby had predicted quite accurately what would be required to build *Royal Sovereign* and her sisters, which displaced 14,150 tons at normal load, and which cost between £915,000 and £980,000.[50]

Apparently suspecting that the Board would recoil from such an outlay, Barnaby also provided 'an outline sketch of a ship of 15½ to 16 knots, armed as ordered, with detached [*ie* separate] citadels, and an armoured conning tower and firing station for each position, of 12,500 tons displacement, and £920,000 for the ship, apart from guns and stores . . .'. This design could be provided with either 20in armour 'on hull, citadels, and turrets,' or 25ins on the

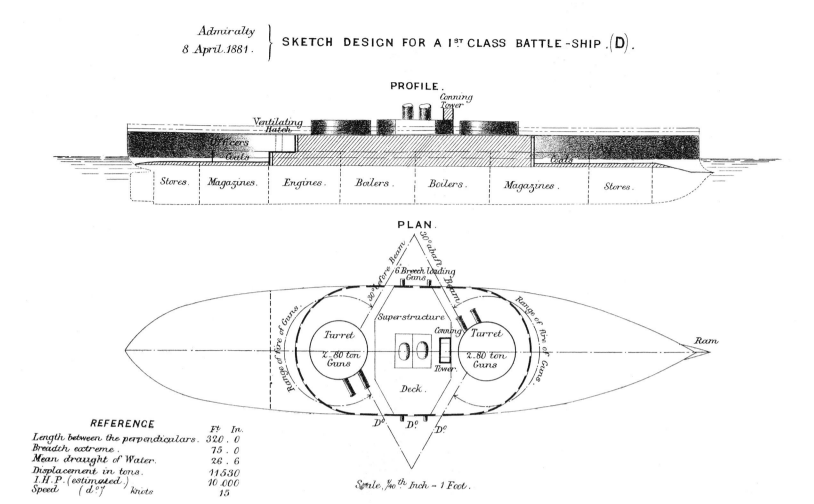

The final design submitted in April 1881 was an improved *Dreadnought*, armed with guns more than twice the weight of those on *Dreadnought* herself.

latter two places 'but with sloping deck armour of 12½ inches instead of vertical armour of 25 ins.' He also forwarded, per the Board's request, an alternative armour scheme for design (A) of his original submission, whereby the heavily armoured 'control position' for the guns was suppressed and the armour redistributed to the barbettes, making it 30 per cent thicker on the latter.[51] He added, however, 'that if large battle ships are tending to become obsolete', the design lacking vertical armour, and it 'alone can be converted into a fast protected cruiser', a remarkable hedging of bets until one recalls the Admiralty's experience with iron frigates in the 1840s, whose hull plates were discovered to be dangerously prone to shattering when hit by solid shot, and which ended up serving as transports, or the first-generation British ironclads, for whom the same proposal was voiced in the event that their armour would not stop shot. Indeed, the parallels are remarkable, for Barnaby also pointed out that '[t]he barbettes and armament could be transferred to smaller vessels, and a spar deck and suitable armament could be given for cruising purposes or war transport'.

Presumably the Board shared Barnaby's aversion to investing so much money in one ship–especially one, as the D.N.C. was fond of pointing out, which could be sunk by a single torpedo–and no sur-

viving evidence suggests that the avenues he sketched out in late May were explored. In July Brassey produced two more memoranda full of his remarkable, often contradictory views on ideal British shipbuilding policy, in which he successively advocated (1) building smaller armoured ships whose possible deficiencies in coal capacity 'could be met by taking up large merchant steamers, to be used in towing those vessels which have only a limited coal supply', (2) reducing armour coverage, since 'if the unprotected vessel has a secure superiority in speed, and is moving at a high rate she will be difficult to hit, and may seldom be struck even in a protracted

49. Cooper Key to Houston Stewart, 19 May 1880; Barnaby to Houston Stewart, 28 May, ibid. Parkes, *British Battleships*, pp354-5. The armour thickness–and consequent cost– was reduced for the *Royal Sovereign*s due to the adoption of nickel-steel alloy plates; the belt was thus only 18ins thick, rather than the 25ins Cooper Key wanted in 1881.

50. Barnaby to Stewart, 28 May 1881, in bound papers relative to decision to build 'Admiral' class, Surveyor's Branch, 1 August 1881, PRO: ADM1/6608.

51. Brassey, 'Remarks Relative to the type of ship required for H.M. Navy,' 2 July 1881, ibid.

battle', (3) building 'an improved *Collingwood* or *Dreadnought*' and 'two types of unarmoured vessels', (4) numerous rams of the *Polyphemus* type, but 'with such improvements as experience may suggest; and among those improvements, not the least will be those which lead to greater simplicity of construction and consequent reduction of cost', and (5) not spending more than £500,000 on individual battleships.[52] Brassey also cited the opinion of former Naval Lord Geoffrey Phipps Hornby, who, when asked whether he would prefer, for a given sum, two *Collingwood* types or three fast, protected cruisers, replied if 'you guaranteed the French would come out in to mid Channel and fight, I might select the former. But if the question were varied slightly, and put in its practical form, viz:– "what addition would you now recommend to the British Navy in view of possible hostilities with France, the money being so limited as to produce two of one class or three of the other?" I should say without hesitation '"build two [protected cruisers] and two *Collingwoods*"', which, of course, was neither of the options offered him. Brassey's arguments regarding design also revealed more concern for cost than for efficiency: he advocated 14kts speed rather than 15 or 16, and only so much armour 'as the preceding conditions [*ie* restricting cost to £500,000] will allow'.

At this point First Lord the Earl of Northbrook also weighed in, asking Houston Stewart to furnish 'the specification of a ship of the *Collingwood* class—Speed, 15 knots . . . Armament, one 80 ton and two 43 ton guns in turrets or modified turrets . . . 6-inch guns, as in *Collingwood* . . . Cost, about £600,000 . . . coal supply may be less than in *Collingwood*'.[53] On 27 July Barnaby replied to this request, providing three alternative schemes, compared to that adopted in *Collingwood*.[54] The first described (no. 3) added turrets 'to the existing barbettes, the latter being converted into armoured-loading chambers', in a manner foreshadowing similar developments in the post-*Royal Sovereign* pre-dreadnoughts of the 1890s. 'The great height of the guns is thus preserved,' Barnaby stressed, but the additional weight of the turrets 'makes it necessary to increase the size of the ship by 1,000 tons, and to exceed the cost of the *Collingwood* [estimated at £567,000] by £100,000.' The second design (no. 2) 'preserve[d] the *Dreadnought* arrangement, and provides in a central citadel armoured protection for discharging torpedoes above water, and a certain amount of armoured protection for range of stability'. On the other hand, Barnaby pointed to notable drawbacks. The citadel armour could not be made thick enough to render it 'impregnable' and thus it was possible 'that both turrets may be disabled by the single shot perforating the side'. Additionally, the central citadel would be 'very cramped and useless as living space', and the guns would have to fire over a lengthy stretch of deck. 'This ship would be the same size as the *Collingwood*, and would cost for hull and engines say £600,000. The height of the armoured glacis [surrounding the base of the turret] from the water is in this case 12 feet, or 8 feet

less than *Collingwood* . . .'. The final design proferred (no. 1) was similar to the first, save that the turrets would be mounted directly on the armoured deck, rather than atop barbettes, 'thus lowering also the armoured glacis to 12 feet out of water [*sic*]. This requires about 9,400 tons, and a cost of, say, £620,000.'

For all of these proposals, Barnaby added, his department had 'taken, as directed, only one 80 ton gun in the fore turret (with 80 rounds of ammunition for it) . . .'. This, he advised was not 'an economical arrangement'. It was acceptable for barbettes, 'because the total depth and weight of [the] armoured structure is much less than in a turret, but in either case the increase in diameter required for a second gun is very small'. Moreover, the price of adding a second gun would not be prohibitive, either in terms of cost or of increased displacement.[55] The D.N.C. also pointed out that '[t]here would appear to be a very satisfactory compromise between the turret and the barbette' which would permit 'the use of the single heavy bow gun instead of a pair of guns, without the sacrifice of economy referred to above'. This compromise would involve;

> plac[ing] one 80 ton instead of two 43 ton guns in the fore barbette of the *Collingwood*, retaining in other respects the bow arrangement of the *Collingwood*, and to employ a turret for two forty-three ton guns at the after end. . . . This would constitute turreted design No. 4. We should endeavour to make the thinnest above-water armour 14 ins., and bring the price down to about £600,000, with a tonnage of about 9,250.

The D.N.O. added his own remarks on 31 July. Design number one, he maintained, 'approaches nearest to what I consider the best type of ship to meet the proposal of [the] First Lord'.[56] Vesey Hamilton agreed with Barnaby as to the economy of mounting two guns in a turret rather than one, but objected to barbettes 'on account of the danger which I consider exists . . . to the mounting from the effect of the explosion of a heavy shell bursting underneath it'. He extended his remarks to the secondary armament, suggesting that its disposition would 'seriously interfere, in the case of the turrets, with the arc of fire of the main battery of the ship', and recommending that it be done away with. Finally, he noted that 'it appears that submerged [torpedo] fire can be obtained forward and abaft [and] above [the] water line on both the broadside and astern, the submerged fire in the latter case being prevented by the twin-screw shafts'.

By this point, the debate over the type of first-class battleship to be built had stretched over nine months and generated no less than eleven discrete design proposals. Yet on the day after the D.N.O. forwarded his opinion along with the last four of Barnaby's designs, Northbrook terminated the process with a succinct directive: 'Two *Collingwoods* to be laid down, one at Pembroke the other at Chatham, the armament to be deferred for the present.'[57]

These vessels were subsequently named *Howe* and *Rodney*. After much deliberation, it was decided to arm both with four 13.5in, 67-ton guns.[58] Continuing concern over French shipbuilding, however, prompted Northbrook and his colleagues to authorise an additional three *Collingwood*-type vessels in 1882, although lack of consensus again plagued their counsels. As of 1 August 1882, when Parliamentary Secretary Henry Campbell-Bannerman described the Board's program, it had been decided that one of the three – *Benbow* – would be a repeat of *Rodney* and *Howe*. Designs for the other two vessels, however, were still up in the air. Campbell-Bannerman matter-of-factly told the House of Commons:

The Admiralty look to the opinions of the officers commanding our ships in the East [Alexandria had been bombarded the previous month] as likely to throw a most instructive light on many problems of practical Naval construction, and thus it is that on this point – as to the type of the new ships to be laid down – I have no communication at present to make to the Committee. The final determination has not yet been made.[59]

Only the following March could he finally inform the House that 'further consideration of the barbette system has satisfied us that it was a wise decision to adopt it in preference to the turret,' and that, consequently, 'the two new ships . . . which were indicated last year will be of this type, and, in fact, sister ships to the *Benbow*.'[60] At the same time, however, the Parliamentary Secretary had to admit that the Board had decided to arm *Benbow* with two 100-ton (ultimately 16.25in, 110-ton) guns rather than four smaller pieces.[61]

The question to pose here is not why the Admiralty went to such trouble and time to consider alternatives to *Collingwood* if that was what it was eventually going to decide to build but, rather, why none of the alternatives was adopted in lieu of *Collingwood*, especially since Barnaby's memorandum of 7 April 1881 implicitly but unmistakably concluded that that vessel did not constitute a viable contender against larger foreign battleships. Northbrook put forward no specific rationale for the course he adopted, but it is not difficult to surmise the factors which impelled it. In 1885 he remarked for the benefit of his successor '[n]o question has probably caused more anxiety to successive Boards . . . or thrown upon them greater responsibility than the course of the designs of first-class armour-plated ships'.[62] His own Board had 'resisted considerable pressure in the direction of an increase in the size' of such ships, noting that both the French and Italians had ceased designing vessels in excess of 10,000 tons. Hence, he concluded, '[w]e have . . . been satisfied with a displacement of about 10,000 tons for our first-class ships.'[63] The perplexed state of naval architecture, exemplified by the profound disagreement evident within the Board and among its professional advisors over size, over the extent, disposition and thickness of armour, and over the preferred method of mounting heavy ordnance virtually mandated, as had been the case with *Collingwood*, that although it was imperative to continue to build battleships, it was also highly desirable that the investment in so doing be kept to the minimum. The 'Admirals' were not the most powerfully armed or armoured, nor the fastest of the numerous designs put forward in 1880-1; they were, however, the least expensive.

---

52. Northbrook to Houston Stewart, 15 July 1881, ibid.

53. Barnaby to Houston Stewart, 27 July 1881, ibid.

54. Barnaby stated that a second gun would add £10-15,000 to the cost, and increase immersion by 7-10ins.

55. Remarks of Vesey Hamilton, 30 July 1881, ibid.

56. Northbrook memorandum, 1 August 1881, ibid.

57. See Henry Campbell-Bannerman's explanation to the House of Commons in *Hansard's Parliamentary Debates*, 3d ser., 273 (1882), cols. 409-10.

58. Ibid, cols. 410-11.

59. Ibid, 3d ser., 277 (1883), col. 607.

60. See Parkes, *British Battleships*, p321. Parkes points to problems at Woolwich as the chief factor for this decision: 'As it was very doubtful if Woolwich would be able to deliver any of the new and untried 13.5-in. B.L. for a considerable period, an alternative heavy gun had to be selected which could be supplied in good time and thus avoid the expense incurred by delay with the contractors [*Benbow* was built in Thames Iron Works' yard].' The choice fell on Armstrongs' 16.25in gun, in order to match the main armament of the Italian *Andrea Doria* class, which were armed with it.

61. Northbrook minute, July 1885, PRO: ADM1/7465c, p13.

62. Ibid, p14.

Chapter 10

THE CRUISER QUANDARY

QUITE ASIDE from the question of what, if any, sort of battleships it should build, the Admiralty had also to deal with the cruiser quandary, a problem of such complexity that it deserves detailed consideration for the manner in which it adumbrates not only the ways in which strategic considerations influenced design policy and the technological limitations with which designers had to contend, but also some of the structural problems within the Admiralty which hindered design success.

Aside from her full sailing rig. *Shannon*'s single propeller shaft and hoisting screw (she was the last British ironclad so equipped) make plain her intended strategic role as a cruiser on distant stations. (National Maritime Museum, London: 19214)

From Swiftsure *to* Shannon

By the early 1870s the strategic rationale for building second-class, cruising ironclads was beset with a clash between tactical and operational needs on the one hand, technological limitations on another, and the strategic imperative of designing such ships for worldwide roles. This clash of conflicting aims and limitations was, before about 1885, incapable of satisfactory resolution, although, as has been the case with the division of the battlefleet into coast-assault and cruising ships, many subsequent commentators have failed to appreciate the degree to which strategic factors confounded the job of British naval designers and administrators during the 1870s.

The Admiralty could and did cease building first-class cruising

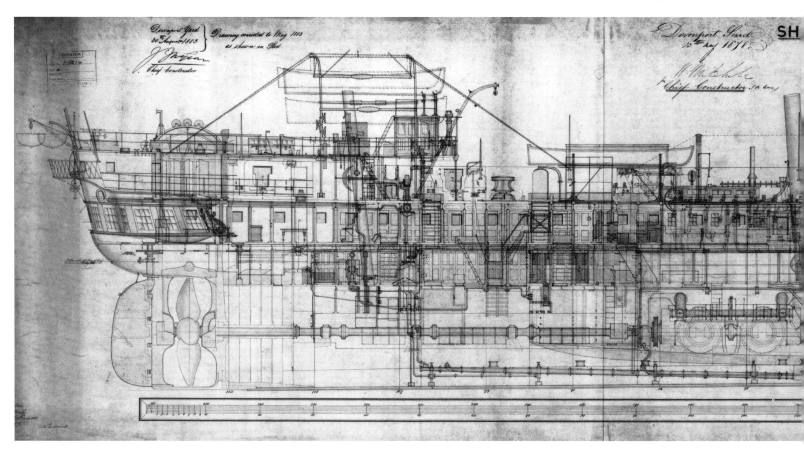

ironclads when the drawbacks of sails were deemed overwhelming, even if steam was not yet sufficiently reliable to effect a complete substitution. Strategically, it was possible to do without the type. Yet the Navy could not dispense with all cruising ironclads, given the threat of *guerre de course*. Indeed, with the appearance of armoured foreign warships designed specifically for commerce-raiding, beginning with the Russian *General Admiral* (laid down 1870), the necessity for a British counter-design became even more pronounced. And as it did the strategic rationale on which British ironclads for overseas stations had been designed shifted, or perhaps more accurately, widened, in marked fashion.

Second-class cruising ironclads had been built during the 1860s with a very specific strategic role in mind: they were designed as economical counterparts to similar foreign vessels, and were thus moderate-sized, iron-hulled vessels. They were either of box-battery or broadside arrangement, often had sheathed hulls (to reduce fouling), and even lighter armament and armour than first-class cruising types. They carried full sailing rigs, since the means for maintaining wholly steam-powered forces on distant stations did not exist, and, like most such sail/steam amalgams, were not particularly fast in either mode. The *Swiftsure* and *Audacious* of the late 1860s epitomised the type. These had been designed principally to meet the challenge posed by the French *Alma* and *La Galissoniere* classes, of which seven of the former and three of the latter were laid down between 1865 and 1869.[1] Other potential opponents, like the Peruvian *Huascar*, were either smaller, slower, more lightly armed, more lightly armoured or, in most cases, a combination of these traits.[2] At the time of their launch, even when completed, therefore, in the course of the duties for which they had been designed the six British second-class cruising ironclads were unlikely to face an armoured foe capable of both outgunning and outrunning them.[3] Potential enemy commerce-raiding operations thus would have either to be undertaken by unarmoured vessels – to meet which the Navy had designed a separate class of vessel, the large and speedy unarmoured frigate *Inconstant* – or else by slow 'station ironclads', which were not only ill-suited for the task, but also liable to fall easy prey to the *Audacious* or *Swiftsure* classes. As late as 1871 the Admiralty Committee on Designs of Ships of War (appointed in the wake of the *Captain* disaster) was of the opinion that;

[w]e believe that reasons of a similar character to those which . . .

1. Chesneau and Kolesnik, *Conway's All The World's Fighting Ships, 1860-1905*, p302. For contemporary evidence on the design of the *Audacious* and *Swiftsure* classes, 'Report of the Committee appointed by the Lords Commissioners of the Admiralty to examine the Designs upon which Ships of War have recently been constructed, with Analysis of Evidence,' *Parl. Papers*, 1872, Vol. 14, ppxiv-xv.

2. *Conway's 1860-1905*, pp116, 118-30, 192, 198, 219-20, 250-52, 274-78, 301-03, 314-21, 344-46, 395-96, 401, 405-08, 410-11, 418-19.

3. In European waters, where many of them served, the situation was different.

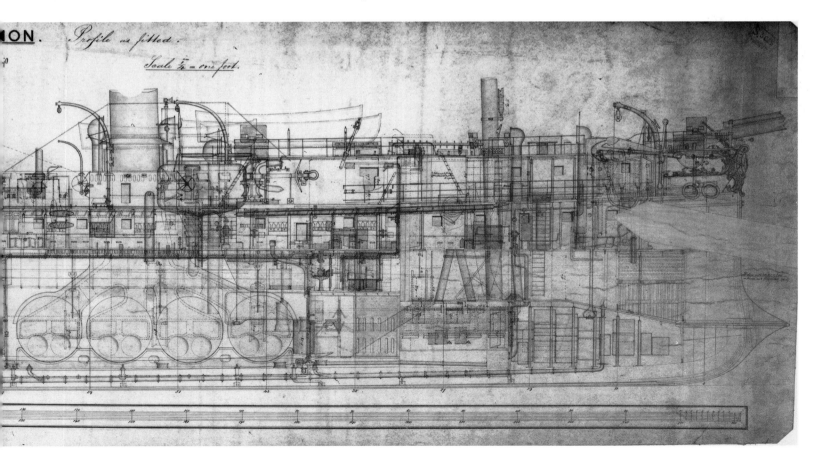

Either *General Admiral* or her sister-ship *Gerzog Edinburgski*. These Russian ships were faster and longer-ranged than other station battleships. (U.S. Naval Historical Center: NH94664)

centrating on their real prey. But with the appearance of the *General Admiral* this course was no longer possible (although the real threat posed by the earliest armoured cruisers was much reduced owing to their deficient engines); from that point forward anti-commerce raiding cruisers required armour, speed, and endurance. The first was detrimental to achieving the second, and as of 1870, 1880, or even 1885, the last was unattainable in a purely steaming vessel if destined for service outside European waters. The Admiralty did not have the technological means at its disposal – not to mention the coaling stations – with which to meet the new strategic paradigm head-on. Faced with the growing vulnerability of first-class cruising vessels they opted to cease building the type. Faced with the threat of *guerre de course* they had to respond, but lacked the means to respond successfully. They were forced to adopt half-measures.

The first product of this insoluble dilemma was HMS *Shannon*, whose design history is unusually well-documented, and which admirably underscores the difficulties the Board of Admiralty experienced in coming to grips with the shifting tactical/operational framework. Nathaniel Barnaby's opening entry for the *Shannon*'s design notes that on 11 March 1873 he was directed to prepare a '[d]esign for an Iron clad . . . to be capable of competing with the second class Iron clads of Foreign Navies with [*ie* in] arrangement with the First Lord, the Controller, and myself . . .'.[5] The D.N.C. was given several parameters: the vessel was to be no longer than 260ft, its breadth a maximum of 54ft, and its mean draught 21ft. He was further instructed to make arrangements for a '[s]ingle lifting screw. *Full sail power.* 13 Knots speed at M[easured] M[ile] Economical Engines, *same coal endurance as Swiftsure class* . . . [and] to be sheathed in wood'.[6] Seemingly the novel threat posed by the *General Admiral* did not enter into the Admiralty's calculations, and it wanted a vessel of the same type as those laid down in the late 1860s.

Thirteen days later Barnaby forwarded a sketch of the proposed design to his superior, Controller William Houston Stewart, which had been prepared 'in pursuance of the arrangement made at the interview with the First Lord on the 11th inst.'.[7] *Shannon*'s sketch was then sent to the D.N.O., Captain Arthur Hood, who Houston Stewart asked to 'give the design your consideration bearing in mind the purpose for which such a ship is proposed'.[8] Hood felt not in the least circumscribed by his title; he made a number of

induced their Lordships to sanction the construction of these ships, must be expected at all times to exist and to require attention; and . . . that for the important services which they are likely to be called upon to perform, they . . . are extremely well-suited as regards displacement, speed under steam and sail, as well as most of the qualities which constitute a handy and useful ship of war.[4]

Even as the Committee's report was being composed, however, the tactical/operational assumptions on which they were constructed were shifting. The Russian navy was building more lightly-armed, but faster and longer-ranged (under steam) proto-armoured cruisers. Against such ships the relatively slow station ironclads would be largely powerless. In the 1860s building two different types of vessels, station ironclads and cruisers of the *Inconstant* type, was a feasible approach (technologically, if not fiscally) to the *guerre de course* problem. Since no potential commerce raider carried armour, the station ironclads had only to contend with similar vessels, and anti-commerce raiding vessels could stay out of harm's way if they encountered station ironclads, thus con-

4. 'Report of the Committee appointed by the Lords Commissioners of the Admiralty to examine the Designs upon which Ships of War have recently been constructed, with Analysis of Evidence', *Parl. Papers*, 1872, Vol. 14, pvi.

5. Barnaby to Constructor's Department, 11 March 1873, NMM: ADM138/43, fol. 1.

6. Ibid, fols. 1-2, 7. Other criteria, such as the thickness and disposition of the armour and the size, number, and arrangement of the guns were also decided at the meeting between Goschen, Houston Stewart, and Barnaby.

7. Ibid, fol. 9.

8. Ibid, fol. 13.

9. Hood to Houston Stewart, 26 March, 1873, ibid, fols. 15-18.

10. Barnaby to Houston Stewart, n.d., 1873, ibid, fol. 23.

11. Remarks of Milne, 2 April 1873, ibid, fol. 19.

12. Remarks of Tarleton, n.d., ibid, fol. 20.

13. Remarks of Seymour, 4 April 1873, ibid.

suggestions on matters unrelated to the ship's armament. Most notably he advocated a full rig, since the *Shannon* would have to make long passages under sail.[9]

From Hood the sketch returned to Barnaby, and at the beginning of April 1873 the latter informed Houston Stewart '[i]n conference with Capt Hood I gave my general concurrence with his views'.[10] With the Controller's covering comments appended, the sketch went before the full Board on 1 April. Alexander Milne composed a detailed minute. 'There has always been,' he wrote, 'an anxiousness at the Admiralty to keep down the large dimensions of our Iron Clad ships, not only from the very heavy expense but also from their being so unwieldy & drawing so much water.'[11] The proposed design meeting this crucial criterion, Milne gave his assent. 'Looking at the proposed plans of this ship,' he added, 'and the advantage which is gained in reduction of size, draft of water, and expense, I fully concur in recommending that the ship should be constructed.' His one caveat involved the sailing rig. Like Hood he preferred a larger spread of canvas than proposed by Barnaby and Stewart. This quibble aside, 'in a ship of this description we will not only have a very useful, but in every respect a very efficient ship of war'.

Second Naval Lord Sir John Walter Tarleton 'entirely concurred' with Milne 'in approval of this design', but pressed for the inclusion of a 'light spar deck' above the gun deck.[12] The deck would, he maintained, allow greater facility for working the sails, would 'protect the guns from the spars falling on them in action and the guns' crews from rifle fire', and would 'afford shelter to officers and crew in all climates'. Junior Naval Lord Frederick Beauchamp Seymour agreed with Milne regarding the rig, but otherwise had no objections to the design, being 'of opinion that a class of ships such as proposed . . . is much required in our service', and 'altogether the design meets [with] my approval'.[13] Finally, First Lord George J. Goschen composed a lengthy minute which set forth not only his views as to the *Shannon*'s design, but also the reasons for directing it to be drawn up, and the intended role of the ship. Having carefully reviewed the ironclad forces of both Britain and other countries, and having considered '[t]he services which our ironclads would be called upon to perform in

Although designed principally for overseas stations, *Shannon* spent most of her service life in home waters, in part because of her limited bunkerage. (U.S. Naval Historical Center: NH65897)

time of war', the First Lord maintained 'it is most desirable that we should possess a certain number of ironclads of the second rank, which may be good cruisers under sail, draw less water than our large ironclads, yet be defended by thicker armour at the waterline and armed with heavier guns than the second class vessels of an earlier period'.[14] 'It would be a waste of power (even if it were possible),' he added, 'to send . . . [first class ironclads] to look after ships of the *Alma* class [of French ironclads], even if there were not other considerations limiting the sphere of operations of our heaviest first-class ships.'

Goschen was simultaneously alive to the perils posed by the march of technology: 'it would not be satisfactory to send ships carrying only 4½ inches [of armour] at the water line to engage vessels with thicker plating.' He concluded;

> These and similar considerations have weighed for some time so strongly with me, that I have urged in concert with the Senior Naval Lord very strongly on the Controller & the Chief Naval Architect the propriety of preparing designs for a second class ironclad of moderate dimensions & light draft of water, ships which should be more than a match for the second class ironclad [*sic*] of foreign powers, but of a character which could be multiplied in a shorter time & at less cost than first class ironclads.

As for the *Shannon*'s design, Goschen opined it 'appears to me admirably adopted . . . to carry out the intentions with which the question of building ships of this class was entertained'.

Shannon's full design took almost two months to draw up. When complete it embodied some, but not all of the Board's recommendations: Tarleton's spar deck, for example, was not adopted. The completed design received the Board's stamp of approval on 27 May 1873.[15] Yet despite the consensus between Goschen, Milne, Tarleton, Seymour, Hood, and Barnaby as to the suitability of the ship for its intended role as a second-class ironclad for service on distant stations, her career suggests how thoroughly the Board had failed to respond to the shifting operational/tactical picture. Of twenty-one years of active service, 'exactly three were spent on foreign stations . . .'.[16] The bulk was spent in reserve or as a coast guard ship. One reason for this fate, Oscar Parkes suggests, related to her armament. Although the vessel was 'very adequately fitted for the Pacific station', she was recalled after only two years, 'probably owing to ammunition difficulties', since no other vessel on the station required 10in shells.[17] Of course, had it been thought worthwhile, the ship's armament could have been altered. But it was not, probably owing to the fact that there were more fundamental objections to the design. First, although *Shannon*'s armament and protection compared favourably with second-class ironclads of foreign powers, with a designed top speed of only 13kts and an actual top speed of barely 12½kts, she was too slow to catch enemy ships bent on commerce destruction.[18] Furthermore '*Shannon* was intended more for sailing than steaming', and this fact, however inescapable given the limitations of contemporary steam technology, coupled with lack of speed rendered the design ineffective in the actual circumstances she would have encountered in the event of war. *Shannon* could outgun any potential rival in the Pacific, it is true, but it was unlikely that she would ever come within range of many of them.

The shift envisioned in the tactical/operation role is best illustrated by comparing the fate and reputation of *Shannon* with her predecessors. *Audacious* and *Swiftsure* were unquestioned successes, even exceeding expectations. Paradoxically, *Shannon*, although over 1000 tons less displacement than her predecessors, superior in terms of armament, protection, and coal capacity and in speed nearly their equal, was judged a failure. The reason, of course, was not that the design was innately inferior to them: rather, it was judged by different criteria. The 'station ironclad' was becoming a *passé* strategic and operational role: what was needed was an armoured cruiser. In another paradox, though, it is clear that the Admiralty was quite aware of the *General Admiral*'s existence, and thus had an inkling of the changing requirements for cruisers. In extending his approbation to *Shannon*'s design, Beauchamp Seymour explicitly stated that '[v]essels like this would be superior to the new Russian vessels of the *General Admiral* type in (probably) speed, in plating, & in armament . . .'.[19] Similarly, when forwarding the initial sketch of the design to Arthur Hood in late March 1873, Houston Stewart described it as a 'partially armoured Corvette for protection of commerce and cruising duties', and scarcely a month before Goschen, Barnaby and Houston Stewart met to discuss *Shannon*'s design, Hood composed a memorandum for Milne warning that in wartime both France and Russia would try to cripple British trade and threaten colonies; '[o]ur policy,' Hood opined, 'would probably be to strain every effort for the protection of our trade (this I look upon as the point of first importance) . . .'.[20] There exists, in other words, unequivocal evidence

14. Remarks of Goschen, 7 April 1873, ibid, fols. 21-22.

15. Houston Stewart to Barnaby, 27 May 1873, ibid, fol. 26.

16. Parkes, *British Battleships*, p235.

17. Ibid, p237.

18. Ibid, p235.

19. Comments of Seymour, 4 April 1873, NMM: ADM138/43, fol. 20.

20. Houston Stewart to Hood, 25 March 1873, ibid, fol. 13; Hood to Milne, *Confidential*, 5 February 1873, Milne Papers, NMM: MLN/144/1/3.

21. Milne, 'New Class of Ship to be laid down to add to the Iron clad Fleet', March 1875, Milne Papers, NMM: MLN/144/5/2.

22. Outline for Modified *Swiftsure*, 23 February 1872, NMM: ADM138/19, fol. 1.

23. Barnaby to Controller, 22 June 1872, ibid, fol. 13.

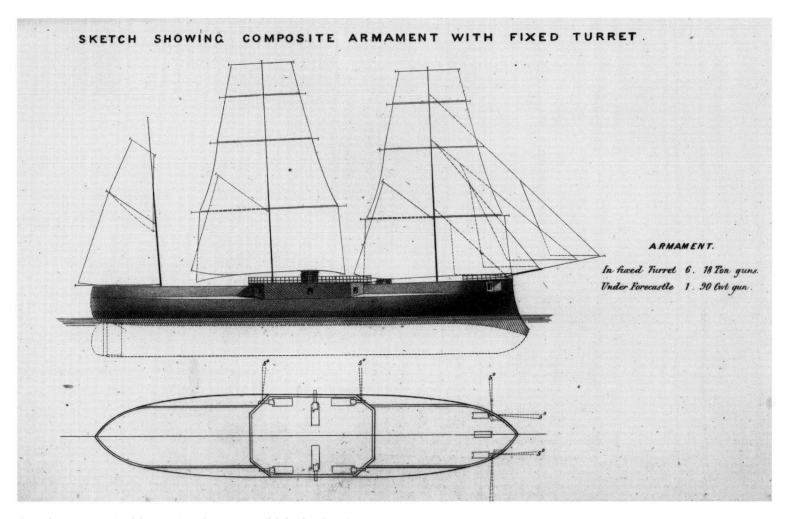

SKETCH SHOWING COMPOSITE ARMAMENT WITH FIXED TURRET.

ARMAMENT.

In fixed Turret 6. 18 Ton guns.
Under Forecastle 1. 90 Cwt gun.

Among the proposals put forward for a 'new *Swiftsure*' (*Temeraire*), this central battery design was most faithful to the original. (National Maritime Museum, London: E2279-3)

that the new tactical/operational context which the Russian vessel's appearance ushered in had been perceived and understood. Yet Seymour's next remark just as clearly revealed his awareness of the strategic context in which such ships would have to operate in the Pacific, Indian, or Atlantic Oceans. *Shannon*, he continued, 'should be efficiently masted and be rigged as a frigate, for with a lifting screw she would then be an efficient cruiser'. And Milne, in considering the design of an ironclad to be laid down two years later repeated his credo: '[f]or Foreign Service sail power will have to be maintained'.[21] As of 1873 sails were essential to any vessel designed for service anywhere in the world, even though they seriously reduced the tactical/operational effectiveness that would enable *Shannon* to counter the Russian-built menace.

Temeraire

Even more than *Shannon*, *Temeraire*'s design history vividly illustrates the tactical confusion that engulfed Admiralty design policy during the 1870s, and also highlights the potential weaknesses inherent in the 'design by committee' approach. In late February 1872 Barnaby was instructed to draw up designs for a 'modified *Swiftsure*'. Accordingly, his guidelines called for medium-calibre

guns in a central battery, a 9in armour belt, and the same rig, lines, and displacement (6522 tons) as *Swiftsure*.[22] Four months later he forwarded two designs to Houston Stewart, one of them a straightforward update of *Swiftsure*'s design, the other based on recommendations made by the Committee on Designs regarding future second-class ironclads. The Committee had objected to the numerous gun ports in the box-battery design, and had suggested in its stead a turret mounting two heavy guns, and a number of lighter pieces ranged along the broadside, unprotected by armour.[23] The Committee had furthermore stressed the importance of fire ahead from the turret guns, plus the desirability of a wide arc of fire on either beam. These qualities, of course, were not easily reconciled with the masts and rigging *de rigueur* in a cruising ironclad. The D.N.C.'s solution was unorthodox: he proposed mounting the turret well forward, and on the main deck, below the impediments of masts and their accoutrements.

Barnaby preferred the traditional box-battery design of the new *Swiftsure*. 'We should,' he wrote in his accompanying remarks,

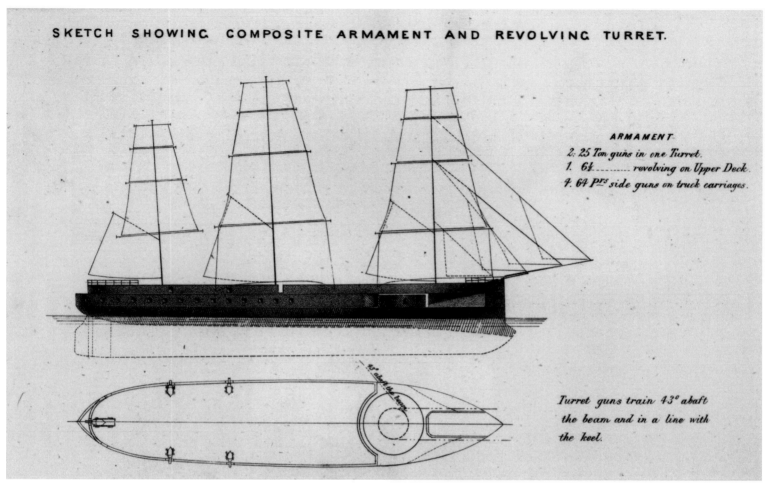

SKETCH SHOWING COMPOSITE ARMAMENT AND REVOLVING TURRET.

ARMAMENT.
2. 25 Ton guns in one Turret.
1. 6¼ .... revolving on Upper Deck.
4. 64 Prs side guns on truck carriages.

Turret guns train 43° abaft
the beam and in a line with
the keel.

The most novel of the 'new *Swiftsure*' sketches was this turret design, the turret being situated well forward on the main rather than the upper deck to prevent the rigging from interfering with gunnery. (National Maritime Museum, London: E2279-1)

'consider that the *Swiftsure* type is, under these circumstances, to be preferred as presenting fewer doubtful features than the turret ship, at very little increase in cost.'[24] The box-battery design had more of its armament behind armour, carried more powerful armament, and was half a knot faster. The turret design, by way of comparison, boasted more powerful fire directly ahead, and was £28,000 cheaper to build, but Barnaby argued the turret guns 'could not be worked satisfactorily when steaming a-head in a heavy sea'. His views were generally shared by the D.N.O., who raised strong objections to the turret design.[25] Among other features, Hood disliked the turret armour, which he maintained was too thin (10ins), the location of the turret, its size, nearness to the water, and limited arc of fire. He also objected to the lack of protection for the secondary armament. Therefore, he stated, 'I should very much prefer an improved "*Swiftsure*" to the proposed turret ship . . .' He was, however, by no means fully satisfied with the proposed *Swiftsure* design: 'in my opinion the fighting powers . . . would be considerably increased' if the guns in the battery were

further apart so as to be more easily worked, if the guns in the bow were 10in calibre rather than 9in, and if the armour belt extended well below the waterline at the bow so as to give 'very considerable protection to the magazine, & render the ship more formidable for ramming purposes'. On 12 July Barnaby replied that he had no objection to any of Hood's suggestions, but carrying them out would slightly increase the ship's size. Otherwise it would not be possible to accommodate the greater weight of the larger bow guns, and the extra armour necessary for an enlarged battery. He maintained Hood that overstated the drawbacks of the turret design, but still expressed his own preference for the box battery.

Slightly less than a month later the Constructor's Department produced a third design – another box-battery ship, with thicker armour, displacing an additional 300 tons. Hood was not happy

24. Ibid, fol. 14.

25. Comments of Hood, 25 June 1872, ibid.

26. Minute by Hood, 24 August 1872, ibid, fol. 17.

27. Minute by Barnaby, 20 September 1872, ibid, fols. 19-20. Why Barnaby was troubled by exposure caused by a greater number of gun ports in one design and not by the complete absence of protection on the broadside in the other is not clear.

28. The seeming discrepancy in the number of guns is explained by the fact that each of the bow guns was capable of being trained around on its respective broadside while the stern gun could be fired on either side.

with it, noting especially that the total weight of guns and ammunition in the design was 376 tons, of which no less than 150 tons was taken up by small (900lb) guns which were all but worthless against armour. '[I]t appears to me,' he stated, 'that disposing of ¾ of the total weight of armament in guns, of value only when engaged with unarmoured vessels, is certainly not advisable. . . .'[26] Instead he recommended suppressing the secondary armament entirely and increasing the heavy ordnance housed in the central battery from four to six 18-ton guns. Of course, the central battery would have to be enlarged to accommodate the increase, but the broadside power would be increased by 50 per cent. Hood concluded:

All points considered, I think the *Temeraire*, as a fighting ship against ironclads, would, if armed with 6 18-ton guns, protected by 10 [inches] of armour plating, be a more useful ship than the improved *Swiftsure* armed with 8 18-ton and 2 12-ton guns [he probably meant six 18-ton and four 12-ton guns, which was what the first design had called for], protected by 5 & 6 inches of armour.

On 20 September Barnaby submitted two further designs. The first embodied Hood's recommendations, although, as the D.N.C. pointed out, it would not be possible to fire all three guns on the broadside other than on a very small angle on either side of the beam. Furthermore, he expressed reservations about the additional weight created by an enlarged central battery sheathed with 10ins of armour, and the exposure created by two additional gun ports. Therefore, he wrote, 'we have sketched out a 5th design, in which the battery is composed entirely of armour-piercing guns, but without any armoured protection to them except an athwartship bulkhead across the bow and stern'.[27] In other words, the central battery was eliminated, leaving armour only on the waterline belt, and on two bulkheads at either end of the gun deck. In place of the weight which would have been taken up by the armour, were eleven, rather than six, 18-ton guns; two capable of firing ahead, one astern, and six on either broadside.[28] Hood left no record of his views on the design.

The second round of 'new *Swiftsure*' sketches included this design, in which the central battery and forward guns were supplemented by eight broadside pieces. The DNO, Arthur Hood, objected to the small calibre of the latter. (National Maritime Museum, London: E2279-2)

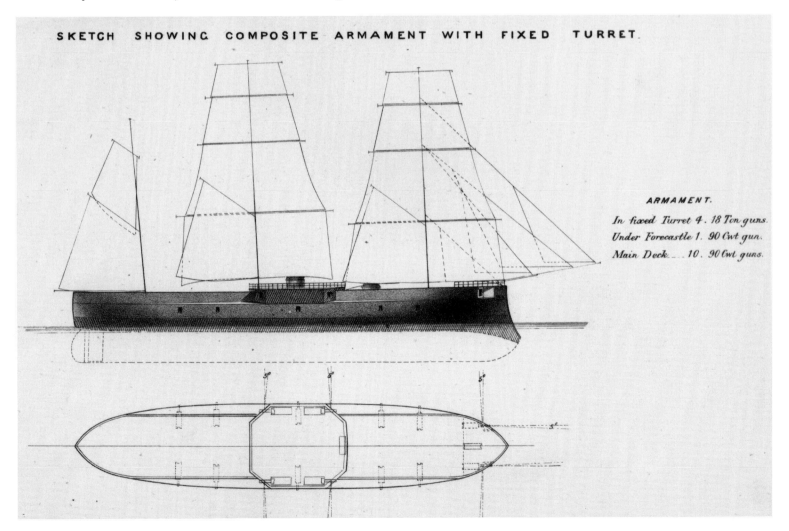

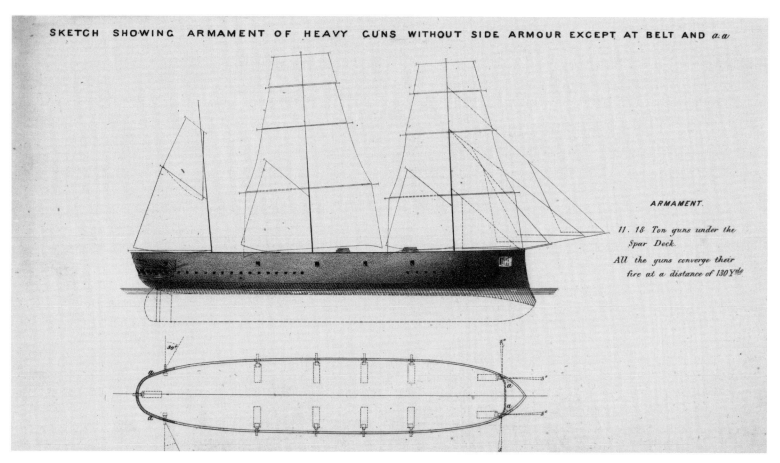

SKETCH SHOWING ARMAMENT OF HEAVY GUNS WITHOUT SIDE ARMOUR EXCEPT AT BELT AND *a.a*

ARMAMENT.

11. 18 Ton guns under the
Spar Deck.

All the guns converge their
fire at a distance of 130 Yds

Nathaniel Barnaby submitted this sketch of a broadside ship with no armour apart from a waterline belt and an armoured bulkhead forward during the 'new *Swiftsure*' deliberations. This armour disposition strongly resembles that of HMS *Shannon*. (National Maritime Museum, London: E2277-4)

On 5 October 1873 Goschen, under the impression that there were only the two original proposals, wrote to Barnaby, asking for the papers relating to *Temeraire*'s design, and instructing him to 'supply the other members of the Board with copies immediately'.[29] 'I am anxious now to come to a speedy decision' wrote the First Lord. The process doubtless took longer than he anticipated. Only on 16 November did Barnaby inform Houston Stewart that he had been ordered to prepare a design based on the fourth sketch; Hood's suggested six-gun box-battery ship. Simultaneously, the Board forwarded its own modifications. First, the number of guns in the battery was to be increased to eight. Second, the guns themselves were to be 25 tons rather than 18 tons each.[30]

Barnaby disapproved the Board's recommendations. The design, he wrote to the Controller, 'has departed from the consideration given to the design in the discussion which you [Stewart] and Capt Hood took part in & we are not prepared to recommend it'. The Board was spurning the advice of the Constructor, Controller, and D.N.O. Moreover, Barnaby added 'the displacement of the ship has increased from 7000 to 8500 [tons] & the cost from £288,000 to £350,000 . . .'. The original criterion of a second-class ironclad of moderate cost had been wholly obliterated by the Board's demand and, as Barnaby pointed out, it was now more worthwhile to compare *Temeraire* to the first-class ironclad *Superb* (later to be renamed *Alexandra*) than to *Swiftsure*. No longer did it

29. Goschen to Barnaby, 5 October 1872, NMM: ADM138/19, fol. 58.

30. Barnaby to Houston Stewart, 16 November 1872, ibid, fol. 94.

31. There is no surviving document in ADM138/19 indicating the exact date of the Board's approval for the first *Temeraire* design, nor is the date recorded in the Admiralty *Digest*. But from later references it is clear that it certainly *was* approved at some point during this period.

32. Barnaby to Houston Stewart, 18 January 1873, NMM: ADM138/19, fol. 172. There is no indication who initiated this idea. Years later, however, Barnaby remembered, relative to the design of the barbette ship *Collingwood*, that 'Sir Houston Stewart had, for many years, desired to mount heavy guns *en barbette*, as the French did . . .'. (Barnaby, *Naval*

Development in the Century, p83.)

33. Cooper Key, 'Report on Foreign and English Guns,' 13 June 1867, PRO: ADM1/6012.

34. Parkes, *British Battleships*, p223.

35. Barnaby to Houston Stewart, 18 January 1873, NMM: ADM138/19, fol. 174.

36. Houston Stewart to Barnaby, 3 February 1873, ibid, fol. 198.

37. Barnaby to Houston Stewart, 3 February 1873, ibid, fol. 199.

38. Hood to Houston Stewart, 5 February 1873, ibid, fol. 204.

bear any resemblance to the 'improved *Swiftsure*' design that the D.N.C. had originally been ordered to prepare. Houston Stewart was no more pleased with the Board's recommendations than Barnaby. On the Controller's instructions two further sketches were prepared, one of a two-deck central-battery design, similar to the *Alexandra*, the other a broadside ship with eight guns on one lengthy gun deck. Neither appears to have met with their Lordships' approval, and sometime between late November 1872 and early January 1873 the enlarged central battery design, mounting eight 25-ton guns, was approved.[31]

Then, in mid-January the Controller asked Barnaby to 'consider whether the upper deck of a ship of the *Temeraire* class could not be armed with one or more complete or partial turrets . . .'.[32] As early as 1867 the then D.N.O. Astley Cooper Key had suggested experimenting with barbettes, indeed, virtually sketching out the design of the *Temeraire*. He noted first that the guns of the *Audacious* class were 'admirably placed – those on the upper deck give a commanding fire in all weathers – while every point of the horizon is covered by guns without moving them from port to port . . .'.[33] Yet, he maintained, 'there is still something wanting in a general action' since an enemy ship might 'place herself close on *Invincible*'s [one of *Audacious*'s sisters] quarter in which position only one gun can bear on her'. To meet this eventuality, Cooper Key 'earnestly recommend[ed] an additional gun in a large iron-clad . . . both fore and aft'. Such a ship, he admitted would have to be specially designed, 'but I consider that a heavy gun on a turntable before the foremast and abaft the mizzenmast – the men protected from rifle fire by a thin iron shield revolving with the turntable would add in an important degree to the offensive powers of that class of ship'. The idea was subsequently picked up by the Committee on Designs. A minority report written by Admiral George Elliot and Rear-Admiral A.P. Ryder, took exception to much of the majority conclusions, arguing, among other things, that heavy guns be 'mounted inside armoured towers on the centre-line in conjunction with a number of smaller unprotected pieces'.[34] Cooper Key's 'thin iron shields' for the protection of the gun crews had become 'armoured towers', but otherwise the principle was unchanged.

Barnaby reported that such a proposal was impossible if the guns were to be mounted in a Coles-type turret. '[T]he weight of such a turret is too great to be planted in the bow and the stern', Houston Stewart was informed, and 'as the turrets are so large it becomes impossible in a moderate sized ship to combine a broadside battery with them . . .'.[35] But, if the guns were mounted *en barbette*, it would be possible to retain the central battery without having to increase the size and displacement of the ship greatly. If the barbette system were employed in *Temeraire*, Barnaby informed his superior, it would be possible to retain a six-gun central battery, as advocated by Hood, albeit with 18-ton rather than 25-ton guns, along with the same armour scheme and thickness as well.

Cramming these features together was possible because of the larger displacement of the Board-approved design. In order to achieve fire directly astern, however, the mizzen mast would have to be discarded.

In early February the question of installing barbettes in *Temeraire* was submitted to the Board for consideration. On the 3rd Houston Stewart instructed Barnaby to 'consider what reduction would require to be made in the Barbette batteries in order to admit of the retention of the present Main Deck Battery as arranged to fire ahead with 25-ton guns'.[36] To meet this requirement, Barnaby replied, 'it will be necessary to effect a considerable reduction in the weight of the Barbette batteries . . .'.[37] The D.N.C. proposed to do so by reducing the rear barbette mounting from two 18-ton guns to one, and by replacing the pair of 18-ton guns in the forward barbette with one of 25 tons. Hood approved the modification, informing the Controller on 5 February:

> I most decidedly prefer the arrangement now proposed for the barbette armament of the *Temeraire* to the former design of the barbette armament; & on the whole, I also prefer it to that of the design first approved of a Central battery on the upper deck. . . .[38]

Finally, on 7 February 1873, Houston Stewart submitted for the Board's consideration three proposed designs:

1. Original approved plan of the *Temeraire*.
2. Proposed Barbette Towers with 4-18 ton guns in towers and 6 in[ch] Main D[ec]k Battery.
3. Altered Barbette Arrangement 1-25 ton gun in Foremost

Temeraire's after barbette gun in firing position. (U.S. Naval Historical Center: NH65899)

Barbette Tower;

1-18 ton After d[itt]o.

2-25 ton guns firing ahead and 4-18 ton guns in Main Deck [Battery].

Main Deck arrangements as in original plan of *Temeraire*.[39]

Milne, Tarleton, and Seymour all preferred the third design, and on the 11th Barnaby was told that it had received the Board's approval.[40] This milestone did not mark the end of his tribulations, though, as the arrangements for mounting the barbette guns still required further consideration, and in late 1874 the Board decided to place a 25-ton gun rather than an 18-ton piece in the after barbette, a modification which necessitated asking the D.N.O. if he would 'be good enough to cause us to be furnished with a revised list of weights &c'.[41]

Why did the Board decide to abandon the second-class design it originally demanded? *Temeraire*'s own cover provides no clues, but

In terms of steaming radius, *Nelson* (pictured) and *Northampton* were great advances on their predecessor *Shannon*, but their cylindrical boilers, operating at 60psi, were nevertheless still too inefficient to permit the abandonment of sail. (National Maritime Museum, London: 19423)

years later, in arguing against the design of *Trafalgar*, Barnaby reminded the Lords '. . . in 1872 the Germans were having two masted ironclads built for them on the Thames, the "*Kaiser*" and "*Deutschland*", which were more powerful than the largest English masted ironclads. This was held to be sufficient reason for building the "*Alexandra*" and "*Temeraire*" against the advice of the Committee [on Designs]'.[42]

It is worth stressing that the substitution did not entail a wholesale departure from the vessel's strategic role as first envisioned. The Board wanted a cruising ironclad, and that is what it got, albeit a much larger and more expensive ship than initially requested. The general strategic dichotomy of the battlefleet was not traduced. The convoluted process of designing *Temeraire* does, however, suggest that the Board had no clear idea of the ship's tactical role. Was it to be analogous to previous first-class cruising ironclads, and generally kept in European waters, or was it to be sent abroad to serve on foreign stations? The initial guidelines, plus the fact that *Temeraire* had a sheathed hull suitable for extended commissions out of reach of graving docks, imply the latter, the approved design as well as the vessel's operational history suggest the former.[43] Finally, the deliberations over *Temeraire*'s design, from the initial instructions to Barnaby to the approval of the mod-

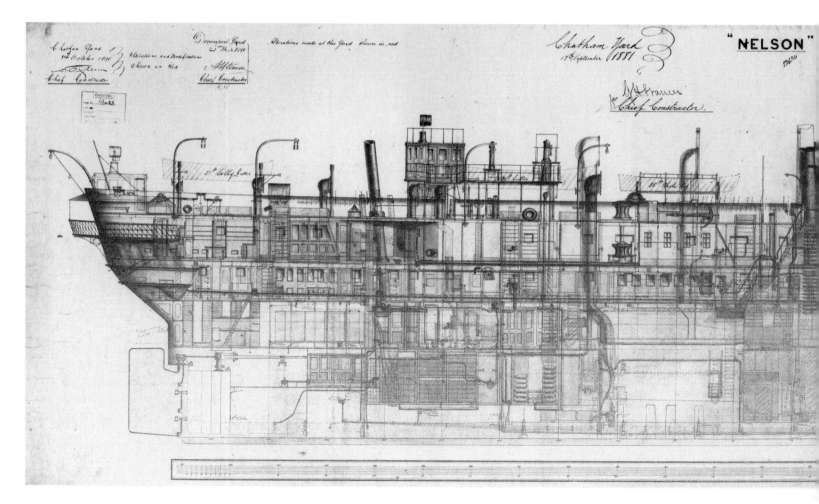

ified barbette design, lasted from February 1872 to February 1873 and fostered the production of no less than nine different designs, further evidence of the lack of consensus, were any necessary. Design by committee certainly involved its share of pitfalls.

Nelson *and* Northampton

The Ship's Cover for the subsequent pair of cruising ironclads, *Nelson* (laid down 1874, launched 1876, completed 1881) and *Northampton* (1874, 1876, 1878) is missing, although it is clear that the fundamental dissonance between strategic and operational ends and technological means was little closer to solution than had been the case in 1873, when *Shannon* was approved. Like the earli-

er vessel, both carried compound engines; the boilers were oval rather than the older rectangular box-type, and the pressure generated – 60 psi – was in line with the standards of the day, in merchant as well as naval applications.[44] Their machinery was, in other words, thoroughly up-to-date. This situation, coupled with a marked increase in coal bunkerage, made possible largely by the fact that the two ships were of 40 per cent greater displacement than *Shannon*, gave *Nelson* and *Northampton* far longer range under steam than their predecessor. *Shannon* could carry, at the most, 560 tons of coal, while *Nelson* and *Northampton* could stow 1150 tons. The upshot was that the latter vessels were capable of steaming 3500 nautical miles at 12kts, 5000 miles at 10½kts, or an impressive 7000 miles at 7kts – forty days of continuous steaming at

39. Houston Stewart to Admiralty, 2 February 1873, ibid, fol. 207.

40. Houston Stewart to Barnaby, 11 February 1873, ibid, fol. 207.

41. Barnaby to Boys, 2 January 1875, ibid, no fol.

42. Barnaby minute, 14 July 1885, to 'Sketch design for First Class Battleship: Type—Improved *Dreadnought*, 9 July 1885', NMM: ADM138/109 (Ship's Cover for *Trafalgar*), S. 5658/85.

43. See Parkes, *British Battleships*, p224.

44. R.H. Thurston, 'A Century's Progress of the Steam Engine', *Annual Report of the*

Smithsonian Institution (1899), p597; Parkes, *British Battleships*, p239. In his article 'British Belted Cruisers' (*Mariner's Mirror* 64/1 [1978], pp23-35), N.A.M. Rodger mistakenly claims that *Northampton* carried simple, rather than compound engines, and that *Nelson* was the first British ironclad to feature the latter type. In fact, *Northampton's* engines consisted of three cylinders of equal size, capable of being operated either in compound mode (one high-pressure and two low-pressure cylinders) or in simple mode, with all three cylinders driven by the same pressure. As for compound engines in general, the small ironclad *Pallas* (launched 1865) had been fitted with them for experimental purposes, the Committee on Designs had subsequently recommended their general adoption, and the Admiralty, as earlier related, had followed this recommendation. All British ironclads from *Dreadnought* onward were engined with compound machinery.

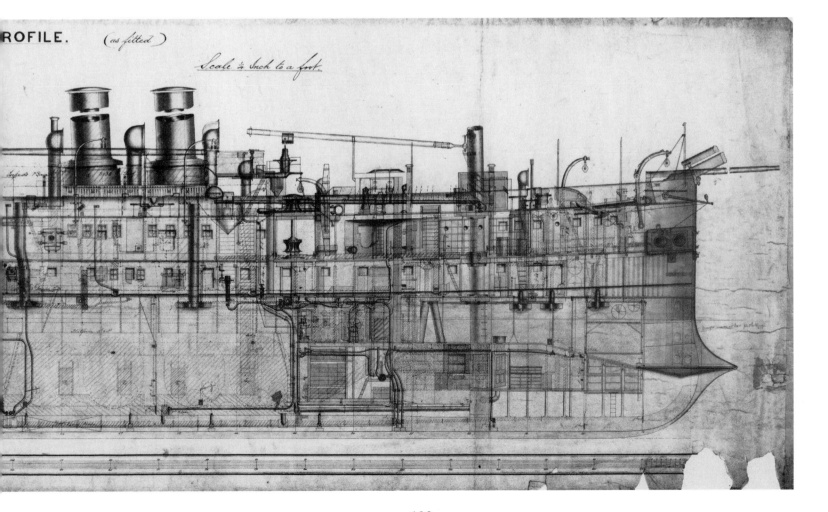

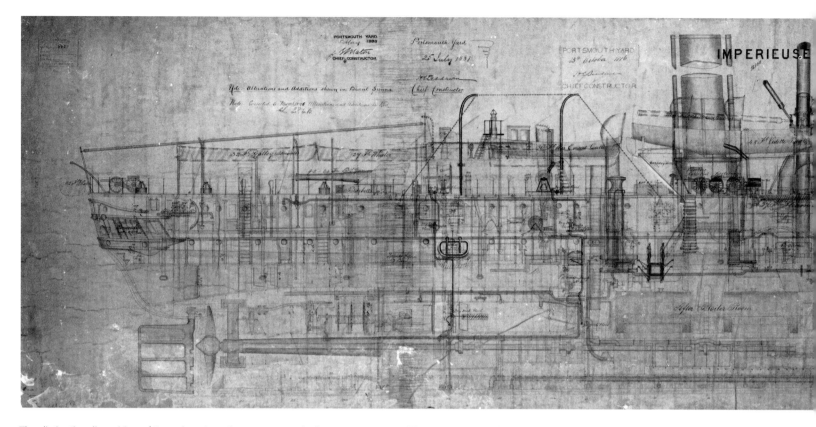

The distinctive disposition of *Imperieuse*'s main armament – single guns en barbette fore and aft, and another amidships port and starboard – was directly imitative of contemporary French cruiser design. (National Maritime Museum, London: 8881)

that speed. Indeed, they carried the largest bunkerage of any masted British ironclad to date.[45] In addition, their top steaming speed – 14kts in *Nelson*'s case, slightly more than 13kts in *Northampton*'s – put them, even in the latter instance, almost a knot above *Shannon*'s best of about 12½kts. For their intended role as commerce protectors they were significant improvements.

But they were nowhere close to the ideal. Although there were faster than their predecessors, they were still too slow to catch the latest merchant vessels, which, according to Russian plans, were to be fitted out as auxiliary cruisers in wartime. Longer-ranged they may have been also, but not so much so that the Admiralty could afford to dispense with masts and sails. Across the vast expanse of the Pacific, where Russian cruisers were expected to operate, the scarcity of coaling stations coupled with the still-inadequate state of steam technology made the retention of sail a necessity, even though it unmistakably harmed both speed and range under steam. There can be no doubt as to their intended function, though. Controller Houston Stewart stated explicitly that the two ships 'were no part of what was called our battlefleet; their object was not to take part in a close engagement but to roam over the seas and drive away unarmoured fast cruisers from harrying our commerce – a flying squadron not for a moment to be confused with our ironclad ships'.[46]

Turning the Corner: Imperieuse *and* Warspite

By the late 1870s, when the Admiralty next considered laying down another pair of armoured cruisers, the technological circumstances had altered still further, and the resulting ships, *Imperieuse* (laid down 1881, floated out 1883, completed 1886) and *Warspite* (1881, 1884, 1888) came far closer to modern conceptions of armoured cruisers than did any of their predecessors.

As early as 1878 Barnaby turned to the matter of increasing the speed of such vessels to render them more suitable for their intended role. In the same memorandum arguing for lengthening *Ajax*-type ironclads to achieve higher speed, he also advocated building a 'cruizing ship' without a 'powerful *protected* battery', which would avail 'herself of a . . . higher speed (15 to 16 knots), in order to employ her ram and torpedoes against battle ships when that may be necessary'. Such a vessel would be 'armed with unprotected armour-piercing, and light guns, but with very few of them, so as not to employ many men about the unprotected decks in action'.[47] Hence, he envisioned;

[T]wo classes [*ie Colossus* and *Imperieuse*], each, say, 350 feet long, but one much wider than the other. Both protected by underwater decks and heavily armoured conning stations; both armed with rams and with bow torpedoes on each side. Both having twin screws and protected steering gear; both armed with guns against armoured and unarmoured ships, but with protection for the guns in the slower ship only.

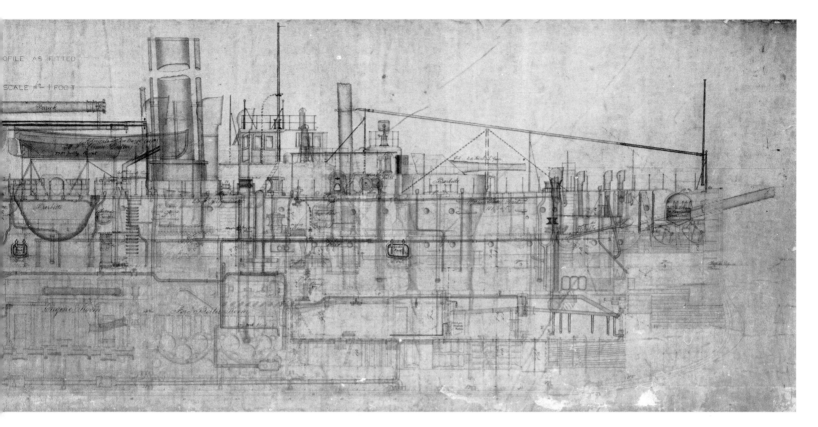

The cruiser, he opined, would 'have a light rig manageable by a small crew, and the battleship to have no sail'.

The Board was no more taken by his argument in favour of building a 350ft cruiser than it was of a 350ft battleship. Barnaby noted that it rejected his and Houston Stewart's arguments to 'adopt a length of 350 feet in a new first-class battle ship, and in a cruizing ship . . .'.[48] Still, the D.N.C. pushed ahead with the proposal for a cruiser, providing an outline of the design at the end of June 1880 under the heading '[i]ronclads to be built in the present programme'.[49] This cruiser would have '16 knots speed and a large coal supply differing from the *Inconstant* and the *Shah* type in having the machinery and magazines protected by an underwater shot proof deck; the floating power protected by a raft body, and the conning station by thick armour'. She would be armed with a ram, torpedoes, 'and a few armour-piercing guns'. Having succinctly sketched out the chief features of what became known as the protected cruiser design, Barnaby maintained, however, that

this, like the peacetime gunboats he envisioned providing a screen for ironclads, would be a dual-purpose ship, which he hoped would 'be able to engage Ironclads with on the whole less risk of being disabled as a completely armoured ship having the moderate thickness of armour which a ship of her size could carry'. Such a vessel would displace less than 8000 tons and would cost, for hull and machinery, about £350,000. The Board was not swayed. None was authorised as part of the programme for 1878-9, or even 1879-80, the Admiralty preferring to invest in *Colossus*, *Edinburgh*, and the third vessel type recommended by Barnaby, a pure coast-defence/assault 'ship of the *Rupert* type of 13 knots speed, with armour from end to end of 11 ins Maxm thickness . . .'.[50]

Only in mid-1880 does the topic of armoured cruisers appear to have been revived, Barnaby reminding the Controller in early August '[y]ou expressed some time ago the opinion that we might give to Portsmouth or Chatham a new *Temeraire* with advantage, still leaving open the question as to the type of ship most suitable

45. Parkes, *British Battleships*, pp239, 243.

46. Quoted in Parkes, *British Battleships*, p239. Barnaby, it might be noted, stressed first their role as station ironclads and their suitability as flagships on foreign stations, yet he added that were also intended to serve as 'protected cruisers'. See Barnaby, 'On the *Nelson* Class,' *Transactions of the Institute of Naval Architects* (1879), p59. Given the evidence available regarding the design of other vessels of the period, there is no doubt that the assumptions of the Board and Controller, rather than the Chief Constructor, informed the design and intended roles of those vessels, and there exists no evidence to suggest that any other was the case with respect to *Nelson* and *Northampton*.

47. Barnaby to Board: 'Considerations put forward by the Director of Naval Construction

preliminary to the preparation of Designs of *Colossus* and *Imperieuse*', [Spring 1878], NMM: ADM138/60 (Ship's Cover for *Ajax* and *Agamemnon*), no fol.

48. 'Memorandum by Director of Naval Construction in June 1878 as to Designs of *Colossus* and *Imperiuse*', June 1878, ibid.

49. Barnaby memorandum, 'Ironclads to be built in the present programme', 25 June 1878, ibid.

50. Ibid. The remainder of the description reads: 'with guns of 38 tons in a single turret protected by armour of 14 ins: with compound engines, a larger coal supply, and a more extensive division into [watertight] compartments. Her displacement will be about 6000 tons (and her cost about £300,000)'.

Like HMS *Rupert*, on which her design was based, *Conqueror* (launched 1881) was intended for coast assault and ramming. (U.S. Naval Historical Center: NH61374)

for meeting the *Italia* until we could get the steam trial of the *Polyphemus*.[51] Barnaby suggested that *Temeraire*'s barbette arrangement might be adopted in the new vessel, albeit fitted with more powerful breech-loaders. Beyond that, he advocated a similar level of protection to *Temeraire*, and 'lengthen[ing] the ship to obtain a higher speed and greater coal endurance with the same power of engines'. He added, too, that '[t]heir Lordships would probably prefer that she should be without sail power, having only lower masts'. If the Controller concurred, 'a design will be put in hand'. No steps were immediately taken, however.

In early November Parliamentary Secretary George John Shaw Lefevre who, as has been noted, was simultaneously pushing for the construction of first-class battleships to compensate for increased French shipbuilding, also addressed the cruiser situation, stressing that Britain had a far greater need for second-class armourclads than any other power.[52] He thus, as has also been noted in conjunction with the decision to lay down the second and third 'Admiral' class ships, recommended building two first-class battleships to contend with analogous French and Italian vessels,

and '2 . . . smaller vessels, of the 2nd class, of not more than 6000 tons displacement at the outside, and even smaller, if possible'.

He took issue with using *Temeraire* as a model for such vessels, considering her too big and expensive. Instead, he called for a curious amalgam which could scarcely have emanated from anyone familiar with naval architecture; a cross between the second-class cruising ironclad/cruiser *Shannon* and the coast-defence turret ship *Rupert*. That the low freeboard characteristic of the latter type was irreconcilable with masts and yards, to say nothing of stability in a moderate-sized vessel, was evidently not an important consideration. In the end, however, he concluded that an improved *Shannon* type would probably best meet Navy needs, although he added 'I think everything should be done to give it the best possible speed even at the sacrifice of the thickness of its armour plates. It would be more than a match for the French vessels of the *Vauban* type, and for the Russian belted cruisers.'

Shaw Lefevre's advocacy of *Shannon* as the model for the new vessel carried the day, and Barnaby's staff apparently started preparing sketches of such a design, without, however, fully heeding the Parliamentary Secretary's injunction about speed. Only on 24 November did the Board explicitly call for two designs to be worked up, both of them to have a speed of 16kts.[53] The first was to be a straight repeat of *Shannon* in almost all respects–

tonnage, firepower and sailing rig—save with less armour at the bow and a speed of 16kts rather than 13kts. The second was, per Shaw Lefevre's preference, to be limited to 6000 tons, and to be fitted with a 2½in armoured deck in place of *Shannon*'s vertical belt.

Two days later Civil Lord Thomas Brassey furnished his own views on the subject, also recommending that the *Shannon* should serve as a model for the new ship and, like Shaw Lefevre, stressing the necessity for higher speed. 'In view of the great activity lately displayed in building fast cruisers for the French and Russian navies it is certain that armoured cruisers, with an advantage in point of speed over the unarmoured ships of foreign services, would be a valuable addition to the British fleet.'[54] 'Great activity' was a species of hyperbole. Brassey presumably meant the French unprotected cruisers *Duquesne* (completed 1878, 16.8kts) and *Tourville* (completed 1877, 16.9kts) and the Russian armoured cruisers *Vladimir Monomakh* (laid down 1880, 15.2kts) and *Dmitri Donskoi* (laid down 1881, 16.5kts). It is difficult to see what else then building in either country's dockyards might have warranted the 'fast cruiser' description. The French *Lapérouse* (four ships) and *Villars* (four ships) classes then under construction were nearer traditional sail/steam 'peacetime cruisers,' with wooden hulls, small coal bunkerage (300-400 tons) and a speed of no more than 15kts.[55] The *Duguay-Trouin* (completed 1879, 15.5kts) was nearer the mark, with an iron hull, but she too carried less than 500 tons of coal, hardly an adequate amount for a vessel designed for wide-ranging commerce destruction. Beyond the two armoured cruisers, neither of them completed until 1885, there was nothing then building in Russia deserving the designation 'fast', almost nothing deserving the name 'cruiser' unless it was the *Pamiat Merkuria* (completed 1881), a 3000-ton unprotected cruiser capable of 14kts and with bunkerage for 300 tons of coal. She was designed for Black Sea operations.

Moreover, the French were not then engaged in building 'armoured cruisers' at all, a fact which certainly contributed to the uncertainty and divided counsels at the Admiralty. The French 'cruising ironclads' then under construction—the *Bayard* and *Vauban* class barbette ships—were second-class station ironclads, comparable more to the decade-old *Swiftsure* than to modern cruisers. They had full sailing rigs, smaller coal bunkerage even than *Shannon*, wooden hulls in the cases of *Bayard* and *Turenne*, and a bare superiority of speed over *Nelson* and *Northampton*—14 to 14½kts for both classes. The first French protected cruiser, *Sfax*,

was not laid down until 1882, the first real armoured cruiser, *Dupuy de Lôme*, until 1888.

Brassey, indeed, wrestled with the dilemma although, characteristically, he seems not to have fully understood the confounding technological factors. Fast cruisers were necessary, he maintained:

> An armoured cruiser steaming 16 knots would be the dread and terror of the foreign vessels, specially designed to cut up British commerce, and would be superior in speed to all the second-class ironclads of foreign powers, while possessing the means of escape from all their first-class ships, save [those] now building for Italy.

However, second-class ironclads were just as necessary, and he pointed to two designs to emulate. First, 'the *Almirante Cochrane*, built for the Chilians [*sic*] from the designs of Sir Edward Reed, is one of the most successful examples of an effective fighting ship of moderate dimensions'. In addition, he advocated designing a scaled-down *Alexandra*, since 'the second-class ironclad must be essentially a cruiser, and consequently a sea-keeping and not merely a sea-going vessel'. *Alexandra* constituted 'the most effective broadside ship in our own or any other navy' and hence might 'furnish a suitable type for reproduction on a smaller scale'.

The former vessel was a central-battery ironclad of about 3500 tons with a battery of moderate-sized guns, 9in armour, and a top speed of around 13kts.[56] What role it might have played in British naval dispositions or strategy is unclear: it would have been suitable for contending with its model, and with the 1860s-era French station ironclads, but with little else; it lacked the speed and the coal capacity (Brassey stated it to be 254 tons) to engage in commerce protection, and was not a match in any important respect for more recent, not to mention considerably larger, station ironclads or armoured cruisers. Likewise, *Alexandra*'s design was by this point the better part of a decade old, and the Admiralty's refusal to build any more such vessels, to say nothing of the proven fallacy of building reduced versions of successful ships, suggests that this too was a blind alley. What tasks would a reduced *Alexandra* perform which could not also be undertaken by an updated *Shannon*?

It is tempting to dismiss these confused, if not outright contradictory, recommendations as manifestations of Brassey's ignorance not only of naval architecture but of strategic and operational factors as well, and on such matters he was certainly not the best-informed member of the Board. By the same token, however, he was not a stupid man, and aspects of his confusion were com-

51. Barnaby to Controller, 4 August 1880, NMM: ADM138/74 (Ship's Cover for *Imperieuse* and *Warspite*), fol. 1.

52. Shaw Lefevre on arrangements regarding dockyards and new construction, 11 November 1880, in the bound papers relative to decision to build 'Admiral' class, Surveyor's Branch, 1 August 1881, PRO: ADM1/6608.

53. Barnaby to Houston Stewart, 30 November 1880, 'New Designs for 1880-81, 82', Precis of Correspondence, nd., ibid.

54. Brassey memorandum, 26 November 1880, ibid.

55. *Conway's 1860-1905*, pp186, 192, 317-19.

56. Ibid, p410.

mon to the Admiralty. It was, in fact, attempting to counter three discrete types of foreign vessels with a single design, although as Brassey's remarks indicate, not everyone was satisfied with this 'solution'. First, as the Civil Lord pointed out, an armoured cruiser needed speed for the task of hunting down swift, unarmoured commerce raiders. Secondly, some degree of armoured protec-

tion, in addition to speed, was mandated for a vessel to fulfil the commerce *protection* role. Yet Barnaby and his staff could not rest easy having to meet only these two criteria; there still remained the French 'station ironclads'; indeed, that nation was building an additional four such vessels, of considerably greater displacement and firepower than earlier versions. These were not armoured cruisers in any real sense of the term; they were 'baby' or 'pocket' battleships, capable of contesting local command of the sea rather than merely nibbling at commerce via *guerre de course*. To match such vessels Britain had built the relatively heavily-gunned and

The French station ironclad *Vauban*. Her construction and that of five similar vessels confounded Admiralty deliberations on cruiser design between 1879 and 1881. (U.S. Naval Historical Center)

armoured *Shannon, Nelson,* and *Northampton*; again in 1880 the need to meet French firepower on equal terms tempted Barnaby to sacrifice speed for guns. Thus, the design he brought forward – a '6000 ton belted cruizer of *Shannon* type of 14 knots speed & with 11-8' B.L. guns' – had clearly been drafted with the French station ironclads foremost in mind.[57]

A note of surprise crept into his tone when, on 24 November 1880, he 'was informed that the basis of the design for such a ship must be not 14 but 16 knots.'[58] Moreover, the DNC was made aware of the 'desire to keep down size of ship to 6000 tons & . . . was instructed to say what ship of the type could be produced with that tonnage & also what tonnage would be req[uire]d if some defensive and offensive power were retained as had been proposed for 14 knot ship of 6000 tons'.

Conversely, a note of dismay was evident in Shaw-Lefevre's account of the meeting. Barnaby, he observed, had designed the new *Shannon* as a second-class battleship rather than as a cruiser.[59] It was, he acknowledged, superior in power to the French *Duguesclin*, but was designed for only 14kts. 'Thus far the *Shannon*,' Shaw Lefevre continued, 'has been considered with reference only to the latest constructions in the French Navy.' This was, to his way of reasoning, a mistake:

> [i]t is even more necessary to keep in view the proceedings of the Russian Naval administration. It was they who led the way in the construction of belted cruisers; and the creation of a squadron [?] of powerful ships of that type, in addition to their far more numerous fast unarmoured vessels, would seem to make a sixteen knot *Shannon* a most necessary addition to our own navy.[60]

The Board's demands, along with its clear preference for the barbette system required some hasty calculations in the Constructor's department. By 29 November, however, Barnaby was prepared with three possible designs, matched up with *Shannon* for comparison. The first two held to the 6000-ton limit: one carried three of its nine main guns in barbettes, the second retaining *Shannon*'s broadside arrangement with armoured bulkheads fore and aft to protect the crews from raking fire.[61] Both featured armoured decks rather than vertical protection.[62] In pursuit of the Board's query as to how much increase in size would be necessary to get 16kts from Barnaby's original 'new *Shannon*' design, the D.N.C. revealed that '[t]o preserve same protection as 14 knot ship was to have, i.e., 10 [inch] & 9 [inch] armour [on the sides], & a 3 [inch] underwater deck forward and aft, raises size to 7000 tons & cost of Hull and Engines to £400,000'.[63] To scale this protection down to remain within the 6000-ton limit while preserving the speed would, alternatively require reducing 'the protection for the guns & vital parts . . . 22% & the underwater deck at the extremities made only for [?7 inch] shot resisting.'

The Board preferred to retain side armour. On 1 December Barnaby informed William White that after discussion by the full Board;

> Their Lordships have decided to day to call for a design of a ship of about 7000 tons displacement with 16 knots speed, with side armour 10 in thick and with protection for the guns of 9" armour (and against machine guns equivalent to 2" of steel). The guns and protection to be of the *Shannon* type say 640 tons weight of guns & protection for them apart from light guns & machine gun protection. The actual distribution of guns & armour to be decided on 8th Inst.
>
> The ship may be brig rigged. She is to be copper sheathed. Design to be got on at once.[64]

D.N.O. Richard Vesey Hamilton, the next to consider the design, pushed strongly for barbettes, 'along the lines of the *Vauban* and *Duguesclin*, but somewhat heavier'.[65] Still, the Board held its hand; the initial design parameters – dimensions: 300ft x 61ft x 24ft 3in,

57. The *Bayard* class carried four 9.4in guns mounted singly in barbettes and two 7.6in pieces; the subsequent *Vauban*s carried the same primary armament but only a single 7.6in gun. Barnaby's proposed new *Shannon* would have had a substantial superiority to either class in weight of fire.

58. Barnaby to Houston Stewart, nd., in 'New Designs for 1880-81-82'. Precis of Correspondence, 30 November 1880, NMM: ADM138/74, (Ship's Cover for *Imperieuse* and *Warspite*), fol. 21.

59. Memorandum to Lord Northbrook, unsigned, but probably Shaw-Lefevre, nd., but probably late November or early December 1880, in the bound papers relative to decision to build 'Admiral' class, Surveyor's Branch, 1 August 1881, PRO: ADM1/6608.

60. Like Brassey, Shaw Lefevre also maintained that the Navy required 'second-class ironclads': 'For second-class battleships several types might be designed – all more or less effective – by adaptations of the most approved first class ships, both English and foreign, with fewer turrets, reduced armament, and limitations of the length of the protected battery. The subject may be dealt with more appropriately when the papers on shipbuilding are circulated for opinions among the members of the Board.' He also stressed the need for speed in this type, to enable them to escape more powerful battleships.

61. Darley to Barnaby, 29 November 1880, NMM: ADM138/74, fol. 11.

62. Running the length of the ship in design 2: only covering the vitals in design 1, which relied entirely on compartmentalisation for floatation in the ends.

63. Barnaby to Houston Stewart, 30 November 1880, in 'New Designs for 1880-81-82.' Precis of Correspondence, nd., NMM: ADM138/74, fol. 21.

64. 'Submitted for Controller's their Lordships' consideration,' 14 December 1880, in the bound papers relative to decision to build 'Admiral' class, Surveyor's Branch, ADM1/6608, 1 August 1881; 'New Designs for 1880-81-82.' Precis of Correspondence, nd., NMM: ADM138/74, fol. 22. 'This arrangement was brought to the notice of the Board on 14/12/80 & discussed at a full Board. It received unanimous approval being recommended by the Controller & D.N.O. and was accepted on the understanding that the dimensions 330x61x24'.3', 7200 tons, 8000 I.H.P. & cost £400,000 for Hull and Engines might require some modification as the design is worked out.' N.A.M. Rodger suggests that William White was responsible for drawing up the design, although the quotation in the text indicates otherwise. See Rodger, 'British Belted Cruisers', p31.

65. Board considers cruiser/2nd class ironclad design and submits it to D.N.O.,1 December 1880, in the bound papers relative to decision to build 'Admiral' class, Surveyor's Branch, 1 August 1881, PRO: ADM1/6608. See also Vesey Hamilton to Houston Stewart, 14 December 1880, 'New Designs for 1880-81-82', Precis of Correspondence, NNM: ADM138/74, fol. 22.

D.N.O. Vesey Hamilton advocated emulating *Duguesclin*'s design. (U.S. Naval Historical Center: NH74969)

7000 tons, 8000 IHP, cost £400,000–were approved on 14 December, yet the Controller was instructed to hold off on producing a design 'as long as possible in order that we might take advantage of the improvements being made' in the type and dimensions of guns, armour, steam technology, and protection schemes.[66]

By 10 December a sketch had been worked up by Henry Darley.[67] Much had been altered in transforming the broadside-armed 'new *Shannon*' to a barbette ship. Most notably, the eleven 8in guns had been supplanted by four 9.4in, 18-ton pieces in the barbettes, supplemented by six (ultimately ten) 6in guns on the main deck, and, portentously, the ship was to carry two masts. The arrangement of the barbettes, as per Hamilton's recommendation, followed that of the four French station ironclads then under construction: a single gun in each of four separate tubes, one at

66. Vesey Hamilton to Houston Stewart, 14 December 1880, 'New Designs for 1880-81-82', Precis of Correspondence, NNM: ADM138/74, fol. 22. The initial design was approved on 14 December 1880.

67. Darley to Crossland & Barnaby 10 December 1880, NMM: ADM138/74, fol. 29.

68. See Parkes, *British Battleships*, pp308-09; *Conway's 1860-1905*, pp302-03. Parkes identifies the *Marceau* class first-class battleships as the models for *Imperieuse* and *Warspite*, but no reference to them appears in the relevant papers. Conversely, there are repeated allusions to the 'second-class' French ironclads of the *Bayard* and *Vauban* types.

69. Barnaby to Houston Stewart, 8 March 1881, NMM: ADM138/74, fol. 90. 'Controller

The design for the armoured cruisers to be built at Portsmouth and Chatham this year is now submitted for final approval.'

'They have a comparatively large number of guns in the armament (10 guns) some of them capable of penetrating, according to the estimate, more than 18 inches of iron armour. The estimated power of the 18 ton 9.2 inches B.L. Guns exceeds that of the 12.5 inches M.L. Guns of 38 tons.

They have steel-faced armour of 10 inches protecting the vitals of the ship that is equivalent to the thickest hull armour of the *Thunderer* and *Devastation*.

The hull is nowhere dependent on such comparatively feeble armour as protects the steering gear of those ships (8" iron) and the barbettes are protected by armour equivalent in power to some of the citadel (p. 91) armour of the *Thunderer* and *Devastation*.

The ships have twin screws, auxiliary sail power, and coppered bottoms.

In arranging the armour considerations as to the protection of stability and buoyancy by means of it have had but little weight attached to them. The armour has been disposed for the purpose for which it was first introduced into ships; viz. to protect the active fighting elements of the ship from shell fire. Under this designation we include propelling and manoeuvring machinery, and the armament and personnel. Efficient arrangements are made, to which the Armour is made to contribute, for preventing alterations of trim, or serious diminution of floating power under continued and effective artillery fire.

The introduction of a barbette armament for the heavy guns in preference to such cover as the *Shannon*, *Nelson*, and *Northampton* have is due to the suggestion of the D.N.O., and the favour of the Controller and their Lordships for such a system, where the guns are B.L. and the ship's speed [needs to be] considerable.

The actual arrangement adopted has our full concurrence.'

70. 'Digest of Papers relating to new Armoured Cruisers', 17 March 1881, ibid, fol. 87. Admiral Hoskins 'Thinks it desirable to have a bulkhead connecting two foremost turrets [barbettes] as protection to [broadside] Battery from raking fire, & 2 additional guns on main deck even if no addl ammunition is carried for them.' Presumably Hoskins meant a diagonal bulkhead running from the front to the wing barbettes, or else a transverse bulkhead between the latter.

71. Comments of Hay, 18 March 1881, ibid.

72. Comments of Cooper Key, 13 March 1881, ibid.

73. Northbrook Minute, 19 March 1881, ibid.

either end of the superstructure, mounted on the centreline, the remaining two on either beam amidships.[68]

The particulars of the design were only forwarded to the Board in early March 1881. Barnaby accompanied the design with a memorandum sketching out the rationale for disposition of armour and the means of preserving buoyancy.[69] To this description Boys and Houston Stewart added their remarks, the latter stating his preference for larger coal stowage but both otherwise expressing general satisfaction with the design. The Board, in turn, forwarded its own recommendations. Junior Lord Anthony Hoskins advocated additional armour against fire from ahead and the addition of two broadside guns.[70] Second Naval Lord John Hay 'concurr[ed] with Admiral Hoskins, but fear[ed] it impossible to add weight to present design, which on whole represents a very good ship, with present information'.[71] Finally, First Naval Lord Cooper Key agreed that it was 'very desirable to provide 2 additional ports for guns in event of possibility to carry them', and urged that the position of torpedo tubes and quick-firing guns be carefully considered 'in construction of ship'.[72] Otherwise, however, he unequivocally stated '[o]n whole this ship is superior to any cruiser afloat or building'. With the unanimous approval of the Board, Lord Northbrook wasted little time authorising *Imperieuse* and *Warspite*.[73]

Despite Shaw Lefevre's insistence on speed, it is clear that Barnaby and the Board, which had mandated the sailing rig, still envisioned a dual-purpose vessel. Sometime following the design's approval the former informed Houston Stewart that '[t]he armoured cruisers to be commenced this year at Portsmouth and Chatham and to be advanced appreciably in 1881-82 will need to be described in general terms for the information of [the new Parliamentary Secretary] Mr. Trevelyan', who would have to provide Parliament with a general description. They were, the D.N.C. stated, 'designed especially for independent service on foreign stations where fast unarmoured ships may have to be opposed', which clearly indicates the Admiralty's awareness of the *guerre de course* role. Yet, as had been the case with *Shannon*, *Nelson* and *Northampton*, the ability to fulfil this role was simultaneously undercut by the requirement that they be able to 'meet and engage . . . the second class Ironclads of our Enemy . . .'. The conflicting design imperatives were even more starkly illuminated in the vessels' specifications:

Imperieuse as completed, with brig rig. (U.S. Naval Historical Center: NH65953)

1. A measured mile speed of 16 knots.

2. A comparatively large number of guns in the armament, some of them capable of penetrating the thickest armour of 2nd class Ironclads at long ranges.

3. To have steel faced armour of 10" protecting the vitals of the ship.

4. The machinery to be of the most economical type with twin screws.

5. To have auxiliary sail power to economise fuel.

6. To have a coppered bottom; to make her independent of docks.[74]

Again, the second and third specifications, to say nothing of the fifth, made the achievement of the first more difficult and seriously reduced fuel economy and range as well.

Imperieuse and *Warspite* are among the most harshly-judged of the Admiralty's designs between 1870 and 1890. Parkes quotes Admiral John Edmund Commerell, who judged them 'amongst the most complete failures of modern ships; badly designed; badly carried out, and absolutely dangerous', adding meekly that 'this was rather harsher criticism than they deserved'.[75] The more recent assessment of *Conway's* is no more positive: '[d]espite their modern features they were intended to fulfil the same function as the early armoured cruisers and were equally unsuccessful, largely due to their being seriously overweight as completed . . .'.[76] Yet, as N.A.M. Rodger rightly notes, they marked a substantial improvement on their predecessors; 'the first belted cruiser in which cruiser qualities had plainly been given priority over all others.'[77] For the first time the British possessed armoured vessels capable of

Imperieuse, with most of her sailing rig removed. (U.S. Naval Historical Center: NH65922)

matching or exceeding the speed of virtually every likely wartime foe.

But the real solution to the cruiser quandary was not increasing the speed of 'station battleships'. Rather, it was three-fold, only one element of which was designing and building cruisers solely for commerce protection. The other two elements–extending the logistical network which made it possible to operate wholly steam-powered vessels anywhere on the world's oceans, and meeting foreign capital ships overseas with the same, rather than trying to match them with vessels designed for three diverging roles–were equally crucial. At the point the Board mandated that *Imperieuse* and *Warspite* carry sail there was a vestigial strategic rationale for the decision. The two were to be boilered at 90-120 psi, and could, with the nominal full coal load of 900 tons steam for eighteen days at 10kts. But they were explicitly designed (at least in part) to meet Russian cruisers which would operate in the Pacific, where only a handful of coaling station scattered about the periphery–Esquimault, Hong Kong, Singapore–and one in the middle–Fiji–provided logistical support for a warship dependent on steam alone. By the time they were completed, in 1886 (*Imperieuse*) and 1888 (*Warspite*), the recommendations of the Carnarvon Commission regarding coaling station defence were beginning to be implemented on a significant scale, and Colonial co-operation in imperial security arrangements was being fostered through such activities as the first Colonial Conference (1887). To be sure, there were cogent naval objections to the brig rig with which *Imperieuse* was saddled–most tellingly that it was no help in moving her in anything less than a fresh gale–but the change in external conditions made discarding her wind trap soon after completion a more practical undertaking in strategic or operational terms than having decided to do without it in the first place would have been in early 1881.

Moreover, during the 1880s and early 1890s the Navy abandoned its efforts to build dual- or triple-purpose vessels. Following *Imperieuse* and *Warspite* only one further class of belted cruisers–the seven *Orlando*s–were laid down: after that the notion of protecting the waterline so that such vessels could tangle with station battleships was abandoned; henceforth the Admiralty devoted its efforts to building protected cruisers such as Barnaby had advocated in 1879, sacrificing the waterline belt to additional speed and range, and relying on an armoured deck to protect the vitals and buoyancy. The prototypes for such vessels–the *Blake* class–'followed the layout of the *Orlando*, having the same armament and a similar appearance', but, thanks to the abandonment of side armour, designer William White 'provided a true first class cruiser with high speed and endurance combined with adequate sea keeping, armament and protection to meet the Admiralty's requirements for a ship suitable for long range trade protection . . .'. They were designed with an operational radius of 15,000 nautical miles at 10kts–over three times that of *Imperieuse* and *Warspite*–and even though that figure was not attained, their working radius of 10,000 miles at that speed was more than double that of the two belted cruisers.[78]

For stations where British warships might encounter foreign battleships, at the end of the 1880s the Admiralty designed and built second-class battleships for that specific role, and when these vessels turned out to labour under the same disabilities as their station battleship and belted cruiser predecessors–too weak to tangle with first-class battleships (although capable of fleeing from them) and too slow to catch cruisers–it bit the bullet and began posting first-class units overseas.[79]

---

74. Barnaby to Houston Stewart, ibid, fol. 66.

75. Parkes, *British Battleships*, p309.

76. *Conway's 1860-1905*, p64-5.

77. Rodger, 'British Belted Cruisers,' p31-2.

78. *Conway's 1860-1905*, p66.

79. Ibid, p33-5. The *Canopus* class battleships (laid down 1896-98) 'were designed partly for the China station . . .'.

Chapter 11

CONCLUSION

Shortcomings

GIVEN THE near-chaos which characterised the technological and tactical spheres, the strong desire to avoid heavy expenditure which followed more or less naturally from it (at least among politicians), and the frequent lack of consensus at the Admiralty, it comes as little surprise to discover that all the major capital ship designs utilised or evolved by the British between 1866 and 1880 were flawed in one or more ways. There is, however, a certain predictability as to why particular designs succeeded or failed, keeping in mind that success and failure were relative and highly subjective in this context, since none of these ships save those which bombarded Alexandria in 1882 saw action. The most successful designs were generally those which attempted the least, those which adhered most closely to one of the prescribed strategic roles: the pure first-class coast assault vessels, such as *Devastation*, *Thunderer* and *Dreadnought*, and the pure first-class cruising ironclads like *Alexandra* and *Temeraire* (despite the utter lack of clarity surrounding the tactical/operational role for which the latter was designed). Less successful were those designs which attempted to combine the qualities of coast assault and cruising: *Inflexible* (to some extent), *Colossus*, *Edinburgh* and *Collingwood*.

The least successful fell into two categories: those in which first-class design features were crammed into second-class displacement, or those which were explicitly designed to fulfil two or more different wartime roles. *Agamemnon* and *Ajax*–'sea-going coast defence ships'–were the cardinal examples of the former, although any vessel, in particular *Colossus*, *Edinburgh* and the 'Admirals', which laboured under tonnage restrictions, could also be added. The succession of armoured cruisers from *Shannon* to *Imperieuse* and *Warspite* exemplified the latter, being built to take on both second-class battleships and commerce raiders. The earlier vessels in the series, *Shannon*, *Nelson* and *Northampton*, also laboured under the additional disability of inadequate steam technology and logistical support, handicapping success in the latter role.

With its lack of masts and sails and in its basic arrangement of two turrets with wide arcs of fire placed on the centreline at either end of a superstructure, the essential layout of the pre-dread-nought battleship had been realised in *Devastation*. In this respect the breastwork monitor type was, as Stanley Sandler argues, 'the prototype of the modern battleship'. Yet Sandler's dismissal of the 1870s as a decade of 'stagnation in British warship design' misses the mark.[1] Far from being a manifestation of conservatism, as he alleges, the Admiralty's refusal to perpetuate the breastwork monitor design in subsequent vessels was just the opposite. Muddled and confused it certainly was, but reactionary–in the generally accepted sense of the word–it was not. And the 'fleet of samples', which N.A.M. Rodger cites as confirmation of Barnaby's lack of qualifications, might be more accurately viewed as a manifestation of the personnel weaknesses of the Board, to which Rodger also calls attention, but more especially as evidence of how far into speculative realms the arrival of the machine age thrust the Admiralty during the 1870s.

Barnaby eloquently touched on the basis of contemporary, and most subsequent, critical assessments of the Navy's design policy in the course of an 1876 lecture to the Institute of Naval Architects. 'It is a frequent remark of journalists that the administrators of the Navy have no plan, and that ships are added to the Navy, at great cost, which, in the course of a few years, will become obsolete.'[2] The D.N.C. freely admitted that '[i]f it could be established that, when the programme of shipbuilding operations for the year is prepared, due heed is not given to the forces of other powers–that would indicate a want of plan culpable enough . . .'.

'[B]ut,' he continued, 'I take it this is not what is meant.' Instead, 'there is a vague idea that the administration should have such foresight as to avoid taking a single step out of the straight road into the position we shall occupy in ten or twenty years hence'. 'This expectation on the part of the public,' he concluded simply, 'does not take due account of the great change in conditions introduced by inventions.' There can be no denying the truth of the last observation. Sandler characterizes the first decade of the ironclad era (1859-69) as one in which 'the Admiralty's constructor's department and the controller were compelled to deal with the problem of warship design at a time of change unparalleled in rapidity and complexity'.[3] By adopting this view, and also

by regarding *Devastation* as the essence of the modern battleship, he implicitly assumes that the major problems of rapid technological change and their incorporation into naval architecture had been solved by 1870. To hold this position, however, is seriously to underestimate the number and complexity of the problems faced by the successors of Reed and Spencer Robinson.

First of all, the Constructor's Department had to contend with the continuing escalation of ordnance size and power. *Devastation* carried 35-ton guns. The same year she was completed (1873) the design of *Inflexible*, calling for 60-ton guns, was approved. This scheme was, within two years, dropped from the design in favour of the new 81-ton guns. Concurrent with ordnance developments, of course, was the increasing thickness of armour, a problem of such gravity (so to speak) as to force the Admiralty to resort to various schemes of reduced coverage – most notably the central citadel and the armoured deck – so as to prevent the weight of a ship's protection from becoming a grave obstacle to both stability and manoeuvrability. In addition, the designers of the 1870s were the first to face the ramifications wrought by the introduction of

Although in many respects pointing towards the pre-Dreadnought design, *Howe* and the other 'Admiral' class ships still suffered from the limitations imposed by displacement restrictions. (U.S. Naval Historical Center: NH60592)

Whitehead torpedoes. The menace thus posed may have been more theoretical than real until the mid-1880s, but the Admiralty could not afford to and did not neglect their potential.

And in one crucial respect, the Constructor's Department and the Board faced a more difficult technological situation during the 1870s than their predecessors had. Reed and Spencer Robinson, after all, had not been dogged by the existence of a counter-discourse which questioned the continued efficacy of ironclads, and which advocated the abandonment of armour, whereas it was a constant factor in the counsels of the Admiralty from 1871

1. Sandler, *Emergence of the Modern Capital Ship*, pp87-8, 248-9.

2. Nathaniel Barnaby, 'On Ships of War,' *Transactions of the Institute of Naval Architects* 17 (1876), p1.

3. Sandler, *Emergence of the Modern Capital Ship*, p46.

The Italian *Duilio* and *Dandolo* (pictured) were the models for *Inflexible*. (U.S. Naval Historical Center: NH74828)

onwards.[4] The view never became the accepted orthodoxy at Whitehall, but it was one which nonetheless exerted its influence on the Board's calculations. Barnaby, theorising in 1876 on the future composition of fleets, felt it necessary to remark that if his premises were right, 'there is still a place in naval warfare for costly ironclads with thick armour and powerful guns'.[5] Perhaps this was not a remarkable statement of itself, but it should be remembered that ten years before 1876 there would have been no reason to make it at all; in 1866 the value of ironclads had been unquestioned. And although the Admiralty never succumbed to the anti-armour arguments of Armstrong and others, doubts about the usefulness of armoured ships clearly influenced the formulation of shipbuilding programmes. It was extremely difficult to sanction the expenditure of £3-400,000 or more on a ship which might be

wholly superseded by the time of its completion. The existence of this particular factor contributed to the small scale of the ironclad building programs of the mid- and late 1870s, and reinforced the preference for ships of moderate dimensions and cost. In sum, the problems confronting Reed's and Spencer Robinson's successors were both more numerous and more daunting than those faced during the 1860s.

In one respect critics of the Navy's design and building policies during the 1870s were and are correct. The Admiralty was generally content to imitate foreign developments rather than lead the way in design innovations. After all, apart from *Polyphemus*, which was an original creation, the two novel battleship designs of the decade, *Inflexible* and *Collingwood*, were novel only insofar as Britain was concerned. Both were openly imitative of foreign vessels. There was a considerable measure of truth in the *Times*' allegation that the Admiralty followed rather than led. Indeed, Ropp has described the British shipbuilding policy of the 1870s as waiting 'passively until a new ship type appeared abroad and then build[ing] two bigger ones like it'.[6] Before condemning this reactionary–in the true sense of the word–policy out of hand, it would be well to consider the basis from which it arose.

In 1871 the Committee on Designs addressed itself to the subject of future shipbuilding policy. Their recommendation is instructive:

> [A] safe method by which the requirements of the British Navy may from time to time be estimated, is to watch carefully the progress of other nations in designing and constructing ships of war, and to take care that our own Fleet shall be more than equal in both the number and power of its ships to that at the disposal of any other power.[7]

A similar approach was recommended five years later by the D.N.O. Captain Henry Boys in rendering judgement on the design for the torpedo-ram *Polyphemus*: 'I submit generally it is desirable only to build ships to fight those now existing and belonging to foreign Powers, and not to venture too far into theories which the experience of war only can determine.'[8]

Reactionary this policy undoubtedly was. It was also unquestionably economical. But it was pragmatic as well. Indeed, it was the sole logical response to the baffling, almost insoluble problems faced by naval architects during the 1870s and 1880s. Given the state of near-chaos in design policy, both at home and abroad, coupled with the virtual lack of foreign challenges after 1870, it is hard to see any alternative policy which would not have resulted in a huge waste of money. Increased ironclad building, in terms of numbers, would have resulted, at best, in a greater number of vessels prone to virtually instantaneous obsolescence and, at worst, not only in rapid obsolescence, but also even more extreme heterogeneity in a battlefleet already beset with disparate types.

Increased size might have helped. Many of the problems of the designs of the 1870s can be attributed to the Admiralty's insistence on moderate dimensions.[9] Yet there were compelling fiscal arguments in favour of the policy. It was foolish to build bigger, more powerful, and more expensive ships if there was no challenge from abroad to justify their construction.[10] As George J. Goschen pointed out in 1873, it made no sense from an economic standpoint to send large and costly vessels to do work which could be successfully undertaken by smaller and cheaper ships (it was also clear to him and others that it would be impossible to have a mastless breastwork monitor serving in the Pacific). Moreover, not all of the arguments in favour of smaller ships turned on financial considerations. So long as ramming was perceived as a viable means of attack, there were cogent arguments in favour of small and (supposedly) handy ironclads. Likewise, the fact that a smaller ship meant a smaller target was relevant whether or not ramming was a part of the tactical picture.[11] And insofar as the insistence on moderate dimensions was a product of penny-pinching, it was beyond the Admiralty's control. It was, rather, imposed on the Navy by successive governments, and hence cannot be attributed specifically to incompetence or blindness at Whitehall.

Finally, the abandonment of moderate dimensions would not have guaranteed an improvement in the quality of the ships the Admiralty constructed. *Inflexible*, after all, had not been circumscribed by tonnage restrictions–it was felt necessary to meet the challenge posed by *Duilio* and *Dandolo* ton for ton–yet she was, owing to changing conceptions of sea warfare and her less-than-ideal ordnance, viewed with as much jaundice as any other design of the decade, with the obvious exceptions of *Ajax* and *Agamemnon*. To overcome the design problem which beset the Navy during those years ultimately required not only the abandonment of moderate dimensions, but the switch to the barbette design, the development of compound armour (to save weight), an unequivocal commitment to building high-seas, as opposed to coast-assault, battleships, the development of breech-loading guns, and, certainly not least of all, much improved maritime steam technology. Only when these important advances were made was forsaking moderate dimensions likely to produce beneficial results. Indeed, this is exactly what happened with the *Royal Sovereign* class battleships.

---

4. Ropp, *The Development of a Modern Navy: French Naval Policy, 1871-1904*, p27. Ropp remarks '[a]t the beginning of the 1870s, there was a vague general feeling among the experts that the battleship was finished, though none of them was quite sure of the way in which its end would come about. Even those who were not yet partisans of a particular new weapon often agreed with the general conclusion that the capital ship had seen its day.'

The same point is made by Arthur J. Marder in *The Anatomy of Sea Power* (New York, 1940; reprint, New York, 1976), pp124-5. 'The enormous destructive power of the torpedo and the apparent impossibility for even battleships to withstand its attack led many to believe that the heavily armoured and armed warship was doomed, and that in the future only small fast ships, armed with light guns and strongly fortified bows for ramming should be constructed.' Indeed, Marder notes that the Admiralty's Parliamentary Secretary stated to the House of Commons in 1886 that *Nile* and *Trafalgar*, two large ironclads then under construction, would be 'the last ironclads of this large type that will ever be built by this or any other country.' As corroboration for this statement, he quoted Sir Astley Cooper Key, who stated in a letter to the *Times* 'I believe the time is approaching, indeed is already arrived, when no more ironclad ships will be laid down.'

5. Barnaby, 'On Ships of War,' p4.

6. Ropp, *Development of a Modern Navy*, p27.

7. 'Report of the Committee appointed by the Lords Commissioners of the Admiralty to examine the Designs upon which Ships of War have recently been constructed, with Analysis of Evidence', *Parl. Papers*, 1872, Vol. 14, pix.

8. Boys minute, 17 January 1876, NMM: ADM138/66, no fol.

9. Marder, *Anatomy of Sea Power*, p114-15. Marder lays particular stress on this point.

10. *Hansard's Parliamentary Debates*, 3d ser., 218 (1873), col. 53.

11. Marder, *Anatomy of Sea Power*, p113. Marder notes that the preference for moderate dimensions was very strong among staunch navalists: '[t]hey preferred medium-sized battleships of about 10,000 tons so that they could have more battleships for the money; also because of the alleged fatuity of putting all one's eggs in one basket, [and] the large battleship presented a large target . . .'.

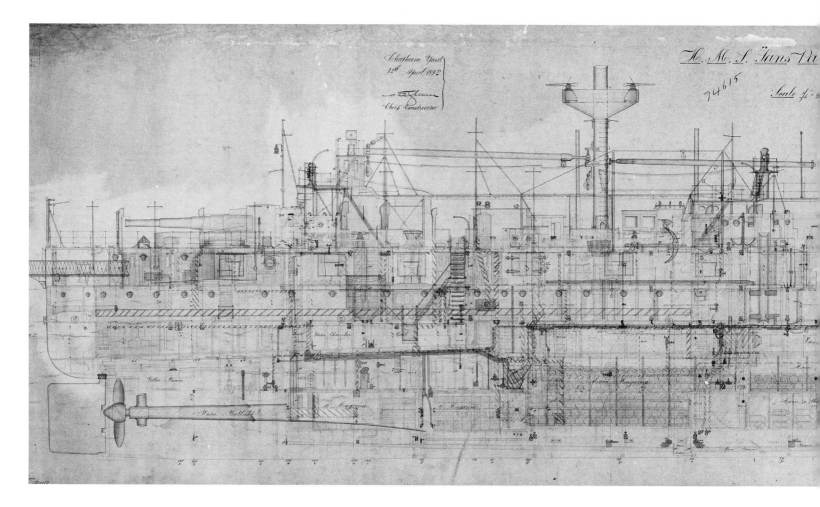

After authorising the six 'Admiral' class barbette ships, the Admiralty signalled its tactical and strategic confusion by reverting to a low freeboard, coast assault turret design for the next two first class battleships, *Sans Pareil* (pictured) and *Victoria* (laid down 1885). (National Maritime Museum, London: 7816)

Keying the incorporation of new technology to the design innovations of maritime rivals, as the British Navy did in the 1870s, usually meant that it maintained, at minimum, technological parity (ordnance excepted), while avoiding fiscal waste by investing in only in the proven technology necessary to uphold its pre-eminent maritime position. In that regard the deliberate pace of technological incorporation reduced – although it certainly did not eliminate – the incidence of problems related to 'working the bugs out' of new weapons and machinery. Furthermore, as is suggested by Boys' memorandum, the policy minimised the investment risk of adopting new technologies which might prove partial or complete failures when put to the test. Finally, and most basically, with the largest investment of any of the maritime powers in existing technology, for Britain itself to have deliberately sped the pace of change by taking the lead in design innovations would have been a policy verging on lunacy.

These factors were recognised by some contemporaries, although many subsequent writers seem not fully to have considered them. In one of its more reflective moments the *Times*, in September 1876, opined that 'the Admiralty are to be congratulated on their resolve to keep continually advancing, so far as can be done without extravagance, side by side with the last improvements in gunnery, and in meeting, as far as possible, the continually varying changes in the conditions of naval warfare'.[12] In short, stated the journal, '[w]e must be content to go on tentatively, making successive improvements as circumstances may suggest.' More authoritative praise for the Admiralty's design policy came the following year from James W. King, Chief Engineer of the U. S. Navy. He wrote:

> The British Navy, charged with the administration of by far the largest and most powerful navy in the world, [is] always cautious in the application of new inventions, rarely adopting any untried plans, but surely accepting the most successful in practical operations. . . .[13]

Finally, though many of the designs of the 1870s may be adjudged overall failures, one should not lose sight of the fact that almost all contained advances which would be incorporated in subsequent designs: *Shannon*'s armoured deck, *Thunderer*'s hydraulic gun loading machinery, *Temeraire*'s barbettes, the electricity and sub-

Profile (as fitted)

merged torpedo tubes of *Inflexible*, *Colossus*'s breech-loading guns, and the essence of pre-dreadnought disposition visible in *Collingwood*. Even *Ajax* and *Agamemnon* contributed to the 'march of progress', being the first British battleships to boast a secondary armament to drive off torpedo boat attacks. Confused the Admiralty's design policy during the 1870s undoubtedly was: stagnant it was not.

Nathaniel Barnaby and His Critics

Nathaniel Barnaby, it has been charged, came to exercise a dominant and none-too-benign influence over Admiralty design policy during the 1870s and 1880s, the consequence of administrative and personnel weaknesses on the Board coupled with his own lack of qualification for the post. The critique has numerous facets: he valued handiness to the detriment of other seagoing qualities, yet ironically many of the ships he designed handled poorly, owing to their beaminess. They were, in Parkes' words, 'mostly unattractive and cumbersome looking', with 'confused and irritating profiles without symmetry, and an ugliness in the matter of masts and funnels which carried no excuse from a utilitarian standpoint'.[14] Worse still, according to N.A.M. Rodger, Barnaby failed to appreciate the distinction between a cruiser's duties and those of a battle-

ship: 'he simply did not accept that difference of function implied any difference of design. An ironclad was an ironclad, wherever she served.'[15] Indeed, so unsuited was Barnaby for his position, that when he managed to design a successful vessel – the dispatch vessel/proto-cruiser *Iris* – the lapse is 'surprising', but the surprise is explained away by the simple expedient of claiming that 'it is not unlikely . . . that the young W.H. White (as his biographer asserts) had the major share in working out the design'.[16] In sum;

[i]f the naval administration of the 1870s, and especially the ships they built, reflected any consistent policy or direction, it was Barnaby's. His was the conception of the 'fleet of samples', of the miscellaneous collection of bizarre and ill-assorted designs which composed the Navy's fleets and squadrons in the middle years of Queen Victoria's reign. In these often misconceived designs, and

---

12. *The Times*, 11 September 1876, p9.

13. James W. King, *European Ships of War and Their Armament, Naval Administration, etc* (Washington, 1877), p190.

14. N.A.M Rodger, 'The Dark Ages of the Admiralty, 1869-1885, Part 2,' *Mariner's Mirror* 62/1 (1976), p44; Parkes, *British Battleships*, p205.

15. N.A.M. Rodger, 'British Belted Cruisers', *Mariner's Mirror* 64/1 (1978), p27.

16. N.A.M. Rodger, 'The First Light Cruisers', *Mariner's Mirror* 65/3 (1979), p211.

The success of HMS *Iris* is usually attributed to W.H. White rather than Barnaby himself. (U.S. Naval Historical Center: NH60125)

in the almost complete lack of any mechanism for strategic planning, are reflected the administrative weaknesses of the Admiralty . . .

These conclusions, however, are impossible to reconcile with the evidence contained in the surviving Ship's Covers. Barnaby's role in sketching out *Shannon*'s design, for example, reveals his ambiguous relationship with the Board. Although he had a far greater knowledge of the parameters of engineering and shipbuilding than the naval members, he was subject to their direction as to the general features, arrangement of armour and armament, and, most importantly, the cost and size of the vessels which it was his job to design. Fault for *Shannon*'s shortcomings, if fault there was, was not Barnaby's. Instructed by the Board to produce an economical design for a second-class ironclad, he had done just that, and what is more, his efforts received its unanimous approval. To absolve Goschen, Milne, Tarleton, and Seymour from responsibil-

ity for the general features of the design is implicitly to argue that they should not be held accountable for their actions.[17]

On a larger scale, it is abundantly clear that Barnaby's freedom of action was severely circumscribed by his superiors. During the 1860s, through close co-operation with the Controller, Spencer Robinson, Edward Reed was often able to carry the Board with him, rather than acting as its servant.[18] The circumstances surrounding the construction of *Captain* and its subsequent capsizing should have further strengthened the hand of the Controller's

17. Rodger, 'British Belted Cruisers', pp26-7.

18. Parkes, *British Battleships*, p150; Memorandum by Spencer Robinson (Copy), 15 February 1869, PRO: ADM1/6138.

19. Considerations put forward by the Director of Naval Construction preliminary to the preparation of Designs of *Colossus* and *Imperiuse*', [cJune 1878], NMM: ADM138/60, no fol.

20. Rodger, 'Dark Ages of the Admiralty, Part 2,' p45.

21. For criticism of Barnaby on this score, see Rodger, 'British Belted Cruisers', p33.

22. Richard Vesey Hamilton, *Naval Administration. The Constitution, Character, and Functions of the Board of Admiralty, and of the Civil Departments it Directs* (London, 1896), p171.

Department, and especially the Chief Constructor, when pressing his views. Perhaps this would have happened had Reed and Spencer Robinson remained at the Admiralty, but the former resigned in 1870, before the *Captain*'s loss, and the latter was forced out of office early the following year. For several years the post of Chief Constructor was held in commission by a team of naval architects overseen by Barnaby, who was given the title of 'President of the Council of Construction'. Finally, in August 1875 he was appointed Chief Constructor in name as well as fact, save that the title was changed to Director of Naval Construction. Spencer Robinson's immediate successor was Captain Robert Hall, followed after barely a year on the job (April 1872) by Rear-Admiral William Houston Stewart. Houston Stewart remained at his post for ten years, Barnaby until 1885. These two men therefore oversaw the Navy's shipbuilding from 1872 onwards. But stability of tenure produced neither the close agreement on design fundamentals which Reed and Spencer Robinson had shared, nor their ability to carry their views with the Board.

Evidence of the degree to which Barnaby was routinely overruled is abundant. The problems encountered in settling on the design of *Temeraire* produced no less than nine different sketches, and the resulting vessel was clearly the product of visions other than Barnaby's. In 1878 his reasoned plea to lengthen the design for the *Colossus* class ironclads to 350ft to secure greater speed was rejected by the Board.[19] And in 1881 he submitted eleven design proposals to the Board only to have all of them turned down in favour of repeating *Collingwood*. Even *Ajax* and *Agamemnon* would have been very different vessels had Barnaby exercised the domi-

nant influence that he is alleged to have possessed, and their chief drawbacks in terms of seaworthiness were unquestionably the consequence of Alexander Milne's dicta, rather than the D.N.C.'s 'professional shortcomings'. To maintain in the face of this evidence that 'the organisation weaknesses of the Admiralty, and the personal failings of his superiors came to give [Barnaby] a dominant influence on questions which he was incompetent to judge' can only be done by ignoring abundant evidence to the contrary.[20]

Future First Naval Lord Richard Vesey Hamilton touched on another aspect of the design process for which Barnaby has been taken to task; the policy of modifying vessels in the course of construction.[21] '[W]hen the ship has been put in hand,' Vesey Hamilton recorded in his volume on British naval administration, 'no changes can be introduced into her, either by the designers or the constructors, without the express sanction of the Board.'[22] It is plain, however, that the Board was more than willing to sanction changes in *Shannon*, to cite but one example, after the ship had been 'put in hand.'

In July 1876 she was to all intents and purposes ready for sea when entering Plymouth Sound, but for the next twelve months the Dockyard laboured to make her better and better. Whiteheads and torpedo fittings with six 20 pdr. guns were added; the armour on the conning tower was increased and it

Although the result of Alexander Milne's criteria, *Agamemnon*'s numerous shortcomings are routinely attributed to Barnaby. (U.S. Naval Historical Center: NH64215)

became part of a considerable deck structure upon which a boat was stowed; armour glacis plates around the lower deck hatchways were thickened; a variety of heavy fittings were installed, and the coal supply was raised from 280 to 470 tons, and crew increased from 350 to 450.[23]

A similar litany could easily be recounted regarding *Imperiuse* and *Warspite.*

More crucially in this context, although the designer could not introduce changes without the sanction of the Board, the latter could do so without the consent, or even the knowledge, of the designer. On 7 September 1877, when *Shannon* was finally complete and ready for her first commission, Barnaby complained of modifications which had resulted in an increase in her draught, modifications made without his knowledge. He wrote;

> I would like to remark that it is a most unsatisfactory state of things to the person in charge of the design that he should be held responsible for the ultimate draft and trim, when he has had no opportunity of suggesting to his Chief [the Controller] a way out of any difficulty which may turn up.[24]

He added that the person superintending the construction should be made responsible for 'follow[ing] the ship through', that is, should be held responsible for adhering to the design. This practice would, argued Barnaby, 'prove more satisfactory for the Service; as such a person would have an especial interest in watching what to him may appear excessive weights and apprise the D.N.C. so as to avoid censure, also he would keep an account of additional weights (which are now lost sight of) to account for excessive draft which may occur'.[25] Finally, and most tellingly, he bluntly informed the Board that 'the *Shannon* has been practically out of my hands from July/74 to the present date'.

The practice of modifying vessels was of course an overwhelming temptation given the desire to keep pace with of technological change during the mid- and late 1870s, a desire which doubtless contributed to the leisurely ship construction of the period. It was a temptation impossible to resist, even in the face of evidence that it often had deleterious consequences for seaworthiness and performance. Clearly something was amiss in the way the Admiralty functioned if the person most responsible for the particulars of a design was not kept informed of modifications. That Barnaby was not even consulted regarding the changes, much less their contributions to the ship's fighting efficiency or its increased immersion, suggests damaging weaknesses in the Board's decision-making process. It also demonstrates unequivocally the degree to which the Constructor's Department in general, and Nathaniel Barnaby in particular, lost control of ship design after the initial criteria were approved.

The points on which Barnaby's reputation warrants vindication, or at least an accurate recounting, range well beyond those already mentioned; so far from advocating masts and sails at all costs, he had concluded by 1871 that such appendages were irreconcilable with fighting power; so far from valuing handiness above every other seagoing quality, especially speed, the memoranda he produced in conjunction with *Colossus*'s design demonstrate precisely the opposite; so far from attaching little value to any ships other than ironclads and merchant auxiliaries in wartime, he was over-solicitous in advocating wartime roles for peacetime vessels, even slow and poorly-protected gunboats; so far from valuing the ram above all other weapons at sea, he explicitly and publicly placed it last, behind guns and torpedoes.[26] And the conjunction of these views led him to conclude by 1878, long before most contemporary naval officers who stated their views on the subject, that future battles at sea would be fought with guns by fleets of ironclads escorted by light screening vessels to protect them from torpedo attacks.

Even Barnaby's insistence on calling *Iris* and *Mercury* 'dispatch vessels' or 'avisos,' rather than cruisers–implying to critics that he was incapable of recognising the latter even were they designed by his department–makes sense when considered in conjunction with their coal bunkerage and range. True, they had the high speed requisite for the cruiser role, but with a maximum bunkerage of 780 tons of coal, they had a range of 6000 nautical miles at 10kts, and only 2000 nautical miles at full speed. By way of comparison, the subsequent class of protected cruisers, the *Leanders*, carried over a thousand tons of coal, enough for a steaming range of 11,000 miles at 10kts. At the time of their construction, therefore, *Mercury* and *Iris* were termed avisos or dispatch vessels for a very pertinent reason. They had the coal endurance to steam at high speed as long as they were heading directly from one place with a coal depot to another where they could fill their bunkers– the sort of duties they would fulfil if used as dispatch vessels. Lacking full sailing rig, they could not, on the contrary, operate in the Pacific, cruising in an anti-commerce raiding role, at least not on completion, given the paucity of coal depots there. The logistical infrastructure to sustain a purely steam-powered cruiser force in the Pacific, in the Indian Ocean, even off South America, was not in place for close to another decade. Not coincidentally, they were reclassified as second-class cruisers in the late 1880s, by which time the coaling station question had begun to receive governmental attention.

Last but not least, criticisms of Barnaby's designs on aesthetic

---

23. Parkes, *British Battleships*, p237.

24. Barnaby to Admiralty, 7 September 1877, NMM: ADM138/43, fol. 185.

25. Ibid, fol. 186.

26. Rodger, 'The Dark Ages of the Admiralty, Part 2', pp43-4.

27. Parkes, *British Battleships*, pp205, 229, 243.

HMS *Mercury* (launched 1878). (U.S. Naval Historical Center: NH88882)

grounds must be viewed in light of the Board's power to dictate design specifications, and should be considered in the context of the normative assumptions on which such criticisms rest as well. First, it is plain that much of *Inflexible*'s 'confused and irritating profile' at which Parkes directed his strictures resulted not from Barnaby's dicta, but from Arthur Hood's. It was Hood, after all, who demanded that the vessel's funnels be moved and the superstructure narrowed. What would she have looked like had

Barnaby's design been accepted? More to the point, it is necessary to ask which ships Parkes means. He expressly excepts *Alexandra* and the 'Admirals' from this criticism, and elsewhere admits that the Board's demands gave Barnaby little scope with regard to *Temeraire*'s design and that *Northampton* (and presumably *Nelson* as well) was 'a handsome and impressive ship'.[27] That leaves only

Shannon, Imperieuse, Warspite and the five central-citadel ships out of Barnaby's creations between 1870 and 1881, and it is likely that Parkes was thinking of the last group when levelling the criticism. To deride the central citadel as misshapen, however, is implicitly to assume some normative standard of what a warship's silhouette is supposed to look like. Have the central-citadel types been condemned because battleships subsequently came to assume a very different shape in the 1890s? Are the early broadside ironclads spared from such criticism because they resemble wooden warships? Is Parkes' criticism, in effect, no more than another way of stating that the central-citadel ironclads are the most unique capital ships in British history?

In short, it is time to confront head-on and refute the allegation that Barnaby came to exercise a dominating influence on Admiralty design policy. Time and time again the evidence compellingly demonstrates that his views and arguments, no matter how strenuously and persuasively argued, were rejected by the Board. We must similarly confront and refute the allegation that he was unsuited for his post. In this respect, though he got much else wrong, Parkes was surely correct in observing that many of the ships of the 1870s would have turned out better had the Board paid heed to Barnaby's arguments.[28] That it did not is enough to demolish the notion that Barnaby exercised influence disproportionate either to his post or his abilities. It also lays to rest the accompanying allegation that the Board's capacity for collective discussion was destroyed by Hugh Childers in the late 1860s. As W.H. Smith's memorandum authorising *Collingwood*, and the voluminous minutes on *Shannon, Colossus, Polyphemus, Temeraire* and the 'Admiral' class make abundantly clear, the members of the Board were quite aware of each others' views. That their awareness did not always produce consensus is not evidence of a poor administrative or decision-making structure at the Admiralty, but simply of the bewildering situation faced by these men.[29]

Barnaby had his weaknesses, to be sure. Perhaps most crucially – in terms of retrospective judgements – he lacked eloquence and forcefulness in writing. Sir George Tryon informed Geoffrey Phipps Hornby in the midst of the *Inflexible* fracas that 'Barnaby damns every cause he seeks to defend – he is very weak on paper & [in] statements before a committee when giving evidence.'[30] He was often convoluted, imprecise, and ordinarily incapable of cutting to the chase. Certainly, too, he lacked Edward Reed's skill and enthusiasm as a controversialist, to say nothing of his power of invective. Yet it is not for his argumentative skills, nor even his deficiency in plain speaking that Nathaniel Barnaby should be judged. He should be judged by his creations, and they must, in turn, be judged in light of the confounding circumstances which gave rise to them. When so considered, the verdict will show that Barnaby was neither a fool nor a man thrust into a position for which he was not competent. Rather, he was faced with an insoluble tactical/technological/strategic quandary of bewildering complexity, one in which, owing to the lack of professional consensus on almost every aspect of it, he was often forced to find his own way. In so doing, he came closer to discerning the shape of naval warfare of the future than many whose training and responsibilities should have forced them to contemplate it. He was not perfect, by any stretch of the imagination, but he was correct much of the time, and under the circumstances that was no mean accomplishment.

---

28. Ibid, p204.

29. For further evidence on this point, see Appendix A, part 5 of the 'Report of the Committee appointed by the Lords Commissioners of the Admiralty to examine the Designs upon which Ships of War have recently been constructed, with Analysis of Evidence', *Parl. Papers*, 1872, Vol. 14, pp301-308. *Devastation*'s design was vetted not only by the entire Board, Edward Reed, and D.N.O. Astley Cooper Key, but a distinguished scientific and professional panel including the Earl of Lauderdale, Sir Hastings Yelverton, Cowper Coles, William Fairbairn, Joseph Whitworth, and Joseph Woolley on 24 March 1869.

30. Tryon to Hornby, 9 August 1877, NMM: PHI/120a/II.

BIBLIOGRAPHY

Manuscripts

Admiralty Papers (Public Record Office and National Maritime Museum)
Cabinet Papers (Public Record Office)
Childers Papers (Cambridge University Library)
Gladstone Papers (British Library)
Hughenden (Disraeli) Papers (microfilm copy, London School of Economics and Political Science)
Home Office Papers (Public Record Office)
Hornby Papers (National Maritime Museum)
Milne Papers (National Maritime Museum)
Stewart Papers (National Maritime Museum)
Tarleton Papers (Liverpool Record Office, William Brown Library)
Wadenhoe (Ward Hunt) Papers (Northamptonshire Record Office)

Published Primary Sources

[Anonymous], *British and French Ships* (London, 1883)
[Anonymous], *Harvey's Sea Torpedoes* (Portsmouth, n.d.)
[Anonymous], 'Nitro-glycerine: The New Explosive', *Westminster Review* 90/34 (1868), pp93-104
[Anonymous], 'On The Present Condition of Our Navy', *Fraser's Magazine* 94 (1876), pp403-18
[Anonymous], 'Our Heavy Guns', *Macmillan's* 18 (1868), pp505-14
[Anonymous], *The Battle of the Ironclads; or, England and her foes in 1879* (London, 1871)
[Anonymous], *The Coming War: England Without a Navy* (London, 1875)
[Anonymous], 'The Progress of Shipbuilding in England', *Westminster Review* 115/59 (1881), pp1-28
[Anonymous], 'The Science of Naval Architecture', *Fraser's Magazine* 97 (1878), pp269-76
Arnold-Foster, H.O., 'Our Position as a Naval Power'. *Nineteenth Century* 13 (1883), pp1-13
———, 'The People of England vs. Their Naval Officials', *Nineteenth Century* 16 (1884), pp702-14
Bacon, Reginald H., *A Naval Scrapbook* (London, 1925), 2 vols
Bagehot, Walter, *The English Constitution* (Reprint ed., Ithaca, NY, 1963)
Barnaby, Nathaniel, 'Armour for Ships', *Transactions of the Institute of Naval Architects*, 20 (1879), pp27-32
———, 'Battleships, A Forecast', *Journal of the Royal United Services Institution*, 27 (1883), pp127-44
———, *Comparison of the Navies of England and France, January 1870* (London: for Admiralty Circulation 1870)
[———], *Comparison between Armoured Ships of England and France as to New Types,* (London: for Admiralty circulation 1880)
———, *Comparative Progress of European Ironclad Navies* ([London], for Admiralty circulation, 1884)
———, *H.M.S. Inflexible* (London, 1878)
———, *Memorandum on the Relative Strengths of British and French Ships* (London: for Admiralty circulation, 1883)

———, *Naval Development in the Century* (London, 1902)
———, 'On Iron and Steel for Shipbuilding', *Transactions of the Institute of Naval Architects* 16 (1875), pp131-46
———, 'On Ships of War', *Transactions of the Institute of Naval Architects* 17 (1876), pp1-12
———, 'On Some Recent Designs of Ships of War for the British Navy, Armoured and Unarmoured', *Transactions of the Institute of Naval Architects* 15 (1874), pp1-21
———, 'On the Fighting Power of the Merchant Ship in Naval Warfare', *Transactions of the Institute of Naval Architects* 18 (1877), pp1-23
———, 'On the *Nelson* Class', *Transactions of the Institute of Naval Architects* 21 (1880), pp59-68
———, 'On the Unmasted Sea-going Ships *Devastation, Thunderer, Fury,* and *Peter the Great*', *Transactions of the Institute of Naval Architects* 14 (1873), pp1-20
———, *The Naval Review of British, French, Italian, German, and Russian Large Ships of War, Being an Inspection of Two Hundred and Fifty-Three Sea-Going Fighting Ships* (London, 1885[?])
———, *The Proper Form and Construction of the Rams or Spurs of Ironclads* (London: n.p., for Admiralty circulation, 1875)
———, *To the Members of the Royal Corps of Naval Constructors, January 1, 1885* (London: n.p., for Admiralty circulation, 1885)
Bower, Graham, 'A New System of Naval Tactics', *Journal of the Royal United Services Institution* 19 (1875), pp503-23
Brassey, Thomas, *Comparison of the French and English Ironclads* (London: for Admiralty circulation, 1881)
[———], *English and Foreign Opinions on the Types of Ships Best Adapted for Modern Naval Warfare* (London: for Admiralty circulation, 1881)
———, 'On Unarmoured Vessels', *Transactions of the Institute of Naval Architects* 17 (1876), pp13-28
———, 'Our Naval Strength and Policy', *Contemporary Review* 27 (1876), pp791-802
———, 'Recent Designs for Ships of War', *Macmillan's* 36 (1877), pp257-66
———, *Naval Annual* (Portsmouth, 1886)
———, *Papers and Addresses* (London, 1894), 2 vols
———, *Recent Naval Administrations* (London, 1872)
———, 'The Administration of the Navy, 1880-1885', *Nineteenth Century* 19 (1886), pp106-26
———, *The British Navy: Its Strength, Resources, and Administration* (London, 1882), 6 vols
———, *The Organization of the Royal Naval Artillery Volunteers Explained* (London, 1874)
[Bridge, Cyprian A.G.], 'Ocean Warfare', *Edinburgh Review* 140 (1874), pp1-31
[———], 'Naval Power in the Pacific', *Edinburgh Review* 152 (1880), pp70-97
———, *Some Recollections* (London, 1919)
[———], 'The Growth of German Naval Power', *Edinburgh Review* 144 (1876), pp1-32

[_____], 'The Naval Strength of England', *Edinburgh Review* 147 (1878), pp495-523

[_____], 'The Navies of the World', *Edinburgh Review* 153 (1881), pp31-63

[_____,], 'The Past and Future of Naval Tactics', *Edinburgh Review* 136 (1872), pp559-89

_____, 'Sub-aqueous Warfare, Ancient and Modern', *Fraser's Magazine* 98 (1878), pp458-70

Briggs, John Henry, *Naval Administrations 1827 to 1892, The Experience of 65 Years* (London, 1897)

Browne, C. Orde, 'Present Position of the Armour Question', *Journal of the Royal United Services Institution* 28 (1884), pp107-26

[Butler, Spencer], 'The British Navy: What We have and What We want', *Blackwood's* 109 (1871), pp357-74

C. [pseud.], 'The Command of the Sea', *Fraser's Magazine* 99 (1879), pp731-40

Chalmers, James, *Armour for Ships and Forts* (London, 1865)

[?Chapman, E. F.], 'Our Ironclad Navy', *Cornhill* 23 (1871), pp55-69

[Clarke, George S.], 'Imperial Defence', *Edinburgh Review* 169 (1888), pp552-91

Colomb, John C.R., *Imperial Defence* (London, 1880)

_____, *Imperial Strategy* (London, 1871)

_____, *Naval Intelligence and Protection of Commerce in War* (London, 1881)

_____, *The Defence of Great and Greater Britain* (London, 1880)

Colomb, Philip H, *Great Britain's Maritime Power: How Best Developed as Regards:- Fighting Ships, Protection of Commerce, Naval, Volunteer, or Supplemental Force, Colonial and Home Defence* (London, 1878)

_____, 'Great Britain's Maritime Power, How Best Developed as Regards Fighting Ships, etc', *Journal of the Royal United Services Institution* 22 (1878), pp1-55

_____, 'Modern Naval Tactics', *Journal of the Royal United Services Institution* 9 (1865), pp1-28

_____, *Naval Warfare: Its Ruling Principles and Practice Historically Treated* (London, 1891)

_____, 'Steam-power *versus* Sail-power', *Journal of the Royal United Services Institution* 22 (1878), pp530-55

_____, 'The Attack and Defence of Fleets', *Journal of the Royal United Services Institution* 15 (1871), pp407-37

[Condor, Francis R.], 'Torpedo Warfare', *Edinburgh Review* 146 (1877), pp281-316

The *Daily News*, London

Dawson, William, 'Future Naval Battles', *Fraser's Magazine* 84 (1871), pp167-81

_____, 'Guns and Armour', *Fraser's Magazine* 87 (1873), pp257-64

_____, 'Modern Seamanship', *Fraser's Magazine* 84 (1871), pp793-801

_____, 'Offensive Torpedo Warfare', *Journal of the Royal United Services Institution* 15 (1871), pp86-111

_____, 'The Naval War Game', *Fraser's Magazine* 88 (1873), pp483-93

Douglas, Howard, *Observations on Modern Systems of Fortification* (London, 1859)

_____, *On Naval Warfare With Steam* (London: n.p., 1857)

Duckworth, A.D. (ed.), *The Papers of William Froude, M,A,, LL,D,, F,R,S,, 1810-1879* (London, 1955)

Eardley-Wilmot, Sydney, *An Admiral's Memories: Sixty-Five Years Afloat and Ashore* (London, 1927)

Elliot, George, *Flotilla, Coast and Harbour Defence, The Gunboat of the Future* (London, 1871)

_____, 'The Ram: The Prominent Feature of Future Naval Victories', *Journal of the Royal United Services Institution* 27 (1883), pp357-78

The *Engineer*, London

Fairbairn, William, *Treatise on Iron Ship Building: Its History and Progress* (London, 1865)

Fisher, John A, *Fear God and Dread Nought: The Correspondence of Admiral of the Fleet Lord Fisher of Kilverstone, Volume I: The Making of an Admiral 1854-1904* (ed. Arthur Marder, London, 1952)

_____, *Memories* (London, 1919)

_____, *Naval Tactics* ([London]: For Private Circulation, 1871)

_____, *Records* (London, 1919)

Fitzgerald, Charles Cooper Penrose, *From Sail to Steam: Naval Recollections, 1878-1905* (London, 1916)

_____, 'Mastless Ships of War', *Journal of the Royal United Services Institution* 31 (1887), pp114-33

_____, *Memories of the Sea* (London, 1913)

_____, 'Side Armour *versus* Armoured Decks from a Naval Point of View', *Journal of the Royal United Services Institution* 29 (1885), pp63-91

Flannery, J. Fortesque, 'On Water-tube Boilers', *Transactions of the Institute of Naval Architects* 17 (1876), pp259-282

Fortescue, Seymour, *Looking Back* (London, 1920)

France, Ministèrie des Finances, *Bulletin de Statistique* (Paris)

_____, Ministèrie des Finances, *Compte Général de l'Adminstration des Finances* (Paris)

_____, Ministère de la Marines et des Colonies, *Revue Maritime et Coloniale* (Paris)

[Fremantle, Edmund R.], 'Are Ironclads Doomed?', *Blackwood's* 141 (1887), pp519-33

_____, 'Ironclads and Torpedo Flotillas', *Nineteenth Century* 18 (1885), pp657-73

[_____(signed E.R.F.)], 'The Loss of the *Captain*', *Fraser's Magazine* 83 (1871), pp68-83

_____, *The Navy as I have Known it: 1849-1899* (London, 1904)

[_____(signed E.R.F.)],'Torpedoes', *Fraser's Magazine* 85 (1872), pp461-76

Gallway, E.P., 'The Use of Torpedoes in War', *Journal of the Royal United Services Institution* 29 (1885), pp471-96

Germany, Kaiserlichen Statistichen Amt, *Statistisches Jahrbuch für das Deutsche Reich* (Berlin)

Goodrich, Casper F., *Report of the British Naval and Military Operations in Egypt, 1882* (Washington, 1885)

Great Britain, Admiralty, *Comparative Progress of the European Ironclad Navies: Comparison of Armoured Ships of England and France* ([London], 1884)

_____, Admiralty, *Condition of the Ironclad Fleet* (London, 1874)

_____, Admiralty, *Course of Instruction in Gunnery Ships for Officers and Seamen* (London, 1875)

_____, Admiralty, *English and Foreign Opinions on the Types of Ships Best Adapted for Naval Warfare* (London, 1881)

_____, Admiralty, *List of the Chief Ports on the Federal Coast of the United States, showing the Shipping, Population, Dockyards, and Defences, as far as known; also how far accessible or vulnerable to an Attack, as far as can be gathered from the Charts, With an approximate Estimate of the Number of vessels required to blockade the several Ports and Rivers* (Confidential, 1861)

_____, Admiralty, *Iron Cased Ships of France: Dimensions, Cost, Armament, &c* (London, 1870)

_____, Admiralty, *Report of the Committee appointed by the Lords Commissioners of the Admiralty to examine the Designs upon which Ships of War have recently been constructed, with Analysis of Evidence,*

_____, Admiralty, *The First-class Ironclad to be Laid Down in 1881-82* (London, n.p., 1881)

_____, Admiralty, *To the Members of the Royal Corps of Constructors: Typical English Battleships, Built and Proposed, Having Unarmoured Ends* (London, n.p., 1884)

_____, Admiralty Torpedo Committee, *Report of the Admiralty Torpedo Committee with Reference to the Defence of Ships against Offensive Torpedoes* (London, 1876)

_____, Parliament, *Parliamentary Debates*, 3rd Series, London, generally known as *Hansard's Parliamentary Debates*

_____, Parliament, House of Commons, *British Parliamentary Papers*, London generally known as *Parliamentary Papers*

_____, Parliament, *Report of the Royal Commission appointed to Enquire into the Civil and Professional Administration of the Naval and Military Departments and the Relationship of those Departments to each other and to the Treasury* (generally known as the Hartington Commission) (London, n.p., 1890, Strictly Confidential)

_____, Parliament, *Report of the Royal Commission appointed to make Enquiry into the Condition and Sufficiency of the Means of the Naval and Military Forces provided for the Defence of the more important Sea-ports within our Colonial Possessions and Dependencies* (generally known as the Carnarvon Commission) (London, n.p., 1881, Confidential)

_____, War Office Committee on Working Heavy Guns: Sub-Committee on Plates and Projectiles, *Report on Experiments with Armour-piercing Projectiles up to 9-inch Calibre, 22nd June, 1880* (London, 1880)

Guedalla, Philip (ed.), *Gladstone and Palmerston* (New York, 1928)

Haddan, J. L., *Iron-clads and Forts: Their Armour, Guns, Propellers, Turrets, &c* (London, 1872)

Hall, William H., *Our Naval Defences* (London, 1871)

Halsted, E. Pellew, 'Iron-Cased Ships,' *Journal of the Royal United Services Institution* 5 (1861), pp121-244

Hamilton, Richard V., *Naval Administration, The Constitution, Character, and Functions of the Board of Admiralty, and of the Civil Departments it Directs* (London, 1896)

[_____], 'The Navy and the Empire', *Quarterly Review* 159 (1885), pp201-19

Harris, Robert Hastings, *From Naval Cadet to Admiral* (London, 1913)

_____, 'The Necessity of Supplementing Armour-Clad Ships by Vessels of Other Types', *Journal of the Royal United Services Institution* 26 (1882), pp24-38

Hay, John Charles Dalrymple, *Lines From My Logbooks* (Edinburgh, 1898)

Henwood, Charles F., 'Ironclads, Present and Future', *Journal of the Royal United Services Institution* 14 (1870), pp148-74

_____, *Sir Robert Spencer Robinson, K.C.B., Edward James Reed, C.B., M.P., and Nathaniel Barnaby, N.A., Arraigned at the Bar of Public Opinion* (London: Printed and Published by the Author, 1874)

[Hobart-Hampton, A.C.], 'The Torpedo Scare', *Blackwood's* 137 (1885), pp737-47

[Hope, C. W.], 'Ironclads and Torpedoes: The *Inflexible* and Mr. Reed', *Blackwood's* 123 (1878), pp153-71

[_____], 'Our Ironclad Ships,' *Blackwood's* 107 (1870), pp706-24

[_____], 'The Progress of Naval Architecture', *Blackwood's* 125 (1879), pp507-24

Hornby, Thomas Geoffrey Phipps, *Squadron Orders for H.M. Ships* (1869)

Hutchinson, W. N., The Ironclad and the Gun of the Future', *Macmillan's* 42 (1880), pp280-89

Inglefield, E. A., 'Naval Tactics, With some Remarks on the Recent Experimental Cruising of the Mediterranean and Channel Squadrons', *Journal of the Royal United Services Institution* 12 (1868), pp483-501

Kemp, Peter (ed.), *The Fisher Papers* (London, 1960)

Keppel, Henry, *A Sailor's Life Under Four Sovereigns* (London, 1889), 3 vols

Key, Astley Cooper, 'Naval Defence of the Colonies', *Nineteenth Century* 20 (1886), pp284-293

King, James W., *European Ships of War and Their Armament, Naval Administration, etc*, (Washington: U.S. Government Printing Office, 1877)

_____, *The Warships and Navies of the World* (Boston, Mass., 1881)

Laughton, John Knox, 'Naval Warfare', *Edinburgh Review* 162 (1885), pp234-64

[_____], 'Past and Present State of the British Navy', *Edinburgh Review* 161 (1885), pp492-513

[_____], 'Thomas Brassey on the British Navy', *Edinburgh Review* 155 (1882), pp477-504

Lean, Francis, 'The Progress of Heavy Artillery', *Fortnightly Review* 32/26 (1879), pp278-93

Lloyd, E.W., and Hadcock, A. G., *Artillery, Its Progress and Present Position* (London, n.p., 1893)

McDougall, Neil, *The Relative Merits of Simple and Compound Engines as Applied to Ships of War* (London, 1874)

Main, Robert, *The British Navy in 1871* (London, 1871)

Maitland, E., 'The Heavy Guns of 1884', *Journal of the Royal United Services Institution* 28 (1884), pp693-729

Mallett, Robert, 'Subaqueous Torpedoes', *Naval Science* 1 (1872), pp269-79

Martell, B., 'On Steel for Shipbuilding', *Transactions of the Institute of Naval Architects* 21 (1877), pp1-32

Martin, Frederic (ed.), *The Statesman's Yearbook* (London)

Merrifield, C. W., 'On Naval Guns', *Transactions of the Institute of Naval Architects* 20 (1879), pp46-58

_____, *Review of the Present Conditions of Naval Design for Commerce and for War* (London, 1872)

Milton, J., 'Strength of Boilers', *Transactions of the Institute of Naval Architects* 21 (1877), pp318-26

Mitchell, W.F., *The Royal Navy* (Portsmouth, 1872, 1881), 2 vols

The *Naval and Military Gazette*, London

Noel, Gerard H. U., 'On Masting Ships of War and the Necessity of Still Employing Sail Power in Ocean-going Ships', *Journal of the Royal United Services Institution* 27 (1883), pp543-75

_____, *On the Best Types of War Vessels for the British Navy* (London, n.p., 1881)

_____, *The Gun, Ram, and Torpedo* (London, 1874)

Paget, John C., *Naval Powers and Their Policies* (London, n.p., 1876)

The *Pall Mall Gazette*, London

Parkes, W., 'On the Use of Steel for Marine Boilers, and some Recent Improvements in Their Construction', *Transactions of the Institute of Naval Architects* 19 (1878), pp172-92

Pellew, Pownall W., 'Fleet Manoeuvering', *Journal of the Royal United Services Institution* 11 (1867), pp527-47

Ramus, Charles Meade, *Rocket Floats and Rocket Rams: A Letter to the Lords Commissioners in Reply to Mr, Froude's report to the Admiralty of Mr. Ramus's proposal of the 20th Day of June, 1872, Proving the Destructibility at Long Ranges of Iron-Armoured Ships* (London, 1875)

Reed, Edward J., *Letters from Russia in 1875* (London, 1876)

_____ (ed.), *Naval Science, A Quarterly Magazine for Promoting the Improvement of Naval Architecture, Marine Engineering, Steam Navigation, and Seamanship* (London, 1872-1875)

_____, 'On Citadel Ships', *Transactions of the Institute of Naval Architects* 18 (1877), pp24-36

_____, *Our Ironclad Ships* (London, 1869)

_____, 'Our Merchant Marine', *Contemporary Review* 44 (1883), pp731-48

_____, 'The British Navy', *Contemporary Review* 46 (1884), pp617-34

[_____], 'The Late Admiralty Committee on Designs,' idem, *Naval Science* 1 (1872), p305

_____, 'What are the most Urgent Measures that should be taken for Increasing Her Majesty's Navy?', *Journal of the Royal United Services Institution* 26 (1884), pp993-1048

_____, and Simpson, Edward, *Modern Ships of War* (New York, 1888)

Rendel, Stuart, *The Question of the Guns as Now Debated* (London, 1875)

Rennie, G.B., 'On the Comparative Merit of Simple and Compound Engines', *Journal of the Royal United Services Institution* 16 (1875), pp196-215

_____, 'On Three-throw Crank Engines of the Compound System—H.M.S. *Boadiciea* and *Bacchante*, *Transactions of the Institute of Naval Architects* 15 (1874), pp136-60

Robinson, E. Kay, 'The Era of the Torpedo', *National Review* 2 (1883), pp205-11

Robinson, Robert Spencer, 'England as a Naval Power', *Nineteenth Century* 7 (1880), pp389-405

_____, 'On Armour-plating Ships of War', *Transactions of the Institute of Naval Architects* 20 (1879), pp1-26

_____, *On the State of the British Navy; With Remarks on one Branch of Naval Expenditure* (London, 1874)

_____, *Remarks on H.M.S. Devastation* (London, 1873)

_____, 'The Dangers and Warnings of the *Inflexible*', *Nineteenth Century* 3 (1878), pp278-95

_____, 'The Navy and the Admiralty', *Nineteenth Century* 17 (1885), pp185-200

[_____], 'The State of the British Navy', *Quarterly Review* 134 (1873), p77-107

Russia, Ministry of Finance, *Bulletin Russe de Statistique, Financière et de Legislation* (St Petersburg: Imprimerie du Ministère des Finances)

Sartorius, George, *The Ram Used Simply as a Projectile* (n.p., n.d.)

Scott, Percy, *Fifty Years in the Royal Navy* (New York, 1919)

Seaton, Albert E., *A Manual of Marine Engineering, Comprising the Designing, Construction, and Working of Marine Machinery* (London, 1907)

Selwyn, J.H., 'On the True Economies of England's Naval Power', *Journal of the Royal United Services Institution* 15 (1871), pp157-75

Sennett, Richard, 'On Compound Engines', *Transactions of the Institute of Naval Architects* 16 (1875), pp91-102

_____, 'On Some Trials of Simple and Compound Engines', *Transactions of the Institute of Naval Architects* 17 (1876), pp283-87

Shaw-Lefevre, George J., 'British and Foreign Ships of War', *Macmillan's* 35 (1877), pp257-65

[Smith, Francis Montagu (signed F.M.S.)], 'Gunpowder and Modern Artillery' *Fraser's Magazine* 82 (1870), pp218-23

The *Standard*, London

Thearle, Samuel J. P., *The Modern Practice of Shipbuilding in Iron and Steel* (London, 1886), 2 vols

Thurston, R. H., 'A Century's Progress of the Steam Engine', *Annual Report of the Smithsonian Institution* (1899), pp591-616

The *Times*, London

The *United Service Gazette*, London

United States, (Lerner, William, et. al., eds.), *Historical Statistics of the United States*, (Washington: U.S. Government Printing Office, 1975)

Very, Edward W., *Navies of the World; Giving Concise Descriptions of the Plans, Armament, and Armour of the Naval Vessels of Twenty of the Principal Nations,* *Together with the Latest Developments in Ordnance, Torpedoes, and Naval Architecture, and a Concise Summary of the Principal Naval Battles of the Last Twenty Years, 1860-1880* (London, 1880)

Watt, Henry F., *The State of the Navy, 1878* (Liverpool, 1878)

White, William H., *A Manual of Naval Architecture* (London, 1877)

_____, 'The Progress in Steam Navigation', *Annual Report of the Smithsonian Institution* (1899), pp567-90

Wilson, Herbert W., *Ironclads in Action: A Short Sketch of Naval Warfare from 1855 to 1895*, (London, 1896)

Young, Charles F. T., *The Fouling and Corrosion of Iron Ships: Their Causes and Means of Prevention, with the Mode of Application to the Existing Ironclads* (London, 1867)

Secondary Sources

Bacon, Reginald, *The Life of Lord Fisher of Kilverstone, Admiral of the Fleet, KCB, KCVO, DSO* (London, 1929), 2 vols

Ballard, George, 'British Corvettes of 1875: The *Inconstant* and *Raleigh*', *Mariner's Mirror* 22/1 (1936), pp43-53

_____, 'British Corvettes of 1875: The *Volage, Active,* and *Rover*', *Mariner's Mirror* 23/1 (1937): 53-67,

_____, 'British Gunvessels of 1875: The Larger Twin-Screw Type', *Mariner's Mirror* 26/1 (1940), pp14-32

_____, *The Black Battlefleet* (ed. N.A.M. Rodger, Annapolis, 1980)

Barnaby, Kenneth, *The Institution of Naval Architects 1860-1960: An Historical Survey of the Institution's Transactions and Activities over 100 Years* (London, 1960)

Bartlett, Christopher, *Great Britain and Sea Power: 1815-1853* (Oxford, 1963)

_____, 'The Mid-Victorian Re-appraisal of Naval Policy' in Bourne, Kenneth and Watts, D.C. (eds.), *Studies in International History* (London, 1967), pp189-208

Baxter, James Phinney, *The Introduction of the Ironclad Warship* (Cambridge, Mass., 1933)

Beeler, John, *British Naval Policy in the Gladstone-Disraeli Era, 1866-1880* (Stanford, 1997)

_____, ' "A One Power Standard?": Great Britain and the Balance of Naval Power, 1860-1880', *Journal of Strategic Studies* 15 (1992), pp548-75

_____, 'Steam, Strategy, and Schurman: Imperial Defence in the Post-Crimean Era, 1856-1905', in Kennedy, Greg and Neilson, Keith (eds.), *Far-Flung Lines: Essays in Honor of Donald Schurman* (London, 1996)

Bourne, Kenneth, *The Foreign Policy of Victorian England* (Oxford, 1967)

Bradford, Edward E., *Life of Admiral of the Fleet Sir Arthur Knyvet Wilson* (London, 1923)

Brodie, Bernard, *Sea Power in the Machine Age* (Princeton, 1947)

Brown, David K., *A Century of Naval Construction: The History of the Royal Corps of Naval Constructors* (London, 1983)

_____, *Before the Ironclad: Development of Ship Design, Propulsion, and Armament in the Royal Navy, 1815-1860* (London, 1990)

_____, 'The Design of H.M.S. *Inflexible*', *Warship* 4 (1980), pp146-52

_____, *Warrior to Dreadnought: Warship Development, 1860-1905* (London, 1997)

_____, 'William Froude', *Warship* 1 (1979), pp212-13

Chesneau, Roger and Eugene Kolesnik (eds.), *Conway's All the World's Fighting Ships, 1860-1905* (London, 1979)

Childers, Spencer, *The Life and Correspondence of the Rt, Hon, Hugh Culling Eardley Childers* (London, 1901), 2 vols

Clapham, J. H., *An Economic History of Modern Britain* (Cambridge, 1926-32), 3 vols

Clowes, William L., *The Royal Navy, A History from the Earliest Times to the Death of Queen Victoria* (London, 1897-1903), 7 vols

Colomb, Philip H., *Memoir of Admiral the Right Honble Sir Astley Cooper Key, G.C.B., D.C.L., F.R.S., etc* (London, 1898)

Courtmanche, Regis, *No Need of Glory: The British Navy in American Waters, 1860-1864* (Annapolis, 1977)

Cowpe, Alan, 'The Royal Navy and the Whitehead Torpedo', in Ranft, Bryan(ed.), *Technical Change and British Naval Policy, 1860-1939* (London, 1977), pp12-36

Crouzet, Francois, *The Victorian Economy* (trans. A.S. Forster, London, 1982)

Dictionary of National Biography (Reprint ed., Oxford, 1967-8), 22 vols,

Egerton, Mary Augusta, *Admiral of the Fleet Sir Geoffrey Phipps Hornby, G.C.B. A Biography* (Edinburgh, 1896)

Elliot, Arthur D., *The Life of George Joachim, First Viscount Goschen 1831-1907* (London, 1911), 2 vols

Fanshawe, Alice E.J., *Admiral Sir Edward Gennys Fanshawe* (London, For Private Circulation, 1904)

Fitzgerald, Charles Cooper Penrose, *Life of Vice-Admiral Sir George Tryon, K.C.B.* (Edinburgh, 1897)

Gardiner, Leslie, *The British Admiralty* (Edinburgh, 1968)

Gardiner, Robert and Lambert, Andrew (eds.), *Steam, Steel, and Shellfire: The Steam Warship 1815-1914* (London, 1992)

Giffard, Ann and Basil Greenhill, *Steam, Politics, and Patronage: The Transformation of the Royal Navy, 1815-1854* (London, 1994)

Goodman, Jordan and Honeyman, Katrina, *Gainful Pursuits: The Making of Industrial Europe 1600-1914* (New York, 1988)

Gordon, D.C., *The Dominion Partnership in Imperial Defence, 1870-1914* (Baltimore, 1965)

Graham, Gerald S., 'The Ascendancy of the Sailing Ship, 1850-85', *Economic History Review* 9 (1956), pp74-88

_____, *The Politics of Naval Supremacy* (Cambridge, 1965)

Gritzen, Edward (ed.), *Introduction to Naval Engineering* (Annapolis, 1980)

Hamilton, C. I., *Anglo-French Naval Rivalry, 1840-1870* (London, 1994)

Hamilton, W. Mark, *The Nation and the Navy: Methods and Organization of British Navalist Propaganda* (New York, 1986)

Hawkey, Arthur, *H.M.S. Captain* (London, 1963)

Headrick, Daniel, *The Tentacles of Progress: Technology Transfer in the Age of Imperialism* (New York, 1988)

_____, *Tools of Empire* (New York, 1981)

Herwig, Holger, *'Luxury' Fleet: The Imperial Germany Navy, 1880-1918* (London, 1980)

Higham, Robin (ed.), *Guide to the Sources of British Military History* (Berkeley, 1971)

Hill, J.R. (ed.), *The Oxford Illustrated History of the Royal Navy* (New York, 1995)

Hodges, Peter, *The Big Gun: Battleship Main Armament 1860-1914* (Annapolis, 1981)

Hogg, Ian and Batchelor, John, *Naval Gun* (Poole, 1978)

Hovgaard, William, *Modern History of Warships* (London, 1920)

Jane, Frederick T., *Heresies of Seapower* (London, 1907)

_____, *Jane's Fighting Ships* (New York, 1897)

_____, *The British Battle Fleet, Its Inception and Growth Throughout the Centuries* (London, 1912), 2 vols

_____, *The Imperial Russian Navy* (London, 1904)

Jelavich, Barbara, 'British Means of Offense Against Russia in the Nineteenth Century', *Russian History/Histoire Russe* 1, pt. 2 (1974), pp119-35

Jenkins, Ernest H., *A History of the French Navy from its Beginnings to the Present Day* (London, 1979)

Kemp, Tom, *Industrialization in Nineteenth Century Europe* (2nd ed., London, 1985)

Kennedy, Paul, *Strategy and Diplomacy 1870-1945, Eight Studies* (London, 1983)

_____, *The Realities Behind Diplomacy: Background Influences on British External Policy, 1863-1980* (London, 1981)

_____, *The Rise of Anglo-German Antagonism, 1860-1914* (London, 1980)

_____, *The Rise and Fall of British Naval Mastery* (Malabar, Fl., 1976)

_____, *The Rise and Fall of the Great Powers* (New York, 1987)

Lambert, Andrew, *Battleships in Transition: The Creation of the Steam Battlefleet 1815-1860* (London, 1984)

_____, 'Preparing for the Long Peace: The Reconstruction of the Royal Navy, 1815-1830', *Mariner's Mirror* 82/1 (1996), pp41-54

_____, *The Crimean War: British Grand Strategy Against Russia, 1853-1856* (Manchester, 1990)

_____, *The Last Sailing Battlefleet: Maintaining Naval Mastery 1815-1850* (London, 1991)

_____, *Warrior: Restoring the World's First Ironclad* (London, 1987)

Lambi, Ivo, *The Navy and German Power Politics, 1862-1914* (Boston, 1984)

Landes, David, *The Unbound Prometheus: Technological Change and Industrial Development in Western Europe from 1750 to the Present* (Cambridge, 1969)

Lant, Jeffrey, 'The Spithead Naval Review of 1887', *Mariner's Mirror* 62/1 (1975), pp67-79

Lawrence, Derek, 'Steel-Clad Champions—The Emergence of the Modern Warship', *History Today* 23 (July 1972), pp462-70

Livezey, William, *Mahan on Sea Power* (Rev. ed., Norman, Oklahoma, 1981)

Lyon, Hugh, 'The Relations Between the Admiralty and Private Industry in the Development of Warships', in Ranft, Bryan (ed.), *Technical Change and British Naval Policy, 1860-1939* (London, 1977), pp37-64

Maber, John, 'The Steam Engine and the Royal Navy', *Warship* 22 (1982), pp93-100

McCord, Norman, 'A Naval Scandal of 1871: The Loss of H.M.S. *Megaera*', *Mariner's Mirror* 57/2 (1972), pp115-34

Mackay, Ruddock, *Fisher of Kilverstone* (Oxford, 1973)

McNeill, William H., *The Pursuit of Power: Technology, Armed Force, and Society Since A.D. 1,000* (Chicago, 1982)

Magnus, Philip, *Gladstone* (New York, 1964)

Mahan, Alfred Thayer, *Naval Administration and Warfare: Some General Principles* (London, 1908)

_____, *Naval Strategy Compared and Contrasted with the Principle and Practice of Military Operations on Land* (London, 1911)

_____, *The Influence of Sea Power upon History, 1660-1783* (Boston, 1890)

_____, *The Influence of Sea Power upon the French Revolution and Empire, 1793-1812* (Boston, 1892), 2 vols

Manning, Frederic, *The Life of Sir William White* (New York, 1923)

Marder, Arthur J., *The Anatomy of British Sea Power: A History of British Naval Policy in the Pre-Dreadnought Era* (Reprint ed., New York, 1976)

Millman, Richard, *British Policy and the Coming of the Franco-Prussian War* (London, 1965)

Mitchell, B. R., *British Historical Statistics* (Cambridge, 1989)

_____, *European Historical Statistics* (2nd ed., New York, 1980)

_____, and Deane, Phyllis, *Abstract of British Historical Statistics* (Cambridge, 1962)

Mitchell, Fred and Dixon, Conrad, *Ships of the Victorian Navy* (Southampton, 1987)

Mitchell, Donald, *A History of Russian and Soviet Seapower* (New York, 1974)

Modelski, George, and Thompson, William, *Sea Power in Global Politics, 1494-1993* (Seattle, 1988)

Monypenny, William F., and Buckle, George Earl, *The Life of Benjamin Disraeli, Earl of Beaconsfield* (New York, 1910-20), 6 vols

Morley, John, *The Life of William Ewart Gladstone* (New York, 1903), 3 vols

Padfield, Peter, *Rule Britannia* (London, 1981)

_____, *The Battleship Era* (New York, 1972)

Parkes, Oscar, *British Battleships, 1860-1950* (London, 1957)

Partridge, Michael, *Military Planning for the Defence of the United Kingdom, 1814-1870* (New York, 1989)

Pemsel, Helmut, *A History of War at Sea* (Annapolis, 1979)

Pollard, Sidney, and Robertson, Paul, *The British Shipbuilding Industry, 1870-1914* (Cambridge, Mass., 1979)

Ranft, Bryan, 'The Protection of British Seaborne Trade and the Development of Systematic Planning for War', in Ranft, Bryan (ed.), *Technical Change and British Naval Policy, 1860-1939* (London, 1977)

Rasor, Eugene, *British Naval History since 1815: A Guide to the Literature* (London, 1990)

Richmond, Herbert W., *National Policy and Naval Strength: XVI to XX Century* (London, 1928)

_____, *Statesmen and Seapower* (Oxford, 1946)

Rippon, P.M., *Evolution of Engineering in the Royal Navy, Volume I: 1827-1939* (London, 1988)

Rodger, N.A.M., 'British Belted Cruisers', *Mariner's Mirror* 64/1 (1978), pp23-35

_____, *The Admiralty* (Lavenham, 1979)

_____, 'The Dark Ages of the Admiralty, 1869-1885', *Mariner's Mirror* 61/4 (1975), pp331-42; 62/1 (1976), pp33-46; 62/2 (1976), pp121-28

_____, 'The Design of the *Inconstant*', *Mariner's Mirror* 61/1 (1975), pp9-22

_____, 'The First Light Cruisers', *Mariner's Mirror* 65/3 (1979), pp209-30

Ropp, Theodore, *The Development of a Modern Navy* (Annapolis, 1987)

Rowland, K.T., *Steam at Sea: A History of Steam Navigation* (Newton Abbot, 1970)

Sandler, Stanley, ' "In Deference to Public Opinion": The Loss of H.M.S. Captain', *Mariner's Mirror* 59/1 (1973), pp57-68

_____, 'The Day of the Ram', *Military Affairs* 40 (1976), pp175-78

_____, 'The Emergence of the Modern Capital Ship', *Technology and Culture* 11, no.3 (1970), pp576-95

_____, *The Emergence of the Modern Capital Ship* (Newark, Delaware, 1979)

Schurmann, Donald M, *Imperial Defence, 1868-1887* (ed. John Beeler, London, 2000)

_____, *Julian S. Corbett, 1854-1922* (London, 1981)

_____, *The Education of a Navy: The Evolution of British Naval Strategic Thought, 1867-1914* (London, 1965)

Scott, J. D., *Vickers, A History* (London, 1962)

Shulman, Mark R,, *Navalism and the Emergence of American Sea Power, 1882-1893* (Annapolis, 1995)

Sokol, Anthony E., *The Imperial and Royal Austro-Hungarian Navy* (Annapolis, 1968)

Sondhaus, Lawrence, *The Naval Policy of Austria-Hungary, 1867-1918: Navalism, Industrial Development, and the Politics of Dualism* (West Lafayette, Indiana, 1994)

Strakhovsky, Leonind, 'Russia's Privateering Projects of 1878', *Journal of Modern History* 7 (1935), pp22-40

Sumida, Jon T., *In Defence of Naval Supremacy: Finance, Technology and British Naval Policy, 1889-1914* (Boston, 1989)

Taylor, A.J.P., *The Struggle for Mastery in Europe, 1848-1918* (Oxford, 1954)

Thornton, A.P., *The Imperial Idea and its Enemies: A Study in British Power* (London, 1959)

Tunstall, W.C.B., 'Imperial Defence, 1815-1870', *Cambridge History of the British Empire* Vol. 2 (Cambridge, 1940), pp807-41

_____, 'Imperial Defence, 1870-1897', *Cambridge History of the British Empire* Vol. 3 (Cambridge, 1959), pp230-54

White, Colin, *Victoria's Navy: Volume II, The Heyday of Steam* (Annapolis, 1983)

INDEX

Page numbers in *italics* refer to illustrations. All ships are British Royal Navy unless otherwise indicated.

Abbreviations

A-H = Austria-Hungary; Chi = China; CSA = Confederate States of America; Fr = France; Ger = Germany; It = Italy; Rus = Russia; USA = United States of America

'Admiral' class battleships 11, 157, 159, 167-8, *170*, 196, 204, 206, 213, 214
  design of 168-81
  sketch designs for *176, 177, 178, 179*
  see also Anson, Benbow, Camperdown, Howe, Rodney
Admiralty, Board of
  attempts to economize on ship construction 97-104
  Boiler Committee (1876-80) 56-7
  criticism of 9-12, 27, 29, 60, 62-4
  policy towards compound engines 57-60
  policy towards ordnance 72-81, 83-6
  policy towards sails 47-51, 64, 183-4, 184-5, 186-7, 202, 203
  policy towards torpedoes 65-9
  relations with the War Office and Ordnance Department 72-83
  ship design policy of 27, 29, 30-46, 87-91, 98-9
  strategic vision of 87-91, 108
  see also Committee on Design of Ships of War, *Inflexible* Committee, Royal Navy, Ship design
Agamemnon 11, 45, 79-80, 83, 100, 104, 117, 125, 127, 156, 157, 160, 162, 175, 204, 207, 209, 211, *211*
  design of 138-43
Agincourt 35
Ajax 11, *45*, 45, 79-80, 83, 98, *99*, 100, 104, 117, 125, 127, *138, 141*, 150, 153, 155, 156, 157, 160, 162, 164n, 170, 175, 194, 204, 207, 209, 211

  design of 138-43
Alabama (CSA) 23-4
Alexandria, bombardment of (1882) 77-8, 83-6, 90, 105, 181, 204
Alexandra *49*, 55, *94, 96-7*, 98, 108-10, *110*, 116, 137, 155, 190, 191, 192, 197, 204, 213
Albemarle 65
Alma (Fr) 21, 103, 183, 186
Amiral Baudin (Fr) *23*, 170, 175
Amiral Duperre (Fr) 162-3
Anson 43, *86, 169*, 172, *175*
  see also 'Admiral' class
Armour 99, 109, 109-11, 173, 180, 211
  arguments for abandoning 46, 88, 143, 157, 205-6
  compound 44n, 45-6, 70, 207
  deck 43-4, *135, 208*
  horizontal *versus* vertical 43-4, 88, 170, 156, *176*
  Krupp 46
  on *Inflexible* 114-5
  steel 44-6
  versus guns 41-3, 205
  wrought iron 44-5
Armoured cruisers *see* Cruisers
Armstrong, William 46, 71, 74, 77, 79-80, 163, 176, 200
Armstrong guns *see* Guns
Armytage, William 92, 106
Audacious 21, *94*, 103, 116, 172, 183, 186, 191
Austria-Hungary, Navy 16, 18, 105-6
Austro-Prussian War 105-6

Bagehot, Walter 27
Ballard, George 9, 91n
Baltic 102, 115
Bange, Captain de 73
Barbettes 118, 138-41, *152*, 159, *165*, 167, 173, 177, 181, 190, 191-2, *191*, 196, 200-1, 207, 209, 212
  versus turrets 160-5, 167
Baring, Thomas G., first Earl Northbrook 174, 180, 181, 201
Barnaby, Nathaniel 11-12, 38, 39, 43-4, 49, 50, 58, 79, 91, 94, 102-3, 104, 106, 108, 116, 136, 168, 170, 206

and *Inflexible* design 113-21 *passim*
and Edward Reed's attack on *Inflexible* 125-37 *passim*
and *Ajax* design 138-43 *passim*
and *Polyphemus* design 143-52 *passim*
  tactical theories of 145-8, 153-5
and *Colossus* design 152-6
and *Collingwood* design 158-68 *passim*
and 'Admiral' class design 170-81 *passim*
and *Shannon* design 184-7 passim
and *Temeraire* design 187-93 *passim*
and *Imperieuse* design 195-202 *passim*
  historical assessments of 11, 167, 204, 209-14
Bartlett, C. J. 14
Bayard (Fr) *95*, 161, 197, 199n
Bellerophon 21, 41, 99
Benbow *41, 59-60, 78, 113, 144*, 172, *176*, 181
  see also 'Admiral' class
Bermuda 52, 116
Bessemer, Henry 39, 82
Black Prince 22, 30, 144
Black Sea 108, 197
Blake 203
Boilers
  Admiralty Committee on (1877-80) 56-7
  cylindrical ('Scotch') 55-6, 57, 192, 193-4
  pressures in 53, 170, 203
  rapid deterioration of 56-7, 60-2
  rectangular ('box') 54-5
  water tube 57-8, 170
  see also Surface Condenser
'Box-battery' ironclad design 42-3, 92-3, *94*, 99, 153, 187-8, *187, 189*
  see also Ship design
Boys, Henry 47, 50, 80, 82, 83n, 84, 86, 91, 105, 123-4, 201, 207, 208
  and Edward Reed's attack on *Inflexible* 129-32 *passim*
  on Polyphemus design 144-52 *passim*
Brassey, Thomas 26, 32, 35n, 51n, 67, 99n, 102, 104, 134, 174, 206

179-80, 197-8, 199n
Bridge, Cyprian 80
Brin, Benedetto 118, 119
Brown, David K. 40, 121

Campbell-Bannerman, Henry 181
Camperdown 98, 155, *172-3, 174*
  see also 'Admiral' class
Canopus 135, 203n
Captain 47n, 83n, 92, 108, 116, 128n, 132, 134n, 135, 136, 183, 210-11
Cardwell, Edward, first Viscount 12, 81n, 82
Carnarvon, Lord *see* Herbert, Henry Molyneux, fourth Earl of Carnarvon
Carnarvon Commission (1879-82) 25, 52, 203
Cecil, Eustace 74-5
Central citadel design 110-13, 125-6, *135*, 138, 167, 180, 214
  see also Ship design
Cerberus 83n, 108
Chen Yuen (Chi) 135-5
Cherbourg 90
Childers, Hugh C.E. 12, 21, 31, 34, 47, 52, 67, 78, 81n, 82, 85, 96, 214
Chile 18, 197
Clapham, J.H. 39, 40n
Coal consumption 53-4, 55n, 193-4, 203, 212
Coaling stations 25, 60, 89, 90, 203, 212
Coast assault strategy 88-95, 102-03, 138, 157, 182, 196
  see also Admiralty, Royal Navy, Ship design
Cobden, Richard 14, 101
Colbert (Fr) *20*
Coles, Cowper P. 29, 92, 134n, 191, 214n
Collingwood *28, 54*, 98, 156, 157, *158, 159, 160-1, 165, 166, 168*, 169, 170, 172, 173, 175, 180, 181, 204, 206, 209, 211, 214
  design of 159-68
Colomb, Philip H. 14, 41, 47, 49, 60, 66, 93n, 106, 107n
Colonial Office Defence Committee (1878) 25

Colossus 11, *27*, 37, 45, 98, 100, *124*, 138, *156*, 157, 158, 162-3, 164, 165, 166, 169, 170, 194, 195, 204, 209, 211, 212, 214
  design of 152-6
  guns for 79-80
Commerell, John E. 165, 202
Committee on Designs of Ships of War (1871) 29, 42, 46, 102, 103n, 106, 116, 132, 134, 136, 143, 153-4, 183-4, 187, 191, 192, 193n
  urges abandonment of sails 50-2, 62-3, 64, 108
  advocates compound engines 57-8
  on end-on fire 91-2
  on central citadel design 111, 125-7, 128
Congress (USA) 105-06
Conqueror 11, *92-3*, 157, *196*
  guns for 79-80
Conservative party 14, 157, 168, 169
Corry, Henry T. L. 30, 31, 35n, 47n, 67, 68, 69, 81n, 89, 103n
Crimean War 30, 65, 78, 90, 105
Cruisers 26, 183-203, 212
  see also Ship design
Cumberland (USA) 105-6
Custance, Reginald 98
Cyprus 52
Cyclops 102, 103n

Dacres, Sydney C. 35, 47, 48, 84, 102
Dandolo (It) *17*, 18, 117, 118, 119, 122, *123*, 125, 143, *206*, 207
Darley, Henry 200
Defence 17
Deutschland (Ger) 192
Devastation 21, 35, 42, 47, 50, 52-3, 63, 91, 93, 95, 97-8, 102, 106, 108, 110, 115, 119, 120, 127, 128, 130, 132, 143, 153, 155-6, 173, 200n, 204, 205
Disraeli, Benjamin, first Earl Beaconsfield 12, 14, 36, 67, 81n, 108, 134
Dreadnought 10-11, 53, 55, 63, *88*, 98, 99n, 108, 110, *112*, 120, 122, 140, 155, 173, 175, 177, 179, 180, 193n, 204
Duguesclin (Fr) 159, 170, 199, 200
Duilio (It) 18, 117, 118, 119, 122, *124*, 125, 143, 206, 207
Dunn, Henry 138-9, 145n
Dupuy de Lôme, Stanislas-Charles-Henri 18-19

Eardley-Wilmot, Sidney 15, 16

Eastern Crisis (1878) 15
Edinburgh (ex-*Majestic*) 11, *37*, 45, *92*, 98, 100, 136, 138, *153*, *154-5*, 164-5, 169, 195, 204
  design of 152-6
  guns for 79-80
Elder, John 54
Elliot, George 107n, 191
Emden (Ger) 25
English Channel 18, 85, 89, 90, 95, 102, 104, 108, 115, 161, 167, 180
Erzherzog Ferdinand Max (A-H) 106
Ericsson, John 101
Esquimalt, Vancouver Island 33, 53, 203
Excellent (Gunnery School) 68, 71, 72

First World War 25
Fisher, John, first Baron Fisher of Kilverstone 14n, 49, 68, 81n, 82, 83n, 85
Fitzgerald, C.C.P. 14, 50
Flannery, Fortesque 57
Formidable 175
Fortescue, Seymour 10
France 38, 67
  Navy *15*, 16, 19-23, 90, 102, 108-9, 180, 186
  and steam power 89
  and sails 63-4
  guns 72-4
  naval policy 22, 26, 30, 45
  and industrial backwardness 21, 35-7
  steel shipbuilding 37
  reconstruction of (1872-83) 157-8, 160-1, 167, 168-9, 175, 181, 194, 196, 197, 198-9
Franco-German War (1870-1) 22, 35, 37, 75, 90, 102, 103n, 157, 168
Froude, William 120-1, 134-5, 136, 165-6

Gathorne-Hardy, Gathorne 74-5
General Admiral (Rus) *25*, 26, 62, 183, *184*, 184, 186
Germany 38, 72-4, 102
  Navy 16, 18, 25-6, 108-9, 120, 168, 192
Gibraltar 51, 52, 122n, 131
Gerzog Edinburghski (Rus) 26, *184*
Gladstone, William E. 12, 14, 15, 27, 30, 31n, 99, 101, 132, 136
Glatton 35, 102, 103n, 149
Gloire (Fr) 18, 20, 33
Goodenough, James 15
Goschen, George J. 21, 48, 51, 52,

56, 63, 81n, 82, 102, 103n, 108, 112, 132, 184, 185-6, 190, 207, 210
Great Britain 12, 20
  Empire 23-4, 169
  naval policy 21-2, 24-6
  naval spending 26n, 26-7
  iron and steel industry 36-41
  Guerre de course 23-6, 183-203 *passim*
Guns 21, 69, 88, 91, 99, 109, *123*, 205, 212
  British 40-2
    Armstrong breechloaders 70n, 71, 72, 74, 91, 156
    arcs of fire 91-2
    breech-loading 65, *72*, *74*, *84*, 122-3, *152*
    problems in obtaining 79-83, 155, 170, 176, 207, 209
    for *Inflexible* 113-4, 117-9, 122-4
  French 40; 72-4
    'gas check' for 78-9, 80
  influence on design policy 91-2
  Krupp (German) 40, 72-4, 78-9
  quick-firing *152*, 165
  shell guns 34, 35n
  steel projectiles 40-1
  versus armour 41-4
  Woolwich muzzle-loaders *71*, *76-7*, 91, 105, 122-4
    comparisons with foreign guns 72-3
    obsolescence of 73-8
    criticism of 74-6
    hydraulic loading machinery for 77-8, 78, 123-4, 208-9
    rifling of 71
  see also Ordnance, War Office, Woolwich Arsenal
Gunnery exercise 85-6
Gunpowder 76-7

Hall, Robert 30, 84, 102, 211
Hall, W. H. 84
Hartington Commission (1887) 60, 81, 82, 83n, 98
Hamilton, Richard Vesey 50, 78-83 *passim*, 134, 158-9, 165, 167, 168, 170, 180, 199, 200, 211
Hampton Roads, Battle of (1862) 105-6
Hardy, W. B. 107
Harvey, Frederick 65-6
Harvey torpedo *see* Torpedoes
Hay, John 201
Headrick, Daniel 52n
Herbert, Henry Molyneux, fourth

Earl of Carnarvon 12, 25
Hercules 21, 35, 41, 42, 61, 83n, 116
Hero 101, 146
Hong Kong 33, 52
Hood, Arthur A. 48, 49, 67, 72, 73, 77, 79, 81, 83, 84, 102, 103n, 124, 157-8, 159, 162-3, 184-5, 186, 188-90, 191, 213
  and *Inflexible* design 116-21 *passim*
Hope, Charles 134
Hope, James 133-4
Hore, Captain 73
Hornby, Geoffrey Phipps 12, 14n, 49, 60-1, 85, 139, 148, 150, 180, 214
Hoskins, Anthony 200n, 201
Hotham, Charles 85
House of Commons 22, 30, 31, 34, 51, 56, 63, 72, 74, 78, 82, 101, 181
  see also Parliament
House of Lords 75-6
  see also Parliament
Howe 50, 60, 106, 172, 181, 206
  see also 'Admiral' class
Huascar (Peru) 183
Hulls
  advantages of wood 33-7
  composite 34
  iron *versus* wood 30-3
  sheathing with copper 33-4
Hunt, George Ward 12, 34, 56-7, 61, 67, 132, 137, 139, 151, 157

Imperieuse 50, *51*, *68*, 104, 170, 171n, *194-5*, *201*, 202, 204, 212, 214
  design of 195-203
Inconstant 32, 183, 184, 195
Independencia (Brazil) 130
Inflexible 9, 17, 18, 42, 43, *44*, 45, 50, 63, *64*, 92, 98, 99n, 100, 104, *105*, *125*, *126-7*, *129*, *135*, 138, 139, 140, 141, 151, 155, 156, 157, 160, 169, 173, 174-5, 177, 178, 204, 205, 206, 207, 209, 213, 214
  design of 110-21
  Edward Reed's attack on 125-37
  guns for 76-7, 122-4
  sails for 116-7
  sketch designs of *117*, *118*, *119*
Inflexible Committee 133-4, 135, 163
Inglefield, E. A. 16
Institute of Naval Architects 38, 39, 43, 46, 91, 119, 122, 128n, 204
Invincible 191
Iris 39, 209, *210*, 212
Ironclads
  coast assault 90-5, 101-3, 204, 206, 207, 208

cruising 92-6, 103-4; 108-10, 182-4, 204, 207
  first-class 96, 204
  second-class 96, 100-4, 182-4, 187-92, 196-9, 201-2, 204, 210
  see also 'Box battery', Royal Navy, Ship design, Turrets
Iron shipbuilding 30-1
  drawbacks of 32-4
Italia (It) 18, *18*, 143, 169, *170*, 175, 196
Italy 16
  Navy 17-18, 105-6, 112, 117, 122, 125, 143, 158, 168, 169, 170, 175, 177, 178, 181, 196

Japan 14
  Navy 18, 33
Jeune École 26, 137, 157, 160
Jones, Gore 16

Kaiser (Ger) 35n, 130
Kemp, Tom 39
Key, Astley Cooper 40n, 41, 67, 137, 139, 157, 164-5, 166-7, 178, 179, 191, 201, 207n, 214n
  and British guns 72, 73, 78, 83
King, James W. 17, 59, 63, 121, 168, 208

La Galissoniere (Fr) 183
Laird, John 31
Lambert, Andrew 32, 34, 35n
Landes, David 37, 38n, 39
Laughton, John K 83n, 136-7
Leander 212
Lennox, Henry 21, 36-7
Lepanto (It) 18, *74*, 143, 169, 170, 175, 176
Liberal party 14, 31, 101, 110, 157, 168-9
Lindsay, William S. 30, 31, 32
Lissa, Battle of 18, 35n, 105-6, 107, 155
Lord Clyde 35n
Louis Napoleon *see* Napoleon III
Luppis, Johann 66

McCord, Norman 14
Magenta (Fr) 20
Mahan, Alfred T. 14
Maitland, Edward 82
Major, John 32
Mallet, Robert 69
Malta 52, 166, 122n
Marder, Arthur J 89, 207n
Marengo (Fr) *19*
Mauritius 52

Meade, Richard J., fourth Earl of Clanwilliam (Lord Gilford) 48, 139, 165
Mediterranean 18, 52, 64, 85, 89, 95, 104, 108, 115, 117, 139, 161, 167
Mercury 40, 212, *213*
Milne, Alexander; 12, 14n, 24-5, 35n, 48, 53-4, 89-90, 91, 98, 102, 108, 109n, 112, 116, 117, 121, 148, 149-50, 154, 157, 185, 186, 192, 210, 211
  on *Ajax* design 139-41, 142-3
Milton, J. 56
Minin (Rus) 17
Minnesota (USA) 105
Minotaur 125, 130, 131
Mobile Bay, Battle of (1864) 65
Monarch 35, 41, 42, 61, 82, 83n, 92, 116
Monitor (USA) 103-6

Napoleon III 18, 20, 22, 30, 118, 119
Napoleon (Fr) 18
Naval Defence Act (1889) 13
Naval Science (journal) 49, 52, 63, 116
Navy *see* Royal Navy *and individual countries*
Nelson 94, 157, 160, *192-3*, 195n, 197, 198, 200n, 201, 204, 213
  design of 193-4
Neptune 49
Nicholson, Captain 35-6, 79
Nile 137, 207n
Noel, Gerard 49, 60, 106
Nolan, Philip 74-5
Normandie (Fr) 35n
Northcote, Stafford, first Earl Iddesleigh 12
Northampton 13, *53*, *94*, 157, 160, 192, 195n, 197, 198, 200n, 201, 204, 213
  design of 193-4

Océan (Fr) 139, *140*
Opal 149
Ordnance 20, 65-86, 87, 170, 208
  influence on ship design 91-3
  see also Guns, Torpedoes
Ordnance Committee (1879) 76, 80
Ordnance Department; 42, 78-84 *passim*, 122n
  see also Guns, War Office, Woolwich Arsenal
Orlando 203
Osborn, Sherard 90
Osborne, Bernal 101
Ottoman Empire 18

Pacific Ocean 33, 52, 103, 104, 186, 187, 203, 207, 212
Paget, Clarence 30, 31, 32, 34-5, 66, 99
Pakington, John 34, 46, 81n
Pall Mall Gazette 22, 136
Pallas 60, 149, 193n
Palmerston, Lord *see* Temple, John Henry, third Viscount Palmerston
Parkes, Oscar 13, 29, 33, 36n, 44, 72, 73, 81, 100, 114, 118, 122n, 135, 138, 142, 159, 167, 168, 181n, 186, 202, 209, 213-4
Parliament 12, 31, 108, 119, 132, 133
  see also House of Commons, House of Lords
Pellew, Pownall 107n
Peru 18, 183
Peter the Great (Rus) 17, 120
Polyphemus 56, 90, 138, *147*, *148-9*, *150*, 153, 157, 158, 162, 170, 171, 180, 196, 206, 207, 214
  design of 143-52
Peto, Morton 101
Porter, David Dixon 16
Preston, Anthony 32
Provence (Fr) 20

Ramming 66, 86, 88, 91, 99, 105-7, 133, 143-52 *passim*, 153-4, 160-1, 171, 196, 207, 212
Randolph, George 91, 107n
Re d'Italia (It) 106
Redoubtable (Fr) 20, *36*, 37, *63*
Reed, Edward J. 42-3, 47, 49, 52, 55n, 63, 92, 93, 94, 97, 99, 106, 107n, 108, 116, 120, 121, 124, 136-7, 197, 205, 206, 210-1, 214
  and central citadel design 110-13, 114, 177
  attacks *Inflexible* design 136-36 *passim*
Rendel, George 133-4, 163
Rennie, G. B. 54
Requin (Fr) 36, 161, *162*, 167, 169, 170
Research 149
Rice, Captain 168
Robinson, Robert Spencer 16, 21, 35, 47, 76, 85-5, 97, 101, 102, 106, 108, 115, 121, 144, 205, 206, 210-1
  attacks *Inflexible* design 132-34 *passim*
Rodger, N.A.M. 193n, 199n, 202, 204, 209-10
Rodman, Hugh 77
Rodney 15, 72, 84, 152, 172, *172*, *173*, 181

see also 'Admiral' class
Ropp, Theodore 36, 40, 73, 163n, 206-7
Rover 145
Rowland, K. T. 54, 55, 57, 59
Royal Navy 33, 70
  and France 18-23, 157-8, 160, 168-9, 178
  and early ironclads 30-7
  expense of 26-8
  historical assessments of 9-12; 13-16, 28, 29, 60, 62-4, 204-9;
  policy towards guns 72-81
  policy towards torpedoes 65-9;
  strategy (1850-90) 87-91, 156, 167, 182-3, 208
  tactical confusion of 104-8, 157-8, 167, 187-93 *passim*, 204, 208
  vis a vis rival navies 15, 16-13, 34-5, 87-8, 95, 157-8, 160, 168-9, 178
  see also Admiralty, Ironclads, Ship design
Royal Sovereign class battleships 46, 137, 155, 167-8, 170, 178, 179n, 180, 207-8
Royal United Service Institution 49, 54, 82, 106
Rupert 195, 196
Russia 14, 65, 90, 91n, 102, 104n, 120
  Navy 16-17, 34, 162
  and *guerre de course* 26, 163, 184, 186, 187, 197, 199, 203
'Russian War-scare' (1878) 25, 50
  see also Eastern Crisis (1878)
Ryder, Alfred P. 70, 73, 107n, 191

Sails 13, 60-4, 183, 184-5, 187, 190, 192
  arguments in favour of 48-50
  versus steam 47-64
Samuda, Joseph 31
Sander, Stanley 29, 34, 38n, 47n, 62n, 63, 75n, 77n, 95, 103n, 107n, 204-5
Sans Pareil 70, 170, *208-9*
Sartorius, George 105, 107, 143-5, 147, 148, 151n
Scandinavia 18
Seaton, A.E. 56, 57n
Seely, Charles 101-2
Sennett, Richard 59
Seymour, Adolphus, twelfth Duke of Somerset 75, 99, 106
Seymour, Frederick Beauchamp, first Baron Alcester 48, 50 , 185, 186-7, 192, 210
Shah 151n

Shannon 11, 43-4, *48*, 48-9, *94*, 98, 116, *182-3*, *185*, 193, 196-7, 198-9, 200, 201, 204, 208, 210, 211-2, 214
   design of 182-7
Shaw-Lefevre, George J. 22, 57, 137, 168-70, 174, 196, 197, 198, 201
Ship design policy 9, 87
   central citadel 110-2, 125-6, 135, 138, 167, 214
   cruiser 182-203
   design modification 97, 104
   historical assessments of 9-12, 9n 27, 29, 62-4, 87-8, 95, 204-9
   imitation of foreign designs 206-7, 208
   influence of economic factors on 96-104
   influence of strategy on 90-6, 182
   influence of ordnance on 91-3
   insistence on handiness 98-9
   iron *versus* wood 30-7
   'moderate dimensions' 97-100, 207
   multiplicity of types 87-104
   sails *versus* steam 47-64
   slowness to switch to steel 37-41
   technological change and 9-12; 29
   wooden shipbuilding 32-4
   see also Admiralty, Turret, Barbettes, 'Box' Battery, Cruisers, Ironclads, Royal Navy
Shoeburyness (Ordnance proving ground) 45
Singapore 52
Sino-Japanese War 135-6
Sinope, Battle of (1853) 34
Smith, Frederic 101
Smith, W.H. 12, 78, 79-80, 81n, 83, 134, 137, 158, 160, 161, 162, 163, 166, 167, 169
Solferino (Fr) 20

Spalding, Augustus 35
Stead, W. T. 14n, 22-3, 136
Steam engines 21, 32, 170
   compound: 53-4, 57-60, 64, 193-4, 207
   confounding influence on strategic thought 89-91, 93-4
   confounding influence on tactical thought 104-7
   simple 52
   triple expansion 61n
   versus sails 47-64
   see also Boilers, Ship design
Steel 96, 156
   armour 45
   boilers 57-8
   shipbuilding
   Britain's slowness to adopt 37-41, 87
   French 27
Stewart, William Houston; 12, 35n, 48, 50, 79, 139, 140, 157, 168, 169, 184-5, 186, 187, 190, 191, 195, 200, 201, 211
   and *Inflexible* design 113-21 *passim*, 123
   and Edward Reed's attack on *Inflexible* 129-32 *passim*
   on *Polyphemus* design 144-52 *passim*
   on *Collingwood* design 160-7 *passim*
   on 'Admiral' class 173-80 *passim*
Suez Canal 15, 115
Sultan 83, 155
Surface condenser 56, 57n
Swiftsure 21, *94*, 103, 182, 183, 184, 186, 187, 188, 189, 190, 191, 192

Tactics 104-8, 157-8
   see also Barnaby, Nathaniel
Tarleton, John Walter 12, 48, 185,

186, 192, 210
Tecumseh (USA) 65
Tegetthoff (A-H) 159
Temeraire 11, 49, *94*, 108-10, *109*, *114-5*, 116, 137, 139, 140, 163, 164 *191*, 195, 196, 204, 209, 211, 213, 214
   design of 187-93
   sketches for *187*, *188*, *190*, *190*
Temple, John Henry, third Viscount Palmerston 30, 31n, 99
Thornton, A.P. 14
Thunderer 63, 75, 77n, 79, 108, 110, 115, 120, 200n, 204, 208-9
Times, The 26-7, 29, 30, 31, 41, 45, 46, 65, 75, 76, 87, 106, 107, 136, 137, 206, 207n, 208
   attacks *Inflexible* design 131-5 *passim*
Ting Yuen (Chi) 135-6
Torpedoes 65, 88, 91, 143-52 *passim*, 153-4, 171, 179, 206, 209, 211, 212
   Harvey 65-6
   spar 65
   Whitehead (self-propelled) 29, *66*, 67-9
Torpedo boats 87, 143-52 *passim*
Torpedo nets *68*, *70*, *144*, 145, *146*
Trafalgar 137, 168, 192, 207n
'*Trent* Affair' 90
Trevelyan, George O. 22, 201
'Truth About the Navy' articles 22-3, 136
Tryon, George 98, 214
Turkey *see* Ottoman Empire
Turrets 92-5
   versus barbettes: 160-5, 167, 187-8, 191

United States 12, 14, 37, 46, 77
   Civil War 15, 37, 65, 91n, 105
   Navy 16, 74

Vauban (Fr) 159, 162, 197, *198*, 199
Vernon (Torpedo school) 68
Victoria 155, 168, 170
Virginia (CSA) 101, 105-6
Vladivostok 26
Volage 32

Walker, Baldwin Wake 20, 30, 31n, 34, 99-100
War Office 25, 39, 42, 69n
   relations with Admiralty 78-84 *passim*
   see also Guns, Ordnance Department, Woolwich Arsenal
Warden, Frederick 107
Warrior 17, 21, 22, 30, 34, 41, 42, 46, 91, 99, 144, 155, 165
Warspite 24, 104, 204, 212, 214
   design of 195-203
Watson, George W. 163-4, 165
Wellesley, George 49, 79, 83, 98, 157, 158, 159
White, William 30, 110n, 113, 155, 165, 166, 167, 199, 203, 209, 210
Whitehead, Robert 66, 69
Whitehead torpedo *see* Torpedoes
Whitworth, Joseph 74, 84, 214n
Wilson, Arthur K. 85
Wooden shipbuilding *see* Royal Navy
Wood, Charles, first Viscount Halifax 12
Woolley, Joseph 46, 116, 132, 133-4, 136, 137, 214n
Woolwich Arsenal 34, 41, 45 , 69, 71, 72, 78-84 *passim*, 104, 122n, 123-4, 155, 167, 176, 181
   see also Guns, Ordnance Department, War Office

Yelverton, Hastings 50, 157, 214n